D0208043

New Plays
from A.C.T.'s Young Conservatory
Volume V

THE YOUNG CONSERVATORY AT
AMERICAN CONSERVATORY THEATER

The Young Conservatory at American Conservatory Theater is a professional theater training program for young people ages eight through nineteen. The faculty are working theater professionals who are passionate and skilled in their working with young actors. The emphasis is on the training of an actor and the development of a young person in relationship to the world and to others. The program provides quality theater training for the beginner—exploring theater and acting for the first time—as well as advanced level study for the young person with previous experience. Classes are designed to develop imagination, concentration, working with others, exploration of character, development of technique in acting, and skills of both the body and the voice. Learning to respect people and the creative process are essentials in the program. The Young Conservatory seeks to empower young people to strive for excellence in their lives, while embracing an atmosphere of safety that encourages creativity. Some students come to explore and discover, others come to define and refine their talents and techniques in order to take themselves further in their quests to become professional actors. The conservatory training frequently extends to the professional company, where students are given the opportunity to play the young roles in main stage productions, learning firsthand from working artists. The Young Conservatory is particularly devoted to developing in young people an appreciation of theater in the making of a more human world, and in the importance of the place young people have in the future of the American theater. To this end, the Young Conservatory's New Plays Program is a center for developing new theater writing by professional playwrights challenged to see the world through the eyes of the young. Critical thinking, feeling, and giving are cornerstones of the program.

OTHER SMITH AND KRAUS BOOKS
BY EDITOR CRAIG SLAIGHT

Great Scenes for Young Actors Volumes I and II

Great Monologues for Young Actors Volumes I and II

Great Scenes and Monologues for Children Volumes I and II

New Plays from A.C.T.'s Young Conservatory Volumes I, II, III, and IV

If you require prepublication information about forthcoming Smith and Kraus books, you may receive our semiannual catalogue, free of charge, by sending your name and address to *Smith and Kraus Catalogue, PO Box 127, Lyme, NH 03768.* Or call us at (800) 895-4331, fax (603) 643-1831. www.SmithKraus.com.

NEW PLAYS
from A.C.T.'s
Young Conservatory

Volume V

Edited by Craig Slaight

YOUNG ACTORS SERIES

SK
A Smith and Kraus Book

For Craig's girls:
Andi, Ann, Carla, Chandra, Cheryl, Chris, Dana, Dianne, Gabriella,
Laurie, Lynn, Nancy, Sheila, Sue, Susan R, Susan WM, and Terri

A Smith and Kraus Book
Published by Smith and Kraus, Inc.
177 Lyme Road, Hanover, New Hampshire 03755
smithandkraus.com

Manufactured in the United States of America
First Edition: March 2009
10 9 8 7 6 5 4 3 2 1

Cover Photo © Tom Haygood
Cover and book design by Julia Gignoux, Freedom Hill Design

Library of Congress Control Number: 2008935715

ISBN-13: 978-1-57525-576-7
ISBN-10: 1-57525-576-6

CONTENTS

THE NEW PLAYS PROGRAM

Since 1990, the Young Conservatory at American Conservatory Theater has been leading the way nationally in new play development for an intergenerational company of actors and audiences. Commissioning some of America's leading dramatists, including such noteworthy writers as Lynne Alvarez, Constance Congdon, Timothy Mason, Jim Grimsley, and Pulitzer Prize–winners Horton Foote and Paul Zindel, the New Plays Program has achieved international recognition for commissioning and producing some of the most exciting new work for young people. *Dramatics Magazine* hailed the New Plays Program as "...*the source of intelligent new scripts for young people in the country.*" For over fifteen years, prominent playwrights have been challenged to write new plays that see the world through the eyes of the young. As a result of the publication of these new plays by Smith and Kraus Books (a leading publisher of theater books in America), subsequent productions have been made available and produced throughout the United States, Canada and the United Kingdom, and Europe.

NEW PLAYS PROGRAM PRODUCTION HISTORY

COMMISSIONS AND FIRST PRODUCTIONS

Across the Universe: The Music of Lennon and McCartney (2006)
    book by Craig Slaight; Music and Lyrics by John Lennon and Paul McCartney
The Rhinoceros with Wings, by Carey Perloff (2006)
Seventh Grade Freaks, by Melanie Salazar Case (2006)
Mullen's Alley, by Timothy Mason (2005)
Nightingales, by Constance Congdon (2005)
Copies, by Brad Slaight (2005)
Shed a Little Light: The Music of James Taylor (2005)
Broken Hallelujah, by Sharman Macdonald (2004)
Anatomy of Gray, by Jim Leonard (2004)
Ladies of the Canyon: The Music of Joni Mitchell (2004)
War Daddy, by Jim Grimsley (2003)
Moontel Six, by Constance Congdon (2003)
Forever Young: The Music of Bob Dylan (2003)
Dusts, by Sarah Daniels (London) (2002)

Dangling Conversations, The Music of Simon and Garfunkle (2002)
The Actor, by Horton Foote (2001)
Illyria, by Bryony Lavery (London) (2000)
Time on Fire, by Timothy Mason (1999)
The Automata Pietà, by Constance Congdon (1999)
When They Speak of Rita, by Daisy Foote (1998)
Second Class, by Brad Slaight (1997)
Analiese, by Lynne Alvarez (1997)
A Bird of Prey, by Jim Grimsley (1996)
Every 17 Minutes the Crowd Goes Crazy, by Paul Zindel (1995)
The Less Than Human Club, by Timothy Mason (1994)
Class Action, by Brad Slaight (1994)
Eddie Mundo Edmundo, by Lynne Alvarez (1993)
High Tide, by Brad Slaight (1993)
Sightings, by Brad Slaight (1993)
Reindeer Soup, by Joe Pintauro (1992)
Windshook, by Mary Gallagher (1991)
Ascension Day, by Timothy Mason (1990)

WEST COAST PREMIERE

Schoolgirl Figure by Wendy McLeod (2004)
Korczak's Children by Jeffrey Hatcher (2003)
Laura Dennis, by Horton Foote (1996)
The Reincarnation of Jaimie Brown, by Lynne Alvarez (1995)

INTERNATIONAL PROGRAMS

In 1999, seeking a wider reach for the New Plays Program, Director Craig Slaight approached Suzy Graham-Adriani, the producer of Youth Programs at the prestigious Royal National Theatre in London with the idea of collaboration on new plays and productions. The Royal National Theatre has been a leader of new playwriting for young people in Europe for the last fifteen years. Without realizing it, Graham-Adriani and Slaight had been simultaneously breaking new ground by commissioning new plays by top professional playwrights for young people in their respective countries. A natural partnership between these two major theaters, both committed to tomorrow's actors and audiences, soon began. This union has already brought new works from America and England to countless theater companies on both sides of the Atlantic. The inaugural work between the two theaters was a commission by A.C.T. of England's Bryony Lavery, a leading British writer. This commission resulted in *Illyria*, which premiered at A.C.T. in August of 2000, under Graham-Adriani's direction. Next up, the young company at A.C.T., featuring a cast of American and British actors, presented Timothy Mason's *Time On Fire* (first commissioned and produced at A.C.T. in 1999), a haunting portrait of young people during the American Revolution, at the National Theatre in London in July of 2001. This was the first American young company to play at the National. In July of 2002 the National and A.C.T. developed two new plays (*Moontel Six* by Constance Congdon and *Totally Over You* by Mark Ravenhill) at the renowned Eugene O'Neill Playwrights Conference, with subsequent productions in both America and England. That same year, the Young Conservatory Company took their celebrated production of *Forever Young: The Music of Bob Dylan* to the National Theatre for a week of performances.

In July of 2003, A.C.T. and Theatre Royal Bath entered into a collaboration to share new play commissions and exchange students. The first co-commission was *War Daddy*, by Atlanta playwright Jim Grimsley. Theatre Royal Bath (T.R.B.) spent two weeks in residence in San Francisco (the young Bath actors stayed with families of Young Conservatory students) working on the play and studying in the Young Conservatory. They then returned to Bath and produced the new play. A.C.T. produced the play in November 2003. In 2004, Bath and A.C.T. co-commissioned *Broken Hallelujah*, a new play by British playwright Sharman Macdonald. In August 2004 A.C.T. traveled to Bath for two weeks, working on the play and studying in the T.R.B. conservatory. *Broken Hallelujah* premiered at A.C.T. in June 2005. Theatre Royal also produced the new play in Bath. The second two-year scheme took place in August 2005 when ten young actors for Theatre Royal Bath and their director Lee Lyford were in residence at A.C.T., taking classes in the Young Conservatory and working on a new play, *Nightingales* (about American and British nurses in WWII) co-commissioned from Constance Congdon, *Nightingales*, which was produced in 2006 by both companies.

As part of the 2005–2006 Season, the Young Conservatory began a new collaboration with the Hochschule Musik und Theater in Zurich, Switzerland, with the commission of a new play, *Only Victory*, by Paul Steinmann, and a residency by the American company in July 2006 in Zurich.

FOREWORD
Director's Biography

Craig Slaight (Director) is an Associate Artist and the Director of the Young Conservatory at American Conservatory Theater. Slaight assumed the leadership of the Young Conservatory in 1988. During his time at A.C.T. Craig has taught in all of the Conservatory programs, served as a resident director on the Geary Theater mainstage and is a member of the artistic team of the company. Slaight began the Young Conservatory's New Plays Program in 1989 with the mission to develop plays by outstanding professional playwrights that view the world through the eyes of the young. To date seventeen new plays are collected in publications by Smith and Kraus publishers, *New Plays from the A.C.T. Young Conservatory, Volumes I, II, III, and IV.* "Volume II" received recognition from the New York Public Library as an Outstanding Book for the Teenage in 1997.

In 1999, Slaight forged a collaboration with the prestigious Royal National Theatre in London, working on developing new plays for young people (writers have included Bryony Lavery, Sarah Daniels, and Sharman Macdonald). In 2000, Slaight's Young Conservatory production of *Time on Fire* by Timothy Mason was the first production by a young American company to ever play the Royal National Theatre. In 2003 the international collaboration was expanded to include co-commissions and shared productions with Theatre Royal Bath. And in 2005, Slaight began a collaboration with theatre companies in Switzerland. With A.C.T.'s Jack Sharrar, Slaight has published ten acting and play anthologies for young actors (Smith and Kraus publishers).

Prior to coming to A.C.T. Craig was an award-winning professional director in Los Angeles (directing such notables as Julie Harris, Linda Purl, Betty Garrett, Harold Gould, and Robert Foxworth). Slaight is a consultant to the Educational Theater Association, the National Foundation for Advancement in the Arts, The Actor's Workshop of Toronto, the O'Neill Playwrights Conference, the Royal National Theatre of London, Theatre Royal Bath, Ten Chimneys Foundation, and he is a frequent guest artist throughout the country. In August of 1994, Slaight received the President's Award from The Educational Theater Association for Outstanding Contributions to Youth Theater. In January of 1998, he was chosen to receive the first annual A.C.T. Artistic Director's Award.

Moontel Six

by Constance Congdon

From left to right: Rachel Burrington, Charles Filipov, Marin Lee, Lawrence
Papale, Rachel Rubenstein and Zach Kenney
Photo credit: Kimberly J. Scott

PLAYWRIGHT'S BIOGRAPHY

Constance Congdon has been writing plays for thirty years, including *Tales of the Lost Formicans*, which has had more than one hundred productions; *Losing Father's Body*, which premiered at Portland (Maine) Stage Company; *Casanova* and *Dog Opera*, both produced at the Joseph Papp Public Theater in New York; *Lips*, produced at Primary Stages in New York; and *The Automata Pietà* and *Moontel Six*, both commissioned by the A.C.T. Young Conservatory New Plays Program. Portland's (Oregon) Profile Theatre devoted an entire season to her work in 2000. She has written five opera librettos, most recently *Earthrise*, for Pulitzer Prize–winning composer Lewis Spratlan, commissioned by San Francisco Opera. Other works include the plays *Native American, Historia Familia: The Children of the Elvi, No Mercy* and its companion piece, *One Day Earlier*, and seven plays for the Children's Theatre Company of Minneapolis. For A.C.T. at the Geary Theater, Connie wrote a new verse version of Molière's *The Misanthrope*, followed by *A Mother*, starring Olympia Dukakis, based on a play by Gorky. Her newest play, *Paradise Street*, is being developed at New York Theatre Workshop. Connie's plays have been produced in Moscow, Cairo, Helsinki, Hong Kong, Tokyo, Berlin, Edinburgh, and London. A collection of four of her plays is in its second printing at Theatre Communications Group, Inc. Acting editions of several of her plays are published by Broadway Plays. She has received an NEA playwriting fellowship, two Rockefeller Playwriting Awards (one for the Bellagio Center in Italy), a Guggenheim Award, a W. Alton Jones grant, and *Newsday's* Oppenheimer Award for the New York production of *Tales of the Lost Formicans*. An alumna of New Dramatists and a member of PEN, she teaches playwriting at Amherst College.

FROM THE PLAYWRIGHT

I was on my way to another story entirely, when this voice, on a loudspeaker, shouted this in my brain: "Kids? Come on out!!! No one's going to hurt you!!" And there I was on another voyage into a story where I was listening for what happens next. I say "listening" because that's what I do and the listening includes images as well. The characters of Meema and Seven appeared and I followed them. I was doing a lot of reading in science, as I do, and was fascinated and horrified by cloning. Having two opposite responses to a subject is a good state for a writer to be in, in my opinion. In my experience, this opposition creates a dynamic that is so electric that it charges what I am writing. I like to think of Dr. Frankenstein pulling the lever to zap his Creature with electricity and the Creature opening its eyes and moving. "It's

ALIVE!!!!" screams the doctor. And that's what I want my plays to be, "ALIVE!!!" And then I just follow them on their halting way into a world they reveal to me. Discoveries in science could not be more amazing right now. I feel so privileged to live in a time like this—where discovery and knowledge of the way the world(s) work are growing at a rate never before witnessed on planet Earth. And, by the way, Seven would use the recent demoting of Pluto as further proof of the vagaries of definition of what constitutes a "planet."

FROM THE ACTOR—Lawrence Papale (Toyn)

When I appeared in *Moontel Six* I was the youngest actor in the company. Instead of feeling scared, however, I was greeted with warm encouraging support. I did not feel any barriers because of my youthful status. I believe this support helped greatly in my efforts to become a better actor. In many ways the experience I had playing Toyn, in this futuristic setting, helped me strengthen my acting and contributed to my later performances at the Young Conservatory and on the A.C.T. mainstage. The unique experiences young actors receive at A.C.T. are unfathomable. It is quite overwhelming, but in a good way. The director and other actors really treat you like a professional, even if you are just an eighth grader. I was treated like an adult, so consequently I learned how to work as a professional and that has informed all of my work at A.C.T. over the five years that have followed.

Moontel Six was one of my favorite productions because there were no limits—it hadn't been done before. As a brand-new play, it was something that could be taken in any direction, and for an eighth grader it was a lot to understand. As a young person, I was being given the chance to create and perform a character that had been written especially for me. It is truly wonderful to work on something that you know has never been done before.

ORIGINAL PRODUCTION

Moontel Six was commissioned and first presented by the Young Conservatory at American Conservatory Theater (Carey Perloff, Artistic Director, Heather M. Kitchen, Executive Director), San Francisco, California, in March 2003. It was directed by Craig Slaight; the set design was by Craig Slaight and Kimberly J. Scott; the lighting design was by Kimberly J. Scott; the costumes were designed by Callie Floor and Maggie Whitaker; the sound was designed by j.j. Bergovoy; the assistant director was Ramsey Williams.

The cast was as follows:

MEEMA . . . . Rachel Burrington
SEVEN . . . . Charles Filipov
UBERBETH . . . . Mairin Lee
TOYN . . . . Lawrence Papale
GEENOMA . . . . Rachel Rubenstein
EMO . . . . Philip Markle
ZIPPER . . . . Chase Oliver
YUSEEF . . . . .Zach Kenney
SARK . . . . .Sarah Grandin
EEBEE . . . . Martine Moore

CHARACTERS

UBERBETH, older female teen. Part luminescent jellyfish. Just began her genitive. A reluctant mother. Skeptical of most people.

ZIPPER, older male teen. Part lizard and part moth. Serious, concerned with his future and the well-being of others.

EMO, male teen. Mixed genes from Earth mammals. Naïve. Given to outbursts of uncontrolled emotion. Sexually ambivalent.

TOYN, boy. Completely human but speaks like a technical manual. Refers to himself in the third person. Suffers from severe allergies and, maybe, asthma. Mature beyond his years but still a boy.

GEENOMA, older female teen. Knows she's beautiful. A genetically warped "valley girl." Wants to be the leader but frequently fails. Comes off as hard but there's a needy child inside.

MEEMA, female teen. In constant quest for answers. Fearless. Knows her power. Capable of holding her own in arguments. A doer rather than a follower.

SEVEN, male teen. Highly intelligent. A math-brain. Logical. Finds comfort in probability. A misfit in a group of misfits.

YUSEEF, older male teen. Human. A protection officer for the human population on the Moon. Recently from Earth. A lost soul desperately looking for a future.

SARK, female Moon being of indeterminate age. Eebee's mate.

EEBEE, female Moon being of indeterminate age. Sark's mate.

SETTING

The play is set sometime in the future, on the Earth's Moon and later on Earth.

MOONTEL SIX

ACT I
SCENE ONE

Meema center stage—channeling.

MEEMA: Fishberries in the starling corn,
    You're monkey tricks for the future,
    So nick a spaceship and fly
    Below to a big blue marble
    Find a sail as big as a city
    So you can catch those solar winds.
    Are you listening, you dirtboys
    And mudgirls?
    Are you listening, you braindance janders?
    Get us on your beamers and i-phones—
    Just tell us where we can go
    And we'll go there.
    (Seven has entered and listened to part of this.)
SEVEN: What was that? Are you picking up transmissions again?
MEEMA: Unless it's Uberbeth or Geenoma planting messages into my consciousness.
    (Said with the purpose of letting this be heard by Uberbeth and Geenoma)
    We've agreed to never do that anymore. It's not our fault we were experiments in paranormal communication. We shouldn't have to live with it all the time.
    We're using spoken speech, RIGHT? Right?
    (Uberbeth enters.)
UBERBETH: I didn't "send" you anything. I wasn't even thinking about you. You're not the center of the universe, Meema.
    (Uberbeth exits.)
MEEMA: Whoa. Look who woke up on the wrong side of the Moon.
SEVEN: Well, Uberbeth and Geenoma had words this morning about whose turn it was to do the laundry. Geenoma lost.
MEEMA: Actually, it was my turn, but I stayed out of it. OK, so I've been seeing this thing in the sky every week or so. And nobody's ever around. So don't move, Seven—you have to be my witness.

SEVEN: Right. I won't move, but—

(Meema lies down on the ground, looking up at the "sky.")

SEVEN:—the probability of you seeing it again is very, very small. And, indeed, we might alter its path by observing it.

MEEMA: Seven, stop thinking so much and just freaking look up?

GEENOMA: *(Entering with a large bag.)* I, like, I, like, I, like, like, like, I can't, like, STAND the, like CHAOS AND FILTH WE LIVE IN ANY MORE!!!

(She dumps the contents of the bag on Meema. It's a zillion pairs of dirty socks. Geenoma exits.)

MEEMA: *(Spitting and wiping her mouth free of sock debris.)* Sock scum! How could she do that to me?

SEVEN: *(Smells them.)* Yeah, they're not even your socks.

(Smells them.)

They're mine.

(Smells them again.)

Well, that one's yours.

(They look at the mess for a beat.)

MEEMA: Well, are you going to help me clean this up?

SEVEN: No, but I'm going to help you understand how it happened. You see . . . when you lose one sock, it leaves behind its mate. Or partner. Let's call it "partner." So you wear the next pair and you lose one of those. Because it's actually more likely that you'll lose one of a matched pair that one of an unmatched pair because you rarely wear an unmatched pair because most people are less likely to wear and then wash the unmatched sock, unless they are us who have stopped washing them all together, so the odds are even greater that the next sock to get lost will be part of a pair. Are you with me?

MEEMA: I hope not. Because this is some flaming convoluted boom-boom you've got going here.

SEVEN: It's important, Meema.

It's important to understand how the world works.

MEEMA: But we're not on the world. The world is a planet. We're on the Moon—a satellite of the Earth. And not a planet.

SEVEN: I know it is futile of me to try to explain this to you, yet again, but: the Moon is a planet. It travels in an orbit, therefore, it is a planet. Just because it doesn't orbit the SUN doesn't mean it is not a planet. It is as much a planet as the Earth is.

MEEMA: You just can't accept the fact that we are satellite dwellers.

SEVEN: If you can't get your total left-brain Nazi to give up your solar-centrism and consider—

MEEMA: Left-brain? Left-brain? I am RIGHT-brain, totally. YOU'RE the left brain, Math Boy! Dweak!!

SEVEN: Try to grok it this way—

MEEMA: Don't you Heinlein me, Seven! That's not fair!

SEVEN: It's a matter of perception. We can be anywhere we want to by using our access to simstem reality.

MEEMA: Seven, you are in denial.

Which is a river on Earth.

Where we are not.

Because we're on the freakin' Moon!

Even Toyn can accept this—

Oops, I said his name.

(Toyn enters. Long beat. He waits for something from them.)

SEVEN: We're sorry, Toyn. Meema just said your name because she likes your name. You go rest now.

TOYN: Don't activate Unit until you are ready to use it.

(Points to them.)

Analogs.

(Takes in the entire community.)

All analogs.

(Points to himself, with attitude.)

Digital.

(He exits.)

MEEMA: Someday he's going to finally accept the fact that he is human. And that we're not. And then he'll hate us like all the rest of humanity seems to.

SEVEN: Meema, you're a lot human.

MEEMA: None of us are, Seven. Not 100 percent. The genetically altered cannot get a human passport. We have bar codes imprinted on our ankles!

SEVEN: But you can't see it.

MEEMA: But they know it's there, Seven. And who knows what's going to happen when we reach our genitive? Uberbeth is part luminescent jellyfish. What if she starts blinking off and on like a lightbulb? She already has a major digestive problem.

SEVEN: She's allergic to lecithin, that's all.

MEEMA: But lecithin is in everything we eat, practically. It enhances shelf life. So, after a few more months, I won't want to live with her—none of us will.

SEVEN: Oh, we can handle it.

MEEMA: Have you been in a closed space with her? Other than here?

SEVEN: I haven't been in a closed space with anyone.

MEEMA: *(She just launches into her next thought.)* And Zipper is part lizard and part moth. You know that lizards eat moths, don't you? What's going to happen there?

SEVEN: If he grows wings, then it'll be all right. If he grew a tail and wings, that would be a problem.

MEEMA: But whatever it is, he can MATE! Doesn't that alarm you?

SEVEN: No.

MEEMA: No wonder they chased us out of Moonstead Estates. And Emo—who knows what's going to happen to him? He has major goat genes and then there's some little dainty animal coded onto his DNA string. I don't know which it is—but I think it's a skittish, scared-to-death little wimpy animal. And Geenoma? Some mess of genes there. Who knows WHAT they were trying to create. We're from the same lab creche and she's always been like that. And then there's me. At least I'm all mammal. And then there's you, Seven. You refuse to talk about it.

(Long beat. Meema waits—maybe this will be the time SEVEN talks about it. But, nooooooo.)

SEVEN: Let's say you have ten complete, but distinct pairs of socks, meaning each pair differs from another, then it will be over one hundred times more likely that the result will be the worst possible outcome.

MEEMA: Seven—this is the Worst Possible Outcome! We're living it! The fact that only an abandoned moontel could be our home! The fact that no one cares what happens to us, except the ones who want us sterilized. Like the wonderful folks in Moonstead Estates who raided our group home and chased us through the hydroponic gardens, through the air tunnels, through the entrails of this community until we ended up in this place. And the Very Worst Possible Outcome is after they find us, which is inevitable—do you deal with inevitabilities in your happy probable world??

SEVEN: The Best Possible Outcome would be seven complete pairs left. Drawing two socks at random even from a drawer full of complete pairs is most likely to produce nothing but two odd socks. And, here's the interesting part—

MEEMA: THERE IS NO INTERESTING PART!!

SEVEN: My point is, if you draw two socks at random from a drawer full of complete pairs of socks you are going to, probably, get two odd socks . . .

MEEMA: Seven, you've got to face some facts. What are we going to do?

SEVEN: I, of all people, love facts. Facts make up the world. So probability is a religious experience. For me.

MEEMA: Well, that's a big help—you were praying. With socks.

SEVEN: With the numbers.

MEEMA: I'm so alone. What am I doing here?

(Sees something in the sky.)

There it is. And you just don't want to face it because you don't understand it. Seven—just look up.

SEVEN: *(Looks up, sees something.)* All right. There's something there.

MEEMA: Lie down.

(He lays down.)

See? There it is.

SEVEN: It's most probable that it's a fault in the dome.

MEEMA: Then why haven't we seen it the million other times we looked up?

SEVEN: Because we haven't paid attention.

MEEMA: No. We didn't pay attention at Moonstead Estates. Since we've been running, we've paid attention.

SEVEN: But not to the sky. *(Sees it.)* Wait.

MEEMA: See it? It moves.

SEVEN: Total Galileo Moment, my Meema.

(Seven jumps up.)

SEVEN: Something is on me!

MEEMA: Oh, Seven, you're such a—

(Sees something on his back.)

Uh-oh.

SEVEN: *(Whimpering.)* "Uh-oh?" "Uh-oh?"

(Meema brushes "it" off and then steps on it.)

MEEMA: *(Noticing similar bugs on the floor.)* Ooo. There're lots of them.

(Meema steps on and pursues lots of "them"—a big killing spree. Seven has freaked out and has escaped somewhere offstage.)

MEEMA: Seven, come on. I killed them all. Come on.

SEVEN: *(Re-entering.)* This place—is getting—uninhabitable, Meema. I still feel like I've got something on me. Indulge me and check.

MEEMA: Turn around.

(Seven turns around and there is a huge bug on his back.)

Just a little dirt, Seven. Just look up and tell me what that phenomenon might be. In the sky. We don't want to miss it.

(Meema removes the bug carefully.)

SEVEN: It looks like someone or something is pinching the sky and then making a crease—And now the crease disappears over the horizon.

(Meema throws the bug offstage.)

However, the probability of that being an actual crease is very low. I purport star surf. A wave. A wrinkle in the sky.

MEEMA: *(Finishing with the giant bug.)* Uh-huh.

SEVEN: *(Suddenly.)* It's a ship, Meema. It's a ship!! See? It's a ship crossing the starfield. Right? And blocking out the stars as it passes, THEREFORE, creating the semblance of a ripple in the sky.

MEEMA: A ship?

SEVEN: Right.

MEEMA: Where is it, then?

SEVEN: It went to the other side.

MEEMA: You mean, the dark side?

SEVEN: Dark in that it doesn't get much sun. And never sees the Earth, in fact. That side of the Moon knows it's a planet.

MEEMA: The question is why would a ship go to the other side?

SEVEN: Visiting a planet.

MEEMA: But, could it be, might it be, a ship that would carry us off this barren satellite—

SEVEN:—planet—

MEEMA:—to somewhere we might, you know, you know, like, be OK.

SEVEN: We'll never be "OK." And, anyway, even if, say if, we found that ship, how could we get to it without air to breathe along the way? And getting everyone to move again—

(Geenoma enters.)

GEENOMA: I, like, like, like, can't stand it, like, one, like, like, like, moment more!!! We are, like, down to shelf life two-thousand-oh-two Ramen Noodles! And, like, that shit is nasty!!! AND WHAT ON BUZZ ALDRIN'S GRAY EARTH IS THIS??

(Geenoma produces the bug that Meema just disposed of and throws it somewhere else and exits.)

MEEMA: I think Geenoma would go.

SEVEN: In a minute. But what about the others? Emo, Zipper—even Uberbeth are trying to believe that we've found a safe place here, as long as we don't bother anybody.

ELECTRONICALLY AMPLIFIED ADULT VOICE: Kids?

We're so glad we found you.

Walk toward the light.

No one will hurt you.

We promise.

Just walk toward the light.

(Start of Muzak music—some Barry Manilow or other bland tune made more bland by Muzak OR something by Nirvana or Pearl Jam done on the cheapest synthesizer possible.)

KIDS: Oh No. They've found us!

(General pandemonium. The kids run around, on and offstage, gathering stuff and bringing it on and taking some off again.)

GEENOMA: Like, like, like, like STOP!!!!

(They all stop where they are.)

OK, like ——. OK. OK. Like, we—all—have to, like,—get into a, like, LINE, and EXIT. Like now. The air tunnels are that way!

(They all exit, led by Geenoma, but Seven gets mesmerized by the light.)

MEEMA: *(Grabbing Seven.)* Seven, look at me, not the light. Now, let's go!

(Long beat.)

(Toyn enters, holding his lovey object and his inhaler. He looks around, isn't bothered, particularly. He waits, takes a hit from his inhaler, waits, looks around, then addresses something that might have an answer for him.)

TOYN: Does the cable you are using have the correct connector?

(Long beat.)

Le câble n'est peut-être pas connecté correctment?

(Beat.)

Do you have the correct cable attached?

(Beat.)

(On to Spanish, and a new tactic to get an answer.)

Sino estan en la casa con las regulaciones—

(Pause.)

— ese unida puede casar descarga electrida de shoke.

(No answer from anything or anybody.)

I don't feel so good.

(He lies down as the lights go down on him.)

END OF SCENE

SCENE TWO

Immediately following. In the entrails of the domed Moon city. The kids are still moving quickly, being pursued, but they're hunkering down, getting into smaller and smaller spaces.

EMO: Where are we going?

GEENOMA: These air tunnels are the only way we can escape!

Like, like, like, keep moving!

UBERBETH: I'm cramped.

MEEMA: Who isn't?

ZIPPER: Are we being followed?

GEENOMA: How did it, like, know our names?

EMO: I don't know.

UBERBETH: Excuse me.

(Smells flatulence.)

SEVEN: Uberbeth!

UBERBETH: I'm sorry—I'm tense. And I just ate some of those Moon Pops we found.

(They look at her, annoyed and shocked. Uberbeth defends herself.)

I was HUNGRY! I have to eat something.

MEEMA: You get in the back of the line.

UBERBETH: There's no room.

ALL: We'll make room!

(They squeeze her past them. She gets to the back of the line.)

UBERBETH: Hey, where's Toyn?

SEVEN: Oh. Well, don't worry.

You said his name—he'll come.

(Silence, they wait and then realize Toyn is gone, then emotional pandemonium.)

ALL: *(Not together.)* Where's Toyn? Oh no! What are we going to do? Toyn! We left him!!

MEEMA: We have to go back.

ALL: *(Not together.)* Right! We have to! Absolutely! Let's go!

(But they have a failure of courage and don't move.)

SEVEN: I'll go.

MEEMA: *(Grabbing Seven's sleeve, surprising herself and Seven.)* No!

ZIPPER: I'll go.

GEENOMA: No. Like, no one will go.

UBERBETH: Geenoma!

GEENOMA: Like, we can't go. All of us are, like, totally genetic freaks and, like, something they, like, want to do away with. Toyn, is, like, 100 percent human. They might be good to him.

ZIPPER: Good? Good???

UBERBETH: She means they won't, you know, fix him.

SEVEN: *(What a stupid word for it.)* Fix?? Fix???

GEENOMA: Like, like, like—

MEEMA: Just spit it out, Geenoma! They want to fix us, they want to sterilize us!! They're afraid we'll pass on our weird genes. And with their precious 100 percent human pure-bred perfect children. No genetically altered genes in their family. All G.A.s must be sterilized!

EMO: Oh, is that all? That's what all of this is about? All the running and the chasing and the hiding? Couldn't we all just take really good showers? I mean, how sterile do they want us all to be? I could use a shower. All of us could. That should be clean enough for them.

(They decided to not inform Emo of what sterilization means.)

UBERBETH: *(Speaks in coded language to protect Emo's innocence.)* Look, I don't mind being really, really "clean." If they wanted to "clean" me, that would be fine.

ZIPPER: Uberbeth, what are you saying? You can't mean that!

UBERBETH: Zipper, I think the flatulence genes should end with me.

(She starts to crawl out of the tunnel, going back in the direction they came from.)

EMO: Uberbeth! Don't go!

ZIPPER: They'll get you!

GEENOMA: I, like, order you to come back here!

UBERBETH: *(Produces flatulence as she exits.)* Oops!

(She's gone, but the odor remains.)

EMO: Woa! Bad one!!

UBERBETH: *(Offstage, about the flatulence.)* Sorry!

GEENOMA: Like, bye, Uberbeth!

(To everyone else.)

This is, like, sad.

MEEMA: I know.

EMO: Maybe they'll let her take a bath instead of a shower. And then she could soak for awhile. Would that be clean enough for them?

SEVEN: I hope so.

EMO: I know baths aren't considered to be all that sterile—

ZIPPER: Can someone tell him??!! Can I tell him???

    Emo, sterilization means they want to—

    (Stops—it's more difficult to tell than he thought.)

MEEMA: Go ahead.

GEENOMA: Explain what they want to do to us.

ZIPPER: They want to—

EMO: Uh-huh. . . .?

ZIPPER: I can't.

SEVEN: They want to take away our ability to pass on our genes.

EMO: How can they do that? All that stuff's inside our bodies. They'd have to—

    (Realization. Overwhelmed. Passes out cold.)

ZIPPER: I think he finally gets it.

MEEMA: Wake him up. We have to get going.

GEENOMA: Like, Meema's right.

ZIPPER: Aren't we going to wait for Uberbeth to bring Toyn back?

    (The others just look at each other.)

SEVEN: The probability of her being successful is very low.

ZIPPER: What is wrong with you guys?? We let her go!!

MEEMA: Zip, we have to think of ourselves.

GEENOMA: They won't, like, exactly, like, kill her—they'll just, like, fix her.

    (Emo comes to.)

ZIPPER: Yeah, they'll spay her, like an earth cat.

    (Emo passes out again.)

ZIPPER: Emo!! Wake up!! Come on!!

    (Emo wakes up.)

    We have to go.

    (Lights down as they all start crawling in line again, continuing their escape.)

               END OF SCENE

SCENE THREE

Back at the moontel. Uberbeth enters—she's just emerged from the entrails of the domed moon community. She looks around, doesn't see Toyn.

UBERBETH: Toyn! Toyn.

    (Suddenly, the electronically amplified voice is right on top of her.)

ELECTRONICALLY AMPLIFIED ADULT VOICE: Geenoma, Meema, Seven, Emo, Zipper, Uberbeth.

You are, like, totally, like, busted.

Walk toward the light.

No one will hurt you.

We promise.

Just walk toward the light.

(Uberbeth hides.)

ELECTRONICALLY AMPLIFIED ADULT VOICE: Geenoma, Meema, Seven, Emo, Zipper, Uberbeth.

You are—

(The announcement stops. Enter a young man, wearing colorful jockey shorts, large fireman-type boots—and nothing else. This is Officer Yuseef Cho-Chee-Buchanan-Stein He carries a small, handheld programming device that he is fiddling with. Uberbeth can't believe her eyes and stands up, then, realizing she's endangering herself, crouches down again, as he reprograms the announcement.)

ELECTRONICALLY AMPLIFIED ADULT VOICE: *(Reprogrammed announcement.)*

Geenoma, Meema, Seven, Emo, Zipper, Uberbeth.

You have gone too far.

You will not survive.

Please turn yourself in.

We only want to take care of you—

(Can't stand the bullshit of the message, reprograms.)

We only want to do a small laser surgery that will leave you unable to ever have children of any kind because we are evil.

(That is satisfying, but he can't do that.)

We only want you to turn yourself in to Officer Yuseef Cho-Chee Buchanan-Stein because he is desperately lonely on this stupid rock that looks so much prettier from the Earth.

(Back to the proper announcement.)

We only want what is best for you and for all of us.

We won't hurt you. We promise.

YUSEEF: OK. Music select.

Anything current on here?

Oh—"I Eat Your Heart and Spit it Out." Too sentimental.

(Finds something.)

OK, here's something from the last five years.

(He programs to play. Out comes a song that is the equivalent of one note

against a complicated repeating rhythm, with a lyric that consists of an occasional shrieked and/or whispered repetition of "Now!" "Sex." He finally rejects that, too.)

OK. Back to old standards.

(Muzak version of some classic rock (Like "The Sunshine of Your Love" by The Cream) hit done à la Muzak pablum and he starts singing to it, but with his own lyrics. He starts to dance to it.)

I hate my job. I hay-ate my job. I hate my job. I hay-ate my job. I hate my job. I hay-ate my job.

(Uberbeth makes herself visible.)

UBERBETH: Then why do you do it?

YUSEEF: What! Wait! You wait right there! You're under arrest!

(He exits, dropping the programming tool. She picks it up. He re-enters, getting into a jumpsuit and grabbing his protective gear—gas mask. She quietly sits and turns off the Muzak.)

All right! You can sit! But don't move!

(She quietly watches as he jumps around, putting everything on, and then grabs his goo gun.)

OK—which one are you?

UBERBETH: What is that thing?

YUSEEF: It's a goo gun. One shot and the perps are encrusted with an invisible goo that makes them stick to ANYONE, including themselves, thereby preventing escape.

(He puts on his gas mask and then throws a can toward her. She picks it up.)

UBERBETH: What is this?

YUSEEF: Stun gas.

UBERBETH: Why would you want to use this in a sealed, domed community with only one source of air that is circulated all over?

YUSEEF: I—I don't know. I was issued a carton of these.

UBERBETH: Aren't you supposed to pull this tab BEFORE you throw it—to activate the gas?

YUSEEF: Don't mess with me, Missy Mutant! You throw that can and you'll be the one not breathing. I have a gas mask on. You don't. So you just forget about exuding your tentacles and zapping me with poisonous spit from you proboscis, because I am protected by the Family Always Serves Community In Setting Things Straight. They have given me my authority to arrest you.

UBERBETH: *(A statement about his sexiness.)* You're really hot.

YUSEEF: An officer does not think about his physical well-being. He only serves to protect the lives and property of the Family Always Serves Community In Setting Things Straight.

UBERBETH: I'm a little peckish. How about you?

(She opens the can. He ducks and covers. She takes out some little snack pretzels and munches on them.)

Mislabled cartons—happens a lot up here. Now, have you seen a small-ish kid with breathing problems? Carries a stuffed creature we're not sure what it is?

(About the opened can.)

Want some? The shelf life on these is usually fairly recent.

(Realizes her mistake. Stops eating them.)

Uh-oh.

(Flatulence.)

Oops.

Oh man. Darn it.

YUSEEF: Now don't think you're not still under arrest, but I'm going to take off my gas mask.

UBERBETH: Oh, don't! Please! You need it!

YUSEEF: The stun gas is a can of pretzels!

(He takes off the mask, anyway. She waits for him to react to the smell of the flatulence and really suffers as he comes closer and looks her over. But he doesn't react.)

YUSEEF: You don't look like a mutant.

UBERBETH: I'm not! I'm just genetically altered, but only slightly.

YUSEEF: They told me you were part luminescent jellyfish.

UBERBETH: I am, but I've never been able to figure out which parts are affected.

YUSEEF: I don't know if it's the extreme heat of this suit they make me wear or just stress in general from being in this very strange environment, but I'm beginning to have just a few little bitty questions about my mission. I'm really hot.

(He starts to unbutton the top of his jumpsuit.)

UBERBETH: That's what I thought when I saw you.

YUSEEF: But I was in my underwear.

UBERBETH: Yeah.

YUSEEF: Wait a minute—here I am, letting my guard down, about to step out of my protective uniform. I know what you're doing. I'm on to you. You are TOYING with me.

(Toyn enters.)

UBERBETH: Toyn!! Toyn!!

(She goes to him and hugs him.)

TOYN: This unit needs to go to technical support. Now.

UBERBETH: No, Toyn. Once we get out of this moontel and into—ah—somewhere else when the air circulation is better—you'll be able to breathe easier.

TOYN: *(About his inhaler.)* Peripheral needs recharging.

YUSEEF: Both of you! Stop! Where are the others? I demand that you take me to the others!

UBERBETH: *(About the inhaler.)* You need a new one. What are we going to do?

(To Yuseef.)

Can you break into the Moon Mall? We've been pilfering his inhalers from there.

YUSEEF: I am an officer of The Family Always Serves Community In Setting Things Straight! And you are NOT going anywhere!

UBERBETH: *(To Toyn.)* Come on. And we can tell the others that there's no need to worry because it's just a rent-a-cop chasing us.

(She starts to exit with Toyn.)

YUSEEF: Rent-a-cop????

(She has exited with Toyn. Yuseef fires his goo gun in the direction of their exit.)

UBERBETH: *(Offstage.)* What? What have you done??!!!

TOYN: *(Offstage.) (Breathing with difficulty.)*

UBERBETH: *(Offstage.)* Toyn, it'll be all right.

(Toyn and Uberbeth hop back onto stage, stuck together.)

Look, what you've done!!!

YUSEEF: I'm so sorry.

(He goes to them, trying to help.)

TOYN: Being sticky is very bad for electronic circuitry!!!

(Yuseef tries to unstick them.)

UBERBETH: You are a horrible person!!!

YUSEEF: I was just doing my job!!!

UBERBETH: I thought you were hot, but you're NOT!! Get away from us!!

YUSEEF: I'm trying to apologize.

UBERBETH: Too late!!! Now leave!!!

YUSEEF: I—I can't.

TOYN: This unit's functioning is further impaired.

UBERBETH: I said, I'm not interested in your apologies! We're your captives—
Big Policeman of the Moon, working for the F.A.S.C.I.S.T.S.
(He doesn't put it together.)
Fascists?
I mean, can you even spell?? Or read???

YUSEEF: I never realized. . .

UBERBETH: Be careful who you work for!! You gotta serve somebody—make
sure it's the Forces of Good. The Earth Prophet Dylan said that. Don't
you even know your own history?

YUSEEF: For your information, that is a Hemisphere Number Two Prophet,
AND it's George Lucas.

UBERBETH: Dylan!

YUSEEF: Lucas!!

TOYN: Gummy is bad for components.

UBERBETH: Get out of here!!! Because of you, we're stuck!!

YUSEEF: So am I.

UBERBETH: What???!!!
(They all try to get unstuck, can't.)

TOYN: I have experienced condensation. It is time to drain my waste liquids.

YUSEEF: What?
*(Uberbeth just looks at Yuseef, totally disgusted with how dense he is. Yuseef
finally gets that Toyn needs to pee. Resigned, Yuseef and the other stuck-
together two hop offstage.)*

TOYN: *(Offstage.)* This unit needs to perform this function in private.

UBERBETH AND YUSEEF: Well, you can't!!

END OF SCENE

SCENE FOUR

Farther down the tunnel. Everyone is progressing. Suddenly, Geenoma, who was toward the head of the line, stops.

MEEMA: What?

EMO: Why have we stopped?

ZIPPER: What's going on?

GEENOMA: I'm, like, getting claustro—

EMO: Don't even say it!

GEENOMA: I mean, like, this looks not too good.

MEEMA: *(To Seven.)* Seven, we may have reached the end. All I see is darkness ahead.

SEVEN: Spare me the metaphors, Meema.

MEEMA: No, really. Look.

SEVEN: Oh no.

EMO: Oh no?

ZIPPER: What.

EMO: He said, "Oh no."

ZIPPER: I'm backing out. I'm heading back.

SEVEN: Wait. We can't go back.

EMO: *(Covering his crotch with his hands.)* No way I am going back.

GEENOMA: OK. OK. OK. So, like, I'm the, like, oldest. So, like, I'm going to go into that dark and find whatever it is. A precipice. A, like, wall. Whatever.

SEVEN: I should go.

MEEMA: No, you're not.

    (She grabs Seven and holds on, surprising them both.)

ZIPPER: I'm going.

    (He heads for the dark.)

    It's time for my chrysalis period, anyway. Something in me seeks a dark place to metamorph.

    (He exits into the dark.)

EMO: Zipperrrrrr!

    (But Zipper's gone.)

GEENOMA: *(Crying upset.)* Oh, like, like, like, that's terrible.

    (Trying to comfort Emo, but can't because he's way down the line.) Like, like, there, there, Emo.

    (To others.)

Pass it on?

(They do.)

Like, Zipper will be, like, all right.

(To others.)

Pass it on?

(They do.)

I, like, hate to see you, like, so upset.

Pass it on?

MEEMA: He totally can hear you, G!

GEENOMA AND EMO: *(Really upset.)* Zipper? Zip?

SEVEN: The probability of us having a good day just keeps decreasing.

MEEMA: For just once, can you keep your facts to yourself?

GEENOMA: I, like, totally apologize. I have, like, totally pulled myself together. Nobody may have ever wanted us. But I'm not going to, like, die crying. I'm going in after Zipper.

(She exits into the dark.)

EMO: Noooo! Zipper! Geenoma!

(He squeezes past and goes in after Geenoma.)

MEEMA: *(Grabbing Seven, who is acting like he's going in, too.)* Stop right there. Haven't you ever seen a horror movie? "Oooo, I'm scared out of my mind. Let's go down to the basement."

SEVEN: Pheasant! You're nothing but a pheasant!

MEEMA: You have the wrong earth bird.

SEVEN: Pigeon!

Turkey!

Ostrich!

Uh—

MEEMA: Chicken. And I'm not.

(She passes him and goes into the dark.)

SEVEN: *(Following her.)* Meema! Why does it always have to be about you? Even our probable death!?

(He follows her into the dark.)

END OF SCENE

SCENE FIVE

Uberbeth, Yuseef, Toyn hop on stage.

TOYN: Ahhh. This unit always operates better after a draining of waste liquids.

YUSEEF: THAT was totally disgusting and embarrassing.

UBERBETH: You have problems with the human body. I can't believe I thought you were hot.

YUSEEF: First of all, you're NOT human. And secondly, I am so hot, I'm sweating!

UBERBETH: I may be a variation on being human, in that I am part jellyfish, but I am still pretty much human. And Toyn is totally, 100 percent human.

TOYN: This unit is an electrical component. This unit is digital. This unit is not human.

YUSEEF: OK. So Toyn is human. I remember reading that in the records, but YOU'RE a freak!

TOYN: Not human, digital.

UBERBETH: Don't upset him.

YUSEEF: I can't stand either of you!! You're a freak and he's insane!!

UBERBETH: Well, YOU ARE A HORRIBLE PREJUDICED DIRT BOY!

YUSEEF: "Dirt boy??" That is so racist!!

UBERBETH: I can smell the dirt on you. You are from the EARTH and you are a DIRT BOY.

Dirt boy! Dirt boy!!

YUSEEF: Genetic freak! Genetic Freak!!

TOYN: Analog!! Analog!!

ALL THREE: I'm getting out of here!!!

(They try to escape from each other and ending up just hopping off.)

END OF SCENE

SCENE SIX

THE DARK SIDE OF THE MOON. Two figures call to each other across the stage.

SARK: Eebee?

EEBEE: Sark?

(*They run to each other and make happy noises.*)

SARK: Ship come.

EEBEE: More trash.

SARK: Good trash.

EEBEE: We make what now?

SARK: More bots. More and more bots.

(*They exit.*)

END OF SCENE

SCENE SEVEN

ON THE DARK SIDE OF THE MOON. ZIPPER enters and looks around.

ZIPPER: Whoa. Cool.

(*Geenoma enters.*)

GEENOMA: Wow. Zipper!

ZIPPER: We're alive!

(*Emo enters.*)

EMO: G, you're OK. And Zip! Zipper, Zipper, Zipper!
Where are we?

(*Looks at the sky.*)

Oh no! Where's the Earth? Where did it go?

ZIPPER: You can't see it from this side of the Moon.

GEENOMA: It's, like, hard to see anything through this dome.

EMO: What company had this dome made?

ZIPPER: Some company that went broke, it looks like.

(*Emo starts to hyperventilate.*)

ZIPPER: Hey, Emo. You're fine. The dome is fine. It works. Look at me—
I'm breathing fine.

(*Emo calms down.*)

GEENOMA: Like, it's, like, if you didn't know, like, the sun existed, like, you
wouldn't, like—

(*Emo grabs her.*)

EMO: Stop saying "like"! Stop it! Never say it again!! Just say what you mean!!

GEENOMA: (*With much struggle.*) No Sun in sky. I here. No see Sun.

ZIPPER: I don't think she can talk another way.

(Sound of scurrying in the dark.)

GEENOMA: Hey, guys? Are there, like, animals on the Moon?

ZIPPER: Nothing but insects that we brought by accident.

(More scurrying.)

SARK: *(Running past.)* Hi!

GEENOMA: Well, I think there might be some, like, really big ones here. Check your bags for glow trash.

(They pull out some glowing, lightee things.)

ZIPPER: See any bugs?

EMO: Thank heaven Seven isn't here. The idea of big bugs would freak him out totally.

(Seven enters.)

SEVEN: I heard my name! I couldn't believe it. I was stumbling in the dark and I heard my name! And then I saw your lights. Where's Meema?

GEENOMA: We haven't seen her.

SEVEN: But she was ahead of me! I have to find her!

(Sound of scurrying.)

Oh, she's hiding in the dark here. Trying to fool me.

ZIPPER: We don't think so.

EMO: No way.

SEVEN: I can see you're lying. You're just covering for her.

(More scurrying—closer.)

I'm going to find her.

(He heads into the dark corners, following the sound of the scurrying.)

GEENOMA: Like, like, totally a bad moment coming.

SEVEN: *(From a dark corner.)* Yikes!!!

GEENOMA: I, like, told you.

SEVEN: *(From the dark.)* Oh, you're kind of cute.

And there are two of you.

(Coming back on, leading a very reluctant Sark, who is squeaking.)

Look what I found.

SARK: *(About the light.)* What this? Ow!!

(Very quickly, Eebee enters, grabs Sark, and exits with her.)

EMO: What was that?

GEENOMA: Some, like, creatures!

ZIPPER: They looked like us—sort of.

SEVEN: But where's Meema?

This is terrible.

EMO: *(About the weirdness of the creatures.)* Zipper, could there be other mistakes—

ZIPPER: Like us? We are not mistakes! Don't ever think that!

EMO: And we don't need any operations.

ZIPPER: Right.

SEVEN: Where is Meema? I've lost Meema.

EMO: Meema's gone!

SEVEN: Where is she? Where is she?

(Seven is frozen with fear.)

GEENOMA: Now, like, OK like OK. Just everybody calm down.

EMO: Seven is calm.

ZIPPER: Seven is catatonic. I've never seen him like this.

GEENOMA: OK. OK. OK. I'm the leader. OK.

(Beat. Then loses it.)

MEEEEEEEEEMAAAAAAAAAAAH!!

EMO: Meema's gone! Meema's gone.

ZIPPER: Everybody!! Chill. Except you, Seven. You need to melt. Wake up. Unfreeze. We're on the Moon. We're on Planet Moon.

SEVEN: Meema?

MEEMA: *(From far off, in the dark.)* Seven?

Seven, are you talking to me from the Next World?

ZIPPER: No, it's more like the next room! Just walk toward our voices!

EMO: Meema's going to be fine.

MEEMA: *(From far off.)* Seven, I've never believed in the Next World and all that.

(Seven is coming to.)

SEVEN: It's all right, Meema. Just follow the sound of my voice.

MEEMA: *(From far off.)* I'm not ready to leave my mortal shell.

GEENOMA: Meema, like, just, like, stand up and, like, walk out here.

MEEMA: *(From far off.)* I hear Geenoma. Is she—there, too?

EMO: Me, too!

GEENOMA: We're all like here, Meema.

MEEMA: *(From far off.)* This is so profound. I was, literally, stumbling in the dark—

SEVEN: Meema, Sweetheart. Just listen to the sound of my voice and walk toward it.

MEEMA: *(From closer.)* It's so scary. To finally be leaving the dark tunnel of life and walking into the light.

ZIPPER: Will you just crawl out of the freaking tunnel and come out here??

SEVEN: Meema!

MEEMA: *(From closer.)* Seven. Now that we're dead, I can tell you that I love you.

SEVEN: You do? Oh, Meema. And I love you—

ZIPPER: Oh for crying out loud!!

> *(Zipper walks to the tunnel opening, reaches in, grabs Meema or some part of her, and drags her out.)*

ZIPPER: Here!

MEEMA: *(Hugs Seven.)* Life and death. They are just a few steps from each other.

SEVEN: Meema, we're not dead.

MEEMA: Keep up your spirits, Seven, that's the spirit. Because we're all spirit now.

EMO: Can someone explain to her?

GEENOMA: Meema, like, we're alive. Like, this is just the, like, DARK SIDE of the Moon.
> OK?
> *(Beat. She gets it.)*

MEEMA: I didn't mean it when I said I loved you.

SEVEN: Me, either.

> *(Light beams down on them from overhead.)*

ELECTRONICALLY AMPLIFIED ADULT VOICE: Kids?
> Thank you for coming.
> We told you we wouldn't hurt you.
> And we kept our promise, didn't we.
> Please get in line.

EMO: No, no, no, no, no!

> *(Zipper grabs him in a hug to calm him down.)*
> Seven
> Meema!

ZIPPER: Emo—hold on to me.

EMO: You're holding me.

GEENOMA: Like like like, this is horrible and I've totally failed as a leader!

MEEMA: Don't look at the light!! Do not look at the light!!

> *(But they can't resist and all look at the light except Meema. The kids line up and start to walk as a subway-arrival-ping sound hits and then the computer voice.)*

ELECTRONICALLY AMPLIFIED ADULT VOICE: Now

Walk Toward The Light.

Walk Toward The Light.

Mind the gap.

Walk Toward The Light.

MEEMA: Seven? Seven? Don't look at the light. Just look at me.

(They look at each other and find that they can break away. Finally, they break away totally.)

SEVEN: What about the others?

MEEMA: I don't know.

(They exit.)

END OF SCENE

SCENE EIGHT

On the light side of the Moon. Uberbeth, Yuseef, and Toyn, still stuck together, are lying down.

YUSEEF: Well. This is great.

UBERBETH: We've fallen and we can't get up.

TOYN: Uhn. Uhn.

YUSEEF: Stop moving that way! It doesn't work and it always hurts me.

UBERBETH: Well. We can't stay here forever!

TOYN: Uhn. Uhn.

UBERBETH: Look, the only way we're going to be able to stand up, is if we work together.

YUSEEF: Oh, please. Spare me the do-gooder globilization mottos.

UBERBETH: I'm serious.

YUSEEF: So am I.

(Uberbeth—flatulence.)

UBERBETH: Excuse me.

YUSEEF: For what??

TOYN: *(Reacting to the odor of the flatulence.)* EEEEEuuuuw. Uberbeth.

YUSEEF: Stop flailing, Toyn!

TOYN: Have to disconnect!! Bad smells are hard on components.

YUSEEF: I showered this morning! OK! It's been a hot day and I can't help it. I sweat!

UBERBETH: You smell OK. You smell kinda good, in fact.

YUSEEF: Well, I wouldn't know. I have no sense of smell.

UBERBETH: Really.

YUSEEF: Yeah. It's some genetic fluke in my family's genes. BUT it happened naturally, after generations of normal, human mating. We're not mutants. Or freaks.

UBERBETH: I'm ignoring the mutant bashing you engage in constantly and have decided to move beyond it because I am a better person, however genetically "Other" I may appear to be. And why this change of heart on my part? BECAUSE you are a freak, too, although you have been assimilated and brainwashed and deprived of the proper conduits to your true culture of the genetically altered. You have the low self image typical of the assimilated because you don't know Who You Are. You are, in fact, Identity-Challenged, and have, in typical fashion, over-identified with the dominant nongenetically altered culture, hence your employment as an officer in the dominant-culture police force.

YUSEEF: Are you finished?

UBERBETH: Yeah, OK.

I'll put my foot here. And Toyn will move that way. Toyn?

TOYN: Instructions received.

YUSEEF: Good. Now, if I put my hand over here, then—

(With a lot of grunting, they cooperate and stand up.)

ALL: We did it!!

(Sound of Muzak approaching and the light.)

TOYN: Digital unit?

YUSEEF: Uh-oh. It's them.

UBERBETH: Who?

ELECTRONICALLY AMPLIFIED ADULT VOICE: Good job, Officer Cho-Chee-Whatever your name is!

You have apprehended the mutants.

(Toyn begins to have a breathing incident.)

UBERBETH: Toyn?

Stay calm.

(To the "voice.")

You're scaring him!! Stop it!!

(To Yuseef.)

I thought YOU controlled the voice.

YUSEEF: Unless it's overridden by my—employers.

UBERBETH: Rent-a-cop!! Rent-a-cop!!

ELECTRONICALLY AMPLIFIED ADULT VOICE: You have been apprehended by the Family Always Serves Community In Setting Things Straight. Prepare for paralyzation to precede sterilization.

Have a nice day.

(Sound of an electronic something revving up.)

YUSEEF: Wait a minute. She's the only mutant.

He and I are human!!

UBERBETH: *(To Yuseef.)* You—horrible human!!

YUSEEF: *(To Uberbeth.)* Get behind Toyn and me.

(To Toyn.)

Come on, Toyn—hop around so we're in front.

UBERBETH: You monster!

YUSEEF: *(Still to Toyn.)* They won't want to shoot humans. Get in front of Uberbeth—we'll be a shield for her. I'm trying to protect you!!! Will everyone just do as I say???

(Electronic sound revs up again and increases. Yuseef gets ready to take the hit. Electronic sound revs down.)

YUSEEF: See? See?

UBERBETH: I saw.

TOYN: Goo deactivated.

UBERBETH: *(Grabs Toyn, then Yuseef by the hand.)* Now let's get out of here.

(They exit.)

VOICE-OVER: Officer Yuseef Cho—whatever your name is.

You are no longer in the employ

Of the Family Always Serves Community In Setting Things Straight.

Have a terrible day.

ÉND OF SCENE

SCENE NINE

Geenoma, Zipper, Emo.

ZIPPER: Where. . . Are. . . We?

EMO: Have they done it yet?

GEENOMA: Like, open, your eyes, Emo.

(Uberbeth gets pushed in.)

ZIPPER: Uberbeth! You're here!

GEENOMA: Uberbeth, are you, like, OK?

EMO: Where's Toyn? Oh, poor little boy—they've fixed him.

UBERBETH: I got recaptured because of him. Have—have any of you seen a policeman?

Tall? Not too ugly?

GEENOMA: Uberbeth, are you, like, OK?

EMO: But where IS Toyn? Poor little boy.

TOYN: *(Offstage.)* This unit does not recognize your operating system! This unit has confirmed that you have experienced information deterioration!

EMO: That's Toyn!

GEENOMA: I, like, never heard him, like, talk so much!

ZIPPER: Who is he talking to?

UBERBETH: He has issues with the Digital Unit that keeps pursuing us. He wouldn't shut up and that's how we got caught again!

ZIPPER: Hey, where are Meema and Seven?

EMO: They've got them first!!! They're lasered and fixed like earth pets!

ELECTRONICALLY AMPLIFIED ADULT VOICE: Please be quiet.

(Beat. Everyone gets quiet.)

Thank you.

You are scheduled for sterilization in twenty minutes.

You are scheduled for sterilization in twenty minutes.

Have a nice day.

(Toyn enters as if pushed.)

TOYN: Bad code!! Bad, bad code!!

ELECTRONICALLY AMPLIFIED ADULT VOICE: Shut up, little boy.

Have a nice day.

UBERBETH: Oh, Toyn, why couldn't you have been quiet? They would have never found us.

EMO: That voice! I can't stand it!

ZIPPER: They're not going to kill us, Emo. And it won't hurt. I promise.

UBERBETH: The flatulence gene ends here.

EMO: I'm too easily upset to be a good father, anyway.

GEENOMA: And I, like, have this, like, bad speech problem.

ZIPPER: We'll just have to be each other's kids, I guess.

UBERBETH: *(To Toyn.)* Do you know what they're going to do to us?

EMO: Don't tell him. Ignorance feels better.

TOYN: This unit . . . will never be replaced . . . by a newer model.

ALL: *(Not together.)* Yeah. That's true. Sad.

(Sark enters from some unexpected place—indicating that Sark and Eebee have infilitrated everywhere.)

SARK: Oh, look! More aliens! Eebee!!

(Eebee enters from some other place.)

SARK: I told you, Eebee! Aliens exist. And I like them. They are pretty.

EEBEE: Tell us. Where are you from? Eggbootle? Zimmertrope?

SARK: You must tell us. And then we help you go home.

EEBEE: You must have many, many trash where you live.

GEENOMA: Yeah, like, like, like we're totally from, like. . . .

ZIPPER: Zimmerdoodle.

SARK: No, no—not Zimmerdoodle.

EEBEE: They are faking, Sark. We go now.

SARK: Where is pretty one who found us?

EEBEE: We go now.

SARK and EEBEE: Dasvedanya.

UBERBETH: Eggtrumple!

EMO: Feeblezom!

ZIPPER: Tropenboop!

(Sark and Eebee are gone now.)

GEENOMA: Help!!!

(Sark and Eebee reappear from somewhere else.)

SARK and EEBEE: You are from Help?

ALL THE KIDS: *(Each one picks an answer.)* Yeah. Absolutely. Of course. That's the place.

EEBEE: Help is fabled city. Dog went there.

SARK: He made us and our world and went to Help to live.

EEBEE: He went to rest because making us and our world was very, very, very tiring.

Maybe you are more of Dog's children.

ALL THE KIDS: Could be. Very possible. I've long suspected it. Oh yeah.

EEBEE AND SARK: We "help" you now.

(They laugh at their pun and then lead the kids out of the prison room. As they go, we see Seven and Meema looking for them.)

SEVEN: I heard somebody laughing.

MEEMA: The probability of them being in one of these corridors is very, very low. I don't know why we're looking.

SEVEN: Meema, you're sounding like me and it's scary.

MEEMA: I hear that rustling sound.

SEVEN: Bugs!!

MEEMA: No bugs. Little Moon creatures, maybe.

(Sark appears, but Seven and Meema don't see her.)

SARK: Pretty one!! Pretty one!!

(Sark runs to Seven and embraces him. Meema peels her off of Seven.)

MEEMA: Get off of him!

(Meema has embraced him to protect him. They both realize and Meema un-embraces him immediately. Eebee enters.)

EEBEE: Sark! Where you go?

(To Kids.)

We find your others.

(Kids enter and see Meema and Seven—much rejoicing.)

EEBEE: You might want to be quiet.

SARK: Bad bots around. No take my pretty one.

EMO: Why did you guys leave us?

SEVEN: To get help.

(That word "help" cracks up Eebee and Sark.)

SARK and EEBEE: This is fun. Now what happens?

(Yuseef enters.)

SARK and EEBEE: More company!! Happy!! Happy!!

YUSEEF: *(To the unseen bad bots.)* Ex-Officer Yuseef here!! And I've come to do the right thing! Because I know evil when I see it. Don't make me use this goo gun.

SARK: Who he?

EEBEE: Hero.

UBERBETH: You're all right!! You found us!!

SEVEN: What are you pointing at, Yuseef?

YUSEEF: They're everywhere, you know. They have surveillance everywhere.

(To the unseen authority.)

I found an entire communication system that someone made from all the trash that YOU, the Family Always Serves Community In Setting Things Straight have been dumping on the DARK SIDE of the Moon for years!

EEBEE AND SARK: *(Not together.)* We made that. No, you made it. I couldn't have made it without you.

YUSEEF: And you've been getting paid a lot of Earth rubles for that illegal, immoral, and horrible practice!!

(No answer.)

And I have reported you via satellite!!

ELECTRONICALLY AMPLIFIED ADULT VOICE: Hang on—the mutants have guns

And satellite connections.
Moving to Enron procedure
And immediate evacuation.
This robot will now self-destruct.
Have a nice day.
(Offstage sound of electrical burn out.)

ZIPPER: It's gone.

EMO: It's gone.

YUSEEF: For now.

TOYN: Where can we go?

SARK: Garbage ship.

EEBEE: Androids drive it.

SARK: We give you bots to help.

EEBEE: You take. We have extras.

SARK: Go to your planet.

EEBEE: Wherever it is.

(They laugh to each other.)

SEVEN: It's just on the other side of here.

SARK: There is nothing on the other side of our planet.

SEVEN: "Our"—what? "Our PLANET."

EEBEE: Our planet is dark.

MEEMA: Well, our TRUE planet is green.

EMO: But it looks blue. From the Moon.

EEBEE and SARK: If you say so.

GEENOMA: Like, like, who made you?

EMO: Did you come from a lab, like us?

ZIPPER: Weren't you genetically altered for space travel or something?

SARK: We come from Map and Pap.

EEBEE: Dog made us.

EEBEE AND SARK: Dog made all.

MEEMA: If you need us—

SEVEN:—to free you—

SARK: You go. Bye-bye.

EEBEE: Ciao-ciao.

(Everyone exits, leaving Sark and Eebee.)

SARK: Eebee, I told you there were aliens.

EEBEE: Good. Now we colonize more planets with our bots.

END OF SCENE

SCENE TEN

On the bridge of the garbage ship. The kids are lying down in a circle, look-
ing up, with their heads touching. They aren't settled yet though, and keep
sitting up and/or standing to talk to each other.

EMO: Is taking off going to be painful?

ZIPPER: No, Emo. And this ship looks reasonably new.

EMO: It doesn't smell all that good.

GEENOMA: Like it's a like garbage ship, Emo.

MEEMA: I wonder if they give smelly ships a name.

SEVEN: How about The Uberbeth?

UBERBETH: Guys.

YUSEEF: I can't smell a thing. I think "Starship Uberbeth" is a great name.

UBERBETH: *(Feels like she emitted some flatulence.)* Oh. Excuse me.

ZIPPER: Hey, I don't smell anything.

EMO: Me, either.

SEVEN: Maybe Uberbeth's changing.

ZIPPER: Hey, I can feel something on my back . . .

EMO: Nubs of wings, bro. I can see them.

UBERBETH: What about you Emo? Feel any different?

EMO: *(In a lower voice.)* No, I feel the same.

ZIPPER: But your voice is lower.

EMO: I'm faking it.

YUSEEF: Wait—who is captain of this ship? Shouldn't we have a human
captain?

GEENOMA: Like, like, you have so much to learn!

ZIPPER: And you're still on trial, "officer."

TOYN: You shot Toyn with goo.

SEVEN: I think Meema should be captain.

MEEMA: Only if you do the navigation, Seven. I mean, numbers, and everything.

TOYN: Computer pilot. All digital.

SEVEN: You know what's really strange? The odds of two lost socks finding
each other is astronomical, but to make pairs from a random collection of odd lost socks, well, that's unheard of. That's all I was trying to
say.

UBERBETH: I feel funny. I mean, not in a bad way, but—

ZIPPER: Check it out!

EMO: No way!

UBERBETH: I feel strange.

GEENOMA: Like, like, like, I'm speechless.

MEEMA: Uberbeth. . .

(*The light on Uberbeth gets brighter and brighter.*)

SEVEN: You're lit up. You're—

TOYN: Luminescent!

YUSEEF: Luminescent!

EMO: You're shining!

ZIPPER: You're glowing!

TOYN: Like a beautiful . . . Person!

UBERBETH: I know. I know!!

YUSEEF: I hear the engines firing. Everyone get ready for take off!

ALL THE KIDS: You're not the boss!

(*Everyone scrambles to lie down and get back into the circle formation with their heads touching.*)

TOYN: We're going HOME!!!

(*They all reach and grab the hand of the persons lying on each side of them.*)

ALL: (*Much quieter, more to themselves.*) We're going home.

(*Sound of the big surge of engines and then take off.*)

END OF ACT I

ACT II
SCENE ONE

The kids run in, dragging Toyn. They try to stand him up, but that doesn't work. They're trying to revive him—he's not breathing. They lay him down and try mouth-to-mouth and pumping on his chest. They open his mouth, put in the inhaler, pump—nothing.

UBERBETH: *(In Toyn's ear.)* Toyn! Toyn! We're home.
> *(Toyn gasps and comes to. He continues to gasp—someone gives him the inhaler—he breathes in. He finally starts to breathe normally. He looks up at the sky. Meema and Seven start looking around.)*

TOYN: This is "home"?

EMO, ZIPPER, UBERBETH: *(Not in unison.)* Yeah. This is it. I guess so.

ZIPPER: It looks blue from the Moon.

UBERBETH: And as I remember, the Moon looks kind of yellow from the Earth.

SEVEN: The Earth looks blue because of its atmosphere. But you don't have to have atmosphere to be a planet. So it's not an impedance to the Moon's classification as a planet that is has no atmosphere.

EMO: I never understand you, Seven. That's why I never talk to you much.

SEVEN: You don't? I never noticed it.

MEEMA: I noticed it Emo. You just have to ignore most of what he says. Listen for the verb.

UBERBETH: Where's Yuseef?
> *(To Meema.)*
> Watch Toyn for me, OK?

MEEMA: Why? He looks OK.

UBERBETH: Seven? Keep an eye on him?

ZIPPER: I'll do it, Uberbeth.

UBERBETH: And no one move out of this area until we're all together.
> *(Uberbeth goes off to look for Yuseef.)*

EMO: I don't really want to move out of this area.

TOYN: It's a biggggggggg dome.

ZIPPER: No dome.

EMO: No dome? There's no dome?
> *(Emo starts to have breathing problems.)*

ZIPPER: We've been through this already, Emo! No dome. Sky.

MEEMA: *(Lifting her feet up and putting them down.)* Seven, check it out. Natural gravity. And the floor is so soft.

EMO: Sky?

ZIPPER: Sky. You remember. When we were little. Sky all the time.

SEVEN: *(About the gravity.)* I forgot. It feels different. And you're right about the floor.

(Seven and Meema start to jump. Testing it.)

TOYN: But this sky is blue. Skies are black.

EMO: He's got a point there, Zipper. What about that, huh?

SEVEN: Emo, move around and try the natural gravity.

(Emo doesn't move.)

MEEMA: Why do you want to be afraid all the time?

SEVEN: Yeah, why is fear your first choice? It's not logical.

ZIPPER: Leave him alone.

SEVEN: This ground is so soft!

(Meema and Seven jump, leap, and move around, experimenting with natural gravity.)

EMO: No, no, I can answer that, Zipper. You see, Seven, it saves time to realize that there's something to fear. I just skip that step and go right on to the fear part. Because I KNOW there will be something to be afraid of in a minute or two.

ZIPPER: Emo—that's kinda good.

EMO: I'm remembering things. I used to have . . . thoughts. And stuff, Zip. Wheels. I used to have wheels. They're important.

TOYN: How do they keep it in?

ZIPPER: What? How do they keep what in?

TOYN: The air.

ZIPPER: It stays here because it . . . has to.

(Realizes he doesn't know how to explain it.)

MEEMA: *(Hopping by.)* It's oxygen and carbon dioxide and they want to stay together.

SEVEN: Actually, Toyn. Oxygen is IN carbon dioxide—that's what "oxide" means. Two atoms of OXYGEN combined with one atom of carbon. And then there's a trace of argon.

TOYN: Toyn thinks those things don't sound very breathable.

ZIPPER: No, no, they are, Toyn. That's what you breathed on the Moon.

EMO: WAIT A MINUTE!! The Moon had a dome. Many domes. Many, many domes—

TOYN:—that kept the air in.

ZIPPER: This air stays where it's put. Don't worry.

SEVEN: It's gravity.

EMO: Does our breath keep it here?

UBERBETH: *(Re-enters.)* Can't find Yuseef. I'm just the least bit worried.

TOYN: Maybe it is breath. Like the breath of a huge animal—

EMO:—who is going to Inhale at any moment! And we'll be sucked into its huge mouth and stomach!!!

UBERBETH: Emo! You'll scare Toyn! Stop it! Zipper, make him stop!

ZIPPER: Have I ever been able to do anything with him? EVER?

TOYN: *(Tries to leave.)* Back on the ship! Back on the ship!! Mama! Daddy!

(This stops Meema and Seven.)

UBERBETH: What did you say?

TOYN: Back on the ship!! Help! Mama!!!

UBERBETH: I'm here, Toyn. Come here.

(Toyn comes to Uberbeth and she holds him, comforts him.)

TOYN: *(Calming down.)* Uberbeth. Don't let Toyn be sucked into—

EMO:—the mouth of a huge animal.

ZIPPER: Emo. That's not going to happen. All right? Clear? Believe me?

UBERBETH: Toyn, you called for "Mommy" and "Daddy." Am I Mommy?

TOYN: No, you're Uberbeth.

ZIPPER: Toyn, did you have a mommy?

EMO: And a daddy? I wonder what that's like.

TOYN: Toyn does not know what that's like. Yet he has a strange memory.

MEEMA: *(Breathing to recover from her frolics with gravity.)* Is everyone breathing? Good. That's the first step. Whoa—it's like being born all over again.

SEVEN: Do you remember that? Being born?

MEEMA: I remember everything. It's a burden, believe me. Elephant genes.

ZIPPER: I'm remembering, too. It comes in pictures. I never had these memories on the Moon.

EMO: Maybe memories are the atmosphere.

TOYN: And we're breathing them.

(Toyn takes in a big breath and breathes it out, and then, says simply—.)
Bicycle.

ZIPPER: *(Breathes in and out.)* Hoops.

TOYN: "Hoops?"

ZIPPER: They're important.

Is all I know.

MEEMA: Rumblings. Deep, deep sounds. Vibrating my tiny body.

SEVEN: I never even knew the owner of the womb I inhabited. I remember it was dark and there was nothing to read.

UBERBETH: I don't remember anything. And I don't know anything about the womb I developed in.

ZIPPER: I know nothing about mine, either. Except she was very thin. There was something about lizard skin and moth wings they were trying to figure out. They didn't consider the fact that lizards eat moths. I'm still very worried about that.

EMO: Mine was a bio-polymer womb controlled by a WINSAC LOGO-RHYTHMIC. I never remembered that before.

UBERBETH: It's because we never talk about this stuff.

ZIPPER: So you didn't even get a mammal. You didn't get something alive to be made inside of.

EMO: It had a heartbeat that they programmed. They showed me the contraption one day when I was six. It was on display in the lobby.

MEEMA: Well, I remember her. Her name was EF—#5783. Or "Jumba." She was thirteen years old. I lived in her womb for twenty-four months, so I grew to be a fairly large baby. I remember being inside. Lots of deep sounds came through me and they vibrated every cell in my body. I still try to make those sounds at night to comfort myself. But with my small lungs and elevated voice box, all I can manage is a medium tone, like singing. All it vibrates is my throat—not enough to lull me to sleep. When I was being born, I remember clearly being pushed along this tunnel toward a light. "Go to the light," I thought, but not in words because I didn't have any then. Then, suddenly, I was surrounded by light and I felt myself dropping, in a cloud, and, plomp, landing on the ground. It was a hard fall, but it bounced something out of this opening in my face. And then, wow!, My chest expands and all this stuff comes in—like dry liquid it was. And then my chest collapses and that stuff goes out. And THEN I have to expand my chest myself because I need more of this dry liquid. And then, it goes out. And I'm breathing. That was breathing. And I still do it all the time without having to tell myself to do it! Now that seems like the most wonderful scientific discovery I've encountered so far. Breathing! And it even goes on when I'm asleep! And now, I'm on Earth, and I can breathe everywhere! I can run in any direction and never, never run out of oxygen!

(Meema runs around them and then runs off in some direction, disappears.)

SEVEN: Meema! Be careful! The probability of you running into something bad for you is very elevated!

(She runs back in and off in another direction.)

MEEMA: It feels so good to remember where I came from!

UBERBETH: I don't think we should be running around just anywhere. We need to stay together!

EMO: She's a brave person.

SEVEN: She's an idiot.

Meema!!!

(Seven runs off to look for her.)

UBERBETH: Those two are so exhausting.

(Geenoma enters, carrying their backpacks.)

GEENOMA: "Like like, where is Geenoma?" "Is she like all right?" "Maybe she got like majorly injured when we like landed or whatever that horrendously painful and scary sequence was."

TOYN: Hello, Geenoma.

There's no dome but it's all right.

See? Oxygen.

EMO: It's blue.

TOYN: But it's not poison gas or anything.

EMO: Or some kind of ionization leak.

It's an ionization leak!

ZIPPER: No, it's not, Emo.

Ionization gas is purple.

GEENOMA: "Thanks, Geenoma, for getting our stuff." "We so like appreciate you carrying eight backpacks through those yellow spikey things that like hurt my feet."

UBERBETH: Where's Yuseef?

GEENOMA: "Gee, Geenoma, it's so good to see that you're all right!"

UBERBETH: Is Yuseef all right?

GEENOMA: What is it? Does Earth's atmosphere like make everyone deaf to like sarcasm?

(Yuseef enters, counting the audience.)

UBERBETH: There's Yuseef!

YUSEEF: Don't bother me! I'm counting.

UBERBETH: Well, excuse me.

GEENOMA: He's counting the bots.

ZIPPER: Yuseef, you know where we are, right?

YUSEEF: I don't think we lost any bots in the landing. Although a couple of them look a little the worse for the journey.

GEENOMA: So, maybe, you could tell me what all that yellow spikey stuff was that I walked through? It hurt my feet.

YUSEEF: Corn.

(Total stunned silence.)

GEENOMA: It's like man-made?

YUSEEF: No. It's made by nature.

GEENOMA: What's it like for?

YUSEEF: You eat it.

TOYN: But it's a solid.

EMO: It doesn't come in a tube. How do you get it into your mouth?

UBERBETH: You use your hand. Like with pretzels.

ZIPPER: Sorry, I cannot eat anything that's just out, laying around. It needs to be packaged in some way.

YUSEEF: We can wrap it up for you. Besides, it's been harvested already. What you were walking on was the stalks.

(Meema re-enters, barely moving.)

YUSEEF: Meema!

UBERBETH: What's wrong?

MEEMA: Gravity.

(She collapses on the ground. Seven re-enters, also dragging.)

SEVEN: Real gravity.

(He collapses, too.)

YUSEEF: We're going to need to get some food. And water.

EMO: Where is the condensation machine? Where are the pipes?

YUSEEF: Emo. Water comes from the sky and is pumped up from the Earth. Don't you remember anything about living on Earth?

ZIPPER: *(Suddenly remembering.)* Rain! But we weren't supposed to stay out in it. It burned our skin.

YUSEEF: Well, that was several years ago and we've cleaned things up. Rain is safe now. And snow, even. And the sun—it's almost OK to have it shine on you without wearing protection.

UBERBETH: *(Finding it in the first-aid bag from the ship.)* Sunscreen!
(Uberbeth starts putting the cream on everyone—their noses and the tops of their ears. She notices that Toyn is grasping his head like he's in pain.)
Toyn?

TOYN: Data. Infinite loop. Won't stop.

SEVEN: There's an extremely high probability you need some downtime.

MEEMA: And then you can re-boot, Toyn. OK?

(But it's not OK. Toyn is still holding his head.)

ZIPPER: What's wrong, Toyn?

EMO: I know. It's all too much.

TOYN: *(Stops, looks up suddenly.)* Skates.

    (Everyone except Yuseef is stopped by this word. Sudden rush of pleasure.)

ALL: *(Except Yuseef.)* Yeahhhhhhhh.

UBERBETH: Are you remembering?

ZIPPER: Something about his childhood, maybe?

YUSEEF: On Earth? Is he from Earth?

UBERBETH: We never knew. He just turned up on our doorstep. In the group home.

MEEMA: Before the Moonstead Estates people evicted us.

GEENOMA: Because they didn't like want us near their like "normal" children. As if!

SEVEN: It was Geenoma they were worried about.

GEENOMA: Well, I am like very attractive. I was made that way.

TOYN: Soccer ball. Football.

ALL: *(Except Yuseef.)* Yeahhhhhhhhhh.

YUSEEF: Enough of this infinite looping you're doing or whatever it is. Now, here's a map that shows you where we are.

    OK, we're in Canamerada. It stretches from the Polar North all the way down to Mexamerica. Where we landed is the Free Grass Range where everything is allowed to grow wild. And the buffalo roam. There used to be cities and towns here, but everything was eliminated from Longdenver to Chi-Pitts and this reservoir of grassland was put in. There are a few small settlements here and there. I'm from one on the edge called Help. It used to have an exclamation point after it, but the Town Mothers had it removed, or, rather, didn't replace it when the wind blew it away. It's a Korean-Navajo-Muslim settlement, but we take anybody in. We're going to walk there—

TOYN: You're not the boss!

YUSEEF: I'm suggesting that we go there because they will have water and food. Yes?

(A large boom heard.)

EMO: *(Diving under everyone.)* Heads down!!

ZIPPER: What WAS that?

SEVEN: Probably not man-made. Resonance uncharacteristic of armaments.

    (BOOM again.)

GEENOMA: I'm not like too happy right now.

UBERBETH: Wait—I recognize that sound.

MEEMA: I smell something—

SEVEN: *(Did she just fart?)* Uberbeth?

MEEMA:—sweet.

GEENOMA: And like very, very clean.

ZIPPER: Something—what's the word?

TOYN: Rain!

YUSEEF: Rain.

ALL: Yeahhhhhhhhhhhhh.

> *(Another big boom that lasts.)*

YUSEEF: Let's dive under the ship.

UBERBETH: Not enough room!

MEEMA: No! No going back! Let's run until we find cover!

> *(She runs off and everyone follows.)*

YUSEEF: This is insane!

> *(Grabbing his map.)*

You don't know where you're going!!

UBERBETH: Yuseef! Come on!

> *(They have all exited, including Yuseef. Sound of rain.)*

END OF SCENE

SCENE TWO

Later. It's getting dark. The kids are under something. Toyn is lying down with his head in Seven's lap. Geenoma is fixing her hair.

TOYN: You don't have a very good lap.

SEVEN: According to the percentages, woman have more fat on their thighs than men—at least of the same test group. This gives them better laps. It's genetic.

> *(Toyn can't get comfortable.)*

Go lie on Geenoma's lap.

> *(Neither Toyn nor Geenoma are comfortable about this, but they adjust. Toyn puts his head in her lap and she attempts to comfort him—by patting him with a flat, stiff hand.)*

GEENOMA: Nice boy.

TOYN: Toyn is not a dog.

> *(Toyn sits up.)*

Dog. Dog dog dog dog. Dog. Toyn had a dog. Sometime. Somewhere. A dog. And her name was . . . was . . .—Toyn can't remember.

SEVEN: You had a—what?

TOYN: Toyn had a dog. A pet. A pet dog.

GEENOMA: It's an animal. You know, like—

(Geenoma imitates a cat lashing out with its paw and making that hissing sound they do. Seven just looks at her.)

SEVEN: What in the world was that?

TOYN: That's a cat. Toyn had a dog.

SEVEN: *(Whispering.)* Where's Meema? She should be back by now.

GEENOMA: They haven't been gone that long.

YUSEEF: *(Entering.)* According to my map and compass and the stars—Meema running off like that with us following her? We're lost.

UBERBETH: But we're on Earth. We'll be fine now. Right? We can go anywhere and breathe and—I am so hungry.

SEVEN: Where's Meema?

YUSEEF: She insisted on looking for some food.

(Meema enters and dumps some stuff she's collected.)

MEEMA: OK.

YUSEEF: None of this is edible.

It's just a lot of leaves and sticks and things.

MEEMA: Well, how am I supposed to know what food looks like when it's not in a package?

YUSEEF: And yet you ran off to look for it.

MEEMA: You're not the boss.

YUSEEF: Yeah. Well, you're not the best supplier of food, are you?

SEVEN: *(Picks up a stick.)* Well, look at this. If you put plastic around it, it would look exactly like a beef stick.

YUSEEF: Oh yeah?

SEVEN: Yeah. I mean, it could easily be that.

Maybe it is.

(Yuseef just looks at him. Seven feels he needs to prove his point, so he bites off a bit of the end of the stick. And then, he chews it slowly as Yuseef continues to look at him.)

Yum.

YUSEEF: OK. I admit it. It's an honest mistake. But we still need to find some real food. We can only live on the stores in the ship for a few days.

(As soon as no one is looking, Seven spits out the stick end with much distaste.)

UBERBETH: Yuseef is right. No more running off. We have to stay together.

MEEMA: And you are—who? Mrs. Boss?

GEENOMA: OK, guys. Stop fighting. We're all like totally tired and we shouldn't like move for a few hours. It's getting dark and like we have some food we brought. Peanut Butter Smoothy tubes. I suggest we like suck on those for a while. And then like go to sleep and like deal with everything in the like morning.

ZIPPER: Geenoma! Leadership!

GEENOMA: Whatever. Like, I'm so tired I can't even be like proud of myself.

YUSEEF: Geenoma is right. We should just sleep here and wait until the morning to decide anything. I know I'm not the boss. I'm just suggesting it.

(Everyone works, spreading a ground cover.)

UBERBETH: It's so beautiful from here. Pure-looking. One color all over instead of blue and white and gray like the Earth. A perfect round circle.

YUSEEF: Tomorrow night it will be smaller.

UBERBETH: No way.

YUSEEF: Way. It has pieces cut out of it every night for many days until all that's left is the smallest little sliver, looking like a smile and then—

UBERBETH: It waxes. And then it wanes again.

YUSEEF: What?

UBERBETH: I have no idea what I'm talking about. I just want you to think I'm smart.

YUSEEF: I thought you thought I was the stupid one.

UBERBETH: No, I just insult people when I'm tense.

YUSEEF: Oh. Oh, that's good to know. So, the Moon. It gets bigger again— that is, we see more and more of it, with bigger and bigger smiles until it's a half Moon and then, soon, a full one again. Fully "waxed." You must remember it when you lived here before.

UBERBETH: I was inside mostly. And then we were in the city and so much light all the time, we couldn't see the night sky. My first night on the Moon, I hid because I was afraid of all that black sky. And then the Earth—so huge and looking like an island. We couldn't see the rest of it.

YUSEEF: Who is "we"?

UBERBETH: All of us experiments. Meema, Geenoma, and me—we're from the same lab creche. And lot of others I don't know what happened to. But we don't talk about it. All of us—the guys, too—we're taught at the group home to forget about the past and only think about the future. Because "we are the future" we were told. And well, Geenoma, in particular, had a lot of trouble with this. Because she knew a lot about the past—she read books—and she was fairly frightened of the future. And really confused about the present.

YUSEEF: Why aren't you and Meema and Geenoma better friends, then?

UBERBETH: Did you have, what do they call it—siblings?

YUSEEF: No.

UBERBETH: Well, we're also very alike—not clones. That would be all we needed—we've got enough to deal with. Anyway, we're bored with one another. Sometimes, I know what they're going to say before they say it.

GEENOMA AND MEEMA: Uberbeth, what are you talking about over there? Are you talking about me? I can feel you talking about me.

UBERBETH: We really need to be in a larger group. Just ourselves? Would never work.

EMO: What is that????

ZIPPER: Wow.

YUSEEF: It's the Moon.

SEVEN: Of course it is.

TOYN: Toyn remembers that.

ZIPPER: Yeah. Seasons. Summer and three or four others.

EMO: The Moon looks like we could run and catch it.

TOYN: Emo, come on! Toyn feels like running!

UBERBETH: No, you don't. Stay here. It's late. Go lie down.

TOYN: *(Under his breath as he obeys.)* Toyn is not a dog.

ZIPPER: Hard to believe that we lived up there for so many years.

GEENOMA: Like, like, it does look like you know cheese. Like, people used to think the Moon was made of, like, cheese.

(They all just look at her then go back to what they were doing.)

UBERBETH: It looks so small.

YUSEEF: Well, it's a satellite—

EMO: Oh no—here we go.

SEVEN: I miss it.

ZIPPER: Are you nuts? Look around you. It's beautiful here! No bugs.

(Sees one.)

Oh. Well, not very many.

SEVEN: Bugs???

YUSEEF: Seven, the Earth is covered with all sorts of bugs. We live with them. And some live on animals and would live on us if we let them. There are probably about a hundred times more bugs on Earth than people. Some people say that bugs are the next evolutionary success story. After humans disappear. Either from causing their own extinction or just because all species eventually fade away to be replaced by other species. It's part of the great mystery of Nature.

SEVEN: I don't like Nature.

I don't like mysteries.

I don't like bugs.

YUSEEF: Like, in this field, there are about thousands of spiders, probably twice as many beetles. When it gets really dark, we can hear crickets. And on a summer day, you can hear that—

(Makes a ticking sound with his tongue against the roof of his mouth.)

And that's usually a locust. And if there's one, there's probably another hundred or so.

(Yuseef lies down on his back.)

Ahhh. It's good to be home. I AM an earthling.

(Yuseef falls immediately to sleep.)

EMO: He's asleep.

ZIPPER: Oh man, that's a good idea.

UBERBETH: He's asleep. He looks so adorable.

GEENOMA: You are like like like so like—

MEEMA: A goner.

(They all lie down except Seven. We should see the decisions about who is next to whom and then the rearranging that happens because of this. After they've all found their spots and settled in, Meema notices that Seven is still standing.)

MEEMA: Seven?

SEVEN: Uh-huh.

MEEMA: Come on.

SEVEN: I prefer to stand.

MEEMA: I'm sure there are no bugs right here. Right now.

(He doesn't move.)

Come on—you lie down next to me.

SEVEN: *(Whimpers.)*

MEEMA: OK. I'll save you this spot.

(Lights down on scene with Seven still standing, then the sound of crickets.)

SEVEN: *(Whimpers.)*

(Silence. A beat or two. Then in the dark, Meema and Geenoma have this conversation, each speaking at the same time.)

MEEMA AND GEENOMA AND UBERBETH: Restless?

    Me, too.

    Are they all asleep?

    Pretty much.

    I guess I'm glad we're here.

    Yeah, we can't be anywhere else.

    It's so strange.

    I guess I'll get used to it.

    (Beat.)

    Good night.

    Good night.

    Good night.

    (They settle back down.)

GEENOMA: Don't bother him, Meema. If he wants to stand all night, let him stand.

MEEMA: I thought we agreed not to read each other's minds.

GEENOMA: Sorry. I'm just—

MEEMA: Yeah.

GEENOMA AND MEEMA: 'Night.

    (Sound of snoring—everyone is out, asleep, except Seven. Then, the sound of a bit of a struggle and Seven trying to speak but being muffled. And THEN the sound of a body being dragged off.)

    (Beat or two.)

TOYN: Uberbeth? Uberbeth?

UBERBETH: What?

TOYN: Toyn has experienced condensation.

UBERBETH: Yes?

TOYN: And, well, he's afraid of draining them out there.

UBERBETH: It's OK. The ground absorbs it.

TOYN: But it's dark.

YUSEEF: It's all right. I'll take him.

UBERBETH: I was trying not to wake you up.

YUSEEF: It's OK. Come on, Toyn.

    (Yuseef and Toyn exit. And then Yuseef reappears in another location.)

TOYN: *(Offstage.)* Yuseef?

YUSEEF: Yeah?

TOYN: *(Offstage.)* How long before we see other people?

YUSEEF: A long time, Toyn. We have to get to Help, my hometown. And then we can communicate with the rest of the world.

TOYN: *(Offstage.)* How many days?

YUSEEF: We can be there tomorrow. It's just over there. I drew a map so I can show everyone where it is tomorrow.

(Toyn enters. He's finished his liquid draining.)

TOYN: And they will have ways for Toyn to find his parents?

YUSEEF: We can run your DNA through a scanner and send it out to see if someone's, you know, looking for you.

TOYN: Toyn doubts that anyone is looking for him.

YUSEEF: Well, you never know. I mean, what do you remember about before you came to the group home in that gated community?

TOYN: Moonstead Estates.

That's all Toyn remembers—Moonstead Estates—the name.

YUSEEF: But who gave you your name?

TOYN: Toyn named himself.

YUSEEF: Well, that doesn't matter. Because your DNA is your identity.

TOYN: Do you think that someone might be looking for Toyn? Mama? Daddy? And Toyn has a bicycle somewhere?

YUSEEF: It's possible. Now, let's try to get some sleep.

TOYN: Where is the map?

YUSEEF: It's next to the food, so people can see it when they get up.

TOYN: Toyn wants to see it now.

YUSEEF: Well, Yuseef is too tired and night is too dark to see and Toyn needs to go back to sleep. Come on.

(They exit to go back to camp.)

(In camp, in the dark.)

EMO: Zipper?

ZIPPER: *(Waking up.)* What?

EMO: Are you all right?

ZIPPER: Yeah.

EMO: Good.

Good night.

ZIPPER: Yeah, whatever. 'Night.

(By this time, Yuseef and Toyn come back into camp and settle down.)

(A beat or two. Toyn gets up very quietly and gets the map and, summoning all his courage, leaves to go find Help himself.)

END OF SCENE

SCENE THREE

Seven is wrapped (swaddled) in garbage-bag plastic and is in custody in some other place.

SEVEN: Make I speak now?
   (Offstage arguing in high-pitched incomprehensible sounds.)
   Who are you? What have I done?
SARK: He is mine.
EEBEE: No, Sark. He belongs to all.
SARK: Mine.
EEBEE: All.
SEVEN: Hello??
   Someone?
SARK: *(Entering, wearing huge sunglasses.)* I will take him! I will take him!
EEBEE: *(Following, also in sunglasses.)* No you won't! No you won't!
SARK: Eebeeeeee. . . .
   He is so pretty.
EEBEE: Sark. He is our god.
SARK: Not Dog.
EEBEE: Dog.
SARK: Human.
EEBEE: Bot. The biggest bot of all. The father of all bots and all Eebees and all Sarks. And all Weezers. And all Terkins. And all Evenzies. And all Oddies. And so on. And evermore, our creator, Dog.
SEVEN: Didn't I meet you on the Moon?
EEBEE: Yes.
SARK: Most certainly.
SEVEN: I thought you liked me.
SARK AND EEBEE: We love you.
SARK: But not for the same reasons.
EEBEE: You are Dog.
SEVEN: I'm Seven.
SARK: A beautiful name.
EEBEE: The name of a god.
SARK: Human.
EEBEE: God.
SEVEN: Could someone untie me?
SARK: Yes.

EEBEE: No.

We have to keep him, Sark. If we untie him, he will skeedaddle.

SEVEN: I promise I won't skeehooble—doodle—hooble doodle.

SARK: He's lying.

EEBEE: I know.

SARK: Human.

EEBEE: Gods lie. Particularly Dog. He told us there was no light. Only a little bit. And dark was better. But we like light.

SARK: Light is good.

EEBEE: So he is Dog. He looks like our image of Dog.

Hair.

SARK: Check.

EEBEE: Nose.

SARK: Check.

But human.

EEBEE: We find out now.

(Sark and Eebee unwrap Seven, making happy noises.)

SEVEN: How are you going to find out?

EEBEE: Blood.

SEVEN: Blood!

EEBEE: Dog was a super-bot. Dog was a Droid.

SARK: Human!!

(And with that, Sark jabs Seven on his thumb.)

SEVEN: Ow!! Ow!!

SARK: He feels pain!

EEBEE: Droids can be programmed to feel pain. They have sensors to protect them.

SARK: Droids don't bleed!

(Sark grabs Seven's thumb and squeezes it to make blood come out of the wound.)

EEBEE: Uh-oh. No blood. No blood, Sark.

(Sark holds on to Seven, not wanting to give him up.)

EEBEE: No blood. Name "Seven." Not a human name. Looks like Dog.

(To Seven who shakes his head "no" to the first four of the following questions.)

Father? Mother? Sister? Brother?

SEVEN: I'm genetically altered. We usually don't have those.

SARK: So are we.

EEBEE: Many erts ago, we were made by Dog. He was a great Bot. And even though we were mistakes, he let us live.

SARK: On the dark planet you call "Moon."

SEVEN: Did you say "planet"?

EEBEE: Planet Luna. Our home.

> *(Sing in close atonal harmony.)*
>
> LUNA, LUNA. YOU ARE OUR HOME.

SEVEN: That's how I feel.

EEBEE: Because you are Dog. And made us in your image. With your thoughts.

SEVEN: Oh, I hope not.

SARK: Don't you remember creating us?

SEVEN: Absolutely not.

EEBEE: No memory, Sark. He is Droid through and through.

SEVEN: But humans forget things all the time. I don't remember my childhood or, really, where I was before I came to the Moon.

SARK: Perhaps you are right, Eebee. He is Dog.

EEBEE: We are so sorry. But we must worship you.

> *(Eebee and Sark get into a worship position.)*

SEVEN: OK. I am a god. You found me out. And my first commandment is for you to take me back to my friends. Now.

SARK: Abuse of power—very like a god. I was so blind, Eebee.

EEBEE: No, Sark. More like a human. I was wrong.

> *(To Seven.)*
>
> You are free to go.

SARK: But I want him!

EEBEE: Our trip here has been pointless. We should have stayed on Luna.

SARK: One thing. Mr. Seven. Where are we?

SEVEN: You're on Earth.

EEBEE: Where is "Earth"?

SEVEN: You can see it from the Moon. Believe me, you can't miss it.

SARK: You can see no planets from our home. Except far, far away.

SEVEN: You cannot see it from the dark side of the Moon.

SARK: But the Moon is all dark.

> *(To Eebee.)*
>
> I can't love anyone who is this stupid, Eebee.
>
> *(But Seven has escaped.)*

EEBEE: We failed in our mission. We should go home.

SARK: Yes. Back to the ship. And home.

> *(They exit.)*

END OF SCENE

SCENE FOUR

Back at the camp. Everyone is asleep, except Zipper. He is listening to Emo talk in his sleep. He's clearly been kept up by Emo's flailing and talking.

EMO: *(In his sleep.)* Wha—wha—furry things—no, no—where are the oranges?
(Zipper finally just gets up, crosses to and rummages in the food tent and finds a Peanut Butter Smoothy Tube, opens it and sucks on it. Seven enters, out of breath.)

ZIPPER: Hey. Shhhh. Everyone's still asleep. Where you been?

SEVEN: Out.

ZIPPER: What did you do?

SEVEN: I was abducted. By Moon women.

ZIPPER: Cool. I'm next, OK?
Look at all of them sleeping. It's been a long time—but we're finally someplace we can feel almost safe. Well, there's the howling

SEVEN: And the Moon women.

ZIPPER: My wing nubs have been itching like crazy. Could you scratch them for me?
(He turns his back to Seven who scratches them. Zipper loves this.)
Thanks.
Peanut Butter Smoothy Tube?
(Seven declines.)

ZIPPER: You hardly ever eat, man. I don't know how you keep yourself going. It's like you're a machine.

SEVEN: Don't say that. Don't ever say that.

ZIPPER: I was making a joke.
Seven, it's me, Zipper. We've known each other for most of our lives, right?

SEVEN: Do you remember when we were kids?

ZIPPER: Yeah. Well, we're still kids.

SEVEN: If I stabbed you in the thumb, would you bleed?

ZIPPER: Tell you what. Why don't you just chill out. Over there, maybe. And breathe.
Breathe. In. Out. 'Kay?
(Breathes in and out again. Seven does the same.)
The air is so good—it's nice to know it hasn't been cycled through hundreds of lungs before it gets to you.

SEVEN: That's right. I do breathe. I breathe, man. I have lungs. I am a breather. Machines don't breathe.

ZIPPER: Are you still on that machine thing? I was making a joke. Forget it. And about the machines don't breathe thing—that's true except for androids. They have a breathing simulation, and heartbeat, and body warmth, and even, you know, some elimination functions. That's all so they can pass. As human. And not embarrass the friends of the families they're made for. Well, the expensive models are like that.

SEVEN: Do the . . . androids believe that they're human?

ZIPPER: I don't know. I'm not an expert. I get the same cyber memos that you do. I just read them when they pop into my head. You need sleep.

SEVEN: That's right. I do need sleep. I can feel it. In my body. Androids don't need sleep.

ZIPPER: Yes, they do. They're programmed for sleep cycles. They go into gray-out and then downtime. Seven, you don't suddenly think you're an android, do you?

SEVEN: Kinda.

ZIPPER: That's it. You're officially boop shooby axelotel mip nurt.

SEVEN: Wha—what?

ZIPPER: Freeman dosher it tell skimgus ming run.

SEVEN: Zipper? Zipper? What's going on?

(Zipper takes Seven's cranium between his hands and gently shakes it.)

ZIPPER: There. That better?

SEVEN: Yes?

ZIPPER: Ever since we were little, you always got a bit delusional when you were overtired. Lie down next to Meema and stay there.

SEVEN: OK.

(Seven crosses to Meema and lies down next to her.)

ZIPPER: Now don't forget to breathe. Even Toyn has been cured by this air. He hasn't had an attack since we got here. And listen—you could always hear him at night, breathing with such effort. Listen—quiet. Very quiet the breathing. It's a little eerie, in fact.

(Crosses over to where Toyn should be sleeping.)

A little unnerving.

(Sees that Toyn is gone.)

Uberbeth? Uberbeth!

UBERBETH: *(Waking up.)* Yes. What. OK.

ZIPPER: Did you take Toyn to empty his fluids recently?

UBERBETH: Yuseef did. A little while ago.

YUSEEF: What? What did I do?

UBERBETH: What's wrong?

ZIPPER: Toyn isn't here.

YUSEEF: Toyn is gone! Oh no!

UBERBETH: Maybe he went by himself. He was embarrassed by having to ask you.

YUSEEF: A box of matches, several Peanut Butter Smoothy Tubes. And, oh no, my map is gone.

ZIPPER: What map?

YUSEEF: The map to Help. I drew it for today and left it with the food for everyone to look at.

ZIPPER: With the food? I was over there this morning and there was no map.

YUSEEF: Oh no!

(Hitting his own forehead.)

Stupid stupid stupid stupid!

UBERBETH: Why? Why are you stupid?

YUSEEF: Because I told him that Help might have information about his parents.

ZIPPER AND UBERBETH: You did what?

YUSEEF: I mean, we were just talking and he asked if I thought someone might be looking for him, like a mama or a daddy.

ZIPPER AND UBERBETH: Yeah . . . ?

YUSEEF: And I said that it's possible. And then he asked how he would find that out. And I said through a DNA scanner and computers like . . .

ZIPPER: They have in Help. Right?

YUSEEF: Right.

UBERBETH: And did he know where the map was?

YUSEEF: I told him.

ZIPPER: Oh man.

UBERBETH: Toyn! We have to go look for him right now!

ALL THE OTHERS: *(Waking up and speaking but not together.)* Quiet! What? What it is? What's going on? Who do we have to find?

UBERBETH: Toyn!

THE OTHERS: Toyn?

EMO: Toyn is missing?!

Zipper? Fix this!! Please?

ZIPPER: Calm down, Emo.

EMO: Why? If I'm calm in a crisis—which this is, big time—then when do I freak out? When everything's OK? That doesn't make sense!!

GEENOMA: We should like like split up and look for him—STOP IT, Meema! LIKE GET OUT OF MY HEAD! LIKE I CAN DECIDE WHAT TO DO WITHOUT YOU LIKE SENDING ME MESSAGES!!

MEEMA: What? What are you talking about?

UBERBETH: Sorry, Geenoma. It was me.

GEENOMA: Well, like that's what we should do. Seven, Meema—like go that way. Emo, Uberbeth, Yuseef—like that way. And like Zipper and I will, like, go this way.

Everybody GO!

(The three parties of people head out, looking for Toyn.)

(Several beats as we hear them call his name and we see them appear in various places in the theater.)

(Toyn enters the camp. He is majorly changed, wearing shades, a cowboy hat, and a jean jacket. He strolls around the campsite, very sure of himself. Makes himself at home.)

TOYN: *(After a beat or so.)* Hey! HEY!! HEY!!!

(That sound stops everyone in their tracks.)

OTHERS: *(From all over the stage areas—not spoken together.)* Did you hear that? What was that? Could it be? It sounded like Toyn?

TOYN: HEYYYYYY!!

OTHERS: Toyn!!

(They all run to the "camp" from wherever they are.)

TOYN: Zappening.

UBERBETH: Toyn!

OTHERS: Toyn! Hey, Toyn? Are you OK?

TOYN: Whoa.

(Making a circle around him with his hands.)

Personal space. Tickets for violation.

UBERBETH: It's him.

Toyn, do you recognize us?

TOYN: Anonymous remailers? Rimbos?

Knowbots?

Braindance Janders.

(Motions to the area around them.)

Starling corn, dirtboys and girls.

MEEMA: Wait a minute. This sounds very familiar.

UBERBETH: Yuseef? Do you know what he's saying?

YUSEEF: *(Translating.)* What's happening. Don't get too close. Are you just some spam or the real thing.

UBERBETH: Knowbots.

YUSEEF: Are you just big dorks on a fact-finding mission?

SEVEN: Yeah, Meema. I recognize it, too.

EMO: Braindance janders.

YUSEEF: Synapses gone wild. And "Janders" are travelers.

ZIPPER: What's starling corn?

YUSEEF: We're standing in it. It's a kind of corn that's only edible for these annoying birds called starlings. So they'll eat it and leave the good corn alone.

MEEMA: I was channeling Earth talk! That's what that was!

SEVEN: It was a premonition that we were going to be here.

MEEMA: But who knew? What good is a premonition if you can't understand it?

EMO: It's not him. It can't be him.

GEENOMA: We come from sky.

(Toyn laughs a lot at this.)

TOYN: Arnoldspeak?

YUSEEF: Some guy from old, old movies who spoke in monosyllables.

TOYN: Bozotic.

YUSEEF: You sound like robot clowns.

TOYN: No bandwidth.

YUSEEF: You lack the capacity to understand.

ZIPPER: I'm going to hit him. That will snap him out of it.

UBERBETH: No!

GEENOMA: Like, I'm the leader—I'll hit him.

UBERBETH: NO!

SEVEN: Toyn? Toyn, I know you're in there, somewhere.

(NO RESPONSE.)

We are your friends, your family, really. Don't you remember? We were all in a home for the genetically altered.

TOYN: G.A.

SEVEN: Yeah, genetically altered.

TOYN: Fishberries. Fishberries.

YUSEEF: That's the Earth word for G.A.s

SEVEN: We were all experiments.

TOYN: Monkey tricks. Monkey tricks for the future.

YUSEEF: Because they used to use monkeys to experiment on—before they switched to humans.

TOYN: Bitstream down.

YUSEEF: Data transference isn't working here.

TOYN: Bozotic!!

MEEMA: Is he laughing at us?

YUSEEF: Oh yeah.

ZIPPER: Make him stop.

Stop!!!

TOYN: Uh-oh. Space rage.

(Zipper takes him down. Uberbeth shouts "no" and tries to pull Zipper off, Emo tries to protect Zipper, then Yuseef tries to protect Uberbeth, then Meema gets involved and Seven tries to protect her. Finally, Geenoma ends up on top of Toyn.)

GEENOMA: Toyn! Like like like BE NORMAL!!

TOYN: MAMA! DADDY! BICYCLE! Mama Daddy Bicycle! Mama Daddy Bicycle! Mama Daddy Bicycle! Mama Daddy Bicycle! Mama— Daddy—Bicycle—.

(Toyn is quiet.)

YUSEEF: Toyn, I'm so sorry you didn't find them. I'll help you look the next time.

(The kids get up slowly and off of him. Uberbeth goes to him to try to comfort him.)

TOYN: No! No. I'll be all right now.

YUSEEF: It's a big planet, Toyn. They could be anywhere.

TOYN: It's all right, Yuseef. I'm fine now.

UBERBETH: No, you're not.

TOYN: I am fine, Uberbeth.

I don't need them.

Now.

UBERBETH: Where's your lovey toy?

TOYN: I burned it. With the matches I took.

It was after I'd given up trying to find my parents.

I sat there. Under the sky. With my small fire.

I added some sticks and leaves because plush and stuffing don't burn very well. I sat there for a long time.

EMO: Weren't you scared?

TOYN: No.

I was scared before.

All the time.

But I realized as I sat there.

"I am Toyn." That's who I am.

And I came back and found you.

And I remembered all my Earthspeak, suddenly.

All the grown-up language I heard when I was little.

So I thought if I used it, I'd be grown-up.

EMO: You seem grown-up, Toyn

You seem more grown-up than me.

TOYN: That would not be all that difficult, Emo.

Maybe it's time for you to give up all your fears.

EMO: That's so scary.

TOYN: Just think about it.

I gave up my fears a little while ago and life has felt so much easier ever since. And then I found this hat and jacket and these shades and I put them on.

And immediately, I felt different. Better.

EMO: Changing clothes always make one feel better.

I hope to be able to change mine someday.

TOYN: Here.

(He dresses Emo in the jacket and puts the shades on him. Toyn keeps the hat.)

EMO: Yo. Yo yo yo.

Yo, Zip!

ZIPPER: Yo, stop talking like that and, yo, take off those ridiculous glasses, yo.

EMO: No, yo.

ZIPPER: "No, yo?" You're "no-yo-ing" ME?

EMO: Yes. Yo.

ZIPPER: *(Crosses and takes the glasses off of Emo.)* Glasses and a different coat don't make you grown up.

EMO: Then what does?

ZIPPER: Well, for one thing, stop trying to get my approval all the time.

EMO: Well, whose approval do I get, then? Yuseef's? Uberbeth's—I think I could get her approval.

ZIPPER: No. The only approval you need to have is Emo's.

EMO: Emo's? Oh, you mean me.

ZIPPER: Yeah. That's the general idea.

EMO: So the only approval I would have would be from me?

ZIPPER: Right.

EMO: That's so scary. So the only approval I would have would be from myself. What? Wha—are you crazy? Do you live like that?

ZIPPER: I'm working on it.

EMO: When I said "crazy" I didn't mean it, Zip.

ZIPPER: Yes, you did.

EMO: No, I didn't.

ZIPPER: Yes, you did.

EMO: You're right. I did mean it. But for only a moment.

ZIPPER: It's a process, this growing up thing.

EMO: Who are you to tell me what's a process or what isn't!

(Zipper is surprised.)

Was that better?

ZIPPER: A little.

EMO: Who are you to tell me what is better and what isn't! And who are you to tell me what is little and what isn't!

ZIPPER: OK.

EMO: How was that? It was a little longer—I split it into two statements. I thought that was a nice touch.

ZIPPER: Is that what you thought?

EMO: No good, huh?

ZIPPER: What do you think?

EMO: I have a headache. I think it was those glasses.

TOYN: Hey, guys. What's that up in the sky?

(They all look up. Long beat.)

EMO: It's a ship!

ZIPPER: It's our ship.

SEVEN: Oh no!!

MEEMA: Yes.

UBERBETH: That's our ship.

YUSEEF: Who's piloting it?

TOYN: Computer. Don't you remember?

GEENOMA: But, like, like, someone has to turn it on.

SEVEN: Moon women.

ZIPPER: Seven. Breathe. OK?

SEVEN: No, really, Zip.

MEEMA: You mean those little creatures who gave us the ship?

SEVEN: Moon women, Meema.

UBERBETH: Eebee and Sark.

SEVEN: Those are the ones. They thought I was a god.

MEEMA: Well, they liked you, Seven, but—

SEVEN: They abducted me. They tied me up. And then they worshiped me.
(They all just look at Seven and some turn away in embarrassment.)
What?

I'm telling the truth. They wrapped me in plastic and this silvery tape.

ZIPPER: He needs a major nap, Meema.

MEEMA: I know.

UBERBETH: Well, it's gone, guys.

ZIPPER: You're the leader, Geenoma. What do we do now?

EMO: The ship is gone! It's gone!

YUSEEF: I think they all know that, Emo.

EMO: Well, yeah. As long as you're sure. Because everyone should know that we're—

YUSEEF:—earthlings. All earthlings now.

EMO: Hold it. That's NOT what I was going to say before you so rudely interrupted me. And I don't want anyone to interrupt me again. Because what I have to say is as important as what anyone else has to say.
(They wait for Emo to finish, but he can't remember what he was going to say.)

TOYN: What was it you were going to say, Emo?
(Trying to cue him.)
"Everyone should know that we're—"

EMO: *(So happy he remembered.)* Stuck! We're STUCK!! We're stuck on this huge planet we know nothing about and with no visible means of support and with limited water and food. And we've never been where we're going.

GEENOMA: Like, thank you, Emo. For that like clarification. So now, my order is, like like like, get used to it, everyone. And, like, that's my final order! Oh, and, like, break camp. And, like, move out! And, like, follow Yuseef!
(To Zipper.)
That is like so tiring, at times.

ZIPPER: Good job, Geenoma. And could you scratch my back? These wings are driving me crazy again. Will I develop an exoskeleton? Man, I hope not.
(She scratches his wing nubs. Everyone starts to pack up. Seven stops and looks up at the sky.)

SEVEN: The Moon is almost white now. Soon we won't be able to see it.

MEEMA: Until tomorrow night.

SEVEN: I still feel I belong on that planet instead of this one.

MEEMA: We could go back someday. When we're older. And, possibly, armed.

SEVEN: They won't own it forever, Meema. And it's still pure and beautiful. Good-bye to the Sea of Tranquility.

MEEMA: Where Neil Armstrong took his first steps.

UBERBETH: Good-bye to the Sea of Rain.

YUSEEF: With the two craters, Copernicus and Kepler. Hey, we all learn about it, even on Earth.

ZIPPER: Good-bye to the Sea of Nectar.

TOYN: And Vapors.

EMO: And Clouds.

GEENOMA: Good-bye to the like Ocean of Storms.

MEEMA: And the Sea of Cold.

UBERBETH: And the Sea of Knowing.

ZIPPER: Good-bye to Emo's crater—

ALL: *(Except Yuseef and Emo.)*—The Sea of Crises.

SEVEN: Good-bye to the Sea of Serenity

MEEMA: Good-bye to the Bay of Dew.

TOYN: Good-bye to the Bay of Rainbows.

(They have all gone except Seven.)

SEVEN: Good Morning, Moon.

See you tomorrow night.

(Meema comes back and fetches him. They both exit.)

END OF PLAY

War Daddy

by Jim Grimsley

Adde Bigelow
Photo credit: Kimberly J. Scott

PLAYWRIGHT'S BIOGRAPHY

Jim Grimsley is a playwright and novelist who lives and works in Atlanta, Georgia. He is currently playwright-in-residence at About Face Theatre in Chicago and Seven Stages Theatre in Atlanta. For his play *Mr. Universe*, Grimsley received the Oppenheimer/Newsday Award for Best New American Playwright in 1988. He has received numerous awards for writing, including a National Theatre Artist Residency from the Theatre Communications Group, the first-ever Bryan Prize for Drama from the Fellowship of Southern Writers, and a Lila Wallace/Reader's Digest Writers Award. A collection of his dramatic work, *Mr. Universe and Other Plays*, was published in 1997 by Algonquin Books. Grimsley is the author of six published novels. He is currently director of the creative writing program at Emory University, where he teaches playwriting and fiction.

FROM THE PLAYWRIGHT

For years I have had a play called *War Daddy* rolling around in my head. What I knew about it was that it involved the son of a general who was fleeing from the general's enemies during an apocalyptic war. The play is an expansion of themes I explored in *A Bird of Prey*, especially in the way that the young people are confronted with an evil that they must confront without the help of adults. Craig Slaight and I discussed the fact that so many young people in the world are caught up in vicious wars in which the children become participants; we both thought that was rich ground for a play. The fact that A.C.T. of San Francisco and Theatre Royal Bath took interest in the idea and provided me with the reality of a large cast to work with allowed the play to happen.

FROM THE ACTOR—Hannah Finnie (Petal)

War Daddy was my first production with A.C.T. and I remember the first reading of the play. W. D. Keith was the director, and before passing out the scripts he gave us all an article about child soldiers in war-torn countries. Looking at the images, I couldn't believe that these were real issues that I barely heard anyone ever talk about. Reading about these children and their behavior, their nicknames (much like the ones in Grimsley's play) and their "motivation" to kill made that first reading even more powerful to me. I suddenly realized that this play was as important as it was unusual. This was a story I wanted to help tell.

In retrospect, Petal was both a perfect character and, simultaneously, quite a challenge for me. At the time we performed the play, I had just endured a difficult illness and had lost my grandfather, so the play itself was cathartic. The nights where I could successfully channel this energy were the nights I also felt emotionally drained, yet the feedback was always better. Meeting Jim and hearing about why he wanted to write this play, it was clear that the themes were not so foreign as they seemed. The hostility and horror felt by these characters was resonant to what was and is happening in Iraq, even within the Bay Area. The more we performed it, the more determined each of us felt to make the play our own and to communicate this message to an unsuspecting audience. We knew this was risky theater—it was dark and unusual and not "safe." But it was also exceptionally beautiful, a true work of art that was rooted in reality.

ORIGINAL PRODUCTION

War Daddy was co-commissioned (with Theatre Royal Bath, England) and first presented by the Young Conservatory at American Conservatory Theater (Carey Perloff, Artistic Director, Heather M. Kitchen, Executive Director), San Francisco, California, in March 2003. It was directed by W. D. Keith, who also designed the set; the lighting design was by Kimberly J. Scott; the costumes were designed by Malia Miyashiro, Katy Simola; and the sound was designed by j.j. Bergovoy. The cast was as follows:

EDDIE	Stephen Cirillo
GUN	Ian Budd Wolff
SANDY	Brooke Bundy
PAT	Charles Filipov
NIX	Aurora Simcovich
GOLEM	Gus Heagerty
PHILBERT	Joshua Schell
MOUTH	Lauren Klingman
FANNY	Morgan Green
LAZY	Aidan O'Reilly
NICKEL	Alexandra Steinman
POKER	Adde Bigelow
PRICK	Max Mosher
PETAL	Hannah Finnie
MOP	Lili Weckler
PALLOR	Jacob Gordon

The Young Peoples Theatre at Theatre Royal Bath in Bath, England, subsequently produced the play the same year. The producer was Kathryn Lazar and the director was Lee Lyford.

SETTING

A small town in a nameless country during the war between General Burly and General Handsome, which is the successor to wars that have been going on so long nobody can remember where they came from.

CHARACTERS

EDDIE, the child of General Burly; he is being pursued by members of General Handsome's Army.

GUN, lover of Eddie and co-leader of the escapees

SANDY, definitely a girl

PAT, speaks only when Nix speaks and often in unison with Nix

NIX, speaks only when Pat speaks and often in unison with Pat

GOLEM, definitely male

PHILBERT, a friend of Eddie and the group

MOUTH, the member of Handsome's Army who speaks

SOLDIERS, members of Handsome's Army, under Mouth's authority, who are pursuing Eddie—Fanny, young, a girl; Lazy; Nickel; Poker, young, a guy; Prick, definitely a guy

PETAL, who lives in the abandoned town; falling in love with Pallor

MOP, cousin of Petal, a girl

PALLOR, their friend who's sick; falling in love with Petal; Pallor is a deserter from General Burly's Army

WAR DADDY

Setting: A ruined interior in a small town in a nameless country during the war between General Burly and General Handsome, which is the successor to wars that have been going on so long nobody can remember where they came from; a small dwelling in the same town.

POKER: I grew up with a gun in my hand. I always knew I had to fight. My dad taught me how to shoot. We were in the backyard. I was a really little kid then, I didn't know anything. We had two rooms in a house, me and my dad and my mom and my sister.

I was just a little kid with the gun. I couldn't shoot it at first because it kicked too hard. It was a pistol, I don't even know what kind.

Where we lived was not in Handsomeland. We were under another general, I was too little to remember the name. Everything was quiet and peaceful and I went to school and learned my letters and numbers with all the rest of the kids and I had friends and enemies and we played together and then General Handsome came and bombed the school and killed most of the parents and put me in one of the recruit camps and because I knew my letters and numbers, I had to teach the other kids in the camp. My sister was there for a while and then they took her away. I never saw her after that. I still look for her sometimes, when I'm in a crowd. I wonder what she might look like.

We were happy and then General Handsome came and nobody was happy any more and now I'm fighting for her and I don't even know why. Except that's what people tell me I'm supposed to do, and that's all I hear. So they gave me this gun, and I have it, and I might as well use it to kill some people, since it's all such a mess out there anyway.

I'm just a kid, like all the rest of the soldiers. People don't live to be very old any more. We hear these fairy tales about how the world used to be, but I'm not sure I believe any of it. I don't believe people really could live to be eighty or ninety, no matter what the books say.

Now I'm on this mission to find General Burly's son and bring him back to General Handsome. I volunteered with Fanny; we like to volunteer for the same assignments, so we can stick together. We're younger than the rest, and the older ones pick on us. When I'm older, I'll get to pick on the younger ones. That's what my life will be like until somebody blows me up.

I wonder who started the war, and why? How long ago was it that the war began? I don't say any of this out loud, and I'm careful with my face so none of these other jerks can tell what I'm thinking. Especially Mouth. I don't want Mouth to know I have any questions. Mouth knows the general personally, that's why he sent Mouth out to hunt for General Potent's son. So I keep quiet, I keep my questions to myself. But I still wonder, who started the war, why did it have to happen, and why couldn't anybody stop it once it started?

SCENE ONE

Lights rise on the interior of a desolate building, a warehouse in a former commercial district abandoned to the war falling to ruin. Enter Eddie, Gun, and Sandy carrying heavy packs. Eddie is lame and walks with the help of a stick. Gun has a gun.

EDDIE: This one has a roof.

SANDY: You sure about that?

EDDIE: It looks like a roof to me. What else would you call it?

SANDY: Something that looks like the bottom side of a roof. But the real test comes when it rains.

GUN: *(Glancing out the door at the sky.)* That's any second now.

EDDIE: *(To Gun.)* This looks good, we can stop here.

SANDY: Where's everybody else?

EDDIE: Coming.

GUN: They're taking their time, all right.

EDDIE: I didn't see anybody on the streets.

GUN: That doesn't mean anything.

> *(Gun is finding a place for Eddie to sit. Sandy is taking off her pack, looking for a place to settle before the others get here. She finds a good corner and starts to unpack. Gun brings an old chair for Eddie, hovers over Eddie while Eddie settles, takes Eddie's pack, and puts it next to Gun's.)*

GUN: How's your leg?

EDDIE: Not bad.

GUN: Hurts?

EDDIE: Some.

SANDY: You think we're going to be here all night? I want to unpack a bit.

> *(Gun shrugs.)*

EDDIE: Where is everybody?

SANDY: I just want to arrange a bit of my stuff if we're going to stay.

GUN: We don't know.

SANDY: Eddie's sitting down.

(Gun shrugs again.)

EDDIE: It's starting to rain.

(Sandy starts to unpack. She has a few personal objects that she uses to make herself feel at home.)

SANDY: A person can't give up, you know. A person has to maintain certain standards.

GUN: What, you're putting out that crap again.

SANDY: These are my treasures. These are to guard me.

GUN: We don't even know how long we're going to be here and you're decorating the place.

SANDY: What do you care, as long as they make me feel better?

(Gun shakes his head and walks back to the door.)

GUN: Here's the rest. All but Golem. Wet as rats.

(Enter Pat, Nix, and Philbert, a little wet, anxious, and subdued as they enter the shelter, looking up at the roof, around at the walls. They are all carrying packs and gear and Philbert is carrying a separate bag of items recently foraged.)

EDDIE: Where's Golem?

PAT AND NIX: *(They speak as a unit, though they need not speak only in unison; the lines may be broken up between the two or spoken together.)* He went off with some people. *(As they speak they are beginning to help each other take their gear off; Pat takes of Nix's gear and Nix takes off Pat's.)*

PHILBERT: *(Setting down his forage bag and looking around for a place to nest.)* We found some food. Cans. They look OK.

GUN: Where'd you go?

PHILBERT: A few streets over. Used to be markets. I dug around in a house that fell down. These shits stood and watched.

PAT AND NIX: I was watching your back. A person can't watch your back and watch your front.

PHILBERT: Nobody saw us.

PAT AND NIX: We're not all framed for taking risks. We were keeping an eye out on the street.

EDDIE: I'm sure you were being very helpful.

GUN: Philbert just likes to make sure we all know how much he's doing.

PHILBERT: That's right, boss.

EDDIE: Who did Golem meet? Where did he go?

PAT AND NIX: These other kids.

PHILBERT: Raggeder than us.

PAT AND NIX: He just went, you know Golem. He hates you anyway, he said.

EDDIE: Did he?

PHILBERT: Shut up, you two.

PAT AND NIX: I'm telling the truth. That's what Golem said.

PHILBERT: That's between Golem and Eddie. That's their business, not yours.

PAT AND NIX: Then Golem shouldn't have said anything.

EDDIE: Where did he go? Is he coming back?

PHILBERT: He met some people who live here. Two kids. They went off.

    (Eddie moves away from the others. Gun is disturbed by this.)

PAT AND NIX: I don't care if he never comes. He was no help. Do you? *(They look at each other.)*

SANDY: I hope he brings back food.

GUN: *(Looking at Eddie.)* I'm with the twins, I don't care whether he comes back or not.

PHILBERT: He didn't say he wasn't coming back.

EDDIE: Did he really say he hates me?

PHILBERT: Yes.

EDDIE: But I got us out of there.

    (Philbert shrugs.)

EDDIE: I didn't know they would follow me.

PHILBERT: It's because of your dad. He hates you because of your dad.

    (Silence for a while. Eddie exits. Gun studies where Eddie was for a while. Pat and Nix set up an area for themselves. Philbert sits down on his pack. Sandy has finished arranging her possessions to make her "apartment.")

SANDY: *(Looking out a window.)* Look at those clouds, will you? Look how red the sky is. Even with the rain falling.

GUN: It's always like that after artillery. It's the smoke from the guns.

SANDY: I haven't heard any guns lately.

GUN: Me either.

SANDY: Or planes.

GUN: *(Shrugs.)* We're pretty far off the main routes. Doesn't mean they won't come.

SANDY: Do you know where we are?

GUN: Not exactly. We drove the van east on some roads Eddie knew about and then he headed up this road and it looked to me like we were still going east, but I'm not sure. Once we ran out of gas, I don't know which way we were walking.

SANDY: Into the country.

GUN: What?

SANDY: We were walking into the country. *(Coming closer to Gun.)* You can stay in here with me if you want to.

GUN: The country's everywhere, every direction. You're nuts.

SANDY: Stay with me anyway.

GUN: In where?

SANDY: In here. In my apartment.

GUN: This junk of yours spread out all over? That's what you call this place?

SANDY: Yes. Because it's my junk. Spread out all over.

GUN: And you're inviting me to stay here. I'm touched. But I'm right over there, see? There's my pack.

SANDY: With Eddie.

(Gun refuses to answer.)

SANDY: Where did he go, anyway?

GUN: Out back, I think. There's a yard in a fence, like. Shitty but green.

SANDY: Watch your mouth. You can't talk like that in my house.

PHILBERT: *(From his own part of the space.)* Cut the crap, Sandy.

SANDY: I mean it. No filthy language.

PAT AND NIX: She's crazy. Listen to her. She's always been crazy.

SANDY: You've only known me a year. So how do you know what I've been like, always?

PHILBERT: This is one big room and we're all in it and we can all hear each other. You can have your little part of it but I'm not playing some stupid game with you about how it's your apartment and this is my apartment and all that. Last night was enough of that.

(Silence a moment. Eddie enters.)

SANDY: But this is my apartment.

PHILBERT: Whatever makes you happy.

PAT AND NIX: I told you she was crazy. We told you.

(Eddie moves to his own pack, opens it, pulls out a gun, looks at it; no one remarks on the gun or pays much attention to what he does beyond noting. He checks to make sure the gun is clean, loaded, ready to fire, puts on the safety, puts the gun back in his pack, pulls out a book, sits and starts to read. Pat and Nix are the cooks and start to prepare food. They have a portable stove and cans of fuel.)

PAT AND NIX: I only have a few cans left. The stove's no good when the fuel runs out.

EDDIE: You think you can find any more cans?

PAT AND NIX: We had more in the van.

EDDIE: The stuff in the van is gone.

PAT AND NIX: We had more food there, too.

EDDIE: We could only carry so much.

PAT AND NIX: Maybe we should stay here, near the van.

EDDIE: Somebody's found it by now.

PAT AND NIX: But what happens when the food runs out? I could stay near the food in the van.

EDDIE: Nix, it's not there any more. The food's not there. Somebody found it as soon as we left. It's just not there.

GUN: If it wasn't for the rain we could go back for another load. But it's not worth it, like Eddie says.

PAT AND NIX: But what happens when we run out?

EDDIE: I don't know. We have to keep moving.

PHILBERT: You have to keep moving.

GUN: Shut up, Philbert. We all have to stay together.

PHILBERT: But it's true. Just like Golem said. They're chasing us because of you. Because of your dad.
(Silence.)

SANDY: What are we having for dinner?

PAT AND NIX: Yams and beans and corn. Cans we found. So we don't have to eat our good food yet.

EDDIE: That's good thinking.

SANDY: Gross.

PAT AND NIX: We don't have any salt to spare so you'll have to eat them the way they come out of the can. We only have two pots so we have to mix the beans and corn together. Beans and corn kept the Aztec alive, and their slaves, in the long ago. *(They look at each other, vaguely surprised.)* We learned about that in Ancient History, in school.

PHILBERT: That's from Ms. Landrew's World History, not Ancient History. That's where I learned it, anyway.

GUN: I thought you said you hated school.

PHILBERT: I hated our school, sure.

GUN: But now you miss it. Lousy as it was. *(Shakes head.)* I guess you never know when you're well off.

PAT AND NIX: They had war all the time. Like we do. The Aztec.

(Philbert laughs, pulls on headphones, starts to listen to music.)

PHILBERT: Throw something at me when the beans are hot. I don't want to miss my beans.

SANDY: Where are we going?

(Silence. At some point during the quiet everybody glances at Eddie.)

SANDY: Where are we going, Eddie?

(Blackout.)

END OF SCENE

PRICK: I don't like to talk. Some of the other jerks do, but I don't. We're all jerks in this squad except Mouth. Mouth gives the orders, Mouth knows the high commander personally. Mouth asked for volunteers for this mission and I was the first one to sign up.

Me, I like the killing part. Other people think the war should be over. I don't. I like the war. It gives me what I want. It gives me a gun. It gives me people to use it on. I'm strong because of the war. The war needs me, and I need it, and that's the way it is.

There was a time when I felt different. When General Burly and General Handsome were working together to get rid of the renegades, I thought we were really trying to do something. Really trying to change things. But then General Handsome attacked General Burly, and I saw what the war was really about.

War all the time. War every day. That's the slogan. I heard it since I was a kid. My dad would say it. My granddad would say it. War all the time. We can't do without it.

Why do we fight? All that crap. We talk about it all the time. You probably heard it already, us or some other dumb jerks. We fight to be free. The price of liberty is never free. Crap. If you have to kill to be free, what's free? It's crap, that's what. Killing's just killing. Plain as that. And that's who I am, the one with the gun. That's the only ambition I have.

You think you're better than me? You don't live here.

SCENE TWO

Lights rise on Petal and Pallor. Pallor is lying in a bed, ill. Petal is beside Pallor, giving Pallor water.

PALLOR: That's nice

PETAL: The bucket of water was right here. You could have had some.

PALLOR: I didn't know if I should.

PETAL: You're welcome to water in my house.

PALLOR: If you say so. I don't know if I believe you. *(Pause.)* What did you say this guy's name is?

PETAL: Golem. He's with a bunch of kids who're hiding out here.

PALLOR: *(Laughs, weakly.)* Here?

PETAL: Yeah.

PALLOR: They picked a great place.

PETAL: They're not staying. They're heading out tomorrow.
(Pallor hears but does not respond; Pallor is disturbed by what Petal says.)

PETAL: Did you hear me?

PALLOR: Yes.

PETAL: We should go with them.
(Pallor is silent.)

PETAL: Did you hear me?

PALLOR: Yes. *(Pause.)* Where are they going?

PETAL: I don't know.

PALLOR: Did you ask?

PETAL: *(Shaking head.)* No. but it doesn't matter. I just want to get away from here. Things have gotten so bad lately.

PALLOR: Where is this guy? Is he coming?

PETAL: He went out with Mop looking for food.

PALLOR: I hope they find something.

PETAL: How do you feel?

PALLOR: Like crap. I keep running to the shitter. Can I have some more water?
(Petal gets the water. Enter Mop and Golem. Mop is limping. They're both out of breath.)

MOP: I don't think he saw us turn in here.

GOLEM: No.

MOP: That asshole.

GOLEM: You all right?

PETAL: What happened?

MOP: We had a run-in with this guy.

GOLEM: Mop was trying to steal his food.

MOP: He had a gun and chased us all the way here. I fell and hurt my leg some.

PETAL: He chased you here?

MOP: Yes.

(Pallor is agitated and tries to get out of bed, eventually does, and begins to look for clothes and put them on.)

PETAL: Who was it?

MOP: I don't know.

GOLEM: Looked like army to me.

PALLOR: Which army?

GOLEM: *(Shrugs.)* Does it matter?

PETAL: Mop, you sure it wasn't somebody from around here.

MOP: Petal, I know everybody who's left around here. I'm sure.

PETAL: Keep your voice down.

GOLEM: *(To Pallor, who is getting sick again.)* What are you doing?

PALLOR: Trying to find my clothes.

PETAL: Relax. Look, we'll be fine.

PALLOR: If some army guy busts in, I don't want to be lying here naked.

MOP: Whoever it was didn't see us come in here, I swear.

PETAL: You're so freaking stupid sometimes, Mop. What did you have to steal the guy's food for?

MOP: I didn't even steal it, I just tried.

GOLEM: It was still pretty stupid. You don't steal from army. They steal from you. This country has a system, that's the way it's supposed to work. *(Mop giggles.)*

PETAL: *(To Golem.)* So do you know how to find your friends?

GOLEM: I think so.

PETAL: Where are you going?

GOLEM: We haven't decided. East somewhere.

PETAL: Where did you come from?

GOLEM: A school. We were all in school together.

PETAL: Where?

GOLEM: None of your business. *(To Pallor.)* What's wrong with you?

PALLOR: I got the shits like crazy. Don't get between me and the bucket.

GOLEM: You look like crap.

PALLOR: Thanks.

GOLEM: You with these guys?

PALLOR: No.

GOLEM: Where you from?

PALLOR: Like you told Petal. None of your business.

GOLEM: You look like a soldier to me.

PALLOR: Crap.

GOLEM: *(Shrugs.)* So don't tell me. Who cares?

> *(They hear a sound at the same moment. Enter, onto another part of the stage, Prick, fully armed. Searching the building. Mop, Petal, Pallor, and Golem go silent. Mop and Petal gather up a few belongings very quietly. They sink into the back of the stage out of sight or disappear in some other way. Prick walks through the stage, including the place where the bed is. Prick stands looking at it in a distinct way, looks around that room carefully, looks at the floor, scouting for tracks in the dust. Prick backs out of the room, backs out of the building, exits stage. After a moment the others come out of their hiding places.)*

PALLOR: We need to get out of here.

PETAL: *(Following a few steps in the same direction as Prick's exit.)* He'll be back, you think?

PALLOR: He went for help. You two get your stuff together, whatever you want to take.

GOLEM: That guy wasn't much older than me.

PALLOR: Handsome's army. What are they doing so far east?

GOLEM: Looking for us. Me and my friends.

PALLOR: Why?

GOLEM: They chased us all the way from People's School.

PALLOR: You were in school?

GOLEM: My pa worked there. I got some classes.

PALLOR: Why would Handsome's army chase you all that way?

GOLEM: There's really only one of us they want. This kid Eddie. He's supposed to be in General Burly's family.

PALLOR: He's with you?

GOLEM: Yeah.

PALLOR: *(To Petal and Mop.)* You ready?

PETAL: We don't have much that's worth saving. How are you feeling? Can you walk?

PALLOR: I feel rotten. But I can walk. *(To Golem.)* You ready?

GOLEM: I guess.

PALLOR: General Burly's family, you said?

MOP: General Burly?

PALLOR: That's who he's traveling with. Somebody from General Burly's family.

GOLEM: His son, or something.

(By now they are offstage but can still be heard talking.)

MOP: No wonder these guys are looking for you.

PETAL: Did you hear him? He said he came from a school. A real one. I bet he can read.

(The stage is empty for a moment. Then the Soldiers appear: Lazy and Fanny, Nickel and Poker. They have been watching the others for a while, and Fanny goes to watch their direction. Enter Mouth, who makes a hand signal. Fanny and Lazy head offstage after Petal, Mop, Pallor, and Golem. Nickel and Poker search the stage. Lights down.)

END OF SCENE

NICKEL. My ma says she always called me nickel because I wasn't worth a dime. My ma was American, a nickel is American money, or it was. She died after General Burly invaded Handsomeland. He sent tanks and infantry through my town. Ma and me were living on the street, begging and stealing. Mostly stealing because begging didn't do much good any more, nobody had anything to share. Ma wasn't cut out for that kind of a life, she didn't last long.

My dad disappeared a long time back. We figured one of the armies picked him up. He was a big mouth, my ma used to say. Dreaming about better times. He was like a lot of the adults, he believed General Handsome and General Burly were going to get rid of all the other generals and make a decent country again, a decent place to live. Then all that went to hell and General Handsome and General Burley started fighting each other. So much for dreamers, my ma used to say.

I can remember being hungry. Sometimes we had nothing to eat for so many days I lost track. Everybody was so thin you could see their bones through their skin. These days we might skip a meal, sometimes; but that's nothing like what I used to go through. These days I get a little hungry on a march, but in those days, I would get hungry enough my stomach would knot into a marble right here, right in my gut, and even then I wouldn't get anything to eat.

We eat pretty good in the army. We eat a lot of beans and potted meat and bread that's usually pretty stale. Who knows the difference when you never get it fresh? You get used to stale bread after a while.

When we're on patrol like this we eat dry rations. It's like gnawing ropes with the flavor of meat. But I even like to eat that.

Give me a sweet any day. Give me candy or a nice piece of fresh fruit like we hardly ever get any more. Give me canned peaches or a bar of chocolate, and I'll shoot anybody you want me to. I'll shoot my own mother, who never wanted me to be in the army in the first place. I guess she wanted me to starve to death, like she did.

SCENE THREE

Lights on Eddie and Gun. They're talking in some area of the warehouse away from the rest of their party.

EDDIE: You think we're going to make it out of this town?

GUN: I was worried. When the van ran out of gas. That last big can, when we used it up.

EDDIE: I wish we could get more.

GUN: These guys aren't tough enough to walk very far. These are school kids, Eddie. And your leg is hurt.

EDDIE: My leg's been like this for a long time. I'll be fine.
    (Silence.)

EDDIE: Philbert's pretty solid.

GUN: That's one out of the crowd. One.

EDDIE: Pat and Nix are pretty helpless.

GUN: You think there's any chance we could find some gas in this town?

EDDIE: I don't know. Anybody who's got any is hoarding it. The only other way you get gas is from a truck and there's not a lot of traffic out there.

GUN: Maybe we could steal it.

EDDIE: Maybe. If it was just you and me, I'd try. *(Pause.)* If the van's still there. If there's even enough gas left in this town to steal. What do you think happened to all the people?

GUN: *(Shrugs.)* The last town we saw that had people on the street was close to school, way west of here.

EDDIE: This place got hit pretty hard.

GUN: I guess.
    (Pause.)

GUN: What's that smell?

EDDIE: Our beans, I guess. Our dinner.

GUN: That smells pretty good.

EDDIE: The twins can cook.

GUN: Smells like it.

EDDIE: They used to cook all the time on our hall in the dorm. I used to have dinner with them. That's how I met Philbert.

GUN: You could cook in the dorms?

EDDIE: Sure. A lot of kids did. It was the only way most of them could afford to eat.

GUN: But not you.

(Eddie does not answer.)

GUN: But not you, right?

EDDIE: No. Not me.

GUN: Because you had plenty of money.

EDDIE: Right.

GUN: Because you're the general's son.

(Silence.)

EDDIE: Does that bother you, too, now?

GUN: No. I didn't say that.

EDDIE: That's what it sounds like.

GUN: Nobody would be chasing us if you weren't the general's son. That's all I mean. That's what they're all thinking. And the only thing that bothers me is that they're likely to blame you for this mess we're in.

EDDIE: I know that.

GUN: Even though you didn't make the mess.

EDDIE: I know that, too.

GUN: What are you going to do about it?

EDDIE: This is such a mess. We had good life at the school. We liked living in the dorm. We liked classes. What was happening to the rest of the world didn't make any difference. *(Pause.)* I don't get along with the general. With my dad, I mean.

GUN: Yeah?

EDDIE: My mom split up with him a long time ago, when he was just a captain, a long time before he was famous.

GUN: Did you ever live with him?

EDDIE: When they were married, my mom and him, I mean.

GUN: Do you ever visit.

EDDIE: Sometimes. *(Pause.)* I don't like to talk about him.

GUN: You don't have to. I won't push.

EDDIE: It's all right. I don't mind with you. *(Pause.)* My mom didn't like what he was doing, setting himself up to rule the country, she said. She didn't want to have us exposed like that, she said.

GUN: Exposed?

EDDIE: Being the captain's wife was getting to be a pretty public job. So she told him she wanted to leave him, she wanted him to find us a place, me and her, and that's when he told her about the school.

GUN: Doesn't sound like he minded your leaving very much.

EDDIE: *(Shrugs.)* I don't know what he thought. I don't feel like I knew him very well.

GUN: I know how that is.

EDDIE: Is that how it was for you, with your folks?

GUN: I don't even remember my folks, Eddie. Maybe a bit, with my mom. There's a face I dream about sometimes, and I think it's her.

EDDIE: Sorry.

GUN: No need. *(Pause.)* At least I found somebody nice. It took a while, but I did.

(They are quiet together for a moment.)

GUN: So how did you hurt your leg? You never told me.

EDDIE: Gunshot. One of the generals sent some people after me and mom, when we were going to visit my dad once. My mom never got over my dad, quite, and for a while we would go and visit. You know how dangerous it is to travel. Well, these soldiers caught us. *(Eddie goes silent.)*

GUN: Is that when she died?

EDDIE: Yes.

GUN: They shot you, too?

EDDIE: I think they thought I was dead. My mom was holding me and she told me to keep still. That was the last thing she ever said. I laid there till she got cold. Then I crawled into some bushes. I'd have died if some people hadn't found us.

GUN: I'm glad you didn't.

(Silence.)

EDDIE: You look tired.

GUN: I am.

EDDIE: You didn't have to drive the whole way. Somebody could have helped you.

GUN: I don't like riding. I like driving. Besides, that won't be a problem any more. No more gas.

EDDIE: Unless we stay here to look for some.

GUN: Is that what you think we should do?

EDDIE: I don't know.

GUN: Maybe Golem will know something about the place when he gets back. He went off with a couple of locals.

EDDIE: Maybe. If he comes back.

GUN: He was just surprised, Eddie. We were all surprised, to find out about your dad.

(Silence.)

EDDIE: It's so peaceful out here. I wish the world was like this all the time.

GUN: Me, too.

EDDIE: You ready to go back inside?

GUN: Somebody needs to stay awake all night. I'll go first. *(Pause.)* You get a good view of the street from here, and it's not so obvious as standing out front.

EDDIE: I'll go next. Who else? Philbert?

GUN: He's the only one I'd trust. Unless Golem shows up.

EDDIE: I'll go talk to Philbert.

GUN: Tell him to move around some, to sit out here some and then to walk out back, in the alley. He should wake up you and me if there's any trouble. Same when you're on the shift, you should wake up me and Philbert if there's any trouble.

EDDIE: I'm starting to get used to this. Keeping watch, and stuff.

GUN: You've just been lucky up to now. But I guess the easy life is over.

(Enter Sandy, in time to hear this last exchange. She has come outside for a little air.)

SANDY: I guess we were lucky and we never really thought about it.

EDDIE: We had it pretty easy, all right. But you'd never have thought so by the way we whined and complained about the school all the time.

SANDY: People like to complain. I do. It gets you attention.

GUN: How are things inside?

SANDY: Quiet. The twins are sitting on their sleeping bags staring off into space, like usual. You think they're talking to each other when they're like that? With their brains or something?

(Gun shrugs.)

EDDIE: Maybe. Who knows? They act like they can read each other's minds, and I guess they have to practice sometimes.

SANDY: I think they're creepy.

GUN: Come on, Sandy.

SANDY: I mean it. Finishing each other's sentences and stuff. It's not right.

EDDIE: There's nothing wrong with them, they're just close, that's all.

SANDY: You're an idiot, Eddie. You're a nice guy, but you're an idiot.

GUN: Keep your voice down out here.

SANDY: Sorry. *(She is genuinely afraid for a moment, shakes it off.)* Anyway, they're not really twins.

GUN: What does that matter to you?

SANDY: They stick so close to each other, it's disgusting.

EDDIE: Why don't you just sit down and enjoy the night without talking for a minute, Sandy. *(Gestures to a place for her to sit.)*

SANDY: *(Sitting.)* I wish I had a cigarette.

GUN: Man, I wish you wouldn't bring that up. Just thinking about a cigarette gives me the shakes.

SANDY: I keep having this fantasy that we'll find a pack, like in a crate or something.

GUN: Shut up.

SANDY: Embassies or B&Hs or Camels.

EDDIE: You're making Gun drool, Sandy. You really ought to stop.

SANDY: I think Philbert's got a pack that he sneaks. He's probably out front smoking one right now.

GUN: Are you kidding? Have you seen him smoking?

EDDIE: Listen to the two of you.

SANDY: No, I haven't seen him exactly. I just suspect him.

GUN: So, in other words, this is another one of your fantasies.

SANDY: Maybe.

(Enter Philbert.)

PHILBERT: Did I hear my name?

GUN: Yeah, Sandy says you're sneaking smokes and not sharing. She says you've got a pack in your pack.

PHILBERT: Sandy says that?

GUN: She's having nicotine deprivation fantasies, I think.

PHILBERT: I don't have any cigarettes.

SANDY: You liar.

(The sound of gunfire is heard, people fighting in a nearby street. Everyone moves closer together by instinct.)

GUN: Everyone get inside. No lights, no candles, nothing.

SANDY: What is it?

EDDIE: It's people shooting, Sandy. Do what Gun says.

PHILBERT: They've found us, haven't they?

EDDIE: I don't think so. Not yet.

GUN: It's just more people killing each other, Philbert. You should be used to that by now.

(All are exiting into the warehouse.)

PHILBERT: Yeah. You'd think I'd be used to it. But I'm not.

END OF SCENE

LAZY: I kill people because I like it. The other jerks in the squad think I'm lying. They think it's just talk, because I'm trying to copy Prick. But I really am just like Prick, only lazier. I like what we do, I like fighting in the army, and I wouldn't change a thing about it. I got no theories. But I got this difference with Prick, I don't like to work so hard.

The one I really want to shoot is Mouth. I think about that all the time. Sticking the barrel of my gun between those lips and shooting. Man, I'm so sick of hearing it day in and day out. I mean, I'm here, I'm in uniform, I'm doing my part for freedom and justice and the boss' bottom line, but I still have to hear this crap all the time. The individual is the atom of history. Even the smallest person's sacrifice can make a difference. We can win if we all pull together. Now is not the time to question our leaders. You're damn right it's not. Not while I'm out here waiting to get my ass blown up.

I mean, sure, I'm all right with killing people. But I'm not so all right with the idea that somebody might do the same to me. Prick doesn't seem to care, Prick acts like nothing can kill him. But I think I could die from cutting myself while I'm shaving, I think it's like that. Your life wants to get away from you, it wants to bleed away like that. That's the kind of stuff that goes on in my head that makes me not such a good killer, like Prick. I'm too worried that I might be the one to get it.

My dad used to talk about what we would do when the war was over. He was simple like that, my dad, he believed in things. But he got killed right in front of me, by some stinking bandits. And after that I didn't believe the killing would ever be over. It sends a person inside himself, to think a thing like that.

Mostly what I like to do is to lie around and think about stuff. Like dirty stuff. Or like what I want to eat. Or like what I would tell my dad if I ever saw him again. Or if I had a brother and sister, what that would be like. Mostly that's what I like to do, think about stuff.

SCENE FOUR

Pat and Nix are sitting together on their sleeping bags. The sound of gunfire is going on in the background. In the beginning of this scene Pat and Nix speak separately. Later, in the speeches marked Pat and Nix, they speak as before.

PAT: It's a kind of rain

NIX: In my head it is

PAT: A pitter-patter sound

NIX: I hear it, too

PAT: I wish you would stop thinking so loud.

NIX: I'm talking, not thinking. That's why you can hear it.

PAT: Oh.

NIX: So it's all right.

PAT: Don't let the others hear you.

NIX: Why?

PAT: They don't think we need to talk to each other any more.

NIX: Oh. Do we?

    (Silence.)

PAT AND NIX: Once upon a time we were in a warehouse. The warehouse was big and dark and spooky like one of those ghost stories Eddie used to tell. Pat and Nix were in a warehouse and outside was the sound of rain or guns or something that made pitter patter in their heads. Inside everybody had the lights out and the candles out and they were all sitting in the dark. Pat and Nix were sitting in the dark side by side.

PAT: They're still calling us twins.

NIX: You're not even in my family.

PAT: You're not in mine, either.

NIX: Don't start that again.

    (Silence.)

PAT: Do you think they can hear us when we talk like this?

NIX: I doubt it.

PAT: So do I.

NIX: Why did you ask? Is there something you want to talk about?

PAT: No. I just wonder about things. I have a very scientific mind.

NIX: So I noticed.

PAT: I have very regular thoughts.

NIX: I agree. It's all right angles and straight lines in there.

(Silence.)

PAT AND NIX: Outside was a world gone crazy. People were shooting each other and stealing food. They were stealing all sorts of food from one another, candy bars and cakes, doughnuts and truffles, puddings and pies and biscuits of every kind. They were stealing nice clothes and shoes and stockings with no holes in them and clean, folded underwear with well-sewn seams and no unsightly stains. The rain was falling and the sound of the rain blended with the sounds of the bullets, with the sounds of the people screaming as the soldiers snatched their food right out of their hands.

NIX: They can hear that part.

PAT: I expect they can, because we're saying it out loud.

NIX: I agree, we are.

PAT: Do you think they like our story?

NIX: I don't even think I like our story.

PAT: There's not much going on in it.

NIX: The same old thing, war all the time.

(Silence. They sit side by side without saying anything.)

PAT: Do you remember how we got like this?

NIX: No, never. Not quite, anyway.

PAT: I do. I was walking in the woods one day and I fell down a kind of hole and there you were.

NIX: Well, if you're going to be that way about it.

PAT: What way?

NIX: How would you like it if I made a story where I put you at the bottom of a hole.

PAT: It's only made up.

NIX: But still, it says something about who you think I am.

(Silence.)

PAT AND NIX: Pat and Nix were born a long time ago, on the same day, in the same town, at the same exact second. They knew who they were as soon as they got out of their moms and looked around. Each of them knew that at least half of them was missing, because the other one had that part. And so they started to look for each other and they found each other after a long, long time. It was like a fairy story, that one day they were in the peaceful school where everything was nice and they were in a room and they were together for the first time and they knew as soon as they heard each other speaking each other's sentences that they would never be apart again.

PAT: It's like love.

NIX: It's not like that at all.

PAT: It's like the truest sort of love.

NIX: Sometimes I don't even like you.

PAT: Well, then, it goes without saying

NIX: Oh, don't say it, then. I already know you don't like me either. I already know it's Sandy you wish could read your mind. Because of her big boobs and all. You like Sandy's big boobs.

PAT: It's been a long time since you said that much without me.

NIX: We're being honest with one another.

PAT: No, we're not.

NIX: We're revealing our true feelings.

PAT: Oh, stick a sock in it, won't you?

(Silence.)

NIX: When you take off my clothes, I don't feel a thing. It's like my own hands are doing the job.

PAT: I feel exactly the same way.

NIX: We'll never get married at this rate.

PAT: Besides. I know you're sweet on Philbert, anyway.

NIX: You're just saying that because I accused you of wanting to touch Sandy's boobs.

PAT: Oh no. I know you like Philbert. When we were having the famous dinner parties in our room at school, you always gave him the best bits.

NIX: He's too skinny for me.

PAT: Well, Sandy's too top-heavy for me.

NIX: She's very well proportioned and you know it.

(Pause.)

PAT: You did give Philbert the best bits. Even tonight you gave him the crusty part of the refried beans.

NIX: You want me to like Eddie. Isn't that right?

PAT: Well, I like Eddie. That's true.

NIX: You're a brownnose.

PAT: Am not.

NIX: Kissing up to Eddie because he's the general's son.

(Silence.)

PAT AND NIX: Once upon a time there were six people in a warehouse waiting for the war to be over. But they knew perfectly well it would never be over. Because when you win one war somebody starts another.

Because when you kill one general, there's always two more who spring out of the ground, already wearing their boots.

PAT: I like that part.

NIX: Nobody said anything.

PAT: I'm not even sure they're listening.

(The sound of guns, which has been going on intermittently throughout the scene, swells as the lights darken on Pat and Nix.)

END OF SCENE

MOUTH: Where I grew up there was plenty of everything. I come from a good family. My grandmother was still alive when I was little. I wasn't the only kid who still had a grandmother, either. We lived on a farm near a village where a lot of people settled to get away from the fighting. There was no fighting where we lived for a long, long time. We had it pretty nice, I guess.

We were the better sort of people, my mom let me know that. We were an old family and we owned the land we lived on. We had a big house and a lot of slaves to run it for us. Maybe you won't like my talking about the slaves like that, like we deserved them, but we never asked them to attach themselves to us, they just did. People who had nowhere else to go, nobody else to turn to, but us. So we took care of them. We put them to work in the fields and we helped them keep a bit of a roof over their heads and we looked after them. My dad used to say they were like our children, the slaves. We had a responsibility for them, we had to look after them.

People aren't all the same. There are people who understand how the world works and keep it working, and there are people who just stumble along letting bad things happen to them. There are people who are noble and good, like General Handsome, and there are the rest, the sheep, the slaves, the ones who end up in the camps. Even the ones serving in the army, I guess. They need people like me, to keep them in line, to keep them moving forward.

I always knew I'd be an officer in the army, since I come from the better sort of people to begin with. I'm young for an officer. That's because so many adults are dead now, even the people I grew up with. My mom and dad are dead because of General Burly. He gassed most of the countryside where we were living. I wasn't there at the time or I would have been dead, too. That's why I hate General Burly, that's why I'd do anything to hurt him.

General Handsome is a good person. I met her a long time ago, when she was friends with my aunt. I lived with my aunt after my folks died, and General Handsome came to visit. She was the most noble woman I had ever met. She was nice to me. I wanted to be like her. I still do.

If there's any hope for us, it's General Handsome. She's tough enough to do what's necessary to get rid of General Burly and the rest. People say she's ruthless but she has to be. The world is a mess. You can't fix it by being virtuous and good. You have to be willing to do the hard things.

I've killed a lot of people, I've watched a lot of people die. I don't let myself get soft about it, there's no use in that. A lot more people will have to die before the war is over, before General Handsome wins. The quicker we get this over with, the better. So I go on doing my part. I even enjoy it a bit. There's no sin in that, is there?

SCENE FIVE

Enter Mop, Pallor, Petal, and Golem, running to hide behind some kind of barricade. The sound of gunfire is much louder here.

PALLOR: Get down behind this stuff.

GOLEM: Are you crazy, this is nothing but wooden crates, a bullet can go right through.

PALLOR: They're not shooting at us. Right, Petal?

PETAL: It's the Scrubs and the Scrims.

MOP: They've been fighting over this part of town for a while.

GOLEM: They're gangs or something?

PETAL: They've been here the last few months. They rob people on the highway and hole up here in between.

MOP: The Scrubs have a lot of food in that big building over there. The Scrims want to get at it.

PETAL: That's the story, anyway.

GOLEM: *(To Mop.)* You're sure?

MOP: I talked to one of them. This guy who runs with the Scrubs. He used to be my sweetheart.

PETAL: You never had a sweetheart.

MOP: Oh shut up, you. He was crazy about me. He gave me two packs of mints.

PETAL: Because your breath smells like the back end of a horse, that's why.

MOP: You're just jealous because nobody ever liked you like that.

PETAL: *(Glancing at Pallor.)* Shut up, Mop.

PALLOR: Both of you shut up. Or at least keep it down. You want them to hear us?

GOLEM: How long does this usually last?

MOP: Not long. An hour. Maybe—

(Mop is interrupted by a new sound. Pallor becomes instantly more alert and starts trying to search the sky from their hiding place.)

PALLOR: Those are helicopters. What the hell?

GOLEM: Helicopters?

MOP: Oh, man, look at that.

PETAL: Where did the Scrubs get a helicopter from?

(The sound of gunfire increases.)

PALLOR: Get down flat on the ground. Now.

(As Golem, Petal, and Mop begin to obey there is the sound of a huge explosion, lights flash painfully bright, the sound goes on for a while, some of the boxes crash over, smoke fills the space. There are several explosions, intense. The sounds ease away. Golem, Petal, Mop, and Pallor look at one another. Slowly start to get up from the ground.)

PALLOR: Somebody called in an air strike.

MOP: Those gangs don't have that kind of metal, nobody around here does.

PALLOR: It's army, it has to be. Handsome or Burly, one of them.

(Enter, out of the smoke, from the direction of the blast, Prick, alone. Enter, from other directions, Fanny, Lazy, Poker, and Nickel. Guns trained on Golem, Pallor, Petal, and Mop. The soldiers gesture for the prisoners to stand. Last of all enters Mouth.)

MOUTH: Very good. Very good. Fanny, call off the helicopter and give it my thanks.

FANNY: Yes, sir. *(Fanny has the radio and uses it.)* Air one, air one, over. Target is down.

MOUTH: *(Signals to Poker and Nickel who search the prisoners for weapons.)* Who do we have here, anyway?

MOP: That helicopter was yours?

MOUTH: Yes. Well, not mine, exactly. The helicopter and I both work for General Handsome. *(To Golem.)* But you'd probably already figured that out, hadn't you?

GOLEM: Me?

MOUTH: Yes. You. You're from the People's School, aren't you?

GOLEM: School? There aren't any schools any more.

MOUTH: Yes there are. Of course there are. I don't know your name, but I know who you are. You're from Hilltown and the People's School and my command and I have been following you for the last week. *(Looking at the others.)* Who are your new friends?

GOLEM: I don't know what you're talking about.

MOUTH: Of course you do. *(Looking at Mop and Petal.)* You're locals, right? You live around here?

(Petal is terrified and can't speak.)

MOP: Yeah. We grew up here.

MOUTH: *(To Pallor.)* And you?

PALLOR: No.

MOUTH: No, what?

PALLOR: No, I'm not from around here.

MOUTH: Are you going to make me pull this out of you one question at a time? I'm a patient person, but my associates aren't so patient.

MOP: He's my cousin. Our cousin. He's staying with us, now.

MOUTH: Us?

MOP: *(Gesturing to Petal.)* Us. We're family.

MOUTH: *(To Petal.)* You're really afraid of me, aren't you?

(Petal nods.)

MOUTH: *(Pleased.)* You should be. I'm very frightening. *(To Golem.)* And you. What lie do you want to tell me?

GOLEM: You said you already know who I am.

MOUTH: Well, at least you have some intelligence. I suppose all that schooling wasn't wasted on you.

GOLEM: You called in that helicopter just to get to us?

MOUTH: That's a bit vain. Don't you think? All that artillery, all that hardware?

GOLEM: The gangs were in your way.

MOUTH: The gangs are hoodlums. Enemies of order. General Handsome comes to bring order.

MOP: Oh, my God. They're after you and your friends.

GOLEM: Shut up, Mop.

MOUTH: No, don't listen to him. Keep talking. What's your name?

MOP: Mop.

MOUTH: Keep talking, Mop. Tell me everything you know.

MOP: That's all I know. He has friends. He's with them.

MOUTH: And they're somewhere here in town. If you call this a town.

MOP: Yes.

MOUTH: Do you know where?

MOP: No.

MOUTH: Are you sure?

MOP: Really, no. I saw him with them. But I didn't see where the others went. Golem came with us, with me and Petal.

MOUTH: *(To Petal.)* You're Petal?

(Petal nods.)

MOP: So we really don't know anything.

MOUTH: That's too bad. *(Makes a gesture to Prick, that somehow includes Mop.)* Is this the one you were chasing?

PRICK: Yes.

MOUTH: The one who tried to steal our rations.

PRICK: This is the one.

MOUTH: You're sure now? Because I wouldn't want to make a mistake.

MOP: A mistake? What? I didn't do anything. We were together, we were, all of us, I didn't do anything.

(Prick shoots Mop through the head. Mop falls dead. Pallor clasps Petal tight and puts a hand over Petal's mouth.)

MOUTH: *(To Prick.)* I suppose you were sure, then. *(Gesturing to the others.)* Take these into custody. *(To Golem.)* If you want your new friends to stay alive, you won't be quite as ignorant as this one. You'll take me where I want to go. All right?

(Golem can't force himself to speak.)

MOUTH: All right?

GOLEM: *(With effort.)* All right.

END OF SCENE

SCENE SIX

Lights on Philbert and Sandy. They are sharing a cigarette in the alley behind the warehouse.

PHILBERT: You ought to be a bit nicer to me after this.

SANDY: Nicer?

PHILBERT: You're at me all the time about my hair and my clothes.

SANDY: So, what, you want me to pretend I think you're good looking or something? Because you gave me a couple of puffs of a cigarette.

PHILBERT: Keep your voice down.

SANDY: What, afraid Gun will hear you?

(They are silent for a moment, passing the cigarette back and forth, both obviously enjoying it.)

SANDY: Anyway, it wouldn't be honest of me to treat you any differently. That wouldn't be like me. The others would suspect we were up to something, like maybe I was going sweet on you, or something.

PHILBERT: So?

SANDY: So I have my reputation to think of. You're not the sort of boy I would go out with.

PHILBERT: I'm not?

SANDY: You don't keep yourself up.

PHILBERT: Don't keep myself up? Sandy, we're running for our lives from a bunch of soldiers who want to kill us, what do you expect me to do, bathe twice a day?

SANDY: They're not trying to kill us, they're trying to kill Eddie.

PHILBERT: Well, they'll be perfectly willing to take out a couple of us along the way. And, anyway, I don't think they want to kill Eddie, I think they want to catch him.

SANDY: Even so. A person can't let go completely, you know. I mean, you could brush the dust off your trousers now and then. You could do something about your hair.

PHILBERT: I don't know why I let you talk to me like this. I must be crazy. I mean, here I am sharing one of the very last cigarettes in the entire world with you, and you go on about me like I'm some kind of bum living on the street.

SANDY: I wish you wouldn't waste your breath like that while the cigarette is burning.

(Silence; they are smoking again.)

SANDY: You think if we give up Eddie to these people they would leave us alone?

PHILBERT: Are you serious?

SANDY: Why should we be in danger because of something we don't have anything to do with?

(Philbert does not answer but makes it obvious that the idea makes him extremely uncomfortable, likely because it tempts him.)

SANDY: If I were General Burly's daughter, I'd give myself up right away. For the good of everybody.

PHILBERT: But you're not his daughter, now, are you?

SANDY: No. But that's beside the point. *(Pause.)* I can't even sleep at night for worrying about when the soldiers are going to catch us. I can't have any peace in my own head for thinking about what's going to happen. How's a person supposed to live like that?

PHILBERT: But if it hadn't been for Eddie and Gun, none of us would have gotten away from the school to begin with.

SANDY: So?

PHILBERT: Sandy, they stole the van. They loaded it with food. They warned us to get ready when the attack was coming. Doesn't that make you the least bit grateful?

SANDY: I'm sure if we'd stayed nothing would have happened to us at all. The school's probably still there, just like we left it, and everybody's back at their desks complaining about the hairs coming out of Mr. Gunderson's nose. This whole thing is their fault for getting us involved in this mess.

PHILBERT: I don't know.

SANDY: Well, anyway, there's nothing we can do about it, can we? I mean, I can't exactly walk out into the street and start looking for these people who're chasing us.

PHILBERT: But you would if you got the chance.

SANDY: I might.

(Silence. The cigarette is finished.)

PHILBERT: There's that one.

SANDY: Can I have the butt?

PHILBERT: We smoked it down to the filter, Sandy.

SANDY: At least I can sniff it now and then. When I've got the cravings.

PHILBERT: Here. *(Pause.)* But it'll only make the cravings worse.

SANDY: You won't tell, will you?

PHILBERT: About what?

SANDY: Don't be such a dope. About what I said. I don't want Gun and Eddie to know.

PHILBERT: Don't want them to know you'd give Eddie up to the soldiers? To save your own skin? I can see why you wouldn't want that to get around.

SANDY: Shut up.

PHILBERT: The twins would probably poison your food or something. They worship Eddie.

SANDY: I don't know why, he's not so special.

PHILBERT: Anyway, if that's really what you want, all you'd have to do is ask.

SANDY: What do you mean?

PHILBERT: You know Eddie just like I do, figure it out. He's the noble type. If you want him to give himself up to the soldiers, most likely all you'd have to do is ask.

(Exit Philbert, leaving Sandy alone in the light to think about what he said.)

PHILBERT: *(From offstage.)* And you could manage to be a little nice to me, in the meantime. Just in case I have more cigarettes.

END OF SCENE

FANNY: I'm too old for dolls any more. Now I have a gun and a knife. I had fun with the dolls. I had a doll that was a soldier and a doll that was a sailor. The soldier always beat up the sailor because that was what I thought should happen.

I have fun with the gun, too. My sister and I went into the army together, because it was that or go on the street begging or slaving yourself to somebody. I'd rather kill people, my sister said. Her name was Ellen. She was good to me, and she took me with her to the recruiter. We signed up for the recruitment camps.

She says we had more family than just the two of us but I think she was lying, I don't think there ever was anybody else. I know you're supposed to have a mother but I don't think I ever had one. Because I would remember if I did. No matter what my sister says.

Last time I saw my sister she had lost an arm. Her right one. She was having to learn how to do things with the left one, it was driving her crazy. She stepped on a mine, I think. Some kind of an explosion. I really don't know. I just kept staring at her while she was explaining, at the place where her arm used to be, and afterward I was embarrassed to ask what she had said.

Sometimes I pretend Poker is my sister. I don't tell her so, but she knows we're friends, she knows I like her. We hang together a lot; we always volunteer for the same details. It's good to have somebody you can be friendly with. I guess we're actually friends, but we don't talk about it. In General Handsome's army you don't talk about things like that, or people will get the idea you're soft.

When Mouth asks what's the price of freedom, I think about my sister's arm, and I think, well, that's pretty stupid, don't you think? Why would you want to be free without your arm? When Mouth asks why we fight, I think about having a mother, and I think we fight so in the future everybody can have a mother, and both arms, and then I think, well, a war is a pretty stupid way to make that happen, and then I get confused and sit down and clean my gun. I just clean it and get it ready till my questions go away.

I mean, I understand sometimes you need a gun, sometimes you have to fight people. Who could look at the world and not realize that? But I get tired of killing the people who can't fight back. I don't understand that part, really.

I met General Handsome once. She was not handsome. She was really scary, I thought. But I'm really not that old anyway, what do I know?

SCENE SEVEN

Petal and Pallor are being guarded by all the Soldiers except Prick. Mop's body is no longer visible.

PETAL: Where's Mop?

PALLOR: We left the body back there. Remember? On the street.

PETAL: *(Shivering.)* I should go back there.

PALLOR: You can't. Not right now.

PETAL: *(Becoming agitated, then calming at the sound of Pallor's voice.)* I can't just leave Mop lying there. It's the middle of the street.

PALLOR: Hush. Be still. We'll go together and take care of Mop later. OK? We can't go right now.

PETAL: I don't understand.

PALLOR: Mop's dead. You can't help her now.

(Silence.)

PETAL: There wasn't any reason to shoot her like that. *(Looking around at the Soldiers.)* All she did was try to take some food. There wasn't any reason to kill her.

FANNY: She messed with Prick.

PETAL: What?

FANNY: She messed with Prick. You don't mess with Prick. Nobody does.

PETAL: Is he some kind of tough guy or something?

PALLOR: Hush, Petal.

PETAL: No, I mean it. Is he some kind of really tough guy, shooting a little girl like that.

(Fanny and Nickel are vaguely uncomfortable. Lazy turns back to the rest.)

POKER: Prick's just crazy. He likes to kill things. Animals and people.

PETAL: For no reason?

POKER: Yeah. Like that. For no reason.

PETAL: He's no better than an animal.

POKER: What about you? Are you any better than an animal?

PALLOR: Leave her alone. She's just upset.

POKER: No, I want her to answer. Is she any better than an animal, living in this dump of a town? Is she helping anybody?

PETAL: At least I don't go around shooting little girls for no reason.

POKER: What do you do, then? Are you helping?

PETAL: Helping what?

POKER: Are you helping the general make a better world?

PETAL: General Handsome?

POKER: Yeah.

PETAL: Is that what you think you're doing?

POKER: I don't have to explain myself to you.

PETAL: General Handsome's just like all the rest. She's out for what she can get.

NICKEL: You can't say that.

FANNY: No, that's not right.

NICKEL: She's trying to end the war. We all are. That's why we fight.

FANNY: We're not all like Prick.

PETAL: What, you think you're some kind of a hero or something. Strutting around with that gun? You think you helped the world when you killed my sister?

FANNY: I didn't kill your sister, Prick did.

PETAL: What difference does that make to me?

PALLOR: Be quiet, Petal. They'll hurt you, too.

PETAL: No, what difference does it make. They're probably going to kill us anyway. Right? *(Looking around at the Soldiers.)* To make the world a better place. Because that's the way you do it, of course. You kill everybody in it.

PALLOR: Petal, please.

NICKEL: It's all right. We don't care what people say. We know why we fight.

FANNY: I'm sorry about your sister.

LAZY: *(Joining the conversation; to Pallor.)* What about you, anyway?

PALLOR: Me?

LAZY: Yeah. Do you think I don't recognize you?

PALLOR: What? I don't know what you're talking about.

LAZY: I been sitting here thinking I knew you from somewhere. Does your friend here know about you, Pallor?

(Pallor is silent.)

PETAL: They know your name.

LAZY: Yeah. We know Pallor, all right. Fanny and Poker don't, they're new. But me and Nickel. You recognize Pallor, don't you, Nickel?

NICKEL: Not really.

LAZY: Pallor's one of us heroes. Fighting to save the world for General Handsome. Right, Pallor?

PALLOR: That's not true.

NICKEL: *(Taking a closer look.)* You're right, Lazy.

LAZY: Damn right I am.

NICKEL: Hair's a bit longer, clothes are a bit dirtier. *(To Petal.)* So your friend here is one of us. Regular army. Another murderer, just like us. What do you think about that?

PALLOR: I'm not.

LAZY: You're not?

PALLOR: No.

NICKEL: Well, I guess you're right, you're not. You're a deserter.

(Pallor refuses to respond.)

PETAL: Is it true?

(Pallor shakes head.)

LAZY: It's true, all right.

NICKEL: What happened, Pallor? You find out you're too good for the rest of us? You find some other way of getting a regular meal?

PALLOR: I don't know what you're talking about.

NICKEL: Oh, don't worry. We might not tell Mouth about you. We might keep your secret. You never know.

LAZY: Us? We're just killers, like this one said. We're just animals.

FANNY: Knock it off, Lazy.

LAZY: Supposing I don't want to knock it off. Supposing I'm feeling a bit twitchy in the finger myself. I haven't killed anybody today. Makes me a bit jumpy.

FANNY: Knock it off.

NICKEL: Fanny, this is a deserter. The worst kind of criminal.

FANNY: Just because you say so? I don't think that's right.

LAZY: *(To Pallor.)* Fanny likes you. You've made a friend.

FANNY: Nobody's my friend. I just don't want to kill anybody without a reason.

NICKEL: Then you're in the wrong business, aren't you?

FANNY: *(Swinging gun to point at Nickel.)* I know what business I'm in.

NICKEL: Point that thing somewhere else.

FANNY: I'm pointing it exactly where I want to point it. You don't like it, try shutting your mouth.

LAZY: The young ones are a bit restless tonight.

FANNY: Just sick of your shit.

> *(Lazy starts to move toward Fanny but Poker points a gun in Lazy's direction.)*

POKER: Don't do it, Lazy.

LAZY: *(Backing off.)* Don't do what? I was just getting more comfortable.

POKER: I'm sick of you older ones bullying us all the time.

LAZY: Poor baby. So mistreated.

POKER: Stuff it. That's enough.

NICKEL: But we've caught a deserter, Poker. Think about the reward you'll get for that.

POKER: What reward? More money that I can't spend because I'm stuck in the frigging army? We'll just wait for Mouth to come back. Mouth will know what to do.

> *(Silence.)*

PETAL: You're nothing but a bunch of kids.

LAZY: What's that supposed to mean?

PETAL: You're not even real soldiers. You're a bunch of kids playing at it.

LAZY: *(Advancing on Petal suddenly, pointing gun at her.)* Oh yeah? Is this a toy? Is it?

FANNY: Leave the kid alone, Lazy.

LAZY: And what are you going to do if I don't?

FANNY: Shoot you where you stand.

> *(The moment ends abruptly. Lazy backs off. Fanny and Petal look at each other.)*

PETAL: All I meant was, you're not any older than I am. How are you going to fix the world and win the war if you're not any older than I am.

POKER: It's all a big mess. We're just doing what we're told. Like everybody else.

FANNY: And waiting for somebody to come along with a real plan.

PALLOR: You can give that up.

POKER: What?

PALLOR: You can give up waiting on someone else to figure out what to do. Especially if you're thinking it's General Handsome. Why do you think I left?

NICKEL: What, all of a sudden you want to talk about it?

LAZY: I told you he was a deserter. I told you.

PALLOR: I recognized you right away, Lazy. Hard to miss that stupid look on your face.

LAZY: *(No longer confident enough to point the gun.)* You're not in a position to be insulting people, if I were you I'd watch your mouth.

PALLOR: If you were me you wouldn't still be waving that gun around. You'd be out here. You'd be free, like I am.

NICKEL: Free?

LAZY: You don't look very free at the moment.

PALLOR: But I am. You can kill me if you want to, I know that. But I won't go back to being what you are.

NICKEL: You've got it so cozy where you are, these days?

PALLOR: Your sarcasm's wasted on me, Nickel. I know you, remember? I know the kind of saving the world you're here to do. You're in the army to get yourself fed. The lot of you. You're in the army for your belly, or because you can't think of anything better to do. So was I. *(Pause.)* But I figured it out, finally. Back when General Handsome turned on General Burly in the first place. There's no point to being where you are.

LAZY: Looks like you've got it all figured out, all right. Sitting there like you're about to crap your pants.

PALLOR: I might be about to crap my pants, but it's because I'm sick, not because I'm afraid. I won't be afraid any more. Not of you or Prick or jerks like Mouth or anybody else. That's how free I am. You don't have any power over me, except to kill me, and I'm ready for that.

NICKEL: In fact, you look like you're halfway there already.

PALLOR: Get a clue, Nickel. You can't insult me with that kind of bullshit. The war taught me how to be free, all right, but it wasn't by trying to win. It was by walking away.

END OF SCENE

SCENE EIGHT

Lights on Prick and Golem.

PRICK: You're not nervous, are you?

GOLEM: What do you think?

PRICK: Mouth won't hurt you much. Mouth doesn't have much stomach for hurting people directly.

GOLEM: What about you?

PRICK: I have the stomach for it, all right. You don't have to worry about that.

GOLEM: So that's how this is going to go?

PRICK: All you have to do is answer the questions when Mouth asks. That's all.

(Enter Mouth.)

MOUTH: That's right. Answer my questions and everything will be fine. What's your name?

(Golem does not know whether to answer or not.)

MOUTH: There's your first question. Here's where you get to decide how much this is going to hurt.

GOLEM: My name is Robert Jernigan. People call me Golem.

MOUTH: People do.

GOLEM: Kids at school.

MOUTH: Golem. Something out of a comic book.

GOLEM: I guess.

MOUTH: Everybody has a nickname these days. Mine is Mouth. Do you know why? Can you guess?

(Golem shakes head.)

MOUTH: Tell him, Prick.

PRICK: *(A bit irritated.)* Because you give the orders, I guess.

MOUTH: *(Paying no attention to Prick's reaction.)* That's right. Because I give the orders. *(To Golem.)* Do you like my name?

GOLEM: I suppose.

MOUTH: But you don't like me, much. You don't have to answer that. I already know you don't. Nobody likes me much. Because I do what's necessary, and that's never very pleasant or popular. Like here, today. Chasing you and your friends. Did you know we were chasing you?

GOLEM: Yes.

MOUTH: Who knew? You? Eddie?

GOLEM: Gun, actually. Gun figured it out.

MOUTH: I don't know Gun.

(Golem shrugs.)

MOUTH: But I'm sure I will. Soon. (Pause.) So, Golem, do you like Eddie? Is he your friend?

GOLEM: I suppose.

MOUTH: You don't sound very sure.

GOLEM: He was my friend at school, yeah. Only he thought he was better than me. My dad was a cleaning man, he worked at the school. So I wasn't like the rest. I got my classes because of my dad cleaning toilets and such.

MOUTH: But you had a dad.

GOLEM: Yeah. So?

MOUTH: Most people don't. My parents were killed a long time ago. Did you like your classes? Did you enjoy learning?

GOLEM: Sometimes. (Pause.) Is this what you brought me here for? To ask me a lot of questions about my life?

MOUTH: Am I making you impatient?

GOLEM: I just wish you would get on with it.

MOUTH: With what?

GOLEM: With whatever you're going to do. (Pause.) I can take you to Eddie if that's what you want.

MOUTH: Really. Just like that.

GOLEM: Yeah. Just like that.

MOUTH: (To Prick.) We're not even going to have to beat it out of him, Prick.

PRICK: Looks like you're right.

MOUTH: Too bad. I always enjoy watching Prick have a bit of fun.

GOLEM: Why should I get myself beaten up for Eddie's sake? He should have told us the truth in the first place.

MOUTH: He didn't tell you he was General Burly's son?

GOLEM: Not until we left the school. (Pause.) Maybe some of the other kids knew. I didn't. (Pause.) So why should I stick my neck out? (Pause.) You're not going to kill him, are you?

MOUTH: Does that make a difference?

(Golem can't figure out an answer.)

MOUTH: That's all right. I don't want to confuse you. No, we're not going to kill him. He wouldn't be much use to General Handsome dead, now, would he?

GOLEM: All right then. (Pause.) What about the others?

MOUTH: The others?

GOLEM: You won't hurt them, will you? *(Golem is looking back and forth between Mouth and Prick.)* There's no reason to hurt them, right?

MOUTH: This is so touching. You're concerned for your friends. You're sitting here planning to betray them, of course, but you're concerned. Like any decent person would be. You're a decent person, aren't you, Golem?

GOLEM: I try to be.

MOUTH: Do you want me to make some kind of guarantee?

GOLEM: Yes.

(Mouth signals to Prick, who whacks Golem across the head with the butt of his gun: The blow should look calculated, not as hard as Prick could hit.)

MOUTH: There's your guarantee, Golem. You can rely on me to behave just like that.

(Silence. Golem is trying to keep himself under control but is terrified.)

MOUTH: Do you want to change your mind about leading us to Eddie, now that you know what's going to happen? *(Looking at Prick.)* I think Prick would like it if you did.

(Golem shakes his head.)

MOUTH: I can't hear you.

GOLEM: I won't change my mind. I'll take you there.

MOUTH: Good. *(To Prick.)* I'll leave you here with him while I gather up the rest of our party. Don't hurt him any more, not for the moment.

GOLEM: *(As Mouth exits.)* I'm doing what you want, aren't I? I'm giving you Eddie.

PRICK: You think that makes a difference?

GOLEM: It ought to. I'm doing the right thing.

PRICK: You're a coward. Look at you, about to wet yourself, with your talk about doing the right thing. You're a weasel and a coward, that's what you are.

(Lights fade on Golem.)

GOLEM: I'm doing what's right. That's all I'm doing. You shouldn't hurt a person for doing that.

END OF SCENE

SCENE NINE

Eddie, Gun, Pat, Nix, Sandy, and Philbert are gathering in a circle in the warehouse. They are about to have a meeting.

GUN: I'd feel better if one of us was keeping an eye on the outside.

EDDIE: I know you would. But we need to talk.

GUN: Right now?

SANDY: Gun's right. It's late and I want to go to bed. I'm tired. Can't we have a talk in the morning?

EDDIE: A lot of things could happen between now and morning. We need to talk now.

PHILBERT: About what?

EDDIE: About Sandy's question from before. Where are we going?
(Silence. They all look at each other.)

GUN: Well, that's fine. But I'm still going to hang back here a bit. Where I can see the door.

EDDIE: That's fine.

PAT AND NIX: Do you have a plan now, Eddie? Is that what this is? Do you know what you want us to do?

EDDIE: So it's me who has to have a plan?

PAT AND NIX: You brought us here. You had the idea in the first place. How are we supposed to know what to do?

EDDIE: That's why we're talking.

SANDY: Oh, Eddie, why bother with this? You're just going to tell us what you want us to do like you always do, and we're going to do it.

PHILBERT: You've changed your tune, haven't you?

SANDY: Shut up, Philbert. Eddie and Gun are the only ones with any idea how to get along out here.

PHILBERT: You're such a little hypocrite, Sandy.

SANDY: I'm just being practical.

GUN: Shut up, the two of you. Right now. Let Eddie talk.

EDDIE: I don't really have much to say.

PHILBERT: What do you mean? Then what are we all sitting round here for?

EDDIE: So you can decide for yourselves what you want to do. *(Pause.)* I mean, I think your choices are pretty clear, when you think about it. You can go back to the school if you want to live under General Handsome, if you trust her. I don't. But you might. Or you can keep going east and see what you find.

SANDY: East? There's nothing east except more of the same, towns like this one and country nobody lives in any more.

EDDIE: That's right.

SANDY: That's no choice.

PHILBERT: You'd rather live in Handsomeland, then? What do you want to be, Sandy? A whore? A slave? A farmhand?

SANDY: If we go back to the school, maybe they'll let us finish classes. Or be teachers, even. Since they killed so many of the teachers, they'll need new ones.

PHILBERT: That's if they're even keeping the school open, Sandy. Use your head.

SANDY: Why wouldn't they?

GUN: Sandy, get real, won't you? General Handsome doesn't bother with schools, or even towns. General Handsome will put you in a camp and put you to work. That's what she did where I came from. You won't like the life in the camps, let me tell you, not a bit. You won't have your bit of space for your apartment there. You won't have anything except work.

PHILBERT: See? Gun knows, Gun was there.

EDDIE: Sandy can make her own choice, if she wants to. Can't you, Sandy? You could go back to Hilltown by yourself, if it came to that.

SANDY: *(With effort.)* No.

EDDIE: No?

SANDY: I don't want to go back there alone.

EDDIE: Then you want to stay with the rest?

SANDY: *(She is growing up as we watch. She is making a choice.)* Yes. Yes, I guess I do.

EDDIE: Because I don't see much other choice, really. You go forward. You keep moving east until you find someplace out of the way, quiet. And you try to make a life there.

GUN: Why are you saying it like this, Eddie?

EDDIE: What do you mean?

GUN: You make it sound like you're not going.

EDDIE: I'm not.

(Silence.)

PHILBERT: *(To Sandy.)* I told you.

SANDY: Eddie

PAT AND NIX: We're afraid. Both of us, equally. Someone tell me what's going on?

PHILBERT: Eddie's not going with us. Eddie's waiting here.

GUN: No. That's not what we planned. We're sticking together.

EDDIE: You know that won't work, Gun.

SANDY: I feel so terrible all of a sudden.

EDDIE: Why? It's what you wanted me to do, isn't it? *(Looking at them all.)* I mean, I don't particularly want to turn myself in. But what happens if I don't and they catch us anyway? Then we're all caught and nobody gets free of this mess. I don't think that makes any sense.

(Golem should enter the space in time to hear much of this conversation. Gun sees him but is too stunned by what Eddie is saying to react.)

PHILBERT: Are you sure?

SANDY: I can't believe you, Philbert. You're ready for him to do this just like that.

PHILBERT: *(A bit flabbergasted.)* Half an hour ago you were ready to turn Eddie over yourself, Sandy.

EDDIE: *(Angry enough to make them all listen.)* That's enough. Just listen. You think I want to do this? You think I want to be the good one all the time? It's a bloody bore is what it is. But you all don't leave me much room, do you? *(Pause.)* If the rest of you have been thinking nobody would be chasing us if I wasn't General Burly's son, do you think I haven't noticed? And why is that? Because it's true. So what choice do I have? Keep running till they catch all of us?

GOLEM: Do you really mean that?

SANDY AND PHILBERT: *(Seeing Golem at the same moment.)* Golem.

EDDIE: You're back.

(Golem can't answer, is too ashamed.)

EDDIE: Come and sit down, Golem. We're talking about what to do.

GOLEM: I'm fine here.

PAT AND NIX: We knew he would come. I knew it.

GOLEM: You were right, twins.

PHILBERT: Where are your friends? Did you find anything we can use?

GOLEM: They're coming. No, we didn't find anything. *(To Eddie.)* So you mean to turn yourself over to them. You would do that?

EDDIE: I don't think they'll hurt me. They want to use me to get at my dad. *(Golem has started to shake, and he is crying or starting to cry.)* Golem, what's wrong? I thought this was what you wanted.

(Enter Mouth, the Soldiers, and their prisoners Pallor and Petal.)

MOUTH: He thought it was what he wanted too, Eddie. He was telling me all about it a few minutes ago. Before he led me here.

(Silence.)

MOUTH: Aren't you going to say hello? I've been chasing you such a long way.

EDDIE: Golem.

GOLEM: I'm sorry, Eddie. I'm so sorry.

GUN: You bastard. You perfect rotting bastard.

MOUTH: Don't be too hard on him. People always pay for their mistakes.
(Mouth signals to Prick, who shoots Golem in the back. Golem goes first to his knees and then to the floor, watching Eddie the whole time. The shooting causes a visible reaction in Fanny and Poker. Most of the others are terrified and frozen.)

EDDIE: What did you kill him for?

MOUTH: Isn't that obvious?

EDDIE: No. Not at all. He gave you what you wanted.

MOUTH: I don't like traitors much. Neither does Prick.

EDDIE: He wasn't a traitor. He was doing what he had to do. I would have turned myself over to you anyway. You already heard me, I'm sure you were listening, too.

MOUTH: He's dead now. Water under the bridge. Let's move forward, shall we?

EDDIE: What kind of person does a thing like that?

MOUTH: A soldier, trying to do what she can do to win a war that's gone on too long.
(Eddie laughs.)

MOUTH: Am I funny? Really? Am I being funny?

EDDIE: War all the time.

MOUTH: That's right. War all the time, every day, until we win.

EDDIE: And then what?

MOUTH: Pardon?

EDDIE: When you win? Then what? *(Pause, trying to get control of himself.)* What about the rest of my friends. If I go with you, will you let them go?

MOUTH: What do you mean, if you go with me? You don't have any choice any more. Neither do your friends.

EDDIE: Let them go. Please. They haven't done anything.

MOUTH: I'm afraid I can't do that.

EDDIE: Please. They just want to find a place somewhere. Please. I'm begging you.

MOUTH: *(Gestures to Fanny and Nickel.)* Get the rest of them out of here. I want to speak to Eddie alone.

(Nickel begins to obey. Fanny hesitates, then swings her gun toward Mouth instead. Everyone freezes.)

MOUTH: What's this? Fanny. Do what you're told.

FANNY: I can't. Not one more time.

MOUTH: I'm going to warn you once, and then Prick is going to shoot you.

(During this confusion Eddie lifts his pack. Eddie shoots Mouth using the pistol in his pack, not even bothering to take it out of the pack till the gun is fired. Mouth, stunned, dies. Fanny shoots Prick before he can react. Poker trains gun on Lazy and Gun covers Nickel.)

PETAL: Oh my god.

PALLOR: Hush, Petal.

PETAL: No, I won't. The bastard is dead. *(To Eddie.)* I'll love you forever. She killed my sister.

EDDIE: *(Still stunned at what he's done.)* I'm sorry.

(This next moment can't be completely scripted. Sandy and Philbert come together and hold each other. Gun goes to Eddie and tells him "It's all right," maybe more than once. Pallor and Petal are embracing. Fanny and Poker are moving slowly toward Nickel and Lazy, guns trained on them.)

EDDIE: *(To Fanny.)* Thank you.

FANNY: Don't thank me. I didn't do it for you.

LAZY: I've wanted to shoot her ever since I met her. *(To Fanny, with respect.)* You can put the gun down.

FANNY: Why don't you put yours down instead. You and Poker, both.

POKER: It's all right, Fanny. I'm with you.

FANNY: Put the gun down anyway. Till I'm sure. *(Pause.)* I guess there's a bit of Prick in me. Who'd have thought.

EDDIE: Who's Prick?

POKER: *(Gesturing.)* That one. The one who shot your friend in the back.

EDDIE: Why don't we all put our guns down? All at the same time.

(He's watching Fanny. He lays his gun down. Lazy does the same. All the rest do the same till only Gun and Fanny are holding theirs.)

EDDIE: Put them down. Please. We can't really talk until you do.

(Slowly Fanny and Gun comply. Pat and Nix, without being asked, are gathering all the weapons.)

EDDIE: That's a start.

POKER: I feel quite naked all of a sudden.

NICKEL: *(Looking at Pallor.)* I feel quite free.

LAZY: I was tired of carrying the thing anyway.

FANNY: We'll still need them, won't we?

GUN: What do you mean?

FANNY: *(To Eddie.)* Where we're going. I want to go with you. But I'm sure we'll still need the guns.

EDDIE: Maybe we'll trust each other better by then. But we should put them down for now. So we can talk.

(Fanny slowly lowers her gun and places it carefully on the ground.)

EDDIE: What's your name?

FANNY: Fanny. My name is Fanny.

EDDIE: And the rest of you?

POKER: Poker.

NICKEL: Nickel.

LAZY: Lazy.

GUN: So you want to come with us?

FANNY: I do. I don't know about the rest.

GUN: *(To others.)* What about it?

EDDIE: We're not sure where we're going, you know. We don't have a plan yet. We just want to get away somewhere, as far away from the fighting as we can get.

SANDY: Well, maybe it's time we made a plan, then.

EDDIE: Now?

SANDY: Why not? We know we can't go back. Any of these new ones can leave if they want to. But I'm staying. Till we figure out where to go.

(Silence; they all look at each other carefully.)

EDDIE: All right then. Let's all sit down and talk.

(They all sit. Lights to black.)

END OF PLAY

Anatomy of Gray

by Jim *Leonard*

From left to right: Della Duncan, Martine Moore and Julien Inclan
Photo credit: Tom Haygood

PLAYWRIGHT'S BIOGRAPHY

Jim Leonard writes plays, movies, and television. Published plays include *The Diviners, And They Dance Real Slow in Jackson, V&V Only, Crow and Weasel,* and *Anatomy of Gray.* Jim created and produced the television series *Close to Home, Skin,* and *Thieves.* His filmed pilots include "Internal Affairs," "Fortunate Son," "The People," "Ice," "Eastwick," and "Kilroy." Jim also wrote and produced the television series *Cracker, Night Visions,* and *The Marshal.* His most notable film credit is *My Own Country,* which was directed by Mira Nair. Theatrical honors include two NEA fellowships, a New York Villager Award, the Dramatists Guild Award, and the Midland Writers Award.

FROM THE PLAYWRIGHT

Plays come from mysterious places—at least for me. Here's how this one came to be: First, I learned that my dear friend Jon Geter, who I'd written the role of Buddy for in a play of mine called *The Diviners,* had a disease called AIDS. Like me, Jon grew up in a small town in Indiana. His childhood church did not react well to the news of Jon's illness. The dying they could deal with. The truly frightening part was Jon being gay. Gay equaled damnation: therefore AIDS, therefore death. The irony is that Jon left acting to become a minister and baptized my sons. But that's how folks thought in the early 90s.

At the same time this illness was happening to Jon, Dr. Henry I. Schvey came to New York's Circle Repertory Theatre seeking to commission a play to celebrate the centennial of Washington University's medical school. I have children. I needed the money. I deposited his check, and I proceeded to panic, having no idea what to write about. Then I had a thought: "What would happen if it was only the Christians who got AIDS?" I love Jesus, but that's where I started: The Godly get ill, complications ensue. It's easy to judge the righteous—it's hard to tell a good story.

For the next two-and-a-half years, I wrote and rewrote. Dr. Schvey staged the premiere with a cast of talented students. I rewrote. We mounted a beautiful and simple production in Circle Rep's Laboratory Theatre. I rewrote. I staged it in Arizona. I rewrote. My friend Steven Deitz directed a stunning production at A Contemporary Theatre in Seattle. The audience seemed happy, but I knew something was profoundly wrong with the story, and I didn't know how to fix it. So I put it away.

For ten years.

Now. Time passes, but time heals nothing, it just lets us grow numb to loss. Years after Jon's ashes were spread on the water, I was in a very dark place. I was depressed, I was angry, and I didn't even know I was grieving. Then one night, I had a dream . . . and when I woke up, I knew how to tell the story.

This is the truth: Craig Slaight called from A.C.T. in San Francisco a week later; he wanted to stage an old draft of the play; I told him about my dream; he encouraged me, dared me, goaded me, and gracefully guided me back onto the waters. This time, the play was the river and I was the raft. I combined and complicated characters, and I put a young woman at the center. Her father had died, and she wouldn't shut up about loss and love and grief and sex and longing and landscape and weather. I didn't find the story, the story found me.

FROM THE ACTOR—Julia Mattison (Heartland Ensemble/
   Assistant Director)

It was a tremendous experience to be a part of Jim Leonard's *Anatomy of Gray* as the Assistant Director and performing as a member of the Heartland Ensemble. To be a part of such a talented group of actors working together and becoming a family reminded me of the close-knit community at the heart of Leonard's play. Over the course of the rehearsal process, the actors deepened their individual work, touched by the care and vulnerability written into each part, especially when faced with crisis.

An exciting aspect of the rehearsal process was that pages were constantly changing, and the storyboard was being created as we worked. To not know the conclusion of the play made each scene and each character stand alone in the present. It was a really powerful way to develop and understand the fears and uncertainties of the townspeople.

Being able to keep in contact with Mr. Leonard throughout the process was an honor that helped us deepen our understanding of his goals, and really flesh out each character.

The Heartland Ensemble was a new and exciting addition to this production, consisting of four singers (accompanied by one guitar and one violin), singing songs that might have been found at the center of small town life. We often worked separately from the rest of the cast, developing harmonies and new versions of the songs. When we teamed up with the cast once again, we were able to add a unique layer to the production, acting as distant observers of the actions onstage and providing transitions between the scenes. Staying onstage during the entire production was a real challenge, but in the end it helped us develop our focus and connection, and it allowed us to delve deeply into the world of *Anatomy of Gray*.

ORIGINAL PRODUCTION

Anatomy of Gray (under the original title, *Gray's Anatomy*) was first presented by the Young Conservatory at American Conservatory Theater (Carey Perloff, Artistic Director, Heather M. Kitchen, Executive Director), San Francisco, California, in March 2004. It was directed and designed by Craig Slaight; the music direction was by Krista Wigle; the lighting design was by Kimberly J. Scott; the costumes were designed by Callie Floor and Maggie Whitaker; the sound was designed by Greg Kunit; and Julia Mattison was the assistant director. The cast was as follows:

JUNE . . . . Martine Moore
REBEKAH . . . . Della Duncan
HOMER . . . . Julien Inclan
CRUTCH . . . . Joshua Schell
BELVA. . . . . Hannah Finnie
MAGGIE . . . . Nathalie Gorman
TINY. . . . . Emma Fassler
PHINEAS . . . . Charles Filipov
GALEN GRAY. . . . . Jacob Gordon
HEARTLAND ENSEMBLE . . . Laelena Brooks, Emily Iscoff-Daigian,
Julia Mattison, Aurora Simcovich

SETTING

The play takes place in Gray, Indiana, in the late 1800s. The stage is empty. All that's needed to tell this story is a bench, a stool, and a chair. The actors, except for Galen Gray, might be seated on pew-like benches just offstage throughout the play, in plain view of the audience.

CHARACTERS

JUNE

REBEKAH

HOMER

CRUTCH

BELVA

MAGGIE

TINY

PHINEAS

GALEN GRAY

HEARTLAND ENSEMBLE

ANATOMY OF GRAY

ACT I

We hear an acoustic version of "The Water is Wide," simply, beautifully felt. Lights rise on June who speaks directly to the audience. The Towns-people enter on or just before their lines, or else they are on stage from the beginning. Most of this section is told right to the audience.

JUNE: Once upon a time there was a girl who looked remarkably like me. You know how much weather there is? Well that's how many feelings she had. It's like there was one sky outside her, and a sky just as huge on the inside. She was one of the more interesting people you'd ever want to meet. But nobody knew it. Because she lived in Gray, Indiana. A town which was primarily notable for bein' the most borin' place in the world.

REBEKAH: June. Put a lid on it.

JUNE: Mother, there's nothin' to do here but live here.

CRUTCH: Oh, hell, we got everything right here in Gray a body could need.

BELVA: Mr. Collins, there's no need to curse.

CRUTCH: We got folks to farm—

HOMER: That would be me.

CRUTCH:—and folks to fix thrashers and grub plows and broken-down wagons and such—

HOMER: That would be you.

CRUTCH:—and plenty of folks to fix meals:

MAGGIE: That would be me—

BELVA: And me—

TINY: And me—

REBEKAH: And me—

JUNE: I mainly get stuck with the dishes.

TINY: Breakfast, dinner, and supper, every blessed day, three times a day, 'til the end of foreseeable time.

BELVA: Tiny, you don't have but one soul to cook for.

TINY: I cook for my brother, I cook for myself—

BELVA: What I mean is you don't have a husband, dear.

TINY: Bless you for pointin' that out, Belva.

CRUTCH: And we've got us a soul-fixer!

(Phineas wears wire-rimmed spectacles—one lens is clear, and the other is darkly tinted.)

PHINEAS: Phineas Wingfield, brother to Tiny, Pastor-at-large.

HOMER: That man would baptize a dog.

PHINEAS: I always loved water.

MAGGIE: One time, he got so hepped up with the spirit, he tried dunkin' a cat. That didn't work out too well.

PHINEAS: Hold it! Just rein it in, wouldja?!

(To the audience.)

The reason I dunked every creature in sight, includin' the aforementioned feline, is this: I can't picture heaven without 'em. If heaven ain't much like Indiana, well Lord God forgive me, I don't want to go. But I'm plannin' to go! And I'm plannin' to take this town with me—lock, stock, and cat.

MAGGIE: But Puff wasn't much for the water, you see; she scratched out the preacher's eye.

TINY: Oh, it was awful. She lashed out and gutted it clean from the socket, that cat.

HOMER: I heard tell she ate the eye, too.

TINY: Gobbled it right down, sat there and smiled.

JUNE: You see there? That's just what I'm talkin' about. That right there— that eyeball-eatin' cat is the most interesting thing that ever happened around here.

(Beat, smile.)

At least til my story begins. *Anatomy of Gray.*

TOWNSPEOPLE: Chapter One:

(Lights isolate June.)

JUNE: In the beginnin', we had folks to shod horses and folks to fix houses, folks to fix meals and thrashers and folks to save souls—but the one thing we lacked in our town was a person to fix other people. For Gray at the time was a town with no healer.

(Beat.)

And that's where the death of my father fits in.

(Rebekah has appeared behind June, touched her shoulder, and now they embrace in quiet grief as lights bring us to a funeral, and the Townspeople sing:)

TOWNSPEOPLE: "Softly and tenderly, Jesus is calling,

Calling for you and for me;

See on the portals, He's waiting and watching,
Watching for you and for me.
Come home, come home: ye who are weary come home;
Softly and tenderly, Jesus is calling,
Calling: Oh, sinner, come home."

(They repeat the chorus in harmony as Belva and Crutch tell us the story, so the singing ends up on a lovely "Amen" just as the narration ends:)

BELVA: June lost her pa; Rebekah was widowed; and we lost a good neighbor and friend.

CRUTCH: *(Hat in hand.)* Oh, there wasn't nothin' that man could not grow. His alfalfa used to come in so pretty that grown men would stand before his fields and weep.

BELVA: And then one day, out of nowhere, his heart just gave out.

CRUTCH: It was Juney who found him, still tethered to his plow.

BELVA: Her father's face was dark blue under the white hot noon sun, and the dust of his fields floated around him.

CRUTCH: And so all of us gathered together, like leaves of an autumn together, to turn that man back to the Earth.

TOWNSPEOPLE: *(Singing.)* "A-men."

PHINEAS: The Lord gave, and the Lord hath taken away.

TOWNSPEOPLE: Blessed be the name of the Lord.

PHINEAS: "Ashes to ashes—"

REBEKAH AND JUNE: *(Kneeling.)* "Ashes to ashes."

PHINEAS: "And dust unto dust—"

REBEKAH AND JUNE: "Dust unto dust."

BELVA: *(To the audience.)* It was a beautiful service.

(The Men put their hats on. People give their condolences to Rebekah and June. Rebekah slowly stands to accept their sympathies, but June remains alone on her knees before her father's "grave.")

TINY: He's gonna be sorely missed, Becky.

TOWNSPEOPLE: *(Before exiting, quietly.)*—My sympathies.—Condolences, ma'am.—You're in our prayers.

PHINEAS: *(Kindly.)* Your pa's gone to a better world, June. Don't ever forget that, you hear?

(Everyone exits but June and Rebekah. Lights isolate June.)

JUNE: *(To the theater.)* Throughout the funeral and the well-meaning whispers which followed, I kept chokin' back the urge to just stand up and scream: It ain't right—it ain't fair that my father is gone, and my mother is weepin' alone in her room, I can't even breathe without cryin', and nothin' is ever gonna feel the same to me, ever! And I cannot believe my pa won't see the sun rise again, or be here to give me away when I marry someday, and I would trade every feelin' of happiness I've ever known just to see him again! People say Time heals everything—but Time didn't heal my father; and neither did God.

REBEKAH: So that night June put pen to paper and wrote herself a business-like letter.

JUNE: "Dearest Almighty: I don't want anyone I care about to die again ever. Including, but not limited to me. So, please! Would you send us a doctor?"

REBEKAH: She wrote—

JUNE: And make him a good-lookin' doctor.

REBEKAH: June thought.

JUNE: Because I'm almost sixteen, and I don't think I'm vain, but I know I'm not ugly, and most of the boys around here are just . . . boys around here.

(Sound of distant thunder as June exits and Crutch enters.)

CRUTCH: The day that the healer arrived was precipitous, friends, in a number of ways.

(More thunder, wind sounds sneak in. Homer enters to watch the coming storm.)

HOMER: Would you look at those thunderheads?

CRUTCH: Rollin' in blacker than sin on a Sunday.

HOMER: *(Hopeful.)* Well. Maybe she'll blow right on by us.

CRUTCH: I doubt it, Homer.

HOMER: I don't mind rain, but I hate that durn thunder.

CRUTCH: Aw, it's just the Good Lord up there blowin' His nose.

(Thunder closer now, louder. Wind sounds are rising.)

HOMER: I've seen some hellers in my day, but this takes the cake.

(June runs on, worried.)

JUNE: Mr. Collins, have you seen my dog?

CRUTCH: Nope.

HOMER: If that dog of yours has any smarts, it's hidin' out, Juney.

JUNE: Ma claims she spotted a funnel cloud yonder!

HOMER: A twister?!

CRUTCH: It's weather for twisters, no question there.

JUNE: I gotta find my dog!

(June runs off calling for "Lady." We hear her continuing to call from off-stage as the storm sounds grow even more intense.)

CRUTCH: You best get yourself down to the storm cellar, June!

HOMER: It's fixin' to break any minute!

CRUTCH: *(Exiting.)* I'm gonna head for shelter myself.

HOMER: *(Exiting.)* I tell you, it's blowin' in fast!

> *(The storm breaks wide open. Thunder and lightning echo through the theater. A trap door pops open and Rebekah pokes her head out. Note: If your stage has no traps, just enter.)*

REBEKAH: June!! Come on, honey!?

JUNE: *(Entering, upset.)* I can't find my dog!

REBEKAH: Don't you have enough sense to get out of the weather?!

> *(June sees something in the sky—she's awestruck by the sight.)*

JUNE: What in the world is that thing?

REBEKAH: It's a tornado, June! What do you think it is?!

JUNE: *(Points out over the audience.)* Just look at it, Ma!

REBEKAH: *(Sees "it" now.)* Oh, my heavenly days.

> *(June raps at another "storm cellar" as Rebekah stares at the heavens.)*

JUNE: Preacher? Hey, Reverend?! Come look at this, will you?

> *(The stage begins filling with people, faces all turned to the downstage sky. What they see is an offstage "balloonist" caught in the storm—and nobody has ever seen anything like this before.)*

REBEKAH: What in creation is that?

PHINEAS: Good God Almighty!

JUNE: I think it's a man up there!

TINY: Sweet Jesus!

REBEKAH: It is a man!

JUNE: It's him, Ma! It's him!

CRUTCH: He's blowin' right for us!

TOWNSPEOPLE:—What's all the commotion about?—It's right over yonder!—He's comin'!—What's comin'!?

> *("The Balloon," unseen by the audience, is blowing right for them. They all turn as one body, to follow "it.")*

HOMER AND PHINEAS:—Good God!—It's fixin' to—

BALLOONIST'S VOICE: *(Live, shouted from above:)* Look out below!!

TOWNSPEOPLE:—He'—He's—He's—Oh, my God!—Take cover, ladies!

> *(A boot falls from the sky! The Townspeople gather around it.)*

BALLOONIST'S VOICE: *(Blowing "past" them:)* Helllllloooooo down theeeeeereee!!!

TINY: It's Jesus! He's Jesus!

BELVA: He dropped his boot.

CRUTCH AND HOMER: Look out for the trees!

TINY: He's headin' right for the river!

PHINEAS: The river?!

(*June runs off up left, shouting:*)

JUNE: I got him! I got him!!

(*The Town watches as offstage June grabs an offstage rope and is "lifted" high into the sky.*)

REBEKAH: Juney! Come down from there!!

JUNE: Ahhhhhh!!!

WOMEN: Ahhhhhhhhhh!!!!

HOMER: Hang on, Juney!

(*June and the Balloonist both fall into the offstage "river," up left. Everyone runs off to help except Tiny, who's holding the boot from above.*)

MAGGIE: Oh, my God!

HOMER: *(Exiting.)* Juney!!

REBEKAH: Swim, baby, swim!!

TINY: Somebody save him!

TOWNSPEOPLE: *(Exiting, and offstage voices:)*—I'll get her!—Gangway now!—Juney??—Keep hold of my arm!—Grab him!—He's got him!—Juney?!

TINY: *(Exiting.)* Don't lose him!

(*The stage is empty.*)

TOWNSPEOPLE:—Hold on!—We got him!—Jesus in heaven!—Look out folks!—Make way!!

(*The Balloonist half stumbles, perhaps helped by Phineas and Crutch. We assume he's soaking wet, but no real water or damp clothes are necessary. He falls to the floor, gasping for breath. The Townspeople rush back on and gather around him. Note: The worst of the storm has passed, but there's still plenty of wind and rain.*)

TINY: Is he alright?

CRUTCH: Don't crowd him now—

PHINEAS: Give him air, people!

BALLOONIST: *(Gasping.)* Where am I?

BELVA: You're in Gray, stranger!

BALLOONIST: Gray?

TINY: You want your boot back?

(*Commotion upstage as Rebekah and Homer enter—Homer carries a lifeless-looking June in his arms. The attention shifts to June.*)

REBEKAH: Oh, my Lord! Oh, God!

HOMER: Pastor, come look at her!

PHINEAS: Juney?

HOMER: I don't think she's breathin'.

    (Everyone except the Balloonist is gathered around June now.)

REBEKAH: Somebody help her!

PHINEAS: *(Patting June's hand, frantically.)* Juney, come to!

HOMER: Breathe, Juney.

REBEKAH: *(Crying.)* Oh, my God, baby.

BELVA: She's fixin' to die!

BALLOONIST: *(Alone.)* Is her heart beating?

REBEKAH: What?

BALLOONIST: *(Crossing to them.)* Does she have a pulse?

REBEKAH: *(Panicked.)* I don't know—I just—

CRUTCH: Give him room, people—let the man through.

REBEKAH: Juney?

BALLOONIST: Ma'am, stand back—I'll do what I can.

PHINEAS: Lord God, we ask you to heal and bless her.

    (Crutch speaks to the audience, as the action continues:)

CRUTCH: This stranger among us—this man from the sky—knelt down
    beside her and took that girl's face in his hands—and then, an amaz-
    ing thing happened:

TINY: Sweet Jesus . . .

CRUTCH: He held to that child and blew his own breath in her body.
    And I mean to tell you, the very same moment she opened her eyes,
    the wind ceased to howlin' and the rain stopped to fallin' like that.
    *(Crutch snaps his fingers once—the rain and wind instantly stop! June
    coughs.)*

BALLOONIST: She's breathing.

TOWNSPEOPLE:—She's breathin'.—She's breathin'!—Praise God, she's alive!

HOMER: Was he kissin' her?

CRUTCH: Oh, for the love of God, Homer.

BELVA: Say, what's your name, Mister?

BALLOONIST: Ma'am, I don't know as I quite comprehend it myself, but the
    fact is my name's Gray.

BELVA: Gray, you say?

TOWNSPEOPLE:—Gray?—G-R-A-Y???—He says his name's Gray!

GRAY: *(The Balloonist.)* Galen P. Gray, Ma'am. The pleasure's all mine.

PHINEAS: If that's not the darndest thing I ever heard.

TOWNSPEOPLE:—Where do you hail from?—I mean to shake that man's hand.—It's a genuine honor.—Isn't that somethin'?

CRUTCH: I tell you, he plain resurrected that child!

GRAY: Sir, let's not overstate the case, please. Resurrection and resuscitation are two entirely different kettles of fish. Now: Having been somewhat involved in the past with various anatomical endeavors, I'm sure you'll understand why I'm loathe to have the term *resurrectionist* attached to my person, if not my reputation per se.

CRUTCH: No offense intended.

GRAY: None taken.

PHINEAS: What in the world was that flyin' contraption?

GRAY: It's called a balloon, Mister—?

PHINEAS: Wingfield. Pastor Phineas Wingfield.

GRAY: Pastor, it holds a voluminous amount of heated, and hence, pressurized gaseous matter—

HOMER: What?

MAGGIE: A load of hot air, Homer.

GRAY: Precisely. It's technically known as an aerostat, Ma'am. They're really quite common in France.
(Rebekah has been tending to June, who's half-sitting-up now on the far side of the stage.)

REBEKAH: Mr. Gray, I don't know how to thank you.

HOMER: Are you alright, June?

JUNE: *(Staring at Gray.)* I feel a little lightheaded.

GRAY: *(He examines her eyes.)* You go home and get some rest, June. Everything's gonna be fine.
(To Rebekah.)
You might give her a dosage of hot tea and sorghum to ward off any chance of the croup, Ma'am.
(Rebekah and Tiny help June off.)

REBEKAH: Hot tea you say?

GRAY: Hot tea's the ticket.

HOMER: Just take her one step at a time.

GRAY: *(Turns to the men.)* Well. I don't know about you, but I could sure do with a stiff drink.

CRUTCH: If you're drinkin', Mister, I'm buyin'.
(The Men exit toward town.)

PHINEAS: *(As he exits the other direction.)* Hard drink is the downfall of civilized man.

(Maggie speaks to the theater.)

MAGGIE: I don't cotton to whiskey and I can't abide smoke—but unlike a lot of good Christians, I'm willin' to tolerate both in the name of commerce. And so, Mr. Galen P. Gray made his way down to the Corner Cafe.

(As Homer and Crutch join the narration, they enter with a stool, a chair, and empty glasses, etc. There's no need for either liquids or a table.)

CRUTCH: Which ain't quite a cafe, but more of a tavern.

HOMER: It ain't even on the durn corner.

(Gray enters during the speech below and turns his chair around backwards, so he straddles it, facing the men.)

GRAY: Now diet—

MAGGIE: He said—

GRAY: —holds the key to constitutional fortitude, friends. It just stands to reason that what you put into your system is what will eventually work its way forth.

MAGGIE: The privy's out back, if that's what you're hintin' at.

GRAY: I think my gastrointestinal tract is holding up fine for the time being, Ma'am. What are your specials this evening?

MAGGIE: Meat and potatoes.

GRAY: I'll try the beef.

MAGGIE: How do you want your beef cooked?

GRAY: Well-done, please.

MAGGIE: I like it rare myself.

GRAY: Lot of folks do.

MAGGIE: Meat doesn't taste right if there's not just a little blood runnin'.

GRAY: Blacken it, please.

MAGGIE: You want that seared on the outside, pink in the middle then?

GRAY: Ma'am, would you please cook the steak through and through?

MAGGIE: If that's how you want it—

GRAY: That's how I prefer it, Ma'am. Thank you.

MAGGIE: *(Exiting.)* Perfect waste of a good piece of meat . . .

CRUTCH: Thank God they don't have the vote.

(The Men clink glasses.)

HOMER: Doc, why do you take your steak black?

GRAY: It kills all the bacterial matter.

HOMER: Bacterial matter?

GRAY: Parasites, germs, and amoebas, that's right. Germs are like dust, see? They're everywhere. They carry diseases around like a puppy totes slippers.

CRUTCH: I don't see nary a one.

GRAY: They're microscopically small, Mr. Collins, but they are tenacious.

HOMER: There's germs in the Corner Cafe?

GRAY: From the looks of it, I'd say a few million have set up housekeeping in this very room.

CRUTCH: Good God Almighty!

GRAY: No call to panic. Whiskey's a fine way to keep them at bay. Serves to sterilize the system, you understand.

HOMER: What about soda pop?

GRAY: Carbonated beverages, consumed in moderation, have actually proven to benefit the metabolism, son.

HOMER: That doesn't surprise me.

(Maggie enters with an empty platter, a fork, and a knife.)

MAGGIE: I hope you brought your appetite with you.

HOMER: Good Lord, if that don't smell tasty, I don't know what does.

MAGGIE: I cooked it up beautiful for him.

GRAY: Madam, I told you—

MAGGIE: Oh, now—it's barely pink, Doctor. Here. Cut it.

GRAY: I've seen cows hurt worse than this get better.

MAGGIE: It's not bloody—it's juicy. It's tasty—just taste it.

(Gray looks like he's going to be ill.)

CRUTCH: Doctor Gray?

GRAY: If you'll excuse me, I have some rather pressing business I need to attend to.

(Gray exits with all the dignity he can. Beat.)

MAGGIE: Well. Good Lord.

HOMER: It don't look too germy to me.

(Homer follows the plate off as Maggie exits. Townspeople might sing a few lines of "There is Power in the Blood" to serve as a transition. Then June steps into a "narrative" light.)

JUNE: Now Galen P. Gray might have been a mite squeamish—but havin' a bona fide healer in town was a new thing for people, and I don't mind tellin' you, we couldn't wait to get sick.

(Tiny enters from one side, and Gray from the other. The scene becomes Gray's "office." He doctors in street clothes—no stethoscope.)

GRAY: What seems to ail you, Miss Wingfield?

TINY: I'm just a tad on the peaked side, Doctor.

GRAY: Peaked, you say?

TINY: Yes, sir, I've got no more pep than a dog in the sun.

GRAY: Maybe you've picked up a bit of a bug.

TINY: You know what the funny thing is? No matter how worn out I get, I can't seem to sleep. I toss, turn, up, down, pacin' the floorboards all night. I guess I'm just naturally nervy. I always have been.

GRAY: Stick out your tongue and say "ahh" for me, please.

TINY: Ah.

GRAY: Ahhhhh . . .

TINY: Ahhhhhhhhhhhhhhhhh . . .

GRAY: Tonsils look normal.

TINY: I've never been to a doctor before. I want you to know I'm enjoyin' it.

GRAY: Good.

TINY: I can't help but notice you don't have a ring on your finger. I take it you must be a widower, Doc?

GRAY: Never known the privilege of marriage.

TINY: Guess what? We have somethin' in common. I never been married myself.

(Gray hands Tiny a small glass jar.)

GRAY: Miss Wingfield, I want you to take this jar out to the privy, and relieve yourself in it.

TINY: *(Doesn't move.)* You want to trot that thought by me again?

GRAY: I need to examine your urine, Ma'am.

TINY: What kind of animal are you?!

GRAY: I am merely trying to ascertain the root cause of your chronic insomnia.

TINY: Oh, my God. I have insomnia?!

(Belva, Crutch, and Maggie instantly enter as Gray exits.)

BELVA: Tell me about it.

TINY: I've suspicioned for years I had somethin' drastically wrong with me, Belva—I just didn't know what it was.

MAGGIE: Guess what I have? I have migraines.

TINY: Oh, you poor thing, you.

CRUTCH: What do you do for it?

MAGGIE: Hot compress.

BELVA: Migraines ain't nothin'. Mr. Collins has—what do you call it, dear?

CRUTCH: It's a dyspeptic ulcer—dear.

BELVA: I have arthritis. It's right here in my hand.

TINY: Oh, my dear God!

BELVA: *(Dry.)* It's incurable.

(More Townspeople enter, forming sort of a chorus-line of ailments.)

TINY: Insomnia.

MAGGIE: Migraines.

BELVA: Arthritis.

CRUTCH: Ulcers.

HOMER: Rheumatism.

JUNE: Menstruation.

REBEKAH: Indigestion.

TINY: Etcetera.

JUNE: From all across the county they came—

HOMER: The lame—

(Rebekah, Crutch, Tiny, and Belva each exit after their lines:)

REBEKAH: The infirm—

CRUTCH: The sickly—

TINY: The peaked—

BELVA: The down in the mouth—

JUNE: People flocked to the healer like birds flock to crumbs! There was somethin' wrong with you if you didn't have somethin' wrong with you.

PHINEAS: (Entering.) I tell you, I wouldn't set foot near that man!

(Lights change as June, Maggie, and Homer cross to Phineas. The scene might be the pastor's front porch.)

JUNE: Why not?

PHINEAS: Cause he's nothing but trouble, that's why. I may not be able to read, but I have committed the bible chapter and verse to my heart. Now you've got your leprosy—you've got your demon possession—and you've got your plagues by the score, but there isn't one single germ in the bible.

HOMER: Folks felt a lot better before that man came to town, Pastor. It's true.

PHINEAS: I wish he'd float back to whence he came, Homer.

MAGGIE: Have you got somethin' personal against him, or is it just biblical?

PHINEAS: Well. I hate to talk, Margaret.

MAGGIE: I know you do, Pastor—I hate to talk, too.

PHINEAS: But Tiny told me—my own sister told me he told her to disrobe herself! And right there in front of him, too.

JUNE: Did she do it?

PHINEAS: I'm not at liberty to say. But what kind of scoundrel'd ask a fine woman, a good Christian flower to do such a thing!? I tell you, it stinks to the core.

JUNE: Personally, I'm all in favor of nudity.

MAGGIE: June.

JUNE: When I went to see him, I took all my clothes off—every last stitch—
he stripped right down to his birthday suit, too. Then we danced around
a fire and sacrificed small animals and house pets till the sun came up.

PHINEAS: Juney: Don't josh.

HOMER: If I had a wife or a sister or a girlfriend or . . . something, I sure as
heck wouldn't let her go near him.

JUNE: I best be heading for home, Pastor.

PHINEAS: Mind yourself, Juney.

HOMER: Bye, June. I'll see you at church, I hope.

JUNE: *(Homer is boring.)* Bye, Homer.
(Homer calls after her:)

HOMER: I'll buy you a soda pop sometime.

MAGGIE: Pastor, where's Tiny been keepin' herself? She wasn't to service on
Sunday nor choir practice on Wednesday.

PHINEAS: That durn doctor told her to sleep in the daytime and stay up all
night.

MAGGIE: Well I never heard such a thing.

PHINEAS: Tiny told me she saw him late last night—and just take a guess
where he was.
(Dramatic beat.)
Graveyard.

MAGGIE: The graveyard?

HOMER: What in the world was Doc doin' out there?

MAGGIE: Did he have a shovel?

PHINEAS: Oh, he's some kind of secretive Free-Thinker, Maggie—there's no
tellin' what he could do! Dig up dead people—desecrate bodies—just
for curiosity's sake.

HOMER: He wasn't diggin' up dead people, is he?

PHINEAS: I don't think we've sunk to that yet. But I know a preacher who
knows of a fella who talked to somebody who lives in the city—

MAGGIE: And?

PHINEAS: Apparently, there was a doctor he knew, kept a whole jar of gizzards—and I'm talkin' human-type gizzards—PICKLED right there on
his desk!

HOMER: Pickled 'em?

PHINEAS: Pickled 'em, that's what he did! Just like a Godblessit cucumber,
Homer! I tell you, it gives a man pause.

MAGGIE: *(Exiting:)* I don't know what this world's comin' to.
(Tiny enters with a length of rope as Phineas and Maggie exit.)

TINY: *(To audience:)* Shhhh. In reality, I'm sound asleep right now. But for purposes of telling this story: I am a tree.

HOMER: *(To audience:)* I'm a tree with a swing in me.

TINY: This is a clothesline.

HOMER: And this is June's yard. And in case you ain't guessed it by now, I am one tree with a real bad crush on the prettiest girl in the county. *(They stretch the "clothesline" between them as Rebekah and June enter with a basket of laundry to hang on the line. Note: We don't need too many articles of clothing to get the point across.)*

JUNE: Mama?

REBEKAH: Yes, June?

JUNE: Do you think you'll ever get married again?

REBEKAH: I doubt it.

JUNE: Why not?

REBEKAH: Because I'm still in love with your father, that's why. I imagine I always will be.

JUNE: But, Ma, just supposing you met somebody you liked a lot, and he liked you back, and he asked you to marry him? What do you think you'd do then?

REBEKAH: Honey, that's not gonna happen.

JUNE: But what if it did?

REBEKAH: It won't.

JUNE: I ain't sayin' it will, but it's possible, ain't it?

REBEKAH: June. What's your point?

JUNE: I think we should ask Doctor Gray over for dinner.

REBEKAH: No.

JUNE: Why not?

REBEKAH: Because I have no interest in courtin' that man. None whatsoever.

JUNE: Well what if I do?

REBEKAH: Oh, Lord, June.

JUNE: I like him. I really do, Ma. I mean I really, really like him.

REBEKAH: Juney, he's too old for you.

JUNE: You were in love at my age.

REBEKAH: Yes, but your Pa was no older than me.

JUNE: I'm old enough to know how I feel.

REBEKAH: Honey, you don't even know Doctor Gray.

JUNE: Then why don't we ask him to dinner and rectify that?

REBEKAH: No, June.

JUNE: But, Ma—

REBEKAH: I said no, honey.

JUNE: *(After a moment.)* Maybe he could just make a house call or somethin'.

REBEKAH: You're not sick.

JUNE: Well you are.

REBEKAH: I am not ill in the least.

JUNE: Then how come you keep throwin' up in the mornin'?

(Off her mother's look:)

Are you havin' a baby?

REBEKAH: *(After a moment.)* I don't know.

JUNE: What do you mean you don't know?

REBEKAH: I mean I don't know if I am or not yet.

JUNE: Maybe you should ask Doctor Gray.

REBEKAH: We've already spoken about it. At length.

JUNE: What did he say?

REBEKAH: I don't want to talk about this.

JUNE: You sure act like you're havin' a baby.

REBEKAH: Honey, look at me. We don't need another mouth to feed. Right now, it's all I can do to look after you and take care of myself, honey. Do you understand what I'm telling you?

JUNE: No.

REBEKAH: *(After a moment.)* I'll explain it sometime when you're older.

(Rebekah exits. June turns to audience:)

JUNE: The first thing I'm plannin' to do when I'm older is move to the city, and set up housekeepin' with Galen P. Gray. He'll teach me to nurse. I'll help him with patients. And we'll live in a real nice house with a nice little office downstairs. I'll cook him nice meals, he'll buy me nice clothes, and we'll have lots of lots of children—which means we'll need to spend an inordinate amount of time in the bedroom. And that's just the way it's gonna be.

(Homer turns to audience as June exits:)

HOMER: If oak trees could talk, I'd be cryin'.

(Night. Belva and Crutch rush on stage. Belva carries a lantern. Crutch has a red rag wrapped around his hand, signifying that he's cut himself. Belva knocks, or we hear the sound of her knocking, as:)

BELVA: Doctor Gray? Doctor, wake up!

CRUTCH: You know it's the funniest thing, Bel—it don't hurt at'all.

BELVA: *(Knocks again.)* Doc? Are you decent?

GRAY: *(Offstage.)* Be right with you, people!

CRUTCH: Sorry to wake you.

(*Gray enters, barefooted and buttoning his shirt. He's just woken up.*)

GRAY: What's wrong, Mrs. Collins? You taking ill?

BELVA: It ain't me, it's him, Doc. He's cut his hand bad.

GRAY: Oh, no . . .

CRUTCH: I was tryin' to sharpen a plow.

BELVA: I went to bed early; I went to sleep directly—

CRUTCH: I's intendin' to plant by the light of the moon.

BELVA: Next thing I knew, Mr. Collins is standin' there bleedin' all over my clean sheets.

GRAY: (*Avoids looking at it.*) How bad is it?

CRUTCH: Well. It's a gash, Doc, there's no question there.

GRAY: How deep is it?

CRUTCH: Well look at it. Isn't that somethin'? You see all them—what do you call 'em?—them innard things?

BELVA: Tendons, I reckon.

(*Gray passes out. Beat.*)

CRUTCH: Doc?

BELVA: Good Lord, he's fell back to sleep.

CRUTCH: Honey, I don't believe he's sleepin'. I think the man fainted flat out.

BELVA: I'll fetch some water—we'll bring him around.

(*Belva exits.*)

CRUTCH: (*Privately.*) Hey, Galen—snap to now—let's sober up, buddy.

GRAY: (*Groggy.*) What . . . ?

CRUTCH: (*Calls.*) He's comin' around, Belva!

(*Belva enters with a bucket.*)

BELVA: Just hold on—I'll give him a dowsin'.

GRAY: What? . . . ho—ho—whoa!—hold it a second! Just let me clear my mind, will you?

(*Pulling himself together.*)

Mr. Collins, if you'll dip your hand in that bucket and clean it off for me, I can't tell you how much that would aid my examination.

CRUTCH: Sure, I can swush it around.

GRAY: You got a knife on you?

CRUTCH: Bel, fish it out of my pocket here for me.

BELVA: You feelin' alright, Doc?

CRUTCH: (*Her hand is in his pocket.*) Watch it there, Belva.

GRAY: I'm gonna be fine, Ma'am.

(She gives him the pocket knife. Gray cuts a strip or two off of his button-down white shirt, as they talk.)

CRUTCH: Good Lord, this water is gettin' dark fast.

BELVA: Doc, how to manage to—?

GRAY: Operate, Madam? I don't. I can't do it. That's all there is to it.

BELVA: What kind of doctor can't cut on nobody?

GRAY: Dead folks I don't have much trouble with, but live ones just take the starch out of my system in two seconds flat.

BELVA: Must make it difficult for you.

GRAY: It curses me, Ma'am. It's a terrible failing, it truly is.

CRUTCH: Doc, if you want, I'll just go home and let 'er stop bleedin' alone.

GRAY: *(It's tempting, but . . .)* No. No, you might get infected, I'd hate to have that. Just hold it out here and I'll try to bind it up properly.
(To Belva.)
Take his arm for me, please.
(Gray can hardly bear to look at the "gash." Crutch's hand shakes a little.)
If you could steady it, Ma'am . . . I'm trying to put myself in a mind of cadavers.
(Gray binds Crutch's hand, as:)

CRUTCH: It's a wonder to me it don't hurt anymore than it does.

GRAY: It might be you sliced a nerve open. You feel numb?

CRUTCH: No.

GRAY: Wiggle your fingers.
(Crutch does.)
I think you're gonna be fine. Main thing's to keep the skin grafting together.

BELVA: Doc, what is this mark on his arm?
(The mark is invisible To audience.)

GRAY: Could be a mole or a birth mark.

CRUTCH: I never noticed that, Belva.

GRAY: You got any others?

CRUTCH: Not that I know of.

BELVA: Look! There's a mark on me, too.

CRUTCH: I'll be dog gone.

GRAY: Could be some type of eczema, I suppose. Does it itch?

BELVA: No.

GRAY: Let me know if it changes shape any or gets any bigger.

CRUTCH: You tie a right handsome knot, Doc.

GRAY: Keep it dry. Keep it clean. Don't try to plow, for God's sake. You show infection the crack of a door, it barges right in like a Mormon. Good night all.

CRUTCH: I thank you again, sir. Sleep tight.

(Gray exits.)

BELVA: I'm too young for age spots.

CRUTCH: I'd call it a beauty mark, Belva.

BELVA: A beauty mark?

CRUTCH: What do you say you and me take the long way home, honey?

BELVA: Mr. Collins, are you spoonin' me?

CRUTCH: This much excitement at this time of night, just puts a man of a mood.

BELVA: I think you should hurt yourself more often.

(Music. Lights rise on Rebekah, who speaks to the theater. Music supports her thoughts, her speech.)

REBEKAH: In the long days that followed the death of my husband, I dreamt about him near every night. In my dreams, my husband rose up from the earth; the dust fell from his eyes; and his voice was so familiar and lonesome, it scared me. Sometimes I could feel his breath through the window. I could feel his touch in my sleep. *(Then.)*
And so, when I found myself dreaming in tears, and I woke up alone, I went to the graveyard to see him.

(Gray enters the graveyard, late at night. We barely see him . . . more shadow than presence. He takes a yarmulke out of his pocket, puts it on, and softly begins to say Kaddish.)

GRAY: *(Half-whispering.)* "Yis-gad-dal v'yis-kad-dash sh'meh rab-bo, b'ol-mo di'v-ro kir'-u-seh v'yam-lich mal-chu-seh, b'cha-ye-chon u-'yo-me-chon u-v'cha-yeh d'chol bes yis-ro-el—"

REBEKAH: What are you sayin'?

(She's startled him. He takes his yarmulke off.)

GRAY: Mrs. Muldoon. Fancy meeting you here.

REBEKAH: What are you doin'?

GRAY: I'm saying Kaddish, Ma'am.

REBEKAH: Say what?

GRAY: It's a kind of a prayer for the dead.

REBEKAH: It's a foreign language, ain't it?

GRAY: To some folks it is.

REBEKAH: It sounds beautiful. Who are you prayin' for?

(Gray crouches near the old "grave," which lies flat to the earth.)

GRAY: You see this old stone here? The name's worn away, but I noticed a star on it.

REBEKAH: Oh, nobody knows who that is. We all figured he must of passed on at Christmas. On account of the star.

GRAY: No, Ma'am, that's the Star of David. I figure whoever this is, he must be one of my people.

REBEKAH: You don't mean he's kin to you?

GRAY: Not by blood.

REBEKAH: *(Softly.)* Would you pray that prayer for my husband? For me?

GRAY: I'd be honored to, Mrs. Muldoon.

(They cross to where her husband was buried.)

GRAY: It's a right pretty stone, Ma'am. You've done him proud.

REBEKAH: Thank you . . .

GRAY: This prayer for the dead is all about life. It speaks to the glory of God, but it's said for the living, you see? It's kind of a prayer for us. You understand?

REBEKAH: You're talkin' about what I asked you before.

GRAY: I'm talking about your so-called "indigestion," that's right.

REBEKAH: Dr. Gray, I haven't changed my mind any.

(Near tears, but strong.)

I loved my husband more than I know how to say, but I can't have this child without him. I just can't.

GRAY: Sometimes decisions we make in a moment of grief are decisions we come to regret. Grief does terrible things to a person's mind, Ma'am, believe me, I know.

REBEKAH: I know there's certain things you can do for a woman who wants to be rid of a baby.

GRAY: I think you should give this a little more thought and a little more time.

REBEKAH: The last thing I want to give this is time! Don't you understand that? I'm only a few months along. If you don't want to help me, I'll do it myself.

GRAY: I beg you not to do that.

REBEKAH: I've heard tell of roots and of—

GRAY: Poisons is what they are! Do you want to kill yourself right along with it? Is that what you want? To lie in some field and bleed to death?

REBEKAH: No, sir, I don't. But I need to be shed of this baby. Why won't you help me?

GRAY: *(A near-whisper.)* Because I don't know if it's right.

REBEKAH: *(Meets his eye.)* Then you take it to God in prayer, sir. And you pray for the souls of us all.

(She kneels at the grave and closes her eyes. Gray looks at her for a moment, puts his yarmulke on, looks up, and then begins to pray, letting us feel the loss in this language . . . slowly at first, and then more rhythmically, until the prayer becomes like a song.)

GRAY: *"Yis-gad-dal v'yis-kad-dash sh'meh rab-bo, b'ol-mo di'v-ro kir'u-seh v'yam-lich mal-chu-seh, b'cha-ye-chon u-'yo-me-chon u-v'cha-yeh d'chol bes yis-ro- el, ba-a-go-lo u-viz-man ko-riv, v'im-ru O-Men. Y'heh sh'meh rab-bo m'vo-rach, l'o-lam ul'ol'meh ol-ma-ya: Yis-bo-rcah v'yish-tab-bach v'yis-po-ar, v'yis-ro-mam, v'yis-nas-seh, v'yis-had-or, v'yis-al-leh, v'yis-hal-lol O-men . . . "*

(Gray takes a breath at the end of this phrase, and Rebekah, assuming he's done because it feels like he is, says:)

REBEKAH: Amen.

(He looks at her.)

I thank you.

GRAY: Mrs. Muldoon, I think that someday somebody's gonna come along, Ma'am, and see you for the good person you are. And he'll love this child, whoever he is, because it's a part of you.

(He puts his hand first on her heart, then on her womb, and then on the grave . . . using a line for each:)

GRAY: Life is here. Life is here. Life is here.

REBEKAH: I just asked you to pray, not to preach.

GRAY: Point taken.

(They both stand.)

GRAY: Would it be too terribly forward of me to ask to escort you home, Ma'am?

REBEKAH: I don't think that'd be too awfully terrible, no.

(She takes his arm and they exit. Music might be nice under the following narration:)

MAGGIE: The weather report is as follows:

CRUTCH: Spring turns to summer and summer to fall.

MAGGIE: There's more leaves upon the earth now than stars in the sky.

CRUTCH: And harvest is in the works.

HOMER: Sunrise'll find half the countryside out in the fields.

CRUTCH: They're shellin' up corn now—

HOMER: Thrashin' the wheat like a misbehaved child.

MAGGIE: But here at the preacher's house, nobody's tendin' the fields this day.

CRUTCH: For here at the preacher's house, sickness has found a home.
(Phineas enters, sinks to a chair, and groans softly in pain as Tiny lets Gray in the "door.")

PHINEAS: Ohhhhhhhhh, my Lord.

GRAY: Morning, Miss Wingfield.

TINY: Come right in, Doctor.

PHINEAS: What is he doin' here?

TINY: I sent for him, brother.

PHINEAS: *(Still doubled half-over in pain.)* Well send him away. I don't need no doctorin'.

GRAY: Pastor, you're red as a beet.

PHINEAS: *(Masking his pain.)* I'm fine—I'll be fine, thank you very much. Prayer is the answer.

TINY: Phineas, whatever this is, you can't pray it away.

PHINEAS: It passes in time every time. I appreciate your concern, sir—now why don't you show him the door?

GRAY: Why don't you tell me what's ailing you, Pastor?

TINY: Pain is what's ailin' him.

GRAY: Pain in the abdomen?

PHINEAS: *(Groans, sounds like "lower.")* Loooooord.

GRAY: Lower abdomen?

TINY: *(In confidence.)* Doctor, it's lower than lower.

GRAY: Miss Tiny, could we have a moment of privacy, please?

TINY: But, Doc—

GRAY: *(Walks her out of the room.)* You just wait out in the hall. He'll be fine. You sleeping alright, are you?

TINY: I love the night.

GRAY: Good!

TINY: I'll pray for you, brother.
(Tiny exits. Gray turns back and matter-of-factly announces:)

GRAY: Alright, Mr. Wingfield—drop your drawers, please.

PHINEAS: Never.

GRAY: Come on now. Get out of those trousers.

PHINEAS: Get out of your own trousers!

GRAY: Let's try to be reasonable, shall we?

PHINEAS: I'm not about to slip down to my skivvies in front of the likes of you.

GRAY: Pastor—

PHINEAS: I'm not even kin to you!

GRAY: I can no more examine a patient who's fully clothed, than you'd read the bible blindfolded.

PHINEAS: I know my scriptures.

GRAY: *(Stares at him, then.)* Alright, to heck with you.

(Gray drops his own trousers.)

PHINEAS: What are you doin'?

GRAY: If I can do it, you can do it. Come on, sir. Drop your pants.

PHINEAS: *(Averts his eyes.)* "Blessed is he that walketh not in the counsel of the ungodly, nor standeth in the way of the scornful—"

(Gray knows the psalm, too. Phineas looks up, amazed. After a moment, the preacher drops his own trousers as they recite the psalm together. Both men end up with their pants around their ankles.)

GRAY: "—But his delight is the law of the Lord. And he shall be like a tree planted by the rivers of water, that bringeth forth fruit in his season—"

PHINEAS: *(Word for word overlap.)* "— But his delight is the law of the Lord. And he shall be like a tree planted by the rivers of water, that bringeth forth fruit in his season"

GRAY: Etcetera, etcetera, and so on.

PHINEAS: Amen.

GRAY: Now: Let's see if we can get to the bottom of this, so to speak.

PHINEAS: Don't touch me.

GRAY: I know you're tender.

PHINEAS: Just keep your paws to yourself!

(Gray and Phineas mirror each other, so that Gray examines his own body.)

GRAY: *(Touching his own belly.)* Would you say the pain is localized about here?

PHINEAS: A tad lower.

GRAY: Here?

PHINEAS: South, and a tad to the East.

GRAY: So it's in the region of the groin, if you'll pardon my French?

PHINEAS: It feels like somebody stuck a knife in me.

GRAY: Sharp pain or dull?

PHINEAS: Shootin' clean through to my backside.

GRAY: And does your urine have a . . . darkish hue to it?

PHINEAS: It's bloody as all get out, yeah.

(Gray sits down to think. Starts to cross his legs, discovers he can't—then continues his diagnosis in a businesslike fashion.)

GRAY: Mr. Wingfield, I believe you've got a stone, sir.

PHINEAS: A stone?

GRAY: A kidney stone, likely. It blocks the urethra, causes some swelling, a great deal of discomfort.

PHINEAS: Are you gonna cut on me?

GRAY: Pastor, I'd hope to avoid that, I truly would. First thing to do is to try and relieve the pain.

PHINEAS: Doc, I'd be more than grateful.

GRAY: You know Benjamin Franklin, my personal favorite among the Founding Fathers, suffered from the very same ailment.

PHINEAS: Ben Franklin had stones?

GRAY: Oh, he had a stone the size of Gibraltar. He was plagued with such pain, it just about crippled him. But being a man of some scientific prowess, he relieved himself of it by reversing the gravitational flow, inverting the torso—thereby releasing his stone from the groinular region.

PHINEAS: Meanin'?

GRAY: He stood on his head.

PHINEAS: *(Starts to cross away.)* You got another think comin'.

GRAY: The pain will get worse. Your plumbing backs up, septicemia sets in, and the body begins to poison itself.
(Phineas stops. Gray has his attention.)

GRAY: That stone's lodged as tight as a drum in your tract. But merely invert the torsonic position, put physics to work—and that thing will rise up and free itself, Pastor.

PHINEAS: *(Reluctantly.)* Well . . . if it worked for Ben Franklin—him bein' a Founder and all.

GRAY: Turn around, sir. That's it. Crouch down, put your hands on the floor.
(Phineas crouches. Gray is right behind him. Both men's pants are around their ankles. Phineas glances back, worried.)

GRAY: Trust me.

PHINEAS: I'm tryin'.

GRAY: Upsy daisy now . . . here we go!
(Gray takes Phineas' legs and thrusts them in the air, so the pastor stands on his head. Phineas screams. Tiny rushes in.)

PHINEAS: OHHHHHHHHHHH GOD!!!

TINY: Phineas! Brother, are you alright?!

PHINEAS: Jesus in heaven!

GRAY: Miss Tiny—please! Madam, avert your eyes!

TINY: What in the world are you doin' to him?

(Gray tries to pull his trousers up with one hand while holding Phineas up with the other—it isn't easy.)

PHINEAS: Whoaaaaa!!!

GRAY: If you'd allow us a modicum of modesty, Ma'am—

PHINEAS: Praise God!! I've been healed!!

TINY: You're healed?!

PHINEAS: Oh, blessed relief!!

TINY: *(To Gray.)* What are your pants doin' down?

GRAY: It's all in the interest of science, Miss Tiny. If you'll just give me a hand with his . . . what is this mark on your leg?!

(Gray notices a "mark" on the pastor's calf—like Belva's and Crutch's.)

PHINEAS: Oh, God, I haven't felt this good in ages.

GRAY: Pastor, have you ever scrutinized this?

TINY: I've noticed the same things on me. I got one up here, and another right chere, on back of my drum stick.

GRAY: Tiny, if you'll take his feet for a second—

TINY: Surely.

GRAY:—I'd like to examine that.

PHINEAS: *(As Tiny takes solo leg duty.)* Watch it now—

GRAY: Just keep his toes to the heavens, Ma'am. Keep breathing, Pastor. You doing alright?

PHINEAS: Tiny, this man's an unqualified genius.

GRAY: I hope you don't mind if I—

TINY: Hike it on up there and you take a gander.

(Gray lifts Tiny's skirts up, and examines the back of her thigh.)

PHINEAS: How long you figure I oughta do this?

GRAY: Sooner or later that stone's gonna have to come out. Let's just hope it passes of its own accord, sir.

TINY: See? It ain't bruised, is it?

GRAY: No, Ma'am, it's clearly a mark of some sort.

PHINEAS: Doc, I'm startin' to get a mite dizzy here.

GRAY: Alright, let's let him down.

(Helping Tiny lower him.)

Easy now. There we go.

PHINEAS: Lord.

GRAY: I warn you: The pain's gonna strike again, sir. They say the only thing worse than passing a kidney stone's birthing a baby. Just rise up a tad at a time.

TINY: Leastways he knows what to do for it now.

PHINEAS: Doctor, we surely give thanks.

GRAY: Pastor. Miss Tiny.

(Rebekah enters and Gray crosses as:)

REBEKAH: Of course I don't have any marks on my person.

PHINEAS: *(Exiting with his sister.)* Tiny, I've misjudged him.

(Rebekah is seven or eight months pregnant now, and definitely "showing." The bench from the preacher's house will soon become a "boat." There's a "paddle" built into the side of it, disguised as a cross beam or support. Or else a platform becomes a "boat" or a "raft.")

GRAY: Just next time you bathe yourself, Becky, be sure to look yourself over.

REBEKAH: I never come down with a thing when I'm pregnant. I can't even catch a cold.

GRAY: *(Helping her into the "boat.")* That's just an old wives tale.

REBEKAH: Well I'm an old wife, and I believe it. Be careful, Galen. This old johnny boat's always been tippy. Sit down. Sit down. Sit, sit, sit for Pete's sake!

GRAY: I'm not completely incompetent in matters of physical prowess. I've captained a balloon for God's sake.

REBEKAH: You're facin' the wrong direction, Captain.

GRAY: So I am.

(He turns around so they're facing each other.)

REBEKAH: Mind your balance now.

GRAY: There. That's a little more like it.

(He paddles the "boat" away from the shore, the stage floor is lit with a blue/green wash, and they're out on the river . . .)

GRAY: Bid farewell to civilization, such as it is.

REBEKAH: Adam and I used to picnic on up in that cove over yonder.

GRAY: I'll paddle you somewhere else then.

REBEKAH: *(After a moment.)* Don't get us caught in the current now.

(He paddles for a moment or two; she relaxes, taking in the view.)

REBEKAH: Gosh, it's a lovely day, ain't it?

GRAY: Becky, I've travelled from here to the edge of the sea itself, but I've got to honestly tell you, the scenery I'm taking in right here and now is just about as scenic as scenery can be.

REBEKAH: You mean up in your balloon?

GRAY: The balloon was an interesting means of transportation at an extraordinarily opportune time, but I think I'd just as soon stay a little closer to home from now own.

REBEKAH: Is this home to you now?

GRAY: Home's always been people, not places for me. My pa was a travelling medicine man, you see.

REBEKAH: You mean a doctor like you?

GRAY: No, I mean he was a charlatan, Becky. We used to sell remedies out of the back of a wagon.

REBEKAH: You didn't?

GRAY: Nostrum's Elixer and Medical Cure-All, yes, Ma'am. "A recuperative miracle," Pa used to call it. Oh, he could sell dog shit to cats, that man could.

REBEKAH: What's it do to you?

GRAY: Well, you funnel a mixture of alcohol, prune juice, and cod's liver oil down any man's gullet, it moves him in more ways than one.

REBEKAH: *(Touches her stomach.)* Oh, good heavens.

GRAY: What?

REBEKAH: I feel it. Right here. It's kickin'.

GRAY: *(Pleased.)* Well isn't that something? I wonder if I could hear his heart yet? You don't mind, do you?

REBEKAH: Galen. You're rockin' the boat.

GRAY: I'm not gonna capsize us, Becky.

REBEKAH: Be careful.

GRAY: Good golly, you are a worry wart.

(He places his head on her womb:)

Interesting . . . interesting.

REBEKAH: What do you hear?

GRAY: Hello in there!

REBEKAH: Galen!

GRAY: Hold on—he's tapping out a message.

(Listens.)

He wants to know what his name is.

REBEKAH: If it's a boy, you can tell him I've settled on Galen.

GRAY: *(Looks up, perplexed, disturbed.)* Don't get me wrong here—I feel a foot taller, Becky, I do, but a name is a holy thing. A good name should honor an ancestor. I'd name a son for his father.

REBEKAH: It isn't his child.

(Gray takes this in for a moment.)

It isn't mine neither. It's yours, Doctor Gray.

GRAY: Mine, Ma'am?

REBEKAH: You're the one havin' this baby, not me. You wanted it, Galen—you got it.

GRAY: Now, Becky—

REBEKAH: I done made my mind up—after I birth him, I'll give him to you.

GRAY: That's a mighty sweet thought, it truly is—

REBEKAH: It ain't a thought, sir: It's a fact.

GRAY: Becky, now—

REBEKAH: I think you'll make a fine mother.

GRAY: Becky, I can't raise a child alone!

REBEKAH: Well somebody has to.

(We hear June calling in the distance:)

JUNE: Doctor Gray—?? Doctor?

(Rebekah has the paddle now.)

REBEKAH: We better head for shore, Galen.

GRAY: Diapers and feeding and—Jesus Jehova!

JUNE: *(Closer now.)* Hey, Doctor—??

REBEKAH: *(Calls.)* He's over here, June!

GRAY: Alright, alright you've made your point, Becky, I've had my comeuppance—now let's quit this funning around, shall we?

REBEKAH: Galen: This baby belongs to you.

GRAY: *(Realizes she fully means it.)* Oh, my dear God.

(June appears on the horizon. As Rebekah rows them closer to "shore," the river light recedes . . .)

JUNE: Doc, I been lookin' all over for you!

GRAY: Juney, just hold on a second.

(To Becky.)

If you want a ring on your finger, there's better ways, Becky.

REBEKAH: Don't flatter yourself.

JUNE: Doc, you need to run to the Collins house—right away.

REBEKAH: Juney, what's wrong, honey?

JUNE: Belva's been coughin' just awful. She's runnin' a fever—she can't hardly breathe!

REBEKAH: Oh, my lord.

(To Gray.)

Is there anything I can do?

GRAY: Oh, I think you've accomplished enough for one day.

(Rebekah exits as lights rise on Belva coughing—it's a terrible, deep, soul-wracking cough. She draws long, raspy, labored breaths. Crutch helps her onstage.)

JUNE: You want me to stay on and help you? Cause I've always been interested in nursin' and whatnot.

GRAY: Mrs. Collins?

CRUTCH: Doctor Gray's here now—he'll tend to you, honey.

GRAY: Bring me a basin of boiling hot water.

JUNE: What do you think's wrong with her?

GRAY: Now, Juney.

CRUTCH: Do what he tells you, girl.

(June rushes offstage. Belva coughs deeply. The cough is so intense that it brings her to her knees.)

GRAY: Easy now . . . easy, Ma'am . . . just let it pass.

CRUTCH: God, I don't know what this is.

(Belva takes her hand away from her mouth; she has a small red handkerchief, signifying that she's just coughed up blood . . .)

CRUTCH: Belva?

GRAY: Dear God Almighty.

CRUTCH: Doctor Gray?

GRAY: Easy now, easy . . . just take it one breath at a time.

(Gray turns away, struggling to keep it "together.")

CRUTCH: Doctor?

GRAY: *(Still away.)* Don't let the blood frighten you, Ma'am . . . there is absolutely nothing to be afraid of. You're gonna be just fine, just fine . . . just breathe right on past it and think about something else.

CRUTCH: Don't tell me you're weak in the knees again. You need a drink?

GRAY: *(Gives Crutch his handkerchief.)* Just clean her up a bit for me.
(To himself.)
You just need to slow down and concentrate. Slow down and breathe.

CRUTCH: Good Lord, you scared me to death, honey.

(Crutch wipes the "blood" from his wife's mouth and hand. Belva's breathing sounds almost like an asthma attack—as if each new breath is a struggle. Gray places his head on her back or chest—he almost steadies himself with his patient.)

GRAY: Alright . . . alright . . . we're gonna get through this, I promise. I want you to take a good breath for me, Belva. That's it . . . breathe deep as you can now, and hold it, please. Hold it.

CRUTCH: It seems like choking inside her own body.

(June enters with a steaming basin of "water" and a large enough towel or cloth to cover Belva's head and upper body.)

JUNE: Dr. Gray?

GRAY: Bring it right here.

JUNE: What's wrong with her?

CRUTCH: She's been coughin up blood, Juney.

JUNE: Blood?

GRAY: Alright, turn your face to the light for me, Belva, and let's have a look at that throat. Open wide for me and take a deep breath. Juney, keep out of the way.

CRUTCH: Yesterday evenin' them marks of hers started to seep like a sieve. Then she set into coughin'.

(Sound of distant thunder . . . Gray makes a sort of vaporizer for Belva with the steaming basin and cloth.)

GRAY: I'm gonna cover your head with this, Ma'am, and I want you to breathe in some steam. There we go, Belva. There you go . . . That feels a mite better, I'd think.

CRUTCH: Doctor, d'ja hear me?

GRAY: I heard, sir.

JUNE: It's fixin' to rain.

(June is with Belva. Gray and Crutch step away for privacy.)

GRAY: Last night her marks started to seep, you say?

CRUTCH: Puffed up the size of a damn silver dollar and blistered wide open.

GRAY: Whatever these lesions are, I think they've cropped up and festered inside her. They've spread to her throat, and her lungs. Do you understand what I'm saying to you?

CRUTCH: You're saying I'm gonna come down with this, too.

(It begins to rain . . . not a storm, but a steady rain.)

GRAY: Mr. Collins: I want this house quarantined.

CRUTCH: Quarantine?

JUNE: *(Looking up at the weather.)* Good lord, it's comin' down fast.

CRUTCH: Why has God done this to her?

(Gray crosses back to Belva, whose breathing is labored. For a good moment, all we hear is her struggle for breath and the rain . . . and then June steps downstage.)

JUNE: And so ends chapter one.

(Thunder crashes. Lights to black.)

END OF ACT I

ACT II

Lights rise on several Townspeople. They speak to the theater.

MAGGIE: The weather report is as follows:

PHINEAS: There was thunder—

TINY: And lightning—

PHINEAS: And sickness—

TINY: And dread.

MAGGIE: Everyday somebody found a mark on 'em.

TINY: Every night somebody else took a fever.

PHINEAS: And still, it continued to spread.

JUNE: *Anatomy of Gray.*

TOWNSPEOPLE: Chapter Two:

> *(Lights isolate June.)*

JUNE: This time—this terrible onslaught of sickness—was a frightening time; but secretly, for a girl who was fated to live in the most boring town in the world—secretly it was also the best of times—because she got to spend so much time with Doctor Galen P. Gray. In fact, the doctor and June were together so much, one would think they were practically married. Except for the fact they didn't have sex or sleep in the same bed or kiss or hold hands—there was very little that they did not share. She went where he went; she did what he did. For June had become his assistant.

> *(Gray enters, feeling faint, gasping for air. He ends up next to June.)*

GRAY: Oh, God, oh, God . . .

> *(He puts his hands on his knees. June waves her hand in his face. It's obvious they've been through this before.)*

JUNE: Just take it one breath at a time, Doc, you're gonna be fine. Drink?

> *(Gray pulls a small flask from his jacket. Takes a sip.)*

GRAY: Thank you.

JUNE: Why are you so scared of blood?

GRAY: I don't know.

JUNE: You think you'll ever get over it?

GRAY: Do we have to talk about this?

JUNE: Why do you wash your hands after every single patient?

GRAY: Because it stops the spread of germs.

JUNE: How?

GRAY: I don't know, it just does.

JUNE: Well if washin' kills germs, then why don't you make everybody who's marked take a bath and just wash the marks off 'em?

GRAY: Because it doesn't work that way, June.

JUNE: Why not?

GRAY: Because the marks are an external symptom of an illness that's already inside them, that's why.

JUNE: Then why don't you wash out their innards? Make 'em drink soap and hot water to kill off the germs.

GRAY: That wouldn't work.

JUNE: Why not?

GRAY: Because the sickness has already taken root in the bloodstream and spread through their systems.

JUNE: Is that why you're scared of blood?

GRAY: Can I ask you a question? Why do you ask so many questions?

JUNE: Because you told me there's no such thing as a dumb question, only a dumb answer.

GRAY: Well I love your questions.

JUNE: You do?

GRAY: In fact, I love them so much I want to parcel them out. From now on, I want you to limit yourself to one question a day.

JUNE: One a day?

GRAY: One a day.

(Townspeople narrate the Q and A for us; they're fairly formal about it.)

REBEKAH: Monday:

JUNE: Do you believe in God?

GRAY: Yes.

REBEKAH AND TINY: Tuesday:

JUNE: Do you believe God is good?

GRAY: *(After a beat.)* Yes.

REBEKAH, TINY, AND HOMER: Wednesday:

JUNE: Why?

GRAY: Why what?

JUNE: Why do you believe God is good?

GRAY: Well don't you?

JUNE: I don't know.

(Off Gray's look.)

They say His eye is on the sparrow, but if that's true, then why do people get sick and die? I mean sparrows don't pray. They don't go to church. They don't tithe. They don't do anything but fly around and be sparrows, and if God cares more about them than he does about us, then what good is He?

GRAY: How do you know sparrows don't pray?

REBEKAH, TINY, HOMER AND PHINEAS: Thursday:

JUNE: How come you've never been married?

FIVE TOWNSPEOPLE: Friday:

JUNE: Have you ever had a girlfriend?

GRAY: Yes.

JUNE: Is there anything else you want to say about that?

GRAY: No.

JUNE: *(To audience:)* I wanted to ask him what happened to her—if she died tragically or flung herself from a bridge because he forsook her, or if she forsook him and left him heartbroken, and that's why he couldn't settle down and probably never would settle down til he met the right person, and I thought we both had a pretty good idea who that might be, but then, I was partly afraid the right person might be my own mother, and I couldn't bear to ask about that. Besides which, I'd already used up my question for Friday.

REBEKAH: Which brings us to—

SIX TOWNSPEOPLE: Saturday:

JUNE: Doc? What happens after we die?

GRAY: I don't know.

JUNE: Can I take back that question and ask a new question?

GRAY: Yes.

JUNE: If you believe God is good, then do you believe in heaven? And if you do, do you think I'll see my father again? And if I do, how old do you reckon I'll be when I see him? Cause I'm plannin' to live as long as I can, so I'll be a lot older than him when I die, and that'll be weird cause I'll look like his mother, but feel like his daughter, except by then, I'll probably have kids of my own, and they'd get confused if I ended up younger than them—so how do you think all that sorts itself out?

GRAY: I think you'll always be your pa's daughter, no matter how old you are.

JUNE: You think I'll ever stop missin' him?

GRAY: No. I think you'll miss him for the rest of your life.

JUNE: I don't need eternity. I'd give anything just to spend a day with him. Or an afternoon even. If I could spend one afternoon with my father, that would be heaven enough for me.

GRAY: And what would you say to him, June?

JUNE: *(Close to tears or in them.)* I don't know. I guess I'd just tell him I love him, and want him back.

(He puts his hand on her shoulder.)

REBEKAH: June, bein' June, saved her last, deepest, and most personal question for—

ALL TOWNSPEOPLE: Sunday.

REBEKAH: And once again, she wrote her thoughts down.

(June gives Gray a piece of paper or an envelope, which he opens and reads:)

GRAY: "Do you think I'm pretty? Check this box for 'yes' or this box for 'no'."

REBEKAH: Oh, June.

JUNE: It may be trite and immature to you, Mother, but there's some things you don't ask out loud.

GRAY: *(Hands her the paper back.)* Juney, I think you're fifteen.

JUNE: What is that supposed to mean?

GRAY: It means I'm not gonna answer that question. Now, if you don't mind, I have patients to tend to.

(Maggie enters. June, of course, feels slapped in the face.)

MAGGIE: Doc, I know you're busy as a three-legged cat in a sandbox, so I won't take up much of your time, but my head hurts so badly I can't barely see.

GRAY: Do have any fever? Aches and pains?

MAGGIE: No.

GRAY: Are your glands swollen?

MAGGIE: No, I don't think so.

(Maggie takes a seat, Gray checks the glands in her neck.)

GRAY: June, will you fix a hot compress, please?

JUNE: No.

MAGGIE: Oh, I've practically soaked my durn head in hot water—it ain't helpin' any. It's probably just what you said, Doc, it's probably just worry is all.

(To June.)

You comin' to choir tonight?

JUNE: Not if I can help it.

GRAY: Maggie: I found a mark on you.

MAGGIE: Where?

GRAY: On the back of your neck.

MAGGIE: *(A worried smile.)* I can't be marked—I haven't done anything wrong.

JUNE: Well neither has anyone else.

MAGGIE: Preacher's too prideful. Belva's a gossip. Crutch drinks like a fish. I read the bible—I pray every day.

GRAY: If God sent down lightning to strike everybody who misbehaved, we'd have theologians predicting the weather.

MAGGIE: Well you tell me what's causin' it then!

GRAY: It's a disease—it's spread by germs, not by God!

MAGGIE: I never heard of these germ things before you came here.

GRAY: Maggie, germs have been here since the dawn of creation.

MAGGIE: I didn't have this before you touched me.

GRAY: Yes, you did, Maggie.

MAGGIE: *(Backing away from him.)* No, I didn't—I couldn't—I know it! *(Maggie exits.)*

GRAY: Maggie?! Maggie, come back here!
(Turns to June, frustrated.)
Would you go talk sense to that woman? Maybe she'll listen to you.

JUNE: Why would she listen to me? I'm just a kid.
(Lights bring us to evening "choir practice." Tiny, Rebekah, Homer, and Phineas. Maggie is the choir director.)

HOMER: *(Soda pop in hand.)* Hey, June, aren't you goin' to choir?

JUNE: *(Exiting.)* No.

CHOIR: *(Singing this hymn or another.)* "A mighty Fortress is our God, A Bulwark never failing; Our helper He amid the flood Of mortal ills prevailing: For still our ancient Foe doth seek to work us woe; His craft and power are great, And armed with cruel hate, On earth is not his equal."

MAGGIE: *(Crossing away before the verse ends.)* I can't do this. I just can't go on like this as if nothin's happened at all. I can't concentrate, and I don't know how any of you can.

PHINEAS: Now, Margaret—

MAGGIE: *(Touching her "mark.")* I'm tellin you, somethin is terrible, terribly wrong with that man.

REBEKAH: Oh, now, Doctor Gray's done a world of good here. You know that as well as I do.

MAGGIE: You call bringin' sickness upon us a good thing to do?

TINY: He surely did wonders for me.

MAGGIE: He's got the poor Collins locked up in their own house.

REBEKAH: That's because he's trying to keep the rest of us from catching it.

MAGGIE: Well guess what? It ain't workin'.

PHINEAS: If you think this through in a factual fashion—

MAGGIE: You want the facts, Preacher? I'll give you the facts. Fact one: He touched me. Fact two: He marked me. And fact three: It's happened to you and you and now me and you know it.

HOMER: I don't have any marks on me, Maggie.

MAGGIE: You had any truck with the doctor?

HOMER: I talk to him, sure.

MAGGIE: Did he touch you?

HOMER: Well now that you mention it . . .

MAGGIE: Did he or didn't he?

HOMER: No.

MAGGIE: You see there?

TINY: I went to see him not two days ago.

MAGGIE: And?

HOMER: Did he touch you?

TINY: He examined me head to toe, Homer, and I'll tell you what else—if I felt any better right now, I'd be twins.

MAGGIE: Oh, why don't you go back to sleep for a couple of years?

TINY: Why don't you wake up, Maggie?

MAGGIE: You are so smitten with him you've gone blind! And you, too!

REBEKAH: Would I let my daughter near him if I thought he was causin' this?

PHINEAS: Ladies—ladies!—sisters, please!

(He has their attention.)

Sickness is a hard thing to fathom, I grant. But I believe the Lord God is a loving creator. I figure the Good Lord has put this mark on us to test us, don't you see?

HOMER: Test us how, Pastor?

PHINEAS: It happens right and left in the scriptures. All the saints suffer. Think about Shadrach, Meshach, and Abednego—look at how God tested Jonah and Job.

MAGGIE: Then why don't He mark Doctor Gray? He's a Jew. They claim to be God's chosen people.

TINY: Oh, everybody claims to be God's chosen people.

PHINEAS: The Jews are a bible-totin' people, course they only tote half of it. When the Rapture comes, I doubt your Jews'll be going to heaven. Maybe God don't want to waste His time on him.

REBEKAH: That's about the most small-minded thing I've ever heard.

HOMER: There's a mark on you, Rebekah.

REBEKAH: Oh, there is not.

PHINEAS: Where?

MAGGIE: There's a mark on her?

REBEKAH: Where?

HOMER: *(Touches his own face.)* It's right there.

MAGGIE: I don't know how he does it, but somehow he does it.

PHINEAS: Well, I've always been somewhat suspicious of him.
  (Crutch enters.)

CRUTCH: Pastor?

MAGGIE: *(To Rebekah.)* I'd keep your daughter away from him.

CRUTCH: Pastor?

PHINEAS: What is it? What's wrong, Mr. Collins?

CRUTCH: It's Belva. She's gone from us . . .

TINY: Belva? Dead?

MAGGIE: Oh, my lands.

CRUTCH: You've gotta have a strong talk with that doctor—he won't let me
  bury her.

PHINEAS: What do you mean?

CRUTCH: I mean he's wantin' to carve on her, sir.

HOMER: Carve on a dead woman!

PHINEAS: We'll put a stop to this, Crutch—don't you worry.

HOMER: I'll come with you, Pastor.

CRUTCH: I tell ya, the man's in a frenzy.

REBEKAH: Dear Lord.

MAGGIE: *(Following the men.)* I knew it, I told you!

TINY: *(To the theater.)* The news spread like a fire that night. A fire that was
  fueled by rumors, by fear, and by the fact that now even Rebekah was
  marked. Rebekah with child was marked. If she could be marked, then
  anyone could. First Juney Muldoon lost her father, now her mother was
  marked, and soon, she feared, soon she would be left with no one. Her
  boring little town wasn't boring anymore, it was dying, and it was rag-
  ing, and boiling with fear. Men raced with lanterns and guns through
  the countryside looking for the cause of this illness: the man from the
  sky. The Jew. The teacher. The coward. The healer. The spreader of germs
  and the locus of fears: Dr. Galen Gray.
  *(Night sounds . . . we hear dogs barking and howling in the distance. And
  then, the sound of horses—not galloping, but neighing, and stomping softly
  in the darkness as the scene becomes the "livery stable." Gray enters quietly, deeply worried, in a hurry. He's wearing a jacket; he carries a halter.
  He might have a carpet bag slung over his shoulder. He doesn't see June in
  the shadows.)*

JUNE: Are you runnin' away again?

GRAY: June. Is that you?

JUNE: Doc, I wouldn't do that if I was you.

GRAY: Wouldn't do what?

JUNE: I might skip town, but I sure wouldn't steal a horse. If Crutch Collins finds out you not only killed his wife, but went and took his best stallion, they'll hang you for sure.

GRAY: I didn't kill Belva—that's crazy talk.

JUNE: It may be crazy, but that's what they're sayin'.

GRAY: What do you recommend I do?

JUNE: Take me along with you.

GRAY: No.

JUNE: Why not?

GRAY: Because!

JUNE: Because why?? Are you mad at me?

GRAY: No, I'm not mad at you.

JUNE: I'm sorry I didn't stand up for you when you found a mark on Maggie. And I'm sorry I was fishin' for compliments with that stupid check-here-for-yes-and-check-here-for-no thing—and I'm sorry I ask so many dumb questions—now will you please take me with you??

GRAY: No!

JUNE: Is it because I'm not Jewish?

GRAY: Oh, for God's sake.

JUNE: Because I can turn Jewish. I think I've always felt Jewish. I just never had a name for it before. But I'm like you. I look like everyone around here on the outside, but on the inside I've always known I was different.

GRAY: June, take my word for it: You don't need to convert just because you're an oddball.

JUNE: See? Even you think so!! Doc, I can't live here the rest of my life. I belong in the city. I want to go to museums and libraries and temples and whatnot. Gray is just . . . flat. Everywhere you look, it's flat. Even the hills are flat.

GRAY: You're only fifteen—

JUNE: Sixteen in March.

GRAY: Your ma's having a baby—she needs you.

JUNE: Well she needs you, too.

GRAY: Juney, my future is feathers and tar. Now I have to go.

JUNE: Will you just answer one more question before you run off? Just one more, that's all.

GRAY: What??

JUNE: Is everybody who's marked gonna die?

GRAY: I don't know. But I fear they will. You're not marked, are you?

JUNE: No. But my mother is.

HOMER: Shhhhhh!!!

GRAY: *(Reacting to the news.)* Oh, no. Oh, God . . .

JUNE: Does that mean her baby's marked, too?

GRAY: Shhhhh.

(Homer has a lantern; Phineas brandishes a small pistol, which he isn't used to using. They enter.)

PHINEAS: My, my, my, my.

HOMER: I toldja he's down to the livery stable.

PHINEAS: Just hold it right there, Doctor Gray.

HOMER: June, has he harmed you?

JUNE: My virtue's intact, Homer, thank you for askin'.

PHINEAS: Go fetch Mr. Collins, and tell him to bring a rope, son.

(Homer exits.)

JUNE: Oh, for pity's sake, Pastor, you're not gonna hang him.

PHINEAS: Did you know he tried to carve poor Mrs. Collins into little tiny pieces right after she died?

GRAY: I just wanted to do an autopsy on her, that's all.

JUNE: What's an autopsy?

GRAY: June, this really isn't the best time for questions.

PHINEAS: It's the devil's work, that's what it is.

GRAY: It's an examination of the internal organs to determine the course of disease and the cause of death, sir—which wasn't me.

JUNE: Are you alright, Pastor? You look kinda flushed.

PHINEAS: It's been a long night.

(Phineas indeed, looks a bit pale, and his kidneys have seen better days.)

JUNE: Doc, you're not makin' him sick, are you?

PHINEAS: What?

JUNE: All he has to do is just look at you cross-eyed, and boom—it's the mark of the beast.

PHINEAS: Juney: Don't josh.

JUNE: He's the devil and I'm in league with him!!

GRAY: I really wish you hadn't said that.

(Phineas sort of backs away, and begins praying a version of the 27th Psalm, quickly, fervently:)

PHINEAS: "The Lord is my light and my salvation; whom shall I fear? When the wicked, mine enemies come upon me to eat my flesh, they stumble and fall—!"

(Etc. As June overlaps with:)

JUNE: *(Overlapping, warning.)* Don't look at him. Don't meet his eye.

PHINEAS: "— Hide not thy face from me, put not thy servant in danger; thou has been the help of my fleeessshhh—!!

(Phineas groans and sinks to his knees—his stones are plaguing him again. June grabs the gun out of his hand.)

GRAY: *(Concerned.)* Pastor Wingfield?

PHINEAS: *(Doubled over in pain.)* Keep away from me!!!

JUNE: Go, go, go, go!

PHINEAS: *(Trying to crawl away.)* Somebody help me!

GRAY: Just hold still and let's have a look at you, sir.

JUNE: Are you crazy? Get on a horse and get out of here!

GRAY: Juney, just hold on a second.

(Checking Phineas.)

You tender here, are you?

PHINEAS: Jesus Almighty!

HOMER: *(Calls out.)* He's right over here!!

GRAY: Pastor, that stone's gonna have to come out.

(Homer and Crutch enter with a fifth of whiskey and a shotgun, which Crutch levels at Gray. Somebody might also have a hanging rope. Phineas is in mortal pain . . . he moans.)

HOMER: Good lord, he's killed the damn preacher!

JUNE: He hasn't killed anyone, Homer.

GRAY: I'm trying to help him.

CRUTCH: *(Levels his shotgun.)* Just get away from him.

PHINEAS: Oh, God—I'm dyin'!

CRUTCH: Doc, I'd like nothin' more than to shoot you right now.

(June aims the small pistol at Crutch.)

JUNE: If you shoot him, I'll shoot you.

CRUTCH: Juney, what's gotten into you?

GRAY: Let's all of us just put the firearms down. If you kill me, he's gonna die, Mr. Collins.

JUNE: And so are you. So make your choice, and say your prayers.

PHINEAS: *(In excruciating pain.)* Oh, God, have mercy!!!

GRAY: I might be wrong, but I think his kidneys are backing up on him.

HOMER: You know how to save him?

GRAY: I do.

(Homer looks at Crutch.)

CRUTCH: Then save him. And get out of town.

GRAY: June, get me a saddle blanket.

(June rushes offstage.)

HOMER: I hope you know what you're doin'.

(Gray opens his carpet bag to look for his scalpel, which he keeps in a small leather case.)

GRAY: I think I got everything I need with me.

CRUTCH: What're you rootin' around for?

GRAY: Mr. Collins, would you point that damn gun at the ground before somebody gets his gonads blown off?!

(June runs back on with a saddle blanket.)

JUNE: Where you want it, Doc?

GRAY: Just spread it out right here.

(To Homer.)

Don't just stand there, son. Give me a hand with him, will you?

PHINEAS: Don't move me!

(Homer gets in position to help.)

GRAY: Ready?

PHINEAS: Oh, God . . .

GRAY: One, two, three.

(Phineas screams as they roll or lift him onto the blanket.)

PHINEAS: Jeeeesus!!!!

JUNE: Careful, now, careful.

CRUTCH: Good lord, he's tender.

HOMER: Are you gonna cut on him, Doc?

GRAY: Give me that bottle.

(June takes it from Crutch and gives it to Gray.)

JUNE: Here you go, Doc.

GRAY: Pastor—now I'm gonna give you some whiskey. It'll help the pain, sir.

CRUTCH: He ain't took a drink in his life.

(Gray takes a drink himself.)

GRAY: There's a first time for everything.

(He offers the whiskey to Phineas, who grabs the bottle and guzzles it.)

HOMER: *(After a moment.)* Just think of it as medicine, Preacher.

(Long pause as they watch him drink.)
GRAY: That's it.
(Phineas keeps drinking. Finally stops.)
Now get his shirt open.
CRUTCH: He's got the damn bottle half emptied already.
(Phineas nearly passes out. Gray takes the bottle from him.)
GRAY: Hold that lantern up, would you?
(Crutch still has the shotgun leveled at Gray. Homer holds the lantern up, too. Gray pours some whiskey on his scalpel.)
JUNE: I hope to God this plague ain't in the bloodstream or you're gonna catch it for sure.
HOMER: How can you catch it? You're the one givin' it, ain'tcha?
GRAY: Homer, I'm so damn stupid I thought you were smarter than that.
(He hands the bottle back to June.)
GRAY: Here. Funnel another dose down him.
HOMER: It's gonna hurt like hell, Pastor.
(June funnels another good, long drink of whiskey down Phineas.)
JUNE: Doc, have you ever done this procedure before?
GRAY: Only to dead people, Juney.
HOMER: *(Whispers to his Pastor.)* Keep drinkin'.
(It's important that Phineas pass out. His body is turned slightly upstage, so the audience can't see his belly. Gray takes a deep breath.)
GRAY: Alright. Whatever you do, don't let him start flailing around on me.
JUNE: You got a grasp on him?
HOMER: I hope to God so.
CRUTCH: Boy, that's quite a knife.
HOMER: Ain't it?
GRAY: *(Having trouble.)* Get a grip on yourself.
(Gray says a quick prayer in Yiddish, then:)
GRAY: Here we go, Pastor.
(The Pastor's undershirt, of course, is red, pre-soaked with the color to signify blood. Gray makes his "incision" and turns away.)
GRAY: Oh, God . . . I'm gonna pass out . . .
HOMER: You can't quit on him now, Doc—you got him wide open!
JUNE: Here—take a drink, take drink!
(Gray drinks.)
HOMER: Lord, would you look at that blood gushin'?!
GRAY: Homer, go fetch us a pail of water.
HOMER: Right now?

GRAY: Don't make me beg you, son—do what I say!

CRUTCH: *(As Homer takes off.)* Go to the well at the church.

> *(Homer exits.)*

GRAY: June, do you think you can follow instructions?

JUNE: I usually make 'em up as I go along, Doc.

GRAY: I'll make 'em up as you go along.

> *(Gray hands the scalpel to June.)*

CRUTCH: Good lord, he's comin' to!!!

PHINEAS: *(Screams.)* Ahhhhhhhhh!!!

JUNE: Ahhhhhhhhh!!!

GRAY: Whiskey!

CRUTCH: Whiskey!

JUNE: Whiskey!

GRAY: Drink, drink, drink!

> *(Gray holds the bottle to the preacher's lips. Phineas drinks again. Passes*
> *out again. Gray pours a little more whiskey on the scalpel.)*

GRAY: *(To June.)* You alright?

JUNE: Uh huh. What do you want me to do?

GRAY: Do you see that darkish thing there?

JUNE: This'n?

GRAY: Don't cut that!! You'll kill him!!

JUNE: Calm down!

GRAY: Darkish-blue—right by the gall bladder. See it?

JUNE: Which one's the gall bladder?

> *(Crutch moves the lantern closer. He's set his shotgun down by now and is*
> *getting involved in the surgery.)*

GRAY: *(Quietly, concentrating.)* There, June. Don't touch the mesenteric artery.
You see that darkish mass?

JUNE: This thing right here?

GRAY: No, right beside it. Mr. Collins, there's a needle and thread in my coat
pocket.

CRUTCH: Got it.

GRAY: Thread it.

JUNE: You want me to cut it?

GRAY: Wait a second . . . give me that whiskey.

> *(He dumps a little more whiskey in the incision.)*

GRAY: There now—you see it?

JUNE: Yeah.

CRUTCH: Lord God, it's ugly . . .

GRAY: That's it . . . you're doing just fine . . . don't press the knife on it. Love with it . . . That's it . . . let the blade do your work.

JUNE: You got any tweezers?

GRAY: *(He has them ready.)* Here.

JUNE: Look at that thing—it's the size of a walnut . . . !

CRUTCH: No wonder it pains him.

GRAY: There we go—that's it—I'll pinch the vein for you. Keep your hand steady.

(Total concentration. Then:)

JUNE: I got the little devil!

(Homer enters with a bucket and a dipper.)

HOMER: I gotcha that water, Doc.

CRUTCH: Good for you, Juney!

GRAY: *(To Homer.)* Bring it on over. Give me that needle and thread, Mr. Collins.

CRUTCH: I'd say this calls for a drink.

GRAY: *(Re: the whiskey.)* Don't you dare waste a drop of that.

(Re: the water bucket.)

Dip a little water in there to rinse out the incision—then I'll close him up.

(June does so.)

That's it. And now a little whiskey to kill off the germs.

(Gray pours some "whiskey" on the surgical wound.)

Whiskey and water, June . . . whiskey and water's the key.

HOMER: I hate the taste of water.

GRAY: Water's the best thing to purify the system. You can't live on nothing but soda pop, Homer.

HOMER: I do.

JUNE: You're not half bad with that needle, Doc.

HOMER: I always thought sewin' was kind of a female art.

JUNE: Just like repairin' a ripped up old sofa.

(Pause. Gray sews.)

GRAY: June, can you cut that thread for me?

(She does so.)

Thank you.

JUNE: You're welcome.

CRUTCH: You finished?

GRAY: *(Finishing.)* Thank God.

HOMER: You did a fine job, Doctor Gray.

GRAY: No, she did a fine job.

(*Then.*)

Let's just hope he lives through it.

(*Everybody shakes everybody else's hand or pats them on the back.*)

JUNE: I didn't think you had it in you, Doc.

HOMER: What do you know about that?

GRAY: Mr. Collins, I beg of you: Let me do an autopsy on Belva. Let me learn what I can from her, please.

CRUTCH: It ain't right to cut a dead person, Doc. I can't letcha do it. She's suffered enough as it is.

(*There's no changing his mind.*)

GRAY: Alright, let's get this man home to his bed. Mr. Collins, if you'll get his feet for me, please. And Homer, you prop up the middle.

JUNE: Careful now.

GRAY: Ready. Set.

(*The three men lift Phineas and carry him off.*)

CRUTCH: I'm too damned old for this.

GRAY: Try not to jostle him. Easy, boys.

JUNE: Good lord, this blanket's a mess.

CRUTCH: Hey, June bug, will you get my gun for me?

JUNE: Surely.

GRAY: Watch it now, watch your step.

(*And they're gone. June is alone on stage. She picks up the shotgun, and the water bucket or lantern. Then turns to face the theater:*)

JUNE: After my father died, I felt so angry, and sad, and confused that I sat down and wrote a long letter to the Powers that Be. I wished for a doctor. I prayed for a healer. But I had no idea that the doctor I'd wished for was me.

(*Tiny and Maggie enter. They speak to the theater as June exits.*)

MAGGIE: The weather report is as follows:

TINY: First it got colder and then it got warm.

MAGGIE: The first sign of illness was fever.

TINY: I felt like my very soul was on a scavenger hunt to find God.

MAGGIE: You're gettin' warmer and warmer and warmer and warmer.

(*Gray enters.*)

GRAY: Let's have a look at your eyes, Tiny.

TINY: Why?

GRAY: Just look at me, please. Hold still.

TINY: You are the nicest individual.

GRAY: Pupils are dilated.

TINY: Dilated. What does that mean? Is that bad or good?

GRAY: I think you better lie down for a spell.

TINY: I don't have time to lie down—I need to look after my brother.

GRAY: Your brother's just fine. June's watching after him.

TINY: June's just a child! She can't barely look after herself.

GRAY: Let's just worry about you for right now.

MAGGIE: You're gettin' warmer and warmer.

    (Lights change. Tiny's attitude changes. She is in pain.)

TINY: I don't know what's wrong with me.

MAGGIE: After the fever set in, the markings would blister.

TINY: I feel like I could crawl out of my skin.

GRAY: Let's check your vitals.

TINY: No. Thank you.

GRAY: I need to examine you, Tiny. I've got other people to see today.

TINY: I just want to get better. Don't you understand that?

GRAY: We've got to get that damn fever down.

TINY: I'll change. I can change. I can be a new person—

GRAY: Tiny.

TINY:—Whatever I'm doin', I'll change it, I swear—

GRAY: I made a salve for you.

TINY: I'll change everything!

GRAY: *(To the point.)* Tiny.

TINY: What?

GRAY: Hush up and sit down, right now.

TINY: I'm doin' it—right now. I'm sittin', I'm hushin', I'm healin', I'm changin', I'm gonna be fine, ain't I? What in God's name are you doin' to me?

GRAY: It's only a salve, Ma'am.

TINY: It's burnin'.

GRAY: Everything good for you has a price. Now hold still and just let me work on you.

    (She relaxes a tiny bit.)

TINY: You missed a spot.

GRAY: Thank you.

    (June brings on a basin and a wash cloth for Gray.)

MAGGIE: First Belva, then Tiny—

JUNE: Then all across the countryside people began to take ill.

    (Night. Tiny is lying down now; fevered, trembling. Gray tends to her;

washing her forehead and arms with a cool, damp cloth. More Townspeople enter, becoming like a chorus of witnesses behind them, alternately commenting on Tiny's story, and caught up in their own.)

TINY: What is happening to me?

MAGGIE: You're gettin' warmer—

CRUTCH: *(Entering.)* And warmer.

TINY: I've got to get myself straight with the Lord.

MAGGIE: And warmer—

HOMER: *(Entering.)* And warmer—

TINY: I ain't ready to go yet.

> *(Tiny sinks to her knees to make her final bargains with God during the scene below. Although Gray is focused on Tiny throughout this dying chapter, he is now part way across the stage, as the situation grows in intensity:)*

JUNE: Doctor Gray?

HOMER: Doctor, I know it's late.

TINY: I've got to take care of my brother . . . he don't even know how to cook.

HOMER: Doctor, I'm worried.

CRUTCH: I'm sorry to wake you.

JUNE: Doc, Mr. Collins ain't well at all.

TINY: Oh, God . . . I have sinful thoughts in me.

JUNE: Just tell me how to take care of him, please.

TINY: Shameful things runnin' through me like a river.

CRUTCH: I thought I told you to go fetch the doctor.

HOMER: Have you seen the doctor?

TINY: I mean to be better.

JUNE: Doc, she's been coughin' up blood all night long.

MAGGIE: I can't get any nourishment down him.

TINY: I want to be healed.

JUNE: She just can't stop coughin'.

TINY: Forgive me!

MAGGIE: Doctor, please.

TINY: Oh, God, forgive me!

JUNE: I don't know what to do for it!

HOMER: Doctor Gray?

CRUTCH: Doctor?

JUNE: There's so many people.

MAGGIE: I just hate to see him in pain.

HOMER: Doc, they need you to come by the house right away.

JUNE: My God, can't you do somethin' for her?!

(We begin to slow down now, the tone changes . . . Tiny has died.)

MAGGIE: You're gettin' warmer:

CRUTCH: And warmer—

JUNE: And warmer—

HOMER: And warmer.

GRAY: I'm sorry.

(Belva enters, extends a hand. Tiny simply sits up, takes her hand, and exits. If Gray remains on stage, he is lost in his own dark thoughts throughout the following:)

MAGGIE: It was like as if the fevers turned into a fire that consumed every soul in its sight.

HOMER: Doctor Gray told us to burn everything that the sickness had ever had part in.

CRUTCH: As the weather grew colder and the darkness grew longer, fires were burnin' all over the country.

HOMER: Fires and fever is all I recall.

MAGGIE: But into the into the midst of this illness—

CRUTCH: This terrible markin' upon us, as if like a mark upon Cain—

MAGGIE: A life came upon us—

(Rebekah enters with a swaddling blanket she holds close: This blanket is her newborn "baby." She sings a made-up lullaby to it, softly, sadly. There's a moment as the Storytellers hear a few lines of her song.)

REBEKAH: (Sings.) "Go to sleep, my baby; go to sleep, my love . . . Go to sleep, my pretty little child, in the arms above . . . "

MAGGIE: (Overlapping from "love.") A child is born.

HOMER: A beautiful—

CRUTCH: Beautiful—

MAGGIE: Perfect young baby.

JUNE: That's my little sister we're talkin' about.

(Rebekah continues to hum to her "baby" as the story continues. Maggie, Homer, and June exit.)

CRUTCH: The baby was born on a night when so many stars jeweled the sky, you just wanted to reach up with both hands and take a few home. (Then:) She was born on the same night I died.

(Belva is waiting. They leave the stage together. Gray crosses to Rebekah.)

GRAY: Rebekah? . . . Rebekah, are you alright?

REBEKAH: I'm just fine.

GRAY: What about the baby?

REBEKAH: She's beautiful, Galen. She's just . . . perfect.

GRAY: Is she alright?

REBEKAH: She's not marked, if that's what you mean.

(This is huge news, just huge, but he reacts to it quietly.)

GRAY: Thank goodness. Thank goodness.

REBEKAH: She looks just like her pa.

GRAY: Every newborn looks like a constipated Eskimo to me.

(Off Rebekah's smile.)

What're you naming her?

REBEKAH: You take her.

GRAY: Rebekah.

REBEKAH: Galen, I'm marked. I can't keep this child, even if I wanted to—
which I think I do—I just can't. You know that as well as I do. Just
take her, please.

GRAY: Becky.

REBEKAH: I can't bear to fall in love with her anymore than I already have.

(Rebekah gives Gray the "baby.")

REBEKAH: I want you to take her and take Juney, and leave.

GRAY: You want me to take both your children?

REBEKAH: Cross the river and never look back.

GRAY: No, Ma'am, I'm not gonna do that.

REBEKAH: *(Verging on tears.)* I don't want my children to die!

GRAY: Well I'm not gonna leave you here to die alone.

REBEKAH: What good can you stayin' here possibly do?—except to sacrifice
that little baby and June! You don't know the cause, you don't know
the cure—you don't know anything!

GRAY: For the first time in my life I know I'm a doctor. And I reckon a blind
man could see my feelings for you.

REBEKAH: You think I don't want you to stay? You think I'm not terrified?
If you stay here on my account, and if my children catch this and die,
I swear to God I will never forgive you.

(The "baby" starts fussing. Gray looks at Rebekah, makes his decision.)

GRAY: I'm gonna give her to June and stay here and take care of you.

REBEKAH: You will do no such thing.

GRAY: Juney?? Hey June?

(The "baby" starts crying.)

JUNE: *(Enters with a bottle.)* Oh, for Pete's sake, she's just squallerin' cause
she's hungry, Doc. Just give her a bottle, that's all she wants.

GRAY: Here. Why don't you give her the bottle?

(June takes the "baby," gives her the bottle.)

JUNE: Oh, stop your fussin'.

(The "baby" does. There's a "moment" as Rebekah watches her daughters together.)

JUNE: There you go, that's a girl, that's a good baby . . .

GRAY: You know what I think?

JUNE: No, but I bet you're gonna tell me.

GRAY: I think she's taken a shine to you.

JUNE: I think she's got our pa's eyes. Don't get me wrong—she's prettier than him—

REBEKAH: Thank the Lord.

JUNE:—but it's just like he's starin' right back at me, Mama.

(Maggie and Phineas once again talk to the theater. Note: Phineas is still recovering from his surgery; he's weakened.)

MAGGIE: And so, in the fullness of time, June and her family walked down to the water's edge.

PHINEAS: As those of us left on the good ground of Shariton County gathered together that evenin' to bury our dead—

MAGGIE: Those who were marked and those who were unmarked did part from each other.

(June, the baby, Rebekah, and Gray are downstage near the "boat." Maggie and Phineas remain upstage in tableau in the "graveyard." Homer enters with a carpetbag that's filled with bottles of soda—although the audience must not hear them clinking yet or realize that's what he has in the bag.)

REBEKAH: Hello, Homer.

HOMER: Evenin', Miz Becky. Doc.

GRAY: Homer.

HOMER: Good golly, is that the new baby?

JUNE: Ain't she the prettiest thing you ever laid eyes on?

HOMER: *(Looking at June.)* No.

JUNE: Hush up.

HOMER: What's her name anyway?

JUNE: I reckon I'll just call her Sister.

HOMER: Hey, little Sister.

REBEKAH: You three take care now.

JUNE: *(Fighting back tears.)* I'll write to you, Mama. I miss you already.

REBEKAH: I miss you, too, baby. Now go on. Get out of here, before I start cryin'.

(Rebekah and June can't and don't touch because of the "mark," although they long to.)

HOMER: *(To Gray.)* I ain't never been nowhere else. What is it like out there?

GRAY: You'll navigate.

HOMER: You're not comin' with us, I take it?

GRAY: No, son. I mean to stay here.

JUNE: I'm not sayin' good-bye to you.

GRAY: Good. I'm not saying good-bye to you either.

JUNE: *(Holds her hand out.)* Doctor Gray.

GRAY: *(Takes her hand.)* Doctor Muldoon. I trust that we'll meet again soon.

(Gray kisses June's hand; then she kisses his hand.)

HOMER: I ain't never been in a boat before neither.

REBEKAH: Just mind your balance. You're gonna do fine.

(Homer sets his carpetbag down before getting in the "boat"—we hear bottles clinking together.)

JUNE: What in the world do you have in there, Homer?

HOMER: Soda pop.

JUNE: Soda?

HOMER: You want one?

GRAY: *(Hands Homer the bag.)* Homer.

HOMER: I figure I'm best off to be prepared, Doc.

JUNE: Here. You mind the baby. I'll do the honors.

HOMER: You want me to hold her?

JUNE: Get used to it, Homer.

HOMER: *(To the baby.)* Hello there.

REBEKAH: Good-bye now.

HOMER: Bye.

JUNE: *(Suddenly tearful.)* Mama? Oh, God, Mama??

REBEKAH: When she's old enough to understand, you tell little Sister I love you both. Now go on, June. You have to be strong now. Don't you ever look back.

(June paddles them onto the river as the lights isolate their "boat" in a gentle blue wash. Gray and Rebekah slowly back away from the "boat" and cross into the funeral. A very soft river sound might sneak in.)

PHINEAS: The river shone bright as a promise that night.

MAGGIE: And so, with the bright stars of evenin' to serve as a guide, they cast themselves onto the water, and travelled off into the world.

PHINEAS: "Ashes to ashes."

REBEKAH/MAGGIE/GRAY: "Ashes to ashes."

PHINEAS: "And dust unto dust."

REBEKAH/MAGGIE/GRAY: "Dust unto dust."

(Gray and Rebekah look back toward the river. June continues to paddle with strength, slowly, elegantly . . .)

GRAY: *(Quietly.)* Water . . .

PHINEAS: Sir?

GRAY: Maybe it's water.

MAGGIE: Well, Doc, it's a river.

GRAY: He doesn't drink water. I boil my water. June does what I do.

REBEKAH: She has since you got here.

GRAY: It's the simplest thing in the world.

PHINEAS: Water.

(They look toward the river again . . . and June glances back at them, too.)

HOMER: Juney?

JUNE: What, Homer?

HOMER: You heard what your mother said: Don't look back.

JUNE: But I want to remember.

HOMER: I know. But it'll just make you miss it all the more.

JUNE: Don't tell me you're already homesick.

(The light is slowly growing fainter on her mother and Gray and the Towns-people, as if they're more and more distant. June continues to paddle at the same steady rhythm.)

HOMER: I never knew a man could miss dirt so much. But I'll tell you somethin': I miss my farm, Juney, I really do. I miss my dirt.

JUNE: I have a baby and I'm a virgin. So don't complain, Homer.

HOMER: Didn't that happen to somebody else one time?

(After a beat.)

Juney?

JUNE: What, Homer?

HOMER: What do you think we might find out here?

JUNE: The rest of the world, I imagine.

(Music, of course, has snuck in by now. The light on the graveyard is fading to darkness as June continues to paddle.)

HOMER: Well. It can't be as pretty as Gray, Indiana.

(Lights focus tighter and tighter on June, until she is the only thing we see . . .)

JUNE: *(To the theater.)* June could not bear to look back on the pain or the beauty of her childhood again, but she never wanted to forget—so at that very moment, under these very stars, and on this very river, she began to compose a story in her mind to tell her little Sister someday. So she'd understand that we all come from loss, and from love. And her story ended and began like this: Once upon a time there was a girl who looked remarkably like me.

(Lights fade to black.)

END OF PLAY

Broken Hallelujah

by Sharman Macdonald

From left to right: Katie Green and Martine Moore
Photo credit: Tom Haygood

PLAYWRIGHT'S BIOGRAPHY

Playwright and novelist Sharman Macdonald was born in Glasgow in 1951. Educated at the University of Edinburgh, she graduated in 1972 and moved to London where she acted with the 7:84 theatre company and at the Royal Court Theatre. While she was working as an actress, she wrote her first play, *When I Was a Girl, I Used to Scream and Shout*, first performed at the Bush Theatre in 1984. The play won the *Evening Standard* Award for Most Promising Playwright. Her other plays include *The Brave*, commissioned by the Bush Theatre; *When We Were Women*, first performed at the Cottesloe Theatre; *All Things Nice*, commissioned by the English Stage Company and performed at the Royal Court Theatre in 1991; *The Winter Guest*, commissioned and directed by Alan Rickman and filmed in 1997 starring Emma Thompson and Phyllida Law; and *After Juliet*, a sequel to *Romeo and Juliet* dealing with Rosalind's story after the death of Juliet, commissioned by the Royal National Theatre for the BT National Connections Scheme for young people. *The Girl with Red Hair* premiered at The Lyceum, Edinburgh, in 2005 and then transferred to The Hampstead Theatre, London. She is also the author of two novels, *The Beast* (1986) and *Night Night* (1988), and she wrote the screenplay for *Wild Flowers* (1989) for Channel 4 Television and the BBC Radio play *Sea Urchins*. A further radio play, *Gladly My Cross Eyed Bear*, was broadcast in 1999. She wrote the libretto to *Hey Persephone!*, performed at Aldeburgh and London's Almeida Theatre, with music by Deirdre Gribbin. Sharman Macdonald has two children and is married to the actor Will Knightley.

FROM THE PLAYWRIGHT

I met Craig Slaight from the A.C.T. Conservatory in San Francisco at the Royal National Theatre in 2000. *After Juliet* was on there in the National's Connections Festival. Craig liked the play. He said would I be interested in writing a piece for him. "Yes, yes," I said and didn't think any more about it. Three years later he phoned up. "Would I write a play for A.C.T. in San Francisco and Theatre Royal Bath?" "I don't have any ideas," I said. "Can I phone you back?" I was reading all I could find about the American Civil War when he phoned. I mean literally when he phoned. The Shelby Foote tomes were open on the black fur rug in the blue room with the phone beside them and me bowed over them cross-legged when the phone rang. The rug's soft, the floor's hard. I should've been writing, I was reading instead. I'd decided to study the Civil War because of the invasion of Iraq. I wanted to understand how we, collectively, could possibly have come to the conclusion that invasion was permissible. I wanted to see where modern America came from. The Civil War seemed like a good place to begin. As I read I fell in love with the cadence of the quick, light voices that whisper still in the diaries and letters of Southerners and Northerners, boys, women, men and girls. I have a son. I couldn't bear it if he was hurt in any cause. There is no "cause" just enough. And my daughter—the North attacked civilians in the South. It was part of their tactics. I phoned Craig back. "Can I write about the American Civil War?" Craig's a man who blesses those around him with his confidence. We went on a joyous journey together. He brought his students to Bath, hosted by Lee Lyford who was directing the Bath production of the play. For ten days he workshopped the piece with his students and I observed. They worked to realize what I'd put down on the page lending it all their talent and commitment. As they worked, it became apparent that the complex time structure I'd conceived for the piece only snarled it up. I rewrote and made it linear. That's the way the play was performed in San Francisco, in Bath, at the Cottesloe as part of Connections in 2006, in Florence and Milan.

FROM THE ACTOR—Martine Moore (Maureen)
We began with meetings every few weeks to discuss the trip and read through the script. The first few days of the trip we were in London where we saw plays and went to museums, which I loved. The city was muggy and beautiful and old-fashioned, a mix of antiquity and historical culture with modern grunge and giant glass buildings. We went to tourist spots like the Tower of London and Westminster Abbey and ate at local pubs and sushi restaurants. Our tour guide, Doug, explained the British monarchy, the current social culture, and how to be a proper British "bloke." After three days in London, we left for Bath by bus and arrived in the afternoon.

Our training started early in the morning with a commedia dell'arte masks workshop with the Bath actors, taught by Lee Lyford, the director of the Theatre Royal Bath Youth Theatre. This was fun work, as we could use our bodies, but not our faces, to convey emotions. The workshop culminated in a public presentation of short scenes performed to music with plots relating to the expression of each mask. My mask was an angry expression and the scene chosen involved my character being stood up for a date. By the end of the scene I could barely see and a thin film of saliva had collected on my chin, but the laughs were worth it. In the afternoons, the American company rehearsed *Broken Hallelujah*. We were aware that British acting techniques focus on articulation, strong stage presence, and loyalty to the text.

It was interesting to compare this to the American emphasis on naturalism—true-to-life acting that involves a more casual, nearly conversational delivery of lines. We had the opportunity to discuss these differences with instructors and the excitement of blending the two styles.

We rehearsed in the upper part of the theater in a room with thick red carpet and white pillars and walls, decorated with posters of past productions. It was there that we met Sharman Macdonald for the first time. She was funny, kind, and trendy, spoke with a soft Scottish accent, and carried a silver cigarette case. When I used my newly minted British slang, she was very receptive. More importantly, Sharman served as an anchor during rehearsals. She was there to answer character and plot questions, to make on-the-spot modifications of lines, and to share her process in writing and visualizing the play.

It was in Bath that the first aesthetic layers of our production came together. For the staged public reading on the last day of our residency, we used a few props, makeshift costumes with rehearsal skirts, and simple blocking that allowed us to carry our scripts. The actors playing Southern characters were asked to experiment with the regional dialect. It was satisfying to see how vivid the characters became after adding this vocal element.

This trip was particularly significant to me because I was disconnected from my identity except as an American A.C.T. student. The British adolescent world was in many ways completely different from ours. They come from a historical countryside; we come from an urban, diverse, and comparatively large city. They grew up at a different pace into a different culture. At the base, however, was a mutual love for theater and a fascination with the lifestyles and habits of one another, and that created strong friendships. I was very close to my host, Hannah, and we are still in contact.

There was a professional quality to the experience in Bath—we worked on projects and went to classes that were all focused on one goal, learning from one another by giving birth to a new play. And despite a severe lack of sleep and so many things to do, it was completely stress-free. I *wanted* to do everything I was doing. Though I inevitably returned to a life with school and obligations, I still hope that my experiences in Bath may mirror a future adult life, one that keeps me moving forward in complete focus on the present and the things I love.

ORIGINAL PRODUCTION

Broken Hallelujah was co-commissioned (with Theatre Royal Bath, England) and first presented by the Young Conservatory at American Conservatory Theater (Carey Perloff, Artistic Director, Heather M. Kitchen, Executive Director), San Francisco, California, in June 2004. It was directed by Craig Slaight; the set design was by Dean Shibuya; the lighting design was by Kimberly J. Scott; the costumes were designed by Callie Floor; the sound was designed by Greg Kunit; and the assistant director was Sarah Grandin. The cast was as follows:

HOSGOOD	Nicholas Padilla
STEWART	Joshua Schell
LOREN	Katie Green
MAUREEN	Martine Moore
HANCOCK	Julien Inclan
BRIDH	Maxie Pulliam
ROWATT	Timothy Smith-Stewart

The Young Peoples Theatre at Theatre Royal Bath in Bath, England, subsequently produced the play the same year. It was directed by Lee Lyford.

SETTING

The play takes place in and around Petersburg, Virginia, September 1864.

CHARACTERS

HOSGOOD, a Northern soldier, eighteen years old
STEWART, a Northern soldier, nineteen years old
LOREN, a Southern girl from Petersburg, thirteen years old
MAUREEN, a Southern girl from Petersburg, fourteen years old
HANCOCK, a Northern soldier, eighteen years old
BRIDH, a Dublin girl, sixteen years old
ROWATT, a Southern soldier from Petersburg, nineteen years old

BROKEN HALLELUJAH

The morning of September 5th 1864 at the siege of Petersburg, Virginia. A gleam of sunlight shines on Northern lines. It hits Stewart in a slum of a dugout, sordid and dirty, beyond the outer defenses of the town. A Northern Soldier, Hosgood, runs low back from the town, leaps roaring onto the lip of the dugout. Stays for three seconds rolls down into the dugout.

HOSGOOD: Gone, see. No Southern trash planter slave-owning son of a whoring-bitch sniper, there. Gone. I'm telling you, gone.

STEWART: Where've you been?

(Hosgood waggles a stick with a hat on the end up there.)

HOSGOOD: There's ways into that town. I could get a whole army in there. Sack old Useless put me in charge and I could.

STEWART: You'd have us all dead with your "ways."

HOSGOOD: Stewart, you are suffering from what is called the siege mentality.

STEWART: Boredom I'm suffering from. Hunger I'm suffering from. The desire to stay alive at all costs I'm suffering from.

HOSGOOD: Like I said.

(The stick with the hat waggles furiously.)

STEWART: Think he's stupid your Southern boy?

HOSGOOD: Think he's gone is all.

STEWART: That's a stick with a hat on the end.

HOSGOOD: I was up there. I was up there for all to see.

STEWART: He's not going to waste shot on a hat and a stick is he?

HOSGOOD: Didn't take a pop at me did he?

STEWART: Getting his aim set is all.

HOSGOOD: He's not there.

STEWART: You're lucky you got through the lines alive. You go back up there now he'll shoot you dead.

(The hat on the stick stabs the air.)

HOSGOOD: He. Is. Not. There.

STEWART: He's waitin'. Like he's fishin' for a fat catfish in a pool. Patience itself he is, sittin' there.

HOSGOOD: I'm going to prove it to you.

STEWART: I don't need proof.

HOSGOOD: I'll make a bet with you.

STEWART: You've got nothing I want.

HOSGOOD: Have though.

STEWART: You've got nothing and I've got nothing. We both got nothing. Nothing to bet.

HOSGOOD: I have something you truly do want and need.

STEWART: You got an itch that's what you got. And there's a Southern boy out there waitin' and willin' to scratch it.

HOSGOOD: Suppose I said I had bacon?

STEWART: You have not got bacon.

HOSGOOD: I got bacon with plenty fat on it and I don't mean army issue. Been through the gates of Hell itself to get it. I mean sweet bacon, whole bacon that doesn't turn to string in your mouth and swell up there with spit til you can't swallow it. Then you do and it rests down in your intestinal tract like a wad of filthy rag waitin' to turn your bowels to water. Know what I'm saying? Saw a man with his stomach shot out, lying there with his stomach in his hands all open to the sky with the contents plain for all to see. Wads of bacon lyin' in it. If he hadn't a been shot the way he was, the bacon would've killed him. Given him a blockage lyin' in there like that and strangulated him. Lucky he was shot. Smoke house bacon I've got here; 'nough fat on it. This bacon I've got it's the best bacon I've ever had the pleasure to behold. Not only does it do honor to the pig that it came from but to all pig kind. My mouth waters at the thought of this bacon. I am salivating. This bacon. There's a yard on the edge of that town. And in that yard there is a secret larder. And in that larder . . . I will wager you this bacon that that sniper has gone.

STEWART: Bacon you say?

HOSGOOD: Sweet smoked bacon.

STEWART: Man might die happy if he had a good few rashers of bacon inside him.

HOSGOOD: Might at that.

STEWART: Suppose I was to take your bet?

HOSGOOD: Your boots against my bacon.

STEWART: You ain't getting my boots.

HOSGOOD: I'll give you mine.

STEWART: I got these off of a dying man. Made my heart cry to take them off him. Dying the way he was. Though he was my enemy. We're all soldiers and he blessed me for giving him a drink as he lay dying and he let me take these boots.

HOSGOOD: Didn't have a choice did he?

STEWART: We're all soldiers in this war one side or the other. Way I see it doesn't matter what side you're on. We're all in the same boat. War won't be over till every last soldier of us is dead. That's what they're aiming at. Only man that valued a soldier's life was General George McClellan whom I take my hat off to. May he be elected president. He'll bring peace. Old Lincoln now he gets back in for a second term we're all dead and gone.

HOSGOOD: You want this bacon?

STEWART: I got a bible here.

HOSGOOD: I don't want a bible.

STEWART: You hear about this bible you'll want it.

HOSGOOD: The sniper hasn't gone you're telling me. If he hasn't gone why don't you wager your boots. You so sure he's not gone you are not going to lose them. No danger.

STEWART: This bible was my ma's bible. I was saying good-bye to her. Course she didn't want me to go but this man paid me three hundred dollars to take his son's place, be his surrogate, my ma knows the value of money.

HOSGOOD: Knew a man was old Abe Lincoln's surrogate.

STEWART: She knows the value of money my ma. Blessed this bible put it next to my heart to keep me safe.

HOSGOOD: We're talking about bacon here. Boots we're talking about.

STEWART: This is a lucky bible.

HOSGOOD: I know, been hit three times, bible's taken the bullet, heart's gone on beating.

STEWART: Only one left of all I enlisted with. Odds are my time is running out. Wouldn't get a betting man to bet on me surviving the next push.

HOSGOOD: Nor any one of the rest of us.

STEWART: I got my bible though. And I'm saying you got a chance of having it.

HOSGOOD: You're trying just too hard to keep your boots. You know that sniper's gone.

STEWART: You get up there on that ridge you'll come back down dead I'll get your bacon anyway you won't get my boots. I'll open my bible and say a few words over you. How about that?

HOSGOOD: There is no one there.

STEWART: So why don't you get up there then and do your roaring thing, your sounding like a stuck pig thing.

HOSGOOD: That's my yell.

STEWART: Rebs have a yell much better than that.

HOSGOOD: Says who?

STEWART: Turns your blood cold when they yell. I've seen men freeze in the ranks.

HOSGOOD: Not me.

STEWART: You going to get up on that parapet?

HOSGOOD: Bet me your boots.

STEWART: I'm not risking my boots even on a sure thing, even to win some bacon.

HOSGOOD: This quiet gets to me. How come it doesn't get to you?

(Beat.)

(Sun's shining.)

(Hosgood roars and leaps.)

STEWART: Hosgood! Hosgood!

(The sunlight's bright almost white. A shot rings out.)

STEWART: Hosgood!

(Hosgood leaps back down.)

HOSGOOD: You were right. He was there.

STEWART: He get you?

HOSGOOD: What?

STEWART: Are you hit man?

HOSGOOD: I wouldn't be a sniper. Would you be a sniper? Dirty thing a sniper. Fighting right out front. That's a man's way. You remember Pickett's Charge. That was a beautiful thing. Watching from up Little Round Top, you and me. Watching the pattern of those troops unfold. Wave on wave. They were the enemy sure enough but you had to admire them for the beauty of their form. That's fighting. Sneaky little runt a sniper. I could've sworn he wasn't there.

(He puts his hand up to the left side of his chest. Touches, looks.)

Can't be blood, can it?

(Stewart and Hosgood stare at each other.)

STEWART: You're hit man.

(Hosgood runs.)

Hey. Hey Hosgood. C'mere man. Come on. I'm not going to hurt you. Come here.

(Stewart catches him. Hosgood struggles.)

HOSGOOD: Nicked me that's all. Flesh wound that's all. I'll just sit still a while I'll be fine.

STEWART: What d'you do it for eh?

HOSGOOD: Have to do something.

STEWART: We need to get you seen to.

HOSGOOD: I'm not going to hospital. I'm not moving from here. More men die in hospital. You get gangrene in hospital. You get fever. It smells bad in there man. The only place you go from there's the embalming tent if you're rich, the shallow earth if you're not. To come popping back up when the rain sets in.

STEWART: More chance there man. In the hospital even so.

(Stewart starts to lift Hosgood. Hosgood gathers himself. Whips out half a side of bacon.)

HOSGOOD: I had you there man? I had you.

STEWART: Eh?

HOSGOOD: I'm not hit.

STEWART: You're hit.

HOSGOOD: I'm not hit man. Here.

My daddy told me always to pay my debts of honor.

STEWART: I'm not taking it.

HOSGOOD: You think I'm a liar?

STEWART: Eh?

HOSGOOD: You don't believe I'm not shot.

STEWART: Come on Hosgood.

HOSGOOD: I take exception Stewart, I do.

STEWART: Hosgood I need you . . .

HOSGOOD: They shot my bacon. Risked my life to get this and they shot it. The fat lady I got it from . . . Risked my very soul. There is the bullet hole.

STEWART: Goes in one side, comes out the other. Where's the bullet.

HOSGOOD: My bacon is now your bacon.

(He puts it down on a stone. Walks to the edge of the dugout.)

STEWART: Where are you going?

HOSGOOD: Taking a constitutional.

STEWART: You're on duty.

HOSGOOD: Why don't you . . . cook your bacon. That's it Stewart cook your bloody bacon. You won it fair and square.

(He slides out of the back of the dugout and he runs, keeping low, hand tight to his chest. Stewart crawls after him.)

STEWART: Hosgood. Hosgood.
(Then he stops. Picks up the bacon.)

(Bright, bright sunlight. So bright nothing can be seen except light.)
(A yard in Petersburg.)
(Southern voices.)
MAUREEN: *(Whispering.)* R. A. P. E.
LOREN: I can spell.
MAUREEN: Didn't say you couldn't.
LOREN: You mean "rape." You say "rape."
(Two girls from the town, walk in a huge yard in the heat. The earth's dry. Now and again Loren scrabbles at the earth. Sometimes she stamps. Listens.)
MAUREEN: Keep your voice down. Ma Tyler hears you she'll be out here with her shotgun. She don't take so kindly to trespassers in her yard. Let alone thieves Loren Maeve.
LOREN: You mean it, you say it.
MAUREEN: My mother she'd make me wash my mouth out if ever I let a word like that escape from it all in one piece.
LOREN: Your mother.
MAUREEN: Don't you use that tone of voice about any member of my family. I've come along to help you out. Help you out with your thievin' which is a sin. I can go home just as easy. I can go home right now and be a sinner no more.
LOREN: You have to say what you mean. You have to say it out loud. That's what I believe. If it's "rape" you mean it's "rape" you say.
MAUREEN: You're not old enough to have beliefs. We neither of us are.
LOREN: Your mother tell you that too?
MAUREEN: Stay young as long as you can my mother says. Even in these days.
LOREN: Go on then go home.
MAUREEN: Well I will.
LOREN: Go on then.
MAUREEN: If I want to I will.
LOREN: Well then?
MAUREEN: I don't want to do I? Do I?
LOREN: You needn't think I need you.

I don't need you. Ma Tyler's got a larder in this yard. And it's just filled with bacon way I hear it. And I'm going to find her larder and I'm going to take that bacon from it to feed my little brother with. She's just a fat old lady after all. And there is no fat old lady on this earth that can scare me.

(Beat.)

MAUREEN: R. A. P. E. They say it that way so's you don't know.

LOREN: Don't know what?

MAUREEN: You and me and all the rest of us if they get into the town. If the town falls what they'll do.

LOREN: I ain't scared of any Yankees.

MAUREEN: Well I'm not either.

LOREN: Never said you were did I?

(Beat.)

MAUREEN: It's what they've been doing.

Rape.

Way I hear it anyway. Everywhere they've been. Because they're dogs the Yankees, no better than. You can tell a Yankee by his smell and of course they don't have much intelligence for which we must pity them. It's an accident of birth after all. What they do, coming into our land, they do it because they know no better.

LOREN: You ever met anybody they've done it to, this rape thing you're telling me of?

MAUREEN: Not exactly.

LOREN: Has your mother?

MAUREEN: Well now I do not think she would tell me if she had.

LOREN: I don't see we've got the proof then that they'd do it.

MAUREEN: It's what mean people do do. Folks they have in their power, they cause them harm.

LOREN: I don't see the proof is all I'm saying.

MAUREEN: You don't know what it is do you?

LOREN: R. A. P. E. you said.

MAUREEN: You don't know.

LOREN: And you do I suppose.

MAUREEN: You just ask me. Go on. Ask me.

(Beat.)

LOREN: Anyway . . .

MAUREEN: What?

LOREN: General Robert E. Lee will not let Petersburg fall I bet.

MAUREEN: He'll sacrifice us is what I hear.

LOREN: He loses Petersburg, he'll lose Richmond. We're his last bastion's what I hear. So I'm not scared of rape or anything any Yankee's going to do when he gets into Petersburg because he just will not be allowed to get in. Besides which we are all a part of humankind.

MAUREEN: Apart from Yankees.

(Loren stamps hard on the ground.)

LOREN: It's hollow somewhere I know it is. That larder's somewhere here and the bacon that's in it.

MAUREEN: They don't shoot. You know that? You know they don't shoot?

LOREN: Who?

MAUREEN: Neither the one side, nor the other shoot.

LOREN: We got a shell through one of the pillars on the porch, near brought the whole house down. I call that shooting.

MAUREEN: That's the big guns. I'm not talking about the big guns. That's shooting at us citizens. They can't see us. Don't mind shooting at what they can't see do they? I'm talking about the soldiers facing each other. All the long lines of them facing. They don't exactly shoot as we understand it. Not as we'd think it.

LOREN: Thought you said they were animals.

MAUREEN: What they do is . . . What they do is they load their guns but they don't fire them off or if they do, they fire to the side, you know, to the side. There were rifles they picked up after . . .

LOREN: Who picked up? Who's they? After what?

MAUREEN: You know what I'm going to say?

LOREN: What?

MAUREEN: You want to know what I'm going to say?

LOREN: Eh?

MAUREEN: You want to know what I'm going to say you have to let me say it. You have to shut your mouth and let me say it.

LOREN: So?

MAUREEN: I could name you battles. I could name you many a battle. The battles I could name you that they picked up rifles after. They picked up rifles and they had never been fired. Gettysburg. Antietam, Cold Harbor even.

LOREN: Benjamin's brother, he died. And his father. My Uncle Samuel died. And Solomon Kirk got his leg chopped off because the bone was smashed into by a lead bullet from an Enfield rifle that the British made and it was so splintered the bone, they couldn't do nothing but take the leg off and he didn't have any ether to take the pain away when they cut. And then they threw his leg onto a bundle with feet and arms and things. And he said he ain't afraid of hell no more because he's been to a far worser place. You think he imagined the bullet in his leg? You think he plain imagined it?

MAUREEN: They faced each other and they never fired.

LOREN: If I was in a battle and I had a rifle and it was loaded and there was a man all lined up opposite me and he had a rifle and it was loaded and he was pointing his rifle at me. I'd fire my rifle. Damn an' I would.

MAUREEN: Don't say that word.

LOREN: Right at him, I would damn well fire it, make no damn mistake.

MAUREEN: You shouldn't say that word, God Almighty will cast you out of heaven.

LOREN: I'm not dead.

MAUREEN: And you'll fall. All the way you'll fall down to the other place that's the Devil's Kingdom.

LOREN: I'm not dead yet.

MAUREEN: And the Devil'll get you and he'll take you and he'll roast you on his spits over the fires of Hell. That's what he'll do an' you say that word.

LOREN: No he won't.

MAUREEN: An' you say that word he will.

LOREN: I'll say what I damn well like.

MAUREEN: It doesn't sit nice in the mouth of a lady.

LOREN: And you know all about ladies. I expect your lady mother taught you.

MAUREEN: I know what I hear is all. I know what I'm told. I listen, Loren Maeve. Which is more than you do. You leave off my mother.

LOREN: She cries every day don't she?

MAUREEN: She's frightened.

LOREN: We're all frightened, we don't cry. No honor in tears.

MAUREEN: My mother's heard too much about honor. And I have. Too damn much.

LOREN: Too "damn" much?

(They giggle.)

MAUREEN: Aren't you the least scared of the Almighty?

LOREN: I can't see Him can I? I can't feel Him. I can't touch Him and He doesn't touch me. Don't seem to me I have much to be scared of.

MAUREEN: Don't you pray?

LOREN: I'm more scared of the Feds than I am of God. And I ain't scared of them at all.

MAUREEN: Don't you pray for your brother?

LOREN: Even General Grant I ain't scared of nor Abe Lincoln himself. Being scared doesn't change what's going to happen way I see it. And it's uncomfortable in your stomach. Might as well not be scared.

MAUREEN: Don't you love your brother?

LOREN: He's my darling and my mother's darling and my father's darling.

MAUREEN: You should pray. If he dies . . . If your little brother dies and you ain't prayed it will be your fault he dies.

LOREN: I held him first when he was born.

MAUREEN: I'll pray for him for you.

LOREN: I don't want you to do that.

MAUREEN: I'd do anything for you. In the cause of friendship.

LOREN: I hear men screaming out there. I hear them screaming in the night sometimes. Don't you pray. Don't you pray to Something that's bad to my brother. Don't you pray to Something that lets men scream like that, all alone in the night. That's Something not worth praying to.

MAUREEN: They're mostly just Yankees.

LOREN: Doesn't matter.

MAUREEN: Our cause is sacred to God.

LOREN: He come down and whisper that in your ear, God?

MAUREEN: Everybody says it is.

LOREN: God came down from the sky and told "everybody" that did he?

MAUREEN: I'm stopping my ears Loren. I'm stopping my ears so I don't hear you. I could go to Hell for hearing you.

LOREN: Why is he sick, my little brother?

MAUREEN: He's hungry.

LOREN: He never did anything to anybody, my little brother.

MAUREEN: Folk get sick when they're hungry is all.

LOREN: I don't see the Almighty making my brother better not for all my prayers.

MAUREEN: You did pray then. You did pray.

LOREN: Not any more.

(Loren stamps on the ground again.)

MAUREEN: There's no larder here. Nor no bacon neither.

LOREN: How come Mrs. Tyler's fat as a hog?

MAUREEN: God made her that way.

LOREN: She's eat herself that way. That's how come. The whole town says there's bacon.

MAUREEN: Send her to prisoner camp. They don't come out of there fat. Good as a reducing diet going to prisoner camp. Never seen a fat prisoner yet my ma says. Skeletal my ma says.

LOREN: Doin' her a favor then. Taking her bacon.

MAUREEN: If we find it.

LOREN: I have to find it. My brother'll die else.

MAUREEN: There are towns south of here. In Tennessee there are towns. In Alabama there are towns and the towns are empty of men. They're just empty of men. All the men from the towns are dead. And the ladies have no husbands. And the children have no fathers. And the girls have no sweethearts. I hear the war will go on and on til all the towns are like that. Til there's only women left in all the towns of the Confederacy. Only then will the war end.

LOREN: How come?

MAUREEN: How come what?

LOREN: If the soldiers don't shoot like you said they don't. If none of the soldiers shoot how come there's all these dead men?

MAUREEN: You have to have a man's weight behind the lead and then the men die. It's the big guns like I said. You don't listen Loren Maeve. The big guns just tear men apart and spread their vitals over the earth til there's lakes of blood and bridges to walk on over the lakes of blood and these bridges they are made of flesh.

(A thud.)

LOREN: There.

MAUREEN: You heard hollow?

LOREN: You didn't believe me did you?

MAUREEN: I didn't hear hollow.

(*Still morning. Still bright.*)

(*In the dugout, Stewart's beginning to cook over a wood fire. Setting stones to heat round it. Putting a trestle over the flames. Taking out a twist of greasy paper with a precious lump of fat in it. Sliding the fat into the slowly heating pan, talking to Hancock, standing watching, all the while.*)

STEWART: Then she says, my ma says, "I'm going to buy the clothes to put upon my back. Just like I'll buy the food we eat. I've cooked all my life," she says. "I'm cooking no more. Your grandma," my ma says, "she wore herself out. She spun the thread, she wove the cloth, she made the clothes, she hoed, she planted, she washed, she scrubbed, she cooked, she died. I don't remember your grandma once singing a song for pure joy," my ma says. "Plenty hymns she sang begging the good Lord above for joy in the life to come. Not a one for joy in the here and now do I remember. Well not me," my ma says. She says, "I'm going to have some joy. Right here. Right now. In this life. For I'm not so sure there is a life to come."

HANCOCK: That bacon fat?

STEWART: She wasn't so sure and neither am I.

HANCOCK: Should use that fat on all the seams of your clothes. All the seams. Keep the chiggers from biting you.

STEWART: You look at them, corpses, lying there, lying where they fall. Watch them swelling up. Watch them rotting. You know there's nothing else. Man's dead he's dead.

HANCOCK: I count that blasphemy.

STEWART: My fire, my blasphemy, your choice.

HANCOCK: Eh?

STEWART: Stay or go.

(Beat.)

HANCOCK: Course you could rub it on your skin, the fat.

STEWART: Still be there when the cooking's done.

HANCOCK: Near as good as salt, bacon fat. Salt-water bathing that would be the thing, keep the beasts from biting you. I'd like to swim in some salt water. We had a water hole back home. Used to swim there in the summer time.

STEWART: Wouldn't be salt.

HANCOCK: Cool though.

STEWART: You've got the James River running over there. Go on down to the river why don't you?

HANCOCK: Sniper'd get me.

STEWART: Maybe not.

HANCOCK: I'd get to that river if I could. See if I wouldn't. I had some salt I'd get there. Wouldn't care though it's fresh water. Rub the salt on my skin see. Use it like soap.

STEWART: No salt, not for any money.

HANCOCK: Think it's green do you, the James? Shady green water? Willows dipping in. Green with silver in it where there's light. Or gold from the sun. Gold and green.

STEWART: No use talking.

HANCOCK: Been quiet today.

STEWART: Quiet enough.

HANCOCK: Don't like the quiet. See my hands.

(Holds them out. They're trembling.)

Like an old man's hands. Like my grandfather's hands. See. See.

STEWART: You want to take up whittling.

HANCOCK: We been judged's what it is. We been judged all right. We been found wanting, else what is all this that's been brought on us. I'm a good man.

STEWART: What's that mean, goodness? Don't mean anything to me. Let them in charge think about goodness I just do what I'm told best as I'm able. I follow orders. One step at a time's enough for me. Right now my orders is to stay put. So I'm staying. I'm heating a pan. When the fat's melted, if I live 'til then. I'll cook some bacon. If I live 'til it's fried I'll eat the bacon. Right now I'm living each melt of the fat in my pan. I'm savouring the melt of the fat. I'm breathing each breath like the precious thing it is.

HANCOCK: Knew a man that cooked. Orderly. Used to be a butler. Mid battle this was. Cold Harbor maybe. They merge. They all merge.

Ask me Grant's a butcher. Bring back McClellan he didn't waste men's lives. Had the pack shot off me at Bull Run. Shell took the pack right off my back. Not a scratch on me. Not a scratch. Miracle they called it. I don't know though. See my hands. See them shaking. My hands think I've had my miracle. I've run out of miracles. Anyway this orderly, my friend the butler. Brass come in for lunch. He has chicken cooked, this orderly, this butler. Old chickens but chickens all the same. Don't know where he got them. He has potatoes cooked. And bread he has. All ready and laid out it is beneath the trees. Hot and savoury as a man could want. Battle makes you hungry. Never understood that. Men dying all around you. They can be friends even. You get hungry. All sorts of hungry. What do you think that is? What do you think?

STEWART: I don't get hungry.

HANCOCK: Hungry, thirsty.

STEWART: I get thirsty.

HANCOCK: Bound to get thirsty.

STEWART: Talking about chickens.

HANCOCK: Brass sits down as well as they can. Aren't enough chairs so they sit on the grass some of them. Barrage starts up just as he's passing the butter, my friend the orderly. For the new baked bread. Shell near cuts him in half, butter in his hand. You'd think a man would die fast cut in two like that. He has time to look around him. See the state he's in.

STEWART: Could put you off butter.

HANCOCK: One way or another it fucked up dinner.

STEWART: They eat the meal?

HANCOCK: Would you?

STEWART: Man spent his last hours cooking it.

HANCOCK: That's so.

STEWART: I'd eat it.

HANCOCK: Man's cut in half though. Not too pretty.

STEWART: Could bury him.

HANCOCK: Dinner would be cold an' you did that.

STEWART: What'd they do?

HANCOCK: Nice question. Nice question.

STEWART: So?

HANCOCK: They left him there. They ate. And they savoured every last mouthful. In his honor. He was nice and fresh and dead see. You don't get that smell not when they're fresh. Buried him after. Proper bacon you got there. Good and proper. Look like you know what you're doing.

STEWART: "You've all got hands to cook and clean with," my ma says. "You get on with it. And while you're about it you can cook and clean for me," she says. "I'm going to read a book, that's what I'm going to do, while I've got eyes to see with. I'm going to read a book in the sun." Read a book, then another and another. Came to Mrs. Beecher Stowe's work that the voice of God himself gave to her if you can believe that. Read *Uncle Tom's Cabin*, became an abolitionist. That woman is a political woman. "All men are created equal." "All men," she says. Then that stuck in her craw. No mention of womankind see.

HANCOCK: This quiet, man. Makes you hear things. Voices you hear. Like home.

STEWART: I loved my ma's cooking. The soups she made, the tarts she made. Gooseberry foule. Elderberry she put in it. Said it was part of the great plan that elderberries came out when the gooseberries did to keep them company in a foule. Like sweet cicely and rhubarb. Almost made her believe in God again.

HANCOCK: Men dying you hear them. Call for their mothers, all the dying men. I can't abide quiet. Makes you soft. You get soft you don't last til the next sunset.

(He holds out his hand, tries to stop it shaking.)

Don't know where I am. What part of the year I'm in. When the sun last shone on me. What day it is? The big tree back home. I don't know if it's flowering. See this quiet.

(Beat.)

I'm remembering July Fourth. You remember? We gave them

something to think about July Fourth. Man that was truly something. That was truly something. Nice boots.

STEWART: Lucky to have them.

HANCOCK: Boots, bacon an' all. You're a very lucky man.

STEWART: Must've spit in a moon-filled puddle.

HANCOCK: You planning on cooking all that bacon? Cutting it down and cooking it?

STEWART: Thought I would.

HANCOCK: All of it?

STEWART: Why not?

HANCOCK: Can't eat all that yourself can you?

STEWART: "Feast all you can. Feast when you can," my ma says. "You got plenty, you eat plenty. Indulge now and then in excess," my ma says, "so you know what it is. You could be dead tomorrow."

HANCOCK: Touch wood when you say that. Throw salt over your shoulder.

STEWART: Leave that to you will I?

(Hancock spits.)

HANCOCK: Feast you say?

STEWART: I do.

HANCOCK: Man could get melancholy if he feasted alone.

STEWART: Could he?

HANCOCK: Mind if I hang around?

STEWART: I do not.

HANCOCK: Well . . .

STEWART: You care for flat bread?

HANCOCK: I am salivating.

(Hancock pokes at the piece of bacon.)

HANCOCK: Where'd you come upon this?

STEWART: Got left it see so's to speak.

HANCOCK: Like in a fella's last will and testament?

STEWART: That's the way of it.

HANCOCK: That a bullet hole?

STEWART: Quit fingering my bacon.

HANCOCK: Bullet hole goes right the way through.

STEWART: Quit mauling it.

HANCOCK: Could say I'm tenderizing it.

STEWART: Tender enough I'd say.

HANCOCK: Pan hot is it?. Stones hot?

STEWART: Bit to go yet. Bit to go.

(Hancock takes a flask from inside his tunic.)

HANCOCK: While we're waiting.

(He offers Stewart the flask.)

STEWART: Hear the Rebs put meat in their brew, give it body. Meat 'mongst other things.

HANCOCK: Don't know what's in this. Don't care. Makes the quiet more bearable, that's all.

STEWART: That fire heats up some. That pan heats up. You won't have quiet anymore—you'll have the sizzle of meat cooking to fill your quiet. The smell of home you'll have. And the smell of home.

(Still hot in the yard.)

LOREN: There.

(She stamps.)

You hear it. You hear it now?

MAUREEN: They're going to say we stole it. Mrs. Tyler will.

LOREN: We're not taking it for us.

MAUREEN: They'll say we stole it anyway.

LOREN: Why should she have food?

MAUREEN: I'm saying what they'll say is all.

LOREN: I'm doing this. Alone if I have to. I won't see my brother die and not lift a hand.

(Beat.)

MAUREEN: I'll dig if you want.

LOREN: Won't take much digging.

MAUREEN: I will if you want.

LOREN: You see no one comes.

MAUREEN: I can dig as well as you can.

LOREN: You can tell me if someone's coming that's what you can do for me.

(Loren digs with her hands.)

MAUREEN: Could feed him rat.

(Beat.)

My mother puts pepper on them. Pepper a rat enough and it tastes like chicken my mother says.

LOREN: She stop crying long enough to cook does she?

MAUREEN: You are plain nasty sometimes you know that Loren Maeve? There is no other word for the way you talk to me.

(Beat.)

LOREN: I'm sorry.

MAUREEN: That's just a word.

    (Beat.)

LOREN: You really think it tastes like chicken, rat?

MAUREEN: Been a while. Been a while since I ate chicken, me. Course my mother won't catch the rats. And my brother won't.

    (Loren stares at Maureen.)

MAUREEN: What?

    (Beat.)

    What?

LOREN: What'll she do when the pepper runs out?

MAUREEN: I'm not going to think about that.

LOREN: I'm never eating rat meat. Never.

MAUREEN: Young rat maybe that's like chicken. Old rats though. Old rats, they need molasses on them.

LOREN: I near can smell the bacon down there.

MAUREEN: You steep an old rat in molasses. Molasses and . . . something . . . old rat needs steeping in molasses and . . . something I forget . . . to make it tender.

LOREN: You got molasses?

MAUREEN: No.

LOREN: They eat the dead bodies, the rats.

MAUREEN: When I'm hungry I just close my eyes and I eat anything mostly. Guess a hungry rat feels just the same way.

LOREN: You eat rats you're eating soldiers. Maybe even Confederate soldiers. Maybe even someone you know, you're eating; if you eat rats.

MAUREEN: I'm always hungry.

    (There's a trapdoor laid bare by Loren's scrabbling.)

LOREN: See now this should just open up.

    (She heaves but the door doesn't budge.)

MAUREEN: Someone's shut that hard.

LOREN: You could help me.

    (They heave together. Nothing happens.)

MAUREEN: What we need is a lever.

    (She works a long stick under the gap in the trap door.)

MAUREEN: A woman's ingenuity is a gift from the Almighty, my mother says.

LOREN: Whatever I find down there I'm taking.

    (She heaves on the stick. It breaks.)

MAUREEN: You hurt?

LOREN: Split my palms is all. No callouses on my hands. A good hand has callouses on. We need something stronger than a stick.

(She searches in the grass for another tool.)

MAUREEN: The biggest enemy of a soldier is his bowels, and his feet, and his lungs. You hear their lungs. In the morning when their drums roll to wake them up you hear the whole army cough. Thousands of men coughing all at once—coughing so hard you can't hear the drums anymore. Can you tell a Confederate cough from a Yankee cough? I can't. That's the strangest thing. We think different, we talk different, we smell different. Wouldn't you think we'd cough different? Measles have killed more men than ever the guns have.

LOREN: Where do you get it from?

MAUREEN: I listen.

LOREN: You never stop talking where d'you get time to listen?

MAUREEN: I'm just going to ignore that Loren Maeve. I'm going to ignore your insult to me and put it down to a cruelty born of your concern over your dying little brother.

LOREN: Don't say he's dying.

MAUREEN: Need to call a thing by it's name, that's what you said.

LOREN: Don't you say it.

(Beat.)

MAUREEN: More men have died of dysentery, and scarlet fever and mumps and the typhus than ever died of bullet wounds. There's a band from a barrel there. In the grass there. You wrap your hands in something case the rust gets in that cut. You get rust in an open wound you'll get the lockjaw.

LOREN: I need your weight here.

MAUREEN: There are prettier ways to die than with the lockjaw.

(Loren tears the hem of her petticoat into a strip. Wraps it round her hands. Maureen swings on the metal.)

MAUREEN: I'm half the girl I was now September's come. I'm half the girl I was on the fifteenth of June when these people started besieging us, my mother says. I'll be half again by the time they go. Then no man will ever want me. A man wants flesh on the bones he holds in his arms. Man sees me half the weight I am now he'll think I've got the galloping consumption and he'll never marry me.

(Loren's finished wrapping her hands. The two girls swing down hard on the metal spar.)

LOREN: I don't want to marry. Marriage brings children. Children bring trouble.

(The trap door swings up. The girls fall.)

LOREN: You all right?

MAUREEN: I've got a bruise. I've bruised my butt.

LOREN: It's dark down there.

MAUREEN: I'm scared of the dark.

LOREN: I am so sick of the sound of that word.

MAUREEN: Scared?

LOREN: Maybe if you didn't say it so often you wouldn't feel it so much.

(She lowers herself into the hole.)

MAUREEN: It's not so bad for you. See. I'm a sinner. I'm already a sinner. Sinners can't go in dark places. One of them might just be the doorway to Hell and a sinner doesn't even need a key to that door. It just flings itself wide open for him and swallows him in.

LOREN: You're not a sinner.

MAUREEN: I am.

LOREN: You are not.

MAUREEN: I am no longer lily white in the face of the Lord.

LOREN: I'm going down there and get Mrs. Tyler's bacon that was cured from her prize hog. That animal had as sweet a disposition as you could wish.

MAUREEN: I am no longer lily white.

LOREN: A sweet-tempered hog makes the best bacon I just bet you he does.

MAUREEN: Don't you want to know why?

(Beat.)

Jem Matthenson put his hand on me.

(Beat.)

I said he put his hand on me.

LOREN: I heard you.

MAUREEN: His father died at Cold Harbor.

LOREN: Doesn't mean he can put his hand on you.

MAUREEN: Think I'll go to Hell?

(Loren's down below. Maureen lies over the hole in the ground calling down to Loren.)

His father was embalmed you know? They put fluid in his veins instead of the blood and sent him home looking like he was alive. That's what Jem Matthenson said. They made Jem kiss his father's dead flesh though he'd died more'n three weeks before. So I let Jem Matthenson put his hand on me when he asked. It was the least I could do. An' I let Jem kiss me too. Tisn't right that a boy should have the taste of dead flesh on his lips so I gave him a living kiss to take the taste away.

LOREN: You'll go to heaven for it. The Almighty will give you wings.

MAUREEN: You find the bacon?

LOREN: No.

(Beat.)

MAUREEN: You find it yet?

LOREN: There's nothing here practically.

MAUREEN: Why'd you ever think there would be? My belt's pulled in three notches from where it used to be.

LOREN: Somebody's taken it.

MAUREEN: What're you talking about?

LOREN: The bacon. Somebody's stolen it maybe.

(A small sack's chucked out of the hole.)

MAUREEN: Think it's flour?

LOREN: Open it and tell me.

(Maureen unties the sack.)

MAUREEN: It's crawling Loren.

LOREN: I don't care about that.

MAUREEN: You can't use it crawling.

LOREN: Pick them out, the crawlers.

MAUREEN: Look like maggots to me.

LOREN: Pick 'em out anyway.

MAUREEN: You pick 'em.

(Loren heaves herself out of the hole.)

LOREN: Look what else.

MAUREEN: Lord Loren that's honey.

LOREN: What can I do? What am I going to do? I needed that bacon for my little brother, to save him. I needed it.

MAUREEN: You got honey. Honey's good for a person. We could make a cake. All we need's eggs and some fat.

LOREN: There isn't a chicken left or a duck on a pond to get eggs from.

MAUREEN: Pie crust. We could make pie crust. And I know where there's blueberries.

LOREN: Blueberries?

MAUREEN: Big fat ones. Down by the river, they are. You know? Where it pools deep and the big willow is. Jem Matthenson told me. Said he'd take me.

LOREN: I don't know.

MAUREEN: Better than nothing Loren. Come on.

(*She walks away. Loren bangs the trapdoor shut.*)

MAUREEN: You bring that flour now.

(*Loren grabs the sack. Runs after Maureen.*)

LOREN: Where'd he put his hand? What part of your anatomy?

MAUREEN: Who?

LOREN: How many have you let touch you?

MAUREEN: Loren Maeve what are you accusing me of?

LOREN: Jem Matthenson you told me.

MAUREEN: It was a sweet moment Loren Maeve and I'm not going to indulge in the kind of gossip that will sour it's memory. For gossip is a pleasure of the moment only, memory lasts forever.

(*Beat.*)

Promise you won't tell.

LOREN: I won't tell.

MAUREEN: Promise or I won't show you where the blueberries are.

(*There's sudden tears running down Loren's face.*)

What're you blubbing for?

LOREN: Ma Tyler eat a whole hog to herself. She could've left one bit. One little bit.

MAUREEN: Keep walking Loren Maeve.

LOREN: It's going on forever. All . . . this.

(*Beat.*)

Feel the quiet.

(*Maureen wipes the tears away with the hem of her dress.*)

MAUREEN: Don't you give in to despair. Don't you ever.

(*Beat.*)

Say, I promise not to tell about Jem Matthenson.

LOREN: I promise.

MAUREEN: Say, if I break my word may the devil take me and roast me on the fiery spits of Hell.

LOREN: May he roast me.

MAUREEN: On my buttocks he touched me then. And on my chest. My left chest. Here. And I don't care a bit that he did. It was a good bit of my life. I treasure the good bits.

(*In the dappled light under the willows by the pond there's a figure. Seems like a young boy. A Northern soldier, far too young to be in uniform. The figure bends down, lifts water in its hands. Holds it there for a moment.*)

Splashes it into the air so that drops sparkle in the sunlight. There's grace in the movement. The soldier unbuttons a faded blue shirt. There's a glimpse of lace beneath.)

(The fire flares in the dugout.)

HANCOCK: You ever made love to a woman?

STEWART: These stones hot enough for dough?

HANCOCK: I'm asking you a question man.

STEWART: 'Course I'm in love with womankind. If my ma taught me anything she taught me that. To love womankind every last one of them. To hold them in reverence and awe on the one hand and on the other to treat them as wantons.

(Beat.)

HANCOCK: Ever made love to a woman?

STEWART: To a girl I made love.

HANCOCK: Can't have been a good girl.

STEWART: Good enough not to want me to die and never have known what it was to make love.

HANCOCK: When'd you last see her?

STEWART: I see her all the time.

HANCOCK: In the flesh man. Not in your mind's eye.

(Beat.)

I'm going to tell you something about your precious womankind. Once you awaken that appetite in them. "Appetite," you know what I mean? Once that appetite is awakened it becomes a fever that has to be sated. Your wanton, that you so reverence, will be off with any man who so much as looks at her. You given her an itch man. She just got to scratch it.

(Stewart leaps up and grabs Hancock.)

STEWART: Take that back.

HANCOCK: I'm telling you man.

STEWART: Take it back.

HANCOCK: I'm telling you for your own good.

STEWART: You'll feel my knife in your throat.

HANCOCK: For your own good man.

STEWART: Now you take back your words.

HANCOCK: I'm telling you the truth.

(Stewart throws him down on the ground sits astride him, forces dirt into his mouth.)

(Hancock chokes.)

STEWART: You swallow them. Swallow the . . . Swallow it. Choke on it.

(Hancock's gagging.)

(Stewart drags Hancock to a sitting position. Hancock spits. Wipes the dirt from his mouth. Watches Stewart. His voice is hoarse when he speaks.)

HANCOCK: Need something to keep you alive I guess. We all do.

STEWART: I'll take that for an apology.

(Beat.)

(Hancock nods.)

STEWART: Stones are hot enough for bread. Put some water in that flour. Some bacon fat. Nice and clear see.

HANCOCK: Nothing like a girl to keep you alive.

STEWART: Work it to a dough why don't you?

(In the dappled light under the willow by the pool, a girl wearing a lace trimmed chemise walks into the water. She ducks under. Comes up into the light shaking the wet from her hair, shorn as if from a recent fever.)

(Loren and Maureen come out from under the shadow of the willows.)

LOREN: Got enough now d'you think?

MAUREEN: What d'you think?

LOREN: You're the cook.

(She's carrying a straw hat full of blueberries.)

   Maureen?

(Maureen's picking through the clothes lying beside the water.)

   They soldier's clothes?

(Beat.)

MAUREEN: We got a Fed here.

LOREN: Where is he?

MAUREEN: He finds us he's going to kill us.

LOREN: He's got no clothes on Maureen.

   He won't kill us—not without his clothes on.

MAUREEN: The good Lord knows what worse he might do to us.

LOREN: Not without his clothes.

MAUREEN: What difference does that make?

LOREN: There's no dignity in it.

MAUREEN: Dignity? Feds Loren. They don't know the meaning of the word. What's that?

LOREN: Splashing see.

MAUREEN: Where?

LOREN: Someone in the water Maureen.

MAUREEN: God save me.

LOREN: Someone swimming is all.

MAUREEN: Light's in my eyes.

LOREN: Ducked under now.

MAUREEN: Is it him? Is it? Loren?

LOREN: There. There. See.

(Hosgood walks slowly through the willows, stands watching a Southern soldier, Rowatt, who sits with his back against a tree whittling at a stick with a knife. Crutches lie at his side. There's a flash of sunlight. He looks up. So does Hosgood. Diamonds of sparkling water are caught in the air just for a moment as the girl splashes in the water.)

HOSGOOD: Nothing like beauty is there?

(Beat. Rowatt turns. Their eyes catch and hold, summing each other up. Then Rowatt turns back to the view.)

ROWATT: That's a—what d'you call it—a chemise she has on there.

(He drags the word out.)

Che—mise.

Now. I have seen my mother in a chemise. And my sister I have seen in a chemise many, many times. Course that's not my sister swimming there. Different thing a chemise when it's not your sister wearing it.

HOSGOOD: Think she knows we're here.

ROWATT: I don't think she'd be so free. You going to shoot me?

HOSGOOD: If I was?

ROWATT: I'd say my prayers.

HOSGOOD: No gun see. You?

ROWATT: Wouldn't like to spoil a quiet day.

HOSGOOD: Sharp knife you got there.

ROWATT: For use on sticks only. I leave knife work to butchers.

(Beat.)

HOSGOOD: Where'd you get yours?

(Rowatt grins at him. Just pats his injured leg.)

I mean the battle you got hurt in that's what I'm enquiring about.

ROWATT: Gettysburg.

HOSGOOD: Where were you?

ROWATT: Peach Orchard. You?

HOSGOOD: Little Round Top. Healing all right is it?

ROWATT: Doing nicely. Thank you kindly for enquiring.

HOSGOOD: How'd you get here?

ROWATT: My daddy brought me home.

Where might your home be?

HOSGOOD: Far away. Too far.

(Beat.)

Bad luck you coming back here to this.

ROWATT: Focuses the mind certainly.

HOSGOOD: The wind blows where I come from. Tang of salt in the air.

Mind if I . . .

ROWATT: You all right?

(Hosgood sits down next to Rowatt.)

HOSGOOD: General Grant whittles like you. Chips away at a piece of wood till there's nothing left of it. Doesn't make anything. That water's good and clear.

ROWATT: Swim if you like, feel free.

HOSGOOD: Might disturb her. Wouldn't want to do that.

ROWATT: Is that blood?

HOSGOOD: No.

ROWATT: Looks like it to me.

HOSGOOD: Had a piece of bacon.

ROWATT: You a devil come to tempt me.

HOSGOOD: Held it against me. Stain is all.

ROWATT: If you say so.

HOSGOOD: Gave the bacon away of course.

ROWATT: Why would you do that?

HOSGOOD: Met a man whose need was greater.

ROWATT: Can't remember when I last saw bacon.

HOSGOOD: Good bacon.

ROWATT: You tell me where it is maybe I'll take my knife and go get me a piece of it.

HOSGOOD: Not worth losing your life over.

ROWATT: I go much longer without any, I might argue that point. I might argue my life will be lost from hunger anyway. Right now my stomach's telling me that my throat must be cut.

HOSGOOD: You got blueberries though.

ROWATT: Help yourself.

HOSGOOD: Maybe I will at that.

ROWATT: Fine blueberries. Fine. I am here to tell you however that man cannot live by blueberries alone.

(A bird cries.)

(Water ripples.)

(Light sparkles.)

(Hosgood and Rowatt watch the girl swim.)

HOSGOOD: Wouldn't be so bad would it?

(Beat.)

Dying. I mean. Wouldn't be so bad if heaven was like this.

ROWATT: There's a hotel in Washington, D.C. my daddy told me. Tobacco spit's thick on the carpet. Senators stay there. Congressmen. Carpet's damp with spit. My daddy never held with the chewing of tobacco. My daddy is a fastidious man. Said to me that for him from then on that foyer was the entrance to hell. And though you might linger in that foyer for all eternity you would never get to heaven through it.

HOSGOOD: Hell's no hotel foyer. Not as far as I'm concerned. When we mined under you. When we blew your lines of defense sky high. When we sent our troops into the crater. When you shot them. When you massacred them. My brother was down there. That was Hell.

ROWATT: I'm sorry for your brother.

HOSGOOD: Lot of good men.

ROWATT: I could tend to that wound for you.

HOSGOOD: I'm watching I tell you.

ROWATT: Sniper's bullet was it?

HOSGOOD: You know something about snipers?

ROWATT: Man has a choice he wouldn't be a sniper.

HOSGOOD: Injured man has no choice that what you're telling me?

(Beat.)

ROWATT: I could try at least to take care of it.

HOSGOOD: Finish the job?

ROWATT: Make you more comfortable.

HOSGOOD: Quiet while I'm watching.

(Loren's picking from a laden bush. Putting some in the straw hat, stuffing some in her mouth.)

MAUREEN: Don't you gorge Loren Maeve. Don't you gorge on these, they'll go straight through you.

LOREN: Never seen so many.

MAUREEN: Don't say I didn't warn you.

   She's got short hair.

LOREN: See these Maureen.

MAUREEN: Look at her with her short hair.

LOREN: Spoonfuls of honey and blueberries. That'll build his strength won't
   it? Spoonfuls of honey will. And pie.

MAUREEN: Loren pay attention.

LOREN: Maybe she had the fever and they cut off her hair.

(On the river bank.)

HOSGOOD: You don't look like a fighting man.

ROWATT: Come in all sorts these days fighting men.

HOSGOOD: I grant you that.

ROWATT: Right you are though. A life of quiet and gentle contemplation of
   the beauties this earth has to offer is what I would choose if I had a
   choice but you have brought trouble to my doorstep.

HOSGOOD: You made the trouble.

ROWATT: You're in my land. I am not in yours.

HOSGOOD: That the only reason you fight?

ROWATT: See. The way I see it. Leaving aside the question of all men being
   created equal for those better qualified than I am to argue, there's no
   viability to slavery in the South. It's run out of it's viability. A man works
   to better his life, his and his family's. Else why would he work? Slave's
   life doesn't get any better no matter how hard he works. So he does as
   little as possible, eats as much as he can. Same as you or me would do
   in his position. He's not stupid, your slave. Low output, high mainte-
   nance. Doesn't make sense. So I'm not fighting for slavery—to keep slavery in the South—I'm not fighting for that. You dictate to us though.
   Righteously. Then you come here. You don't just fight. You burn and
   you steal. Unarmed women and children you pull their homes down
   round them. And I don't see by what right you do that and so . . .

HOSGOOD: You fight?

ROWATT: Need every man we've got.

HOSGOOD: Still fight hurt like you are.

ROWATT: I don't use my legs to shoot with.

HOSGOOD: Good shot are you?

ROWATT: Hunter has to be a good shot less he likes to see suffering.

HOSGOOD: You hunt?

ROWATT: Been known to.

HOSGOOD: Though I am your enemy . . .

ROWATT: I would relieve your suffering. If you were armed in front of me threatening me and mine I would shoot you.

(Hosgood knows he's talking to the sniper. Nods his head.)

HOSGOOD: She's coming out the water. See. Walking out the water.

(Maureen fans herself in the shade.)

MAUREEN: You ever get an intuition?

LOREN: Don't feel the need.

MAUREEN: You never had one?

LOREN: Intuitions make a person give up.

MAUREEN: I'm having one now Loren.

LOREN: We need to go make a pie.

MAUREEN: I got something to say to you.

LOREN: I need to get home. Right now I need to.

MAUREEN: You see her?

LOREN: That chemise is practically transparent.

MAUREEN: There she is with her short hair. There is this bundle of soldier's clothes and no soldier.

LOREN: Don't stare at her like that.

MAUREEN: She can't see me.

(Maureen lifts the clothes and hides them in the middle of a bush. Loren watches.)

LOREN: I need to get these home

MAUREEN: I am going to put something to you.

LOREN: My brother, Maureen. My brother.

MAUREEN: You go then. Go on. Go.

LOREN: Aren't you coming?

MAUREEN: There is a girl with short hair. Here is a bundle of clothes here in the middle of this bush.

Suppose the two belonged together.

LOREN: She's a girl Maureen.

MAUREEN: I know that.

LOREN: Those are men's clothes.

MAUREEN: Get down Loren. Get in here 'fore she sees you.

(Maureen grabs Loren. The blueberries spill.)

LOREN: They've gone all over the place.

(She gathers them up.)

MAUREEN: There's plenty left.

LOREN: I don't want them dirty.

MAUREEN: Get down Loren.

(She grabs Loren's arm and pulls her down.)

LOREN: You're hurting me.

MAUREEN: You watch. Watch her. Watch her now. What she does.

(The girl from the water walks to the place on the bank where the uniform had been.)

MAUREEN: Lookin' for her clothes, see.

LOREN: So what then? So what?

MAUREEN: Jem Matthenson said there were women fighting for the Yankees. Disguising themselves as men.

LOREN: I'm sick of Jem Matthenson.

MAUREEN: I'm talking about women soldiers marching and shooting and fighting like men.

LOREN: Take a brave woman.

MAUREEN: She's a Yankee.

LOREN: Doesn't mean she isn't brave.

MAUREEN: See. See.

(The girl from the pool sits at the water's edge, shivers, wraps her arms round herself, bows her head.)

(Rowatt gets to his feet.)

ROWATT: You going to let me see that wound?

HOSGOOD: She's cold, see.

ROWATT: You let me see that wound.

HOSGOOD: You a doctor all of a sudden.

ROWATT: Sun'll warm her.

HOSGOOD: She needs help.

ROWATT: Your brother died right?

HOSGOOD: Men left in the crater injured, they didn't make a good death.

ROWATT: You got any more brothers?

HOSGOOD: No.

ROWATT: Sisters even?

HOSGOOD: I have no siblings.

ROWATT: Think of your mother and let me help you.

(Beat.)

HOSGOOD: Thing I despise most is a sniper.

(Beat.)

ROWATT: Thing I despise most is a fool.

(Hosgood gets to his feet. It hurts him to do it.)

(The fire flares.)

STEWART: It is a fact that a man with a wound on the losing side in a battle, he dies. Man with the same wound on the winning side lives. Older man with a wound lives, boy with the same wound dies. In the first place the winning side has hope. Hope gives life. In the second place man's been through a lot, knows you can live through pain so he does, he lives. Boy doesn't know enough to live through pain so he dies.

HANCOCK: Man with a dream lives too, that your point?

STEWART: What keeps you alive Hancock?

HANCOCK: Mealtimes. I look forward to them. You know?

STEWART: It's coming. You pass that drink now.

HANCOCK: I don't want to halt any progress toward this feast.

STEWART: This stuff's too weak to halt anything.

HANCOCK: I'm not forcing you to partake.

STEWART: No offense meant.

(Hancock passes his flask.)

(Maureen whispers crouched low.)

MAUREEN: If she's a soldier, right, we might just kill her. One less of them to worry about.

LOREN: I don't know how to kill anybody.

MAUREEN: You must be the only one for miles around here that doesn't.

LOREN: She's not that much older than us Maureen.

MAUREEN: What's age got to do with it?

LOREN: No.

MAUREEN: Don't you want to do something for the cause?

(Beat.)

You and me, we're in this just like everyone else. We've got to do our bit. That's what's expected.

LOREN: No one knows we're out here.

MAUREEN: We know.

LOREN: We haven't got a gun.

MAUREEN: I've got string.

LOREN: You can't kill someone with a piece of string.

MAUREEN: I never come out without string. It's good and strong my string.

LOREN: What d'you use it for.

MAUREEN: Rats.

You don't think they walk into the cooking pot do you? Leap up onto the stove and beg to be cooked? Well they don't Loren Maeve. You have to work to catch your rat and you never know where you might come upon a fruitful spot. If you'd caught rats your brother might not be failing now.

LOREN: Are you going to choke her?

(Beat.)

She's lying down now in the sunlight. She's drying off in the sunlight. You can't kill someone like that. Lying in their chemise in the sun.

MAUREEN: We got to.

LOREN: No.

MAUREEN: For the Cause.

LOREN: I don't know what the Cause is. I never have.

MAUREEN: Course you do.

LOREN: I don't.

MAUREEN: We have the right to keep slaves that no one can ever take from us.

LOREN: We've never owned slaves. Neither have you.

MAUREEN: Doesn't mean we shouldn't have the right. No one can tell me what to do. They take one right away from us what other rights they going to deprive us of? They take our human property away from us. What other property they going to take from us? They going to take the dresses off our backs just because they think they're stronger than we are. Stand there and order us to strip ourselves in the street.

LOREN: We're talking about depriving a person of life, of breath itself.

MAUREEN: A Yankee. I do not know why you are so reluctant.

LOREN: She's a girl in a chemise she's not a soldier.

MAUREEN: I say she is.

Those are soldier's clothes we put in the bushes there or am I having a sainted vision.

LOREN: They're soldier's clothes.

MAUREEN: Does she or does she not have short hair.

LOREN: Yes but we said . . .

(The girl by the water starts to cough, rolls over on her side.)

There. There. See. Fever. Fever passed, but fever all the same.

MAUREEN: A soldier can't have fever then?

LOREN: I just want to save my baby brother's life.

MAUREEN: I will never be your friend again if you don't do this.

LOREN: All right.

MAUREEN: What?

LOREN: Don't be my friend. I can get along without you.

MAUREEN: I always thought you were the bold one. Of the two of us. It was you was bold.

> *(Beat.)*
>
> I will tell the whole town about you. I will tell them you're a traitor.
>
> *(Beat.)*
>
> Loren? With you or without you Loren.
>
> *(Willow branches blow in the breeze. Shadows and sunlight.)*
>
> *(Maureen creeps up on the girl in the chemise, dozing by the pool.)*
>
> *(Gets the string round her neck and pulls.)*
>
> *(The girl fights, scratches, spits, and chokes. Maureen holds on. The girl's stronger than she is.)*

MAUREEN: Loren. I need you. Loren Maeve. You get over here now.

> *(The girl starts to get the better of Maureen. Loren jumps on her back.)*

MAUREEN: You haul on that string. You haul on it now.

> *(Maureen and Loren fight the girl. They are trying to kill her. And the girl begins to fail.)*
>
> *(Hosgood blunders through the undergrowth. Rowatt's behind on his crutches.)*
>
> *(Hosgood hauls Loren off the girl's back. It's not easy for him. Rowatt hits Maureen with his crutch. She passes out.)*

LOREN: What have you done? You've killed her.

> *(The Southern soldier tends to the girl in the chemise.)*

LOREN: She's a soldier.

ROWATT: She's just a girl.

LOREN: She's still a soldier.

ROWATT: I don't kill women.

LOREN: You're a traitor.

> *(Hosgood can't hold Loren anymore. She rushes to Maureen's side.)*

ROWATT: Loren Maeve isn't it?

LOREN: She's hardly breathing.

ROWATT: Your mother know you're out here.

LOREN: *(To Hosgood.)* What're you lookin' at?

> *(To Rowatt.)*
>
> Tell your Yankee friend to take his eyes off of me.
>
> *(Hosgood sinks down.)*

LOREN: What's wrong with him?

ROWATT: *(To the girl.)* You all right?

BRIDH: I reckon.

ROWATT: What's your name?

BRIDH: Bridh.

ROWATT: Irish?

BRIDH: What's that to you? Get off me.

   (Beat.)

   Get your filthy stinking hands off me.

ROWATT: I saved your life.

BRIDH: Am I supposed to say thank you?

ROWATT: Might ease the path.

BRIDH: Why would I want to do that?

ROWATT: You have me there.

BRIDH: You want to look to your friend over there. I can take care of myself.
   Been doin' it long enough.

ROWATT: Pardon me.

   (He stands and bows to her.)

BRIDH: Very graceful.

LOREN: Are you a soldier?

BRIDH: You move away from me.

LOREN: You'll run away if I do.

BRIDH: I want room to breath is all.

LOREN: Maureen says you're a soldier.

BRIDH: That Maureen?

LOREN: What of it?

BRIDH: Look where thinking got her.

LOREN: She says you're a soldier.

BRIDH: She says shite then.

LOREN: Who's side are you on?

BRIDH: Who's on my side?

LOREN: Everyone's on a side.

BRIDH: Not me. Get some water for your hell fire friend there. Wet her
   forehead.

LOREN: Who are you then?

BRIDH: That's a man with a bullet in him.

ROWATT: He says not.

BRIDH: I've seen them deny it before now. Doesn't stop it killing them.

LOREN: You were wearing soldier's clothes.

BRIDH: Where are they?

LOREN: Wasn't my idea, killing you.

BRIDH: That makes me feel a whole lot better.

LOREN: If you're not a soldier . . .

BRIDH: I borrowed the clothes. The man I borrowed them from's asleep in my bed.

(Beat.)

Tell them.

(Beat.)

You.

ROWATT: Beg pardon Ma'am.

BRIDH: "Beg pardon Ma'am" Name's Bridh. Him that calls me Ma'am, he's mocking me.

ROWATT: No offense.

BRIDH: Way I see it.

LOREN: Bridh?

ROWATT: Beautiful name.

LOREN: Bridh what?

BRIDH: I don't think my mammy ever knew that. Or if she did she didn't tell me.

LOREN: It's slaves don't have last names.

BRIDH: That's about placed me then. I'm a slave all right. A wage slave.

LOREN: What's that?

BRIDH: Means I have to eat. Means no one feeds me but me. Means I have to work how I can wherever I can or I don't eat. Means it isn't certain that I will eat. Means every day eating's all I think about.

LOREN: What's your work?

BRIDH: He knows. His lordship over there. He's the sort I work for.

LOREN: He's a Confederate.

BRIDH: He's a man.

LOREN: I don't understand.

BRIDH: I'm Irish. I'm a woman. The piece of stupidity this war is. Think I'd take one side or the other. Whatever side survives that's the side I'm on. I'm an independent.

LOREN: Is that why your hair's short?

BRIDH: It's long to how it used to be.

LOREN: Why'd you cut it.

BRIDH: I saw a fashion plate in a French magazine. Thought I'd be upsides with the French.

LOREN: Is that the truth you're telling me?

BRIDH: You calling me a liar?

LOREN: Did you have a fever?

BRIDH: I didn't.

LOREN: Why's it short then, your hair?

BRIDH: Some folk don't like a soul to be too independent.

> (Beat.)

LOREN: Somebody did that to you?

BRIDH: Take care they don't do it to you.

LOREN: Why would they?

BRIDH: You're consorting with the enemy now. They'll think you're a spy.

LOREN: For talking to you?

BRIDH: It's him I'm thinking of.

LOREN: He hasn't said anything.

BRIDH: You should go home.

> (Beat.)
>
> Give me my clothes and go home.

LOREN: What am I supposed to do with Maureen?

BRIDH: Carry her.

LOREN: She's quite heavy. She says I've got thick ankles but she's the heavy one really.

BRIDH: Why don't you give me my clothes?

> (Loren goes to get the clothes from the brambles.)

LOREN: Maureen might be angry with me.

BRIDH: You've got to be your own person. Much as you can be. Slaves, soldiers, and whores course they're not their own people.

LOREN: Is that what you are?

BRIDH: A slave like I told you.

LOREN: A whore?

BRIDH: Don't like that word.

LOREN: You said it first.

BRIDH: So I did.

LOREN: Are you then?

BRIDH: Are you going to give me my clothes?

> (Loren passes them to her.)

LOREN: My little brother's hungry. He might die he's so hungry. And when we give him things to eat, he can't hold them down. He has pains in his stomach. Like he's been shot he has pains.

> (Hosgood pulls himself up. Shivers.)

BRIDH: Cold creeping up on you?

HOSGOOD: Don't put them on.

BRIDH: This is my day off. My day off I do what I want I don't do what any man tells me.

LOREN: You are a whore.

BRIDH: Not today. I'm bathed and I'm washed clean I'm a new woman today. Good as you are.

HOSGOOD: You're beautiful.

BRIDH: Don't you look at me with those soft eyes.

ROWATT: Group of women I heard of. They got this girl. She was earning her living. Women didn't like it. Tied her to a post and shaved off her hair.

(Beat.)

One thing I hate worse than I hate some men. Some women.

(Beat.)

You need to get that boy's jacket off. Cut that bullet out of him.

HOSGOOD: No.

BRIDH: What's your name?

HOSGOOD: Hosgood.

BRIDH: Kind of name's that?

HOSGOOD: Family came from Devon, England, long time ago.

BRIDH: Family's going to die out if that bullet's left in you.

LOREN: He's got a pink froth on his lips.

(Hosgood wipes his mouth.)

ROWATT: Bullet's in his lung.

BRIDH: I have a proposition for you Hosgood. You want to hear it?

HOSGOOD: Sure. Yes.

BRIDH: You let . . . what's your name?

ROWATT: Rowatt.

(She looks at Loren.)

LOREN: I'm Loren Ma'am. Loren Maeve.

BRIDH: Rowatt and Loren Maeve here, they're going to ease you out of that jacket of yours, then I'm going to tell you my proposition.

(Hosgood starts to laugh.)

As well you can laugh.

HOSGOOD: Better be a good one.

BRIDH: It's a good one. Do we have a deal?

HOSGOOD: Haul away.

(Maureen starts to come to. Bridh sits on her.)

BRIDH: You carry on.

(Loren and Rowatt take the jacket off as gently as they can.)

MAUREEN: Get off me. Get off. Get off.

BRIDH: I've seen people die from a bump on the head.

MAUREEN: You have not.

BRIDH: Moving around too much after that's what they die of.

> *(Maureen spits at her.)*

BRIDH: Well look at you. Big and brave aren't you? Your mammy taught you well.

MAUREEN: Get up. Get off.

BRIDH: Lay him down.

MAUREEN: *(Struggling.)* What're you doing? He's a Fed. You can't help him.

> *(Bridh reaches out and grabs the string twists it round Maureen's ankles and round her wrists.)*

MAUREEN: Are you going to let her tie me up?

ROWATT: Are you going to keep out of the way if she doesn't?

MAUREEN: Take them prisoner go on.

ROWATT: Man on crutches, think I'd win do you.

MAUREEN: Loren'll help you.

ROWATT: You stay right where you are Loren.

BRIDH: You keep very still Maureen. For the honor of the Confederacy.

MAUREEN: I don't like your tone.

BRIDH: Well you know just what you can do don't you.

> *(Beat.)*

> Hosgood?

HOSGOOD: I'm all right. You had a proposition for me.

> *(Maureen tries to roll.)*

BRIDH: Loren you come over here and keep this friend of yours away from us.

MAUREEN: My wrists are getting cut so they are.

HOSGOOD: What's your proposition if I let you cut this bullet out?

MAUREEN: My circulation's stopped. I could get gangrene from this.

> *(Bridh walks over. Crouches down by him. Smooths the hair away from his forehead. Rowatt's sharpening his knife on a stone.)*

BRIDH: You want to know what it is?

> *(She's very gentle with him.)*

HOSGOOD: Tell me.

BRIDH: You really want to know? Will you give us some room here Rowatt. I'm going to give this man a reason to cling on to his life. I am going to put something to him and I want privacy to do it. In a minute I'll need you.

(Rowatt moves away. Turns and watches Hosgood and Bridh.)

(Bridh whispers in Hosgood's ear. There's a silence broken only by the lapping of water, the distant cry of a bird and the pale quiet rustle of Bridh's whispering in the sunlight.)

(Stewart's sharpening his knife on a stone. The bacon sits proud and intact on another stone. The bread's cooking. Hancock's holding out his hand to the flames.)

HANCOCK: See the veins in that. See the blood flowing through the veins in that.

(He takes his hand away.)

Won't be quiet tomorrow. Can't ask for that. Be back to normal tomorrow.

(Stewart saws the bacon into thick slices.)

Hardly rashers these. More like chops.

STEWART: Turn the bread over.

HANCOCK: Least we'll die with our bellies full.

(Spark of sunlight.)

BRIDH: You accept my proposition?

HOSGOOD: It is more than generous.

BRIDH: It's a once in a lifetime. So I won't have you insulting me by turning it down.

HOSGOOD: I would think the less of myself if I did any such thing. Ma'am. Bridh.

(She touches his shoulder. His cheek. He catches her hand kisses it. Holds on to it.)

HOSGOOD: Do what you have to. Whatever it takes.

(Beat.)

BRIDH: I've got the sun in my eyes.

ROWATT: Take my hat.

BRIDH: You ready Hosgood.

HOSGOOD: First name's Edwin.

BRIDH: I like Hosgood better.

HOSGOOD: I'm ready.

BRIDH: Wait. Wait, wait, wait. Wait.

Where's my clothes?

You take anything out the pocket of my clothes?

MAUREEN: We're not thieves.

BRIDH: You bring my clothes to me.

MAUREEN: Don't you.

> *(Rowatt holds her in place with his foot.)*
>
> *(Loren runs to get the clothes.)*

BRIDH: Don't get all pricked by those thorns will you?

MAUREEN: What do you care?

BRIDH: I am so sick and tired of your mouth.

LOREN: What have you got?

BRIDH: There's a bottle in that pocket. Give it to Rowatt.

> *(Loren hands Rowatt a medicine bottle.)*

You see you get a customer from the medical tents. Sometimes. The medicine doesn't always go to the sick.

LOREN: What is that?

BRIDH: Might help him. I don't know. Worth a try. I seen men dreaming on this stuff.

> *(Rowatt holds Hosgood's head. Let's him drink.)*

Nothing wrong with dreaming. Better than pain.

(Bacon frying.)

STEWART: They ain't singing over there. I like it when they sing.

HANCOCK: Think they're planning something?

STEWART: Think we are?

HANCOCK: Guess they'll tell us soon enough.

Good smell. You can feel that smell right in the pores of you.

STEWART: You hear them talking sometimes over there. Night air carries the sound. Yarns they spin.

HANCOCK: I like a good story.

STEWART: Can't ever remember them, I can't. I hear them and they're gone from my head.

HANCOCK: Don't remember ever smelling better bacon than this.

STEWART: I used to have a good memory.

> *(Hancock stretches his hand out to the fire. It's shaking again. He closes his fist.)*

(Loren's crouching by Maureen.)

MAUREEN: What're they doing now?

LOREN: Cutting into him.

MAUREEN: I'm going to be sick.

LOREN: Don't look then.

(Beat.)

MAUREEN: Are they not done yet?

LOREN: There's cloth from his shirt in where the bullet went.

MAUREEN: He's going to die isn't he.

LOREN: Maybe.

MAUREEN: I don't care if he does.

LOREN: He talks different to us. He don't look any different.

MAUREEN: Will you take this string off of me?

LOREN: I don't want him to die and Rowatt doesn't.

MAUREEN: Take the string off.

He ought to look different to us. That would be a whole lot easier.

LOREN: Why would it?

MAUREEN: You know.

LOREN: I don't.

MAUREEN: I want to hate him.

LOREN: I don't want to hate anyone.

MAUREEN: Not even Becky Jennison.

(Beat.)

LOREN: I despise her and I will do all my life long.

(Firelight.)

STEWART: I call this cooked now. It's cooked. Might as well eat.

(Sunlight on the girls.)

MAUREEN: Would you touch a man like that?

LOREN: With a knife you mean?

MAUREEN: You are so stupid sometimes.

LOREN: She's cutting into his flesh with a knife.

MAUREEN: She's touching him with her very heart.

LOREN: How is she?

MAUREEN: Well if you can't see that Loren Maeve. You must be blind.

LOREN: Of course you know everything.

MAUREEN: I know about touching. A little bit I know. Untie me.

LOREN: Say please.

MAUREEN: I won't help you make the pie. So your brother will die after all.

LOREN: Why is "please" so hard to say?

(Beat.)

MAUREEN: I don't need you to sound like my mother.

LOREN: You're just plain stubborn Maureen.

(She starts to untie the string.)

MAUREEN: You know when I had this round her neck, her over there.

LOREN: What about it?

MAUREEN: I did it because . . . That's what you're supposed to do isn't it? Kill your enemies I mean.

LOREN: You wouldn't have killed her really.

MAUREEN: What if I had though?

(Beat.)

See how gentle she is.

LOREN: She's done with the knife now.

MAUREEN: We're friends still aren't we?

LOREN: The way she's looking at him.

MAUREEN: Loren?

LOREN: I suppose we'll always be friends.

MAUREEN: Even if . . .

LOREN: What?

MAUREEN: What'll happen to us when they win Loren?

(Beat.)

(Rowatt picks up his crutch.)

ROWATT: I'm taking you two back.

MAUREEN: Did you get the bullet out?

(Beat.)

ROWATT: You pick up your blueberries.

LOREN: It was in too deep wasn't it?

ROWATT: What you got in that sack? Is that flour in that sack.

LOREN: And honey we've got.

ROWATT: You're rich.

LOREN: How will they get back the two of them.

ROWATT: She'll find her way.

LOREN: And him will he?

ROWATT: Come on now. Come on.

(They go leaving Bridh sitting with Hosgood's head in her lap.)

HOSGOOD: Afternoon's leaving us.

BRIDH: Well it would.

HOSGOOD: About that proposition.

BRIDH: What about it?

HOSGOOD: I won't be taking you up on it will I?

BRIDH: I want you to drink all of this you can.

HOSGOOD: Marry me.

BRIDH: Just like that.

HOSGOOD: It's a good offer.

BRIDH: What do I get out of it?

HOSGOOD: You won't have to put up with any of my bad habits I can promise you that.

BRIDH: I don't see a preacher.

HOSGOOD: I see a cathedral of green what do we need a preacher for?

BRIDH: What about a ring?

HOSGOOD: Take that signet off my finger.

BRIDH: No Hosgood.

HOSGOOD: Take it off my finger.

BRIDH: They'd say I stole it.

HOSGOOD: I'm cold.

BRIDH: I know.

HOSGOOD: Take my ring.

(She eases the ring off his finger. Slips it onto her wedding finger.)

BRIDH: That what you want?

HOSGOOD: You take that home for me. Will you?

BRIDH: Your home?

HOSGOOD: A long way north from here.

BRIDH: It's too big for me.

HOSGOOD: Wear it on a chain round your neck.

BRIDH: I don't have a chain.

HOSGOOD: Find one. Take it home. They'll like to know you at home. They'll like to hear you were with me. They'll take care of you.

(Beat.)

I feel like I've known you all my life.

BRIDH: Here.

(She pulls out a stem of grass. Twists it round his finger.)

That makes it right. Now you're my husband.

(He puts a hand up to touch her hair.)

HOSGOOD: I like your hair.

BRIDH: I'm glad someone does.

HOSGOOD: By the time my folks see you it'll be real fine.

BRIDH: A long way north then.

HOSGOOD: Salt spray and a breeze always blowing.

BRIDH: Hold tight to my hand.

(Beat.)

HOSGOOD: You could kiss me.

BRIDH: Now?

HOSGOOD: I would be obliged.

(She kisses him. A long kiss.)

(Then she sits very still as the sun sets. Just sits there with his head cushioned in her lap.)

BRIDH: Sweet dreams.

(Firelight.)

(Stewart and Hancock wipe their plates with the flat bread.)

STEWART: See. Fat's solidifying.

HANCOCK: No loss then.

STEWART: No loss.

(Away from the river now. Loren, Maureen, and Rowatt are walking back to the town. Loren stops.)

MAUREEN: I'm tired Loren Maeve. Come on.

LOREN: You smell that?

MAUREEN: Come on home Loren Maeve. Right now.

ROWATT: I can smell it.

MAUREEN: It is not right to have secrets from me. It is not kind.

ROWATT: Someone's cooking bacon.

(Late afternoon sunlight shines on enemy lines. It hits Stewart and Hancock by the fire.)

MAUREEN: Yankees.

LOREN: They've stolen it. They've stolen it from my little brother.

MAUREEN: Let's go get it then before they eat it all up.

(Rowatt slides the wrapping off his crutch.)

ROWATT: You stay right where you are.

(The crutch laid bare is a rifle. Rowatt raises it to his shoulder.)

LOREN: I think they've finished the bacon. I think they've finished it anyway.

(Maureen follows his eyeline.)

MAUREEN: Difficult shot.

ROWATT: Long is all.

Squeeze the trigger, that's what my daddy taught me. Don't pull it, squeeze. And what you have in your sights human or animal, respect it enough to shoot it dead.

(The two girls watch Rowatt. Stewart's in the sunlight. Rowatt shoots.)
(A flash of light.)
(Blackout.)

END OF PLAY

Mullen's Alley

by Timothy Mason

From left to right: Nicholas Baefsky, Charlotte Locke,
Jorge Orozco and Isadora Epstein
Photo credit: Tom Haygood

PLAYWRIGHT'S BIOGRAPHY

Mullen's Alley is Timothy Mason's fourth play for A.C.T.'s Young Conservatory, a collaboration with Artistic Director, Craig Slaight, that spans more than fifteen years *(Ascension Day, The Less Than Human Club* and *Time on Fire)*. Tim's other plays have been produced by Circle Rep in New York (where he was a company playwright), Actors Theatre of Louisville, South Coast Rep, Seattle Rep, Victory Gardens, Portland Stage, the Jungle Theatre, and the Guthrie Theatre Lab. A host of wonderful actors have created roles in his plays, including Julie Harris, Mary-Louise Parker, and Timothy Hutton. Tim has written many plays and musicals for young audiences, for the Minneapolis Children's Theatre Company and the Seattle Children's Theatre. His musical, *Dr. Seuss' How the Grinch Stole Christmas!* (with composer, Mel Marvin) is the annual holiday production of San Diego's Old Globe and in October 2006 opened on Broadway. Tim's first novel, a fantasy-adventure for kids called *The Last Synapsid,* is being published by Delacorte Press.

FROM THE PLAYWRIGHT

I've lived for twenty-five years on the Lower East Side of Manhattan, the traditional first home of immigrants to this country. I came there not from another land but from Minneapolis (which is like another land, but that's another story). Still, in my first years in the big city, I felt myself to be in some way an immigrant, and I was from the beginning always interested in the other transplants. The tenants in my building were elderly Jewish and Russian Orthodox immigrants from Eastern Europe. I listened and watched, and counted nine different languages spoken between the front step of my apartment building and the Italian bakery a few blocks away. It was wonderful to me.

Not far from my home is a high-rise housing project, right on the East River, called The Jacob Riis Houses. Eventually I became sufficiently curious to learn who Jacob Riis was, and to discover the amazing photographs he took of the people who had preceded me on this very ground. One of the photos is known as "Mullen's Alley," and almost from the first moment I saw it, I knew I would someday use it in my work.

A bunch of kids stand between two tenements. The children stare at us with a fierce affirmation. Here am I. I am me and no one else. Even the faded figure who seems already to be a ghost speaks to us. I was here, she says, and in some way I will be here always.

Craig Slaight responded immediately to my proposed play, which was trusting of him, since there was no play in my head, and no story, just a photograph. My friend Leo said, "If you're going to write a play about a photograph, you have to read Susan Sontag's essays, *On Photography*." Well, that just made matters more difficult, raising all manner of questions I'd never even considered. What's in a picture? What *is* a picture? A photographic portrait of a person is *not* the person. Which made me wonder about all attempts at capturing and representing human beings truthfully, playwriting included.

Craig was scheduled to begin rehearsing *Mullen's Alley* in the middle of July, 2005, but as of June 1, I hadn't begun writing it. What had I been thinking? The kids in this photo are desperately poor. They're likely sick, some of them. One or more may be starving. How many would survive to adulthood? This was such grim material, I wasn't sure I wanted to *see* the play, much less write it. Fortunately, just at this point, I visited a pair of old friends, back in Minneapolis. One of them had been a poor boy in London's East End, and had almost miraculously gone on to become an MGM child star in the Hollywood of the 1930s and 1940s. He picked up my copy of Jacob Riis' *How the Other Half Lives* and paged through the photos. "This reminds me of my childhood," he said. "This is what I came from. "

Right there, my friend Terry had provided me the key to my story. Hope. Hope, not only for the plucky lad who escapes grinding poverty via a life in show business, but the hope which each of the characters nourishes for himself or herself. Because each of us has that fire within us when we are young. Even if life dims it for some, or extinguishes it eventually, it nonetheless propels us all.

A note: The characters at times speak in verse. I think this may be the verbal equivalent of formal photography, creating both distance and depth, from the artist to his subject. I think. The verse simply showed up in the writing of the play; I tried to get rid of it, but it wouldn't be got rid of, so there it is.

(Oh, yes, I finished writing the play in five weeks and we began rehearsals on time and the production five weeks later was thrilling—thank God for hope.)

FROM THE ACTOR—Nicholas Baefsky (Isadore)
History class, early on a Monday morning. "Please turn in your books to page six," the teacher orders in her water-polo-coach yelp. I flip slowly through, "A New Industrial Age" dreading another day of monotony. Then I see it. A small photograph, glossy, with the caption under it "Mullen's Alley."

As the teacher lectures about life in the tenements on the Lower East Side, I sit at my desk quietly, and allow myself a little smile. "Jacob Riis," she says hoarsely, "arrived New York a young man in 1870," and I fill in the details.

I remember a boy walking briskly, nervously, through the busy streets of San Francisco. He looks up briefly, and enters American Conservatory Theater, not knowing what to expect. As the door swings shut behind him, he is ushered for the first time, into the world of acting. Eyes wide, he out-stretches his hand, slightly embarrassed for the calluses from a year of rowing. It is taken and shook firmly by a short man whose eyes seem to twinkle behind spectacles. "Hello Isadore," I hear him say, "I'm Tim." And thus I was introduced to Timothy Mason, playwright.

I met my fellow cast members and director, and we took the velvet padded elevator to the top floor Garret space, from where one can look down and see the main stage in all its brilliance. We sat at the large table in silence, uncertain of ourselves, some leafing through the scripts provided, others speaking in hushed tones, until the last girl rushed in, mumbling apologies. Then we began work on *Mullen's Alley*, a new play by Timothy Mason.

I remember opening my neon binder multiple times, the click of the silver rings signaling the addition of new pages, pages which would bring further life to those children struggling for hope. Pages still warm from the printer, still warm from the imagination of Tim Mason.

I remember the smell of backstage. I remember the heat of the lights, and the chills I would get night after night, as I craned my neck and imagined Ma Dolan's flight. I remember antics with blood capsules, and I remember laughing with a cast of friends. I remember stifling tears closing night, as Simon and Garfunkel's "America" faded into a "GREAT FLASH!"

I am brought back to class by the bell. "I expect you to know about everything I've covered in class today for the test on Thursday," the teacher shouts over the scraping of chairs and zipping of backpacks.

"Nobody knows Mullen's Alley," I murmur to myself with a chuckle, and gently shut the history book, "No one, and nobody will."

ORIGINAL PRODUCTION

Mullen's Alley was commissioned and first presented by the Young Conservatory at American Conservatory Theater (Carey Perloff, Artistic Director, Heather M. Kitchen, Executive Director), San Francisco, California, in August 2005. It was directed by Craig Slaight, the set design was by Dean Shibuya, the lighting design was by David Robertson, the sound was designed by Greg Kunit, the costumes were designed by Callie Floor and the assistant director was David Morse. The cast was as follows:

ELLEN MARGARET	Keelin Woodell
JIMMY COLAN	Conner Neddersen
RIVERBOY	Jorge Orozco
LILLY	Isadora Epstein
TERRY	Daniel Kennedy
ISADORE	Nicholas Baefsky
REBECCAH	Charlotte Locke

SETTING

The play takes place in and around the Five Points neighborhood of New York City, in 1889.

CHARACTERS

JIMMY DOLAN, fourteen or fifteen
TERRY DOLAN, nine
ELLEN MARGARET, fourteen or so
ISADORE KLEIN, about fourteen
REBECCAH KLEIN, twelve
LILY, fifteen
RIVERBOY, fifteen

MULLEN'S ALLEY

In the narrow canyon which is Mullen's Alley, Jimmy Dolan strides on in a rage, followed by Ellen Margaret.

JIMMY: Oh shite! Oh shite! Shite!

ELLEN MARGARET: *(To audience.)* There's me Jimmy Dolan.

JIMMY: Holy shite!

ELLEN MARGARET: *(To audience.)* Me one true love, ain't he a treat? *(To him.)* Jimmy's upset, is it?

JIMMY: Shut your trap, Ellen Margaret!

ELLEN MARGARET: Try and shut it, booger-nose!

JIMMY: Sister of a whore!

ELLEN MARGARET: Spawn of a bedbug!

JIMMY: Two-penny scrubber!

ELLEN MARGARET: Maggot! *(To audience.)* And no, not an hour and more of this sort of talk it won't be. This is just to give the general idea. *(To Jimmy.)* Stink-hole!

JIMMY: Stop-a-Clock!

ELLEN MARGARET: Dung-for-Brains!

JIMMY: Ah, go soak yer head!

ELLEN MARGARET: Go soak yours!

JIMMY: Give over, will you, Ellen Margaret, for the love of God!

ELLEN MARGARET: So what is it got up yer flue, Jimmy Dolan?

JIMMY: Him with the flash-powder.

ELLEN MARGARET: The camera fella? Mr. Riis? Is it after you he's been?

JIMMY: He brings in some goons with a picture machine—
they bust into rooms, you should hear us all scream.
We're dead to the world, we're trying to sleep—
he sets off a flash—bang!

ELLEN MARGARET: He captures the scene?

JIMMY: He captures my fanny!—what does it show?
You see what he shows you, but hey—it ain't so!
(The other Kids come into the light.)

RIVERBOY: 'Cause nobody knows Mullen's Alley—

LILY: Nobody knows Cherry Hill—

TERRY: Nobody knows the Mulberry Bend—

JIMMY: No one! And nobody will!

ELLEN MARGARET: *(To audience.)* Jacob Augustus Riis, born Denmark, 1849, arrived New York a young man in 1870, hoping to find work as a carpenter.

ISADORE: He did not find it.

REBECCAH: He scrounged jobs where he could, and mostly he could not.

ELLEN MARGARET: He discovered what it was to be homeless, sleeping on the floor in the nasty lodging house run by the police in their own cellar on Mulberry Street. By and by, though, he became a crime reporter, and his beat, how strange, after his god-awful treatment by the coppers . . .

LILY: One of the cops tossed him out in the middle of the night for complaining about conditions, and when his dog growled, the copper beat the dog's brains out on the steps of police headquarters.

TERRY: I don't even want to hear about things like that.

ELLEN MARGARET: As a reporter, his beat was . . .

RIVERBOY: Ironically!

ELLEN MARGARET: . . . his beat was police headquarters. On Mulberry Street. That's how he got to know all of us.

JIMMY: Joker goes around with a camera in the middle of the night . . . He better watch himself, that's all!

ELLEN MARGARET: Don't you do nothing stupid, Jimmy Dolan—don't you get in trouble now!

JIMMY: He busts into people's rooms and sets off a great flash. He set light already to two tenements that way, one of 'em full of blind people. He's a right shite.

ELLEN MARGARET: He put the fires out, Jimmy Dolan, he didn't just let them burn.

JIMMY: Even so.

ELLEN MARGARET: You're going to do something stupid, I can see it writ all over your stupid face.

RIVERBOY: Jacob Riis and the book he got published in 1890, titled *How the Other Half Lives* . . .

JIMMY: You hear that!? Do you hear that?!

RIVERBOY: . . . *How the Other Half Lives,* will do more to bring about tenement reform . . .

JIMMY: I ain't the other half of nothin'!

RIVERBOY: . . . tenement reform than any other social reformer or movement of the era.

JIMMY: He's a shite!

ELLEN MARGARET: And . . . he's a bit of a shite. You never met a more big-oted man.

RIVERBOY: Even for the era, which was, let's face it . . .

ISADORE: Read what he says about the Jews of Jewtown.

JIMMY: The Irish.

TERRY: The Irish.

RIVERBOY: The Italians.

LILY: He says the blacks are better-behaved than any of their European neigh-bors, but according to him, they have their comfort-loving, lazy ways all the same. The Chinese, he truly despises. "John Chinaman," he calls them.

TERRY: Honest—he hates the Chinese, really and truly hates them.

ELLEN MARGARET: I know, I know—but he hates the bad landlords worse! He's working to make all our lives better.

JIMMY: Oh, give over, Ellen Margaret.

ELLEN MARGARET: No one else is, Jimmy Dolan! Working himself to death, Mr. Riis is.

RIVERBOY: He'll not listen to his doctor, or slow down, and in 1914 his heart'll give out and he'll die.

JIMMY: *(To Riverboy.)* Is it you seeing the future again? Stop it, will you! It's annoying!

ELLEN MARGARET: *(To audience.)* So it's complicated.

JIMMY: 1914? That's over twenty years from now, that Danish chump gets to live all that time? He ain't exactly working himself to death, Ellen Margaret, and some of us here are, so *can* that talk, will you?

ELLEN MARGARET: Mr. Riis is angry about how we're treated, how we live. He's angry about landlords making a profit from our suffering, stuffin' ten, twelve, fifteen people into two small rooms, building buildings on top of buildings, crammin' them in with no light, no air, no nothin'. Mr. Riis makes people pay attention with his pictures.

RIVERBOY: And some of us, some of us right here in Mullen's Alley, will sur-vive, honest to God, only because of him.

JIMMY: *(To Riverboy.)* Is it the future again you're seeing? What did I just tell you!

(A great flash of light, revealing the kids posed in Mullen's Alley.)

TERRY: *(To audience.)* This is a play about a photograph.

ELLEN MARGARET: Ain't he the dearest thing? This is *not* a play about a photograph.

REBECCAH: This play is about some people, which are us, in a photograph that became famous.

ISADORE: This play is about the people, Rebeccah, forget the photograph.

ELLEN MARGARET: You think anybody remembers us?! The photograph is all anybody remembers, nobody remembers the people.

LILY: Forget the people, it's all about the photograph.

JIMMY: The photograph is a lie!

(Big flash.)

TERRY: *(To audience.)* This is a play about a lie.

JIMMY: Terry Dolan, I'm telling you, a play is just another kind of lie.

TERRY: So it's a lie about a lie, Jimmy?

ISADORE: Maybe it's not a play, maybe it's a photographic album, like mother and father brought from the Old Country.

REBECCAH: I think it is *like* a photographic album, Isadore, but it is a play.

TERRY: I think a play is like a photograph, it's a lie that's got people in it, and a frame around it.

RIVERBOY: This is a play about a photograph which is like a play. Some people, a frame, and a great big flash!

(A great flash.)

ELLEN MARGARET: He called it "Mullen's Alley."

JIMMY: Mullen's Alley, that's us.

RIVERBOY: We got Irish, Italians, Dutch, Bohemians, a few Chinese, some Jews and one actual honest-to-God family of Iroquois Indians. We, all of us live here.

LILY: *(To audience.)* This is Riverboy. He sees the future.

JIMMY: He smells of fish is what he does.

LILY: Shut up, I love him.

JIMMY: Even so, he smells of fish.

LILY: Stuff it!

JIMMY: I wish he smelt like the fish of the future, maybe they'd be fresher and he wouldn't smell so bad.

RIVERBOY: *(To audience.)* Here in Mullen's Alley . . .

JIMMY: . . . Lily, it's a joke!

RIVERBOY: *(To audience.)* We've had death by cholera, several. Starvation, two that I know of. Drowning, yes, East River, the floaters get snagged near Corlear's Hook, that bend in the river where suddenly you can see the Liberty Statue in all her green glory?

LILY: "Liberty Enlightening the Masses!"

REBECCAH: The Lady with the Fork!

ISADORE: What?

OTHERS: What?

REBECCAH: The Statue of Liberty, the Lady with the Fork.

ISADORE: It's a torch, Rebeccah, it's the Lady with the Torch.

REBECCAH: How embarrassing. I always thought it was a fork.

RIVERBOY: *(To audience.)* Anyway. Corlear's Hook. I'll walk you down there if you like, I'm there all the time. Here in Mullen's Alley we got death by consumption, who knows how many, by smallpox, lots. Infanticide, twice, at least, suicide by hanging, six, suicide by poison, two. Suicide by off-the-building? One glorious ma went sailing while her nine-year-old boy and his older brother was runnin' up the stairs to stop her, too late, chums, too late.

ELLEN MARGARET: Who was that, then, Riverboy?

RIVERBOY: It ain't happened yet. The ma will be reeling laundry out over the airshaft, I guess she'll decide her linens look freer than she ever was, Whoosh, look at me, I'm a bird!

(There's a sudden, somber silence, the kids picturing the woman's flight.)

ELLEN MARGARET: *(To audience.)* Nobody knows Mullen's Alley

REBECCAH: Nobody knows Cherry Hill

TERRY: Nobody knows the Mulberry Bend

JIMMY: No one. And nobody will.

POLICEMAN'S WHISTLE, MAN'S VOICE: "Move along, there, you kids, move along!"

(Kids scatter, lights dim, and then there's a great flash, revealing Isadore and Rebeccah Klein, seated in their tenement home, sewing like they've never done anything else but sew. They react to the flash—their eyes were probably already hurting from the close work they do six days a week—but it's also a little exciting to have one's photograph taken. They speak politely, a little formally. Their Yiddish accent isn't as pronounced as their parents', but it's there. Rebeccah looks to her brother, and he nods.)

ISADORE: Go ahead, Rebeccah, you may speak.

REBECCAH: My name is Rebeccah Klein. Little Beccah is something they call me, "klein Beccah Klein," a play on my name because Klein means small. And I am small, which makes the joke. My brother Isadore and me, we work for our father who makes knee-pants, knickerbockers they are called, a hundred and twenty dozen a week. We are two years apart, Isadore and me, him the elder. Nobody calls him anything but Isadore because my brother is a very serious boy and works hard.

ISADORE: My sister Rebeccah is a beautiful child, but too serious, she works too hard. One must work, of course, but still. I say to her, Rebeccah, you must play with the other children, you must breathe the air. There is not much time for play, but still—she is a child, after all.

REBECCAH: That's my mother, working there, my father is not here right now. And my sisters, two elder, working at the table by the window, and the small children . . . Well, they are here somewhere. That is the baby, you see, sleeping on top of the pile of pants? We make a little fence of finished pants around him, so he does not roll off from up there, he is my favorite after Isadore. I sleep beneath the table, on remnants. Very soft, they make a good bed. I am happy, do you see that with your camera? I am happy.

ISADORE: We are going places in the New World, we are rising. My father used to be a hand, but now he is a sweater himself, and employs three men beside us children and mother. One of the hands is a lodger and lives here with us, so that makes nine of us at 17 Mullen's Court. For the knickerbockers, the manufacturer pays forty-five cents a dozen. The six machines we rent for $2 per month, and the landlord here takes $13. Bread is fifteen cents a day for the nine of us, and two quarts of milk each day at two to four cents a quart, depending on how old it is, and coffee, potatoes, pickles, and one pound of meat for the nine of us almost every day at twelve cents. Pickles are good when meat is short, they stop the children crying. We are on the rise. *(A confidential tone.)* My sister Rebeccah, her lungs . . . You can hear them in the night. I will work hard to give her more meat, so she will grow strong. See if I don't.
(Lights fade on everything but Isadore's face. He stares at the audience, the camera, intensely, his face gaunt, sepulchral, haunted and haunting.)
(Cross-fade to Riverboy and Lily, on a dock at the edge of the East River, the water reflecting on their faces.)

LILY: I hate my life. All I do is work. Sometimes I think I can't get through another day. I mean, if it's all suffering, what's the point?

RIVERBOY: Susan Sontag says that to suffer is one thing; to live with the photographed images of suffering is another, and that it don't necessarily strengthen your conscience or help you to be more compassionate.

LILY: *What?*

RIVERBOY: Susan Sontag says pictures can corrupt your conscience. Looking at pictures of suffering, again and again, can make the suffering seem less real.

LILY: Who is this? Susan what?

RIVERBOY: Sontag.

LILY: And she said all that?

RIVERBOY: She will. She'll write it in a book. She's very smart.

LILY: You like her?

RIVERBOY: Sure. For an essayist. Where are you going?

LILY: What do you care?

RIVERBOY: Lily!

LILY: Get Susan Sontag to keep you company!

RIVERBOY: Lily, wait! You can't be jealous of Susan Sontag, she ain't even born yet! Come on!

(Lily circles back to audience, losing Riverboy, who goes offstage. She stands alone at the edge of the river.)

LILY: For the morning crowd at Rosen's Diner,
from five to nine I clear the scraps and wash the dishes.
From nine to noon I stir the soup and make knishes
for the lunchtime mob who eat at Rosen's Diner.

I'm not a whiner.

But all the time I'm peeling spuds, or elbow-deep in greasy suds,
I'm thinking all that time about a young Italian boy,
knowing all too well that Mama's bound to say, "But he's a goy!"—
as the dinner hordes pour into Rosen's Diner.

The key is minor.

Yes, all the time I'm slicing lox, my heart is with him on the docks,
where Riverboy goes scavenging the jetties and the wharves.
While the smell of cooking cabbage seeps inside my very pores,
I know my Riverboy is on the river.
He makes me shiver.
For the nighttime pigs who rut in Rosen's Diner,
From five to nine I slam the forks and fling the dishes.
I lose my patience and my one and only wish is
For my own dear Riverboy, who smells like fishes . . .

That he'll carry me far away from Rosen's Diner . . .

As I slam the forks and fairly fling the dishes,
that's what my one and fondest only wish is.

Thank you for listening.

(Lily runs offstage.)

(And Jimmy Dolan drags his little brother, Terry, on by the scruff of his neck.)

JIMMY: What do you think you're a-doin', Terry Dolan? What do you mean by it?

TERRY: A fine way to treat your brother! Leave go!

JIMMY: I oughta squeeze you like a pimple!

TERRY: Jimmy, don't!

JIMMY: I will, then! One good squeeze and pop! What were you doin' there? Well?

TERRY: Nothin'.

JIMMY: Liar!

TERRY: Please, Jimmy, I was just watchin'.

JIMMY: I'll give you something to watch, you little wart. You keep away from those Baxter Street Dudes, you hear me?

TERRY: They put on shows, Jimmy, it's spectacular! Costumes, settings, just like the big playhouses on the Bowery.

JIMMY: Yeah, except they stole every bit of it! You keep clear of them, you hear me! That head boyo, he's a right shite. Baby-Faced Willie, I'll give him a face he won't soon forget.

TERRY: He's my friend!

(Jimmy slaps Terry's face. There's a silence.)

JIMMY: And I suppose your own brother ain't?

(Terry doesn't speak.)

JIMMY: I'm just lookin' out for you, kid.

(Silence.)

JIMMY: I couldn't believe it, seeing you come out of that dive.

(Silence.)

JIMMY: Somebody gives himself a moniker like that, "Baby-faced Willie," I mean, come on. He's a punk, Terry, nothing more than a punk.

TERRY: I'm looking out for meself.

JIMMY: I got a duty here.

TERRY: We're different, Jimmy—you and me.

JIMMY: Yeah—you're a pimple and I ain't.

TERRY: Mother was cryin'.

JIMMY: What else is new?

TERRY: She said she's breakin' her heart over you.

JIMMY: Yeah?

TERRY: If you can run all night with the Growler Gang, I don't know why I can't be in a show.

JIMMY: Oh, it's *in* a show you are now? Squeeze—pop!

TERRY: Don't tell Ma.

JIMMY: Ma? I'll tell Pa when he comes, he'll go and pitch you right out the window, and you know it.

TERRY: Pa? Stop talking about Pa, Jimmy. Pa's gone two weeks and more, he ain't coming home. *(A silence.)* I won't tell nobody about you runnin' with the Growlers.

JIMMY: What makes you think I'm running with . . .

TERRY: I'm lookin' out for meself.

JIMMY: Ah, you make me tired.

TERRY: I made a buck fifty last week.

JIMMY: You never did. Doin' what?

(Ellen Margaret comes on.)

ELLEN MARGARET: I want him dead.

JIMMY: Who's that then, Ellen Margaret.

ELLEN MARGARET: He took a picture of me sister. He had a dirty copper with him, the bastard.

JIMMY: Mr. Riis, is it? Change your tune, then? *(To Terry.)* Scram, you!

(Terry runs offstage.)

ELLEN MARGARET: He took her picture, and then the copper run her in, and for what? She wasn't doin' nothin'!

JIMMY: Your sister's always gettin' run in, Ellen Margaret.

ELLEN MARGARET: Is not!

JIMMY: Ellen Margaret, your sister's a whore.

(She slugs him.)

JIMMY: Well . . . ?

(She turns away from him.)

JIMMY: I'm sorry for that, Ellen Margaret. You know I wouldn't hurt you, not on purpose.

ELLEN MARGARET: She's my sister!

JIMMY: I know that.

ELLEN MARGARET: I think it's mostly lies anyway they're saying about her.

JIMMY: Me brother thinks it's with the Growler Gang I'm running, when I don't come home at night.

(Jimmy puts his arms around Ellen Margaret from behind.)

ELLEN MARGARET: And what if it ain't lies? What if it's true, every word? So what?

JIMMY: About Moira? You know it's the truth, Ellen Margaret, I'm sorry but she's not ever gonna get a lot of respect around here.

(She shakes him off.)

ELLEN MARGARET: What of it? I don't care what anyone says about her. She does well for herself. Look at her clothes, will you! She's plump, she eats, she's got food, she earns her bread. And not like our mother, one crust at a time and barely that, her eyes sinking dark into her head like she's a ghoul. Me sister's good looking, she walks straight up, she looks you in the eye. She don't care what they say about her. Respect? Our mother can't put clothes on her own back but she says Moira ain't respectable. Say Moira's name before our father, he'll kick you down the steps, right down, he'll thrash you. But she eats and we don't, she's got money and we got nothin', she sleeps late, in a bed, and our mother is starving, she'll be lucky if she ain't dead in a month. What do they mean when they talk about respect, is what I'd like to know. What are they talking about?

JIMMY: *You* know, Ellen Margaret. I hope you do.

ELLEN MARGARET: Matter of fact, I don't think I do. You tell me.

JIMMY: You're scaring me a little, Ellen Margaret.

ELLEN MARGARET: I want to hurt that bastard, that Jacob Riis fellow. Looking at us through that machine, like he's superior, like that camera makes him better than us and we no better than animals in a cage.

JIMMY: I care for you, Ellen Margaret. I love you.

(Suddenly turning on him in frustration and rage.)

ELLEN MARGARET: And what good is that ever gonna do me? What can you give me? A life like me mother's? You, a boot-black with not a penny in your pocket, always on the run from the coppers yourself! You got nothing! Nothing!

(Ellen Margaret goes, Jimmy watching her.)

A MAN'S VOICE: "HEY, YOU! MOVE ALONG, THERE, MOVE ALONG!"

(Jimmy goes offstage opposite.)

(Riverboy, carrying a lumpy, heavy sack, comes on with Isadore.)

RIVERBOY: It's all good stuff, top quality tools.

(Riverboy and Isadore look around furtively—they're in a narrow alley.)

ISADORE: Where did you get it all?

(Riverboy doesn't answer.)

ISADORE: Let me see.

(Riverboy sets down the sack and Isadore peers into it, both boys always keeping an eye out for the law.)

RIVERBOY: What did I tell you? Mr. Singer himself don't have better tools.

ISADORE: Probably because Mr. Singer himself used to own these.

RIVERBOY: You'll keep your machines in fine running order with 'em, believe me.

ISADORE: How much?

RIVERBOY: "How much?" Will you look at the merchandise first? See what you're getting, then ask how much!

ISADORE: How much?

RIVERBOY: Impossible.

ISADORE: I have seen you with your girl in the Mullen's Alley.

RIVERBOY: Yeah, I seen you, too, and your sister.

ISADORE: She's Jewish, your girl.

RIVERBOY: If you say so.

ISADORE: And you are not. You are an Italian, a Catholic boy.

RIVERBOY: Izzy, I don't know what the hell I am. I follow the river.

ISADORE: My name is Isadore. They say . . . They say there's something about you.

RIVERBOY: You don't wanna listen too much to what anybody says.

ISADORE: I know that, believe me—a Jew knows that. What is it about you?

RIVERBOY: Nothing. Do you want the tools or not, 'cause plenty others will.

ISADORE: There's rust here.

RIVERBOY: Izzy, there's rust everywhere, we're all of us gonna die!

ISADORE: How much?

RIVERBOY: You're worried about your little sister, I can see that. You're worried about her breathing. *(A silence.)* I'm sorry, it's something I do.

ISADORE: Is this a part of the play? Is this one of the photographs of Mr. Riis? Is this the photo album? Or is this something real?

RIVERBOY: *Real*, well, what's that, anyway?

(Rebeccah comes on.)

RIVERBOY: Two bucks.

ISADORE: One.

RIVERBOY: One fifty.

ISADORE: Done.

REBECCAH: Isadore?

ISADORE: Hush!

REBECCAH: You tell me to go out, you tell me to play with the others, but you never let me do it, or you hush me up when I do. *(To Riverboy.)* Hello, sir, I am Rebeccah Klein and this is my esteemed brother, Isadore, with whom you seem already to have made acquaintance. Are you selling him stolen goods?

(A great flash! Isadore grabs Rebeccah's hand and the bag of tools and runs offstage. Riverboy comes down toward us, pocketing his money. He sits on a dock, reflections from the river appearing in his face. Terry comes on and sits with him.)

TERRY: What is it you see when you look at the river? Why are you always here?

RIVERBOY: What do *you* see, kid?

TERRY: Ships. Masts. Smoke. Brooklyn.

RIVERBOY: Yeah?

TERRY: *(After a moment.)* It's like a prison. The river keeps us penned in. I feel trapped, you know?

RIVERBOY: Not me.

TERRY: Well, no, of course not you—you're Riverboy. It's river, river, river with you.

RIVERBOY: So what's your big thing?

TERRY: Getting out.

RIVERBOY: Getting out . . . Think you will?

(Terry doesn't answer.)

RIVERBOY: Sometimes I walk into the river.

TERRY: Sure, we all go swimming.

RIVERBOY: No. I walk around on the bottom, I breathe river water, I look around. Believe me?

(Terry shrugs.)

RIVERBOY: There's a whole world down there. Oyster beds so big you can't imagine. Miles of oysters. Millions of fishes, all kinds. Flat-fish, with both eyes on one side, skimming along the bottom. Great sturgeon. Cod. Whole meadows full of mussels. And wrecks, so many shipwrecked ships down there, Terry, lying where they sank, whole or cracked open, with broken masts, and splintered decks and riggings and the skeletons of thousands. A whole city of the dead down there. When they move with the tide, they clink and rattle, it's like a kind of music, and the eyes of the dead are always staring, whenever I visit, their eye-sockets follow me wherever I go, hungry for news of the world above. Tell us, they say, tell us about the sun. Tell us about houses and paving stones and dry land. Talk to us about coffee, and roast beef, and girls. Tell us.

TERRY: Why do you come back?

RIVERBOY: Well, a fellow's gotta make a living. And then there's Lily.

(Lily comes on, taking off a greasy apron.)

LILY: And then there's Lily.

TERRY: We're talking about the river.

LILY: Oh, what a surprise! What a complete and total shock! The river! Imagine that!

(She sits.)

LILY: Get me out of here.

(The three of them watch the river.)

LILY: *(Finally.)* Remember the poet fellow? Him with the great ratty beard? He must be an old man by now, or dead.

RIVERBOY: That Whitman fellow? He'll die sometime next week.

(Lily and Terry give Riverboy a look.)

RIVERBOY: I mean, maybe. Or not. Who knows?

TERRY: I remember him. The crazy old geezer? Used to stand in Five Points, didn't he, turnin' in circles, lookin' and grinnin'.

LILY: Sure, and he'd come through Mullen's Alley, great big hulk of a fellow, hands stuck in his pockets. One night in Rosen's Diner he had a growler-full of beer with his stew and didn't he stand up and start sayin' poetry, loud, and everybody stopped talkin' and listened to the old drunk.

RIVERBOY: *(Confidentially to Terry.)* This is why I don't stay down at the bottom.

LILY: "The free city! no slaves! no owners of slaves!
The beautiful city, the city of hurried and sparkling waters! the city of spires and masts!
The city nested in bays! my city!"
That's all I remember, it's probably all wrong.

RIVERBOY: This is why I come back.

LILY: Nearly five, I'm late.

TERRY: Nearly five? No. Really?

(Terry, in a panic, takes off running. Riverboy kisses Lily, she pushes him away and stands, putting on her apron again.)

RIVERBOY: You smell like cabbage.

LILY: Yeah, well you smell like fish, together we make a chowder.

(Riverboy kisses her. Isadore Klein appears, staring at Lily from a distance. Lily sees him, Riverboy doesn't.)

RIVERBOY: It's made in heaven, us.

LILY: Gotta get back to work.

RIVERBOY: I'll pick you up after?

LILY: I think Isadore Klein wants to court me.

RIVERBOY: *What?*

LILY: He follows me.

RIVERBOY: He better not, that's all.

LILY: I'm late.

(She goes, Riverboy follows her.)

RIVERBOY: He'll regret it if he does. Lily?

(They are off. Isadore stares after them. He realizes that Rebeccah is there, watching him.)

ISADORE: What are you doing here?

REBECCAH: What are you doing here?

(A guilty silence.)

REBECCAH: Mother sent me for butter.

ISADORE: I'll get the butter—you go on home.

REBECCAH: She sent me out to rest my eyes, the butter was a pretext only. Go!

(Reluctantly, Isadore goes.)

REBECCAH: *(To audience.)* And with the butter money, I bought a ticket to the Baxter Street Show. It was a daring and a wicked thing to do.

(Lights change. We hear hurdy gurdy music and Terry comes striding on, at age nine acting like a seasoned music hall trooper.)

TERRY: You know Mrs. Kelly? . . . *You* know Mrs. Kelly . . . Don't tell me you don't you know Mrs. Kelly! Her husband's that little fat man, always at the corner of the street in a greasy waistcoat, pickin' his teeth . . . Good grief, don't look so stupid, you *must* know Mrs. Kelly! . . . You *don't* know Mrs. Kelly? . . . Well of course, if you don't, you don't—but I thought you *did*, because I thought everybody knew Mrs. Kelly. Oh, what a woman—perhaps it's just as well you *don't* know her . . . In fact, I'm glad you don't know Mrs. Kelly, very glad, I'm elated, I rejoice for you, my friend, in your complete and total ignorance of Mrs. Kelly. . . . Why? Why? Because she's greedy, that's why. You think you know greedy women? You don't know greedy women. If you knew Mrs. Kelly you'd know a greedy woman! *Greedy?* I know for a fact—her little boy, the one who's got the sore eyes and the runny nose, he came over and he told me this himself—Mrs. Kelly had half a dozen oysters . . . and she ate them in front of the looking glass . . . to make them look a dozen. Now *that's* Mrs. Kelly!

(We hear raucous laughter and applause. Someone throws him a cane, and he sings to the tune of an Irish jig.)

TERRY: Oh, McGinty is dead
    And Mahony don't know it
    Mahony is dead
    And McGinty don't know it
    The two of them sleepin'
    In one single bed . . .
    And neither one knows that
    The other is dead!
    (Terry takes his bows. More laughter and applause.)
TERRY: Thank you, thank you, thank you, you've been a great audience!
    Except for you, and you, and especially you! You two were terrible, but
    you . . . were worse! Thank you!
    (Laughter, applause, and Terry runs off. Rebeccah catches him.)
REBECCAH: Hello.
TERRY: Hello. You live in Mullen's Court, don't you?
    (She nods.)
TERRY: You weren't in *there*, were you?
REBECCAH: I think you are wonderfully talented.
TERRY: You're just a kid, you shouldn't be going to places like that!
REBECCAH: I'm years older than you.
TERRY: Yeah, yeah. I'll walk you home, it ain't safe around here.
REBECCAH: Were you frightened when the man threw all those knives at you?
TERRY: These guys knew what they're doin'.
REBECCAH: I could hardly breathe.
TERRY: Yeah, it's quite an act.
REBECCAH: I took a seat in the first row of benches. I don't see very well.
TERRY: Oh, yeah, I remember—the Lady with the Fork.
    (They are offstage.)
    (Night begins to fall in Mullen's Alley.)
    (Jimmy runs on, carrying a large heavy object covered by a ratty old blan-
    ket. He stops beneath a tenement and whistles up at one of the windows.)
JIMMY: Hssst! Ellen Margaret! Hssst! Ellen Margaret, it's me, Jimmy! Will
    you not come out! Please!
    (Jimmy sets the heavy object down.)
JIMMY: Shite.
    (Riverboy appears.)
JIMMY: Ellen Margaret!
RIVERBOY: She ain't there, Jimmy Dolan.
JIMMY: So where is she?

RIVERBOY: How should I know?

JIMMY: He can tell the future, but he can't tell you anything a bit useful.

RIVERBOY: What's that you got?

JIMMY: It's for Ellen Margaret.

RIVERBOY: I didn't ask who it's for, I asked what is it?

(Isadore comes hurrying on, carrying a bolt of fabric.)

ISADORE: *(To Riverboy.)* What is it that you have stolen now?

RIVERBOY: It ain't mine, it's his.

ISADORE: What is it?

RIVERBOY: *(To Isadore.)* I'll tell you what *is* mine, Izzy—my girl is mine, Lily's mine, you got that?

ISADORE: My name is Isadore.

(Terry appears.)

TERRY: What's that then Jimmy?

JIMMY: Have you seen Ellen Margaret?

(Lily comes on.)

LILY: She ain't here.

JIMMY: If I thought she was here, would I be askin' you where is she?

LILY: What's that thing?

(Rebeccah comes on.)

REBECCAH: Isadore? Father's waiting. What's going on?

JIMMY: Oh, fine, now it's the whole building's got to know a fellow's business!

(Terry pulls the blanket off, revealing a massive 1880's camera. There is a collective gasp from the kids.)

JIMMY: Dammit, Terry!

(Jimmy hastily covers up the camera, looking around furtively.)

RIVERBOY: It's his camera.

TERRY: Aww, Jimmy . . .

JIMMY: *(To Terry.)* I oughta take you apart!

RIVERBOY: It's Mr. Riis' camera, you went and stole Mr. Riis' camera!

JIMMY: Shut up, you!

ISADORE: You'll go to prison for that.

JIMMY: Shut up, all of you!

(Ellen Margaret comes on, wearing a pretty shawl.)

REBECCAH: Jimmy Dolan's stolen Mr. Jacob Riis' camera.

JIMMY: Say, pipe down, will you? I'll tell her!

ELLEN MARGARET: What's going on then?

JIMMY: I took his camera, Ellen Margaret.

ELLEN MARGARET: What?

JIMMY: It was that smooth, I wish you coulda seen it. Mr. Riis was comin' along Hester with one of his goons, the goon carryin' the long pole-thing he puts it on, and Riis carryin' the camera, and they looked like they been up all night like they do, and I just took Tufty Biggs and pitched him under a cart-horse, it was brilliant.

LILY: Poor Tufty!—did he live?

JIMMY: Tufty'd do anything for me, it was fine with him.

LILY: And he's not bad injured?

JIMMY: That's not the point. Anyway, it's not you I'm tellin', is it? *(To Ellen Margaret.)* So Riis and the goon went and pulled Tufty out from under the horse and while they were doin' that . . .

(He points proudly to the blanket-covered object.)

JIMMY: I took the bastard's camera!

(He lifts a corner of the blanket, showing her the camera, and then covers it up again.)

ELLEN MARGARET: Why ever did you do that, Jimmy Dolan?

JIMMY: It's for you.

ELLEN MARGARET: What?

JIMMY: The camera.

ELLEN MARGARET: I don't want a camera.

JIMMY: I did it for you.

ELLEN MARGARET: I don't understand.

ISADORE: If you are caught, you will surely go to prison.

JIMMY: What do you know about it? Why don't you mind your own business!

ELLEN MARGARET: What do I want with a camera?

JIMMY: It's worth a lot! I can sell it, I'll give you all the money!

ELLEN MARGARET: Jimmy Dolan, I think you must be mad.

JIMMY: But . . . I thought you'd be happy.

ELLEN MARGARET: I think you're an idiot.

JIMMY: Don't . . . Please . . .

RIVERBOY: Did he see you, Jimmy? Did anybody see you?

ISADORE: On Hester Street? Only several hundred, I'd say.

JIMMY: Hey, clear out, all of you!

TERRY: You'll break our mother's heart, Jimmy.

JIMMY: You—scram!

(Terry runs from him.)

JIMMY: Can't a fellow talk to his girl in private? Clear out!

(Jimmy takes Ellen Margaret by the arm and pulls her downstage. The others stand, watching Jimmy and Ellen Margaret for what follows.)

JIMMY: You said I had nothin' to give you. You said I was worth nothin'.

ELLEN MARGARET: Did I? I was upset I guess.

JIMMY: Don't run away from me, Ellen Margaret, why do you run away from me? Where were you tonight, I went to the factory, they said you weren't there, and you weren't here . . . Why won't you look at me even? *(She evades him.)*

JIMMY: *(Meaning the shawl.)* Where did this come from then? Ellen Margaret?

LILY: It's silk.

REBECCAH: *(Awe.)* Silk . . .

ISADORE: Silk . . .

TERRY: Silk . . .

LILY: She got it given to her in Rosen's Diner.

JIMMY: *(Confused.)* In Rosen's Diner . . .

LILY: A man took her there.

(A great flash! Followed by a terrible silence. Ellen Margaret breaks out of it to appeal to audience.)

ELLEN MARGARET: *(To audience.)* Wait! If this is all about a picture, and whether pictures tell the truth or not, isn't this play just the same?

JIMMY: What man, Ellen Margaret?

TERRY: What play?

ELLEN MARGARET: *(Pointing at Lily.)* This girl there, this girl we're calling Lily, she thinks she sees someone she knows in a place, and someone else who she doesn't know, and she paints a picture of it with her words that makes everybody else see it a certain way which it wasn't! Don't you see?

JIMMY: What man?

ELLEN MARGARET: It could have been anybody! It could have been this girl's, this Ellen Margaret's uncle!

RIVERBOY: Sure, if Ellen Margaret had a living soul in her over-populated family who ever had the scratch to buy himself a cloth cap, never mind a shawl of silk for his niece.

LILY: Which she surely did not.

JIMMY: What man give you that shawl, Ellen Margaret—tell me!

ELLEN MARGARET: All right, I'm sorry, if that's what's being implied here, then I'm not sure I'm willing to play this part. Frankly.

REBECCAH: What's being implied here?

TERRY: Play what part?

ISADORE: Rebeccah, go inside.

LILY: That Ellen Margaret received a gift in exchange for improper favors.

TERRY: Favors?

ISADORE: *(To Rebeccah.)* Go!

(Rebeccah stands riveted.)

ELLEN MARGARET: And I'm not Ellen Margaret, remember, that's just a made-up name for a made-up girl, that's not who I am.

TERRY: *(Realizing.)* Ohhh. I don't even want to hear about things like this.

(Jimmy sinks down on his haunches, his head in his hands.)

ELLEN MARGARET: It's not necessarily true, any of it. Jimmy? It's a fiction. I mean, did Jacob Riis really have his camera stolen?

(Jimmy stands, picks up the camera, and heads offstage.)

ELLEN MARGARET: I mean, do we know that? Does history tell us? Jimmy?

(Jimmy does not look back. He goes off, the others look at Ellen Margaret and then turn and exit—all except Riverboy.)

ELLEN MARGARET: *(Appealing to him.)* I thought this was an exercise. "Jacob Augustus Riis, born Denmark, 1849, arrived New York City . . . " *(She trails off.)* I thought this was just a documentary . . .

RIVERBOY: Who are you talking to? You're being shunned, don't you understand?

(Ellen Margaret pulls the shawl around her like it's her last refuge and exits. Riverboy approaches us.)

RIVERBOY: The poet, Wallace Stevens, will walk these streets compulsively when he starts law school about a decade from now. And years from then he'll write a poem called "Thirteen Ways of Looking at a Blackbird." See, this is just a city version of that. Different ways of looking at what might seem to be the same blackbird.

(Riverboy watches Isadore enter, agitated, followed by Rebeccah.)

ISADORE: I don't believe it!

REBECCAH: Father says it cannot be avoided.

ISADORE: It is too much! We have no room for another lodger! Where is Father going to put him? Where are we to sleep, how are we to live?

REBECCAH: We managed last night.

ISADORE: You think so? You think we managed? Rebeccah? I think we did not!

REBECCAH: What choice did Father have? It's the competition, we are losing business to the competition.

ISADORE: Those stupid shiksas in the sticks!

REBECCAH: Isadore, don't . . .

ISADORE: Stupid farm girls, they think it's a game to sew knee-pants and sell them to the manufacturer for 30 cents a dozen! *Thirty cents*, Rebeccah! They don't care, it's nothing to them, just a little extra work at the end of the day—they furnish their wedding trousseau with the money they steal from us, with the bread they take out of our mouths, oh! life is wonderful on the farm! Meanwhile you lose the only bed you ever knew to the new lodger . . .

(Rebeccah is suddenly alarmed.)

REBECCAH: Isadore . . .

ISADORE: . . . Mama puts you under the stove to sleep, what kind of place is that for a young girl to sleep, under the stove? And you in your health? I heard your lungs all night . . .

REBECCAH: Isadore, look . . .

(Rebeccah takes a hanky from her apron and dabs Isadore's mouth and chin with it—it comes away bright red with blood.)

ISADORE: What?

REBECCAH: Blood . . .

ISADORE: What?

REBECCAH: You're spitting blood, Isadore. It's not my lungs, I'm fine. It's yours.

(Isadore takes the hanky and stares at it.)

REBECCAH: It's yours.

(Isadore drops the hanky on the pavement, stares at it.)

ISADORE: It's nothing.

(Rebeccah stoops to pick up the hanky.)

ISADORE: *Leave it! (After a moment.)* I must get back to work. I was wrong to question Father's judgment.

(Isadore goes offstage. Rebeccah picks up the hanky, folds it and tucks it back into her apron. She speaks to Riverboy as though she were in the middle of a longer conversation.)

REBECCAH: How long does he have?

RIVERBOY: Listen, this is interesting. Over a hundred years from now, in the twenty-first century, this neighborhood will be—guess what?—full of tenement buildings, the same ones, stuffed to overflowing with immigrants, working in tenement sweatshops just like your father's, just like today. A hundred years from now! There'll be millionaires living next door, of course, but still. The immigrants will be Chinese mainly, working from first light to late into the night for survival wages. And *they* will lose *their* work, not to the farm girls of Maine and Vermont, like you folks, but to the Chinese. In China. Ironically. They'll call it "outsourcing."

REBECCAH: How long does my brother have?

RIVERBOY: *(After a hesitation.)* He'll have a chance to do some good things. The labor union movement will be born right here, from these streets, and in the next year or so, Izzy will be a part of all that.

REBECCAH: His name is Isadore. I think it was watching my brother living his life that first made me want to write. I was devastated to see Jacob Riis' camera stolen. I wanted that picture he was making of us, I wanted it desperately, it was important. And then that lovely foolish boy stopped it all. So who would now tell my brother's story?

RIVERBOY: You will. You'll paint a picture.

REBECCAH: But learning my letters, learning to read, was a terrible difficulty, given my eyesight.

RIVERBOY: You'll paint a picture with a pen
of all the women, and all the men . . .

REBECCAH: I came to love this language which was so foreign to my family, this English.

RIVERBOY: You'll show the world the way we lived,
You'll show the lives that might have been . . .

REBECCAH: The world seemed a blur that only words could sharpen.

RIVERBOY: You'll paint a picture with a pen.

REBECCAH: I think it was because it was so hard for me to see
it gave me second sight.
I think it was because of what my brother meant to me
that I began to write.

I think it was because I was invisible to all
that vision came to me.
I think it was because I heard their hearts' imprisoned call
that I was finally free.
(She starts offstage.)

RIVERBOY: You're going to be given a gift.

REBECCAH: I have a gift.

RIVERBOY: No—I mean, another one. A different sort of gift.

REBECCAH: You smell so like the river.

RIVERBOY: I know.

REBECCAH: Are you a character in one of the stories I will write? Or am I a character in one of yours?

RIVERBOY: Maybe the two of us are living our lives in someone else's story, who knows? *(She nods and starts offstage.)* Terry Dolan ain't with the Baxter Street Dudes anymore, if that's where you're headed. He's been discovered. He's playing uptown now, on 14th Street. Tony Pastor's Theatre, all very classy, you don't want to miss the show, do you?

REBECCAH: *(She grins.)* Thank you.

(She runs offstage. Riverboy moves offstage in another direction.)

(Hurdy-gurdy music. A spotlight hits Terry Dolan, dressed in tights and doublet.)

TERRY: Let me not to the marriage of true minds
Admit impediments. Love is not love
Which alters when it alteration finds,
Or bends with the remover to remove.
O no! it is an ever-fixed mark
That looks on tempests and is never shaken;
It is the star to every wand'ring bark,
Whose worth's unknown, although his height be taken.
Love's not Time's fool, though rosy lips and cheeks
Within his bending sickle's compass come;
Love alters not with his brief hours and weeks
But bears it out even to the edge of doom.
    If this be error and upon me prov'd,
    I never writ, nor no man ever lov'd.

(He bows with a flourish and we hear applause from the audience. Then he goes into his signature finish . . .)

TERRY: *(Singing.)* Oh, McGinty is dead
And Mahony don't know it
Mahony is dead
And McGinty don't know it
The two of them sleepin'
In one single bed . . .
And neither one knows that
The other is dead!

(Terry takes his bows. Laughter and applause.)

TERRY: Thank you, thank you, thank you, you've been a great audience! Except for you, and you, and especially you! You two were terrible, but *you* . . . were much worse! Thank you!

(The spotlight switches off. Jimmy comes on, staring at Terry in his costume.)

TERRY: Jimmy, don't hit me!

JIMMY: Look at you!

TERRY: Don't hit!

JIMMY: I ain't gonna hit you, who do you think I am, anyways?

TERRY: My brother.

JIMMY: Am I? *(Jimmy walks around Terry, examining him.)*

TERRY: Where've you been? Ma's that worried, she's sad all the time, Jimmy.

JIMMY: Everybody liked your act.

TERRY: You were in there?

JIMMY: There ain't a law against it, I guess. You learned all them words, then?

TERRY: Yeah.

JIMMY: That's a lot of words.

TERRY: Yeah.

JIMMY: What the hell did they mean?

TERRY: Just some stuff about love. Where've you been, then, Jimmy? You don't look so good.

JIMMY: Yeah, I got that it was about love, I ain't completely stupid, you know.

TERRY: Of course you aren't, ain't.

JIMMY: So what did it mean then?

TERRY: Aw, Jimmy . . .

JIMMY: Go on, what?

TERRY: Only that, you know, real love is steady, it don't go away, it stays.

JIMMY: Yeah, I see. So it was a load of crap.

(Ellen Margaret appears. Terry sees her, Jimmy does not.)

TERRY: Unless. Unless the man who wrote it's sayin' this is what love should be, not what it is. Unless he wrote it 'cause he had his heart broke by love.

ELLEN MARGARET: Jimmy.

(Jimmy, startled, starts to walk offstage.)

ELLEN MARGARET: Jimmy, please . . .

TERRY: Go and talk to her, Jimmy.

(Jimmy smacks Terry.)

TERRY: Don't hit, I said!

JIMMY: I never hit nobody.

(Terry runs off.)

JIMMY: Hey, come back here!

ELLEN MARGARET: You don't have to be afraid to be with me alone, then, Jimmy. You didn't used to be.

JIMMY: I ain't afraid of nothin'.

ELLEN MARGARET: I was forgettin'. You don't look so good.

JIMMY: Yeah, I heard.

ELLEN MARGARET: Did the coppers rough you up, Jimmy?

JIMMY: Who cares if they did? They got nothin' on me, they'll never find it.

ELLEN MARGARET: The camera is it?

JIMMY: What do you care?

ELLEN MARGARET: It wasn't the way they painted it, Jimmy.

JIMMY: What's that then?

ELLEN MARGARET: The shawl, then.

JIMMY: Easy to say.

ELLEN MARGARET: It wasn't, I swear it.

JIMMY: Yeah?

ELLEN MARGARET: The shawl or how I come by it. They got it all wrong, Jimmy.

JIMMY: All of it?

ELLEN MARGARET: Every bit. Every bit.

(Jimmy takes this in.)

JIMMY: Oh, God, Ellen Margaret. Look at me, I'm a fool. I get it wrong, always, me whole life. No matter what I do, it'll be all wrong! I don't know what it is. Things are just, I don't know, too much for me or somethin'. Here I went and lifted that man's camera, I thought it would please ya, now why did I think that? You called me a idiot . . . .

ELLEN MARGARET: Jimmy . . .

JIMMY: . . . and you were right to do it! I am a idiot, a fool, look at me, gettin' it wrong always. Accusin' you of bein' a . . . Oh, God, Ellen Margaret, how can you bear to look at me, I know I can't!

ELLEN MARGARET: It's all right, then, Jimmy.

JIMMY: It wasn't some man give you that shawl after all, God, what a fool.

ELLEN MARGARET: Just an old fella, Jimmy, a poor old man.

JIMMY: What?

ELLEN MARGARET: It was just a sad old man who give it me, I didn't do nothin' for it, he just wanted company . . .

JIMMY: That's what it was, was it.

ELLEN MARGARET: Just someone to sup with, that's all, just a lonely old codger wantin' someone to talk to while he ate his supper.

JIMMY: *(Finally.)* Whore.

ELLEN MARGARET: What?!

JIMMY: I wisht I never clapped eyes on you.

(Jimmy goes offstage.)

ELLEN MARGARET: Jimmy? Jimmy!

(Ellen Margaret goes offstage, opposite.)
(Lily comes on with Isadore. Lily carries her apron.)

LILY: I think it's interesting that your breaks from work always happen at the same time as my breaks from the diner.

ISADORE: Yes, it is a coincidence.

LILY: It makes me wonder if you can see the back door of Rosen's Diner from where you work.

ISADORE: Your parents make overcoats, yes?

LILY: Yes.

ISADORE: That is a great skill. A well-made overcoat can bring a good price.

LILY: Yes.

ISADORE: Not like knee-pants.

LILY: No?

ISADORE: No. Shall we sit? Do you have time?

(Reflections of water on their faces.)

LILY: On the pier? I don't know . . .

ISADORE: I thought you liked to sit here.

LILY: Isadore, are you courting me?

ISADORE: Yes.

LILY: I see.

ISADORE: I don't have much time. For courting, I mean. I can't afford to leave work very much. Shall we sit?

(Lily sits, Isadore sits beside her.)

ISADORE: If you could do anything, what would you do?

LILY: Oh. I don't know. What a strange question, I'll have to think. My sister married a man who moved her uptown and then he moved her all the way to California. He's a dentist and a dentist can do such things, evidently. California, when I think of it, it seems like the other side of the Moon. That's how much I know about it. She writes letters, she describes it, but it's not like a picture, I can't see it. I can't picture it. Anyway, something like that might be nice. To live on the other side of the Moon. What would you do if you could do anything?

ISADORE: Marry you and merge your father's business with my father's and manufacture overcoats instead of knee-pants.

LILY: *(Finally.)* I guess you're not the romantic sort, are you Isadore?

ISADORE: And have lots of children by you, I want lots and lots of children.

LILY: Well. I don't know how a girl could say no to all that.

ISADORE: You mean, I have your permission to speak to your father, you will marry me?

LILY: No. I'm sorry, no, I won't. But thank you.
(She stands.)

ISADORE: He has no occupation, that Italian boy.

LILY: Not really, no.

ISADORE: He smells like fish.

LILY: Yes.

ISADORE: He is a goyim.

LILY: Yes, I know.

ISADORE: He is not your religion.

LILY: Izzy, I'm afraid that might be just exactly what he is. My religion.
(She puts out her hand to shake his—he doesn't take it.)

ISADORE: My name is Isadore.

LILY: Isadore.

ISADORE: That might be blasphemous, what you just said. But I do not condemn you. I just wish it was me you said it of. And that, I *know*, is blasphemy.
(He finally takes her hand.)
Lily. Good-bye.
(He turns and goes, leaving Lily. She puts her apron on. A great flash! She looks into the camera, blinking and startled.)

LILY: *(To audience.)* Get out of here! That was private! I heard you lost your damn camera, and I rejoiced to hear it, I heard it was stolen, but that doesn't stop you, does it? You just get yourself another!
(She turns to leave but Rebeccah runs on and stops her. Rebeccah is very excited—she wears spectacles.)

REBECCAH: Wait! Lily, wait!

LILY: *(Still to the camera.)* Susan Sontag says that taking a person's picture is a form of aggression. That's what my Riverboy says she says anyway. She says it's like . . . interfering with a person. Nasty. She says it's a soft form of murder.

REBECCAH: Lily, let me see you!

LILY: What?

REBECCAH: You're beautiful, I knew you must be, but now I can see it!

LILY: You're wearing glasses.

REBECCAH: Yes, he gave them to me! Terry Dolan! He took me to the Children's Aid Society and a man there put so very many glasses on my face and then, all of a sudden, I could see—I can see, Lily! And the charge was two dollars and Terry Dolan paid it right then and there! I've been all over, looking. You know the great tree on Mott Street, near the church?

(Riverboy comes on.)

RIVERBOY: *(To Lily.)* She hadn't ever seen leaves before—she'd heard the word, but didn't know what it meant.

REBECCAH: I've been living my life seeing only a blur of green. But thousands and thousands of leaves, each leaf sharp and clear and different from every other? This I did not know! And grass is not a carpet painted one color only, grass is blades, there in St. Patrick's churchyard, among the graves, millions of little green soldiers, waving at me, Hello, klein Beccah! Lily, I taught myself to read with the books this close to my face, but now I can walk along the Mulberry Bend and read the signs from where I stand, thousands of words, everywhere I look!

(Rebeccah moves off, looking at all she can see.)

(Reading the signs as she leaves.) "Dutch's Dry Goods." "Hammerstein's Stables." "Rosen's Diner." "Klein and Company, Knickerbockers," I never was so proud!

(She is gone.)

LILY: Riverboy?

RIVERBOY: Lily?

LILY: What would you do if you could do anything?

RIVERBOY: I'd take you and move to the bottom of the harbor
and live underwater with you for the rest of time.

LILY: No, I'm serious, I meant it.

RIVERBOY: So do I. I'd make a house for us of the old Commodore Vanderbilt, the ferry that went down in the nor'easter of '79, all hands lost.

LILY: Please, Riverboy—just for once, think about real life, think about here and now and me . . .

RIVERBOY: It's all brass inside, Lily, and red velvet and mahogany, oh my Lord, it's a beautiful boat. You'd live like a queen, Lily, like an empress of the sea, you'd love it there.

(There's a silence.)

LILY: *(Finally.)* No I wouldn't. No I wouldn't. Neither would you. 'Cause people can't live underwater, Riverboy, people die underwater. What a terrible dream, what an awful thing to hope for. Who are you, anyway? What kind of a name is that, "Riverboy"?

RIVERBOY: I don't know, it's just a name.

LILY: No, it's not. It's not a name. Riverboy is not a name.

RIVERBOY: Lily, what's wrong?

LILY: Don't touch! This is hard enough without . . . Listen, we live in Mullen's Alley, you and me. You can't live on poetry there, you'll starve.

RIVERBOY: I don't understand.

LILY: Obviously. I'm just afraid you won't ever understand. Good-bye.

RIVERBOY: Good-bye? That doesn't make sense.

LILY: How dare you talk about sense!

RIVERBOY: Is it Isadore? Has that bastard been after you, is that's what's wrong here? 'Cause I'll kill him!

LILY: You leave him alone! That poor boy'll be dead in a year, you said so yourself! You just leave him be! It's not him anyway.

RIVERBOY: Then what . . . ?

LILY: It's you, love.

(She touches his face, then tears herself away and runs offstage. Riverboy goes to the end of the pier and looks out.)

(Terry runs on, carrying a piece of paper.)

TERRY: Riverboy! Where's Jimmy? Have you seen Jimmy?

(Riverboy shakes his head "no." Terry looks around frantically.)

TERRY: *(Shouting.)* Jimmy!

RIVERBOY: He ain't here.

(Rebeccah comes on, looking at the world hungrily.)

TERRY: Rebeccah . . .

REBECCAH: It's all because of you! Everything's changed because of you!

(She throws her arms around Terry's neck, then quickly disengages, deeply embarrassed.)

REBECCAH: Forgive me, I'm so sorry.

TERRY: A man came to the stage door and left this for me—he said it was from my ma.

(He gives Rebeccah the paper and she holds it near and far until she can read it through her new glasses.)

TERRY: I'm scared Rebeccah.

REBECCAH: She just says she loves you.

TERRY: Yeah, I'm really scared.

REBECCAH: You must go to her.

(Terry takes back the note and starts to move away.)

TERRY: *(Shouting.)* Jimmy! Jimmy Dolan!

RIVERBOY: *(To audience.)* They won't be in time, she's already on the roof.

REBECCAH: It's her? It's Terry Dolan's mother? The woman on the roof?

(Terry runs to his building and up the first flight of stairs, turns the

corner at the landing and shouts. (e.g., he runs upstage with short, climb-ing-steps, rounds the corner and pauses.)

TERRY: Ma, I'm coming!

(Terry runs flat along the corridor beside the stairs, turns the corner and runs up the second flight of stairs.)

TERRY: Ma!

(Ellen Margaret appears.)

ELLEN MARGARET: What is it then?

(Terry turns the corner and sprints along the corridor, turns that corner and starts up the next flight of stairs. Lily enters.)

LILY: What's going on.

(Jimmy Dolan runs on.)

REBECCAH: It's your mother, go, go, go!

JIMMY: *What?*

RIVERBOY: To the roof, Jimmy—I'm sorry, but there it is.

(Jimmy takes off running, chasing Terry in oblong circuits, making sharp corners, while the others watch.)

RIVERBOY: *(To audience.)* There's no light in the staircase, of course, after the first floor it's pitch black, day and night. There's a drunk passed out on the third-floor landing, and the shoemaker's got his stand and all his tools on the fourth-floor corridor, all that will slow them down.

(Terry pushes through out onto the roof.)

RIVERBOY: Terry will reach the top floor first, he'll push through the door and run out onto the roof, and there his mother will be, staring off over the parapet, staring at the flapping sheets she's just reeled out, surrounded by all the washing she does, for ten or twelve or I don't know how many families.

TERRY: Ma!

RIVERBOY: And then she gets an idea, or she had it already, or forever, I don't claim to know. I don't know if she hears her boy or not.

TERRY: Ma!

RIVERBOY: Whether or no, into the crisp chill air of this autumn evening, the weedy smell of the river penetrating the soot and the smoke, Mrs. Dolan takes flight.

(Jimmy runs out onto the roof.)

JIMMY: Ma!

RIVERBOY: Takes flight.

ELLEN MARGARET: Oh dear God . . .

RIVERBOY: Takes flight.

(There is a great flash!)

(Jimmy sinks to his knees, Ellen Margaret walks directly to him and folds him into her arms, where he silently sobs. All the others of Mullen's Alley are out watching this by now.)

(Terry Dolan does not move. He stands alone, breathing the rooftop air as darkness begins to fall, and the lights of the city wink on. A spotlight hits him, and suddenly he's all we see.)

TERRY: *(Singing.)* McGinty is dead and Mahony don't know it

Mahony is dead and McGinty don't know it

The two of them sleepin' in one single bed . . .

And neither one knows that their mother is dead . . .

(Terry realizes what he's just sung and covers his face. Spotlight off. A dusky light on Mullen's Alley.)

RIVERBOY: *(To audience.)* Nobody ever found Mr. Riis' camera, and the police never charged Jimmy Dolan with the theft. That's not to say that he spent no time in jail in the years to come, by no means. I think the best moments of his life, and there were not many, were those he and Ellen Margaret spent together.

ELLEN MARGARET: *(Gently caressing Jimmy.)* Don't you listen to him, then, what does he know? There were plenty good times, weren't there, Jimmy Dolan, off and on.

RIVERBOY: Lily?

LILY: Yes, Riverboy?

RIVERBOY: I was walking the bottom of the East River, just below the Brooklyn Bridge once, years later, and there it was: Jacob Riis' camera, locked in a skeleton's embrace—Believe me?

LILY: No.

RIVERBOY: You went and married a dentist, how could you!

LILY: An optometrist.

RIVERBOY: Well, I'll bet he couldn't see like me.

LILY: No, Riverboy, he couldn't. No one could, in the whole wide world.

RIVERBOY: *(To audience.)* Isadore Klein you all know about . . .

ISADORE: What? Know what?

RIVERBOY: . . . and yes, Rebeccah his sister, became a published writer, making stories of people living their lives on the Lower East Side.

REBECCAH: Most out of print and forgotten, but still . . .

ISADORE: Everybody knows what about me?

REBECCAH: *(Hugging Isadore.)* You were the one who introduced me to Emma Goldman . . .

RIVERBOY: *(To audience.)* The radical! The anarchist!

ISADORE: "Ask for work. If they give you no work, ask for
bread. If they give you no work or bread—take
bread!"

REBECCAH: Emma was a little wild.

ISADORE: She was a great woman, truly.

RIVERBOY: You gave her the title of her famous memoir.

REBECCAH: *Living My Life.*

RIVERBOY: And Terry Dolan, well.

ELLEN MARGARET: He became a movie star, didn't he, my sort-of brother-
in-law.

REBECCAH: In the earliest days of the movies, when it was all here in New
York—Vitagraph Studios! James Stuart Blackton himself discovered him!

ELLEN MARGARET: He's the little boy in *Burglar on the Roof!*

REBECCAH: And Tiny Tim

ELLEN MARGARET: He became that rich, you couldn't believe it.

LILY: Especially after he moved to the other side of the Moon.

ELLEN MARGARET: He was always slippin' us money when he came to town.
But Jimmy didn't talk to his brother, or hardly at all, ever again—he
blamed himself for the mother.

JIMMY: She broke her heart over me, look what I did to her . . .

ELLEN MARGARET: It wasn't you, Jimmy, love, it was herself.

LILY: It was Mullen's Alley.

REBECCAH: It was Mullen's Alley.

RIVERBOY: Nobody knows Mullen's Alley—

LILY: Nobody knows Cherry Hill—

ISADORE: Nobody knows the Mulberry Bend—

JIMMY: No one! And nobody will!

RIVERBOY: No, Jimmy, she'll paint a picture with a pen
of all the women, and all the men . . .

ISADORE: She'll show the world the way we lived,
She'll show the lives that might have been . . .

REBECCAH: I'll make a picture with a pen.

ELLEN MARGARET: You make a picture with a pen!
You tell the world, and maybe then
they'll see that we deserve to live,
deserve to grow, deserve to win . . .

RIVERBOY: She'll make a picture with a pen.

TERRY: To see the world through others' eyes,
    to see this life and realize
    the value of a single breath—
    to catch it quick before it dies . . .
RIVERBOY: To see the world through others' eyes,
    We'll paint a picture with a pen.
    *(Hurdy-gurdy music. The kids by now are arranged in Mullen's Alley as
    they were for the first photo taken, staring out at the camera.)*
    (There's a great flash! Terry steps forward . . .)
TERRY: *(Somber.)* Thank you. You've been a great audience. Except for
    you . . . And you . . . And especially you.
    (Lights out.)

END OF PLAY

Copies

by Brad Slaight

PLAYWRIGHT'S BIOGRAPHY

Brad Slaight (playwright) has been a contributing writer and producer for many television shows, including: "The Sunday Comics" (FOX); "Comic Strip Live" (FOX); "Into The Night" (ABC); "Evening at the Improv" (A&E); "Haywire!" (FOX); "The Tonight Show"(NBC); "Just the Ten Of Us" (ABC); "Fact or Fiction" (MTV). Brad wrote special comedy material for a National Lampoon CD-ROM computer program and helped create a groundbreaking interactive television network for U.S. West and Time Warner. As a playwright, Brad has written many stage plays (published by Baker's Plays, Samuel French, and Smith and Kraus) that have received hundreds of productions in the United States and all over the world: *Class Action, Second Class, Sightings, High Tide, The Road Taken, L.A. River Anthology, Dancing by Myself, Middle Class,* and many others. Brad is also a professional actor and has appeared in numerous TV shows and films.

FROM THE PLAYWRIGHT

Did you have an imaginary friend when you were a kid? You know, someone who never argued with you, would listen to your deepest secrets, and always took your side when it came to fighting your enemies? They were almost a real part of you. As you grew older, the need for your imaginary friend was replaced by real friends who you shared your life with and who stuck with you through thick and thin . . . well, thin anyway. But a part of you disappeared with your childhood and when it did you were pretty much on your own.

About a year ago, I was reading an article on cloning and started to think about the possibilities the future might hold if they perfected it for commercial purposes. Would I want another Brad running around? Brad Pitt, maybe, but another Brad Slaight? God knows this one has a lot of flaws, what would a copy of me be like? If it were anywhere near the quality of the copies I get at the local copy store it wouldn't even be as good as the Brad that I am. Scary thought. Also, would I want the clone to be a baby? Surely if they had the technology to clone me they could accelerate the copy to be at an age that would be more beneficial to me. You know, someone I could have do the things I don't want to, like take my driver's test, go on blind dates in my place, and show up at family reunions so I didn't have to pretend to like my aunt's runny lime green Jell-O with the mystery vegetables in it.

The setting for *Copies* takes place at an orientation camp for new teenage clones. They are sent to "Camp I.M.U" fresh from the lab to make a transition into the world of the "Originals" who have ordered them made. The newest *Copy* (a word they prefer to *clone*) to arrive is a very bright and positive teenager named Michael who soon realizes what the other copies in his cottage have known for awhile—that their stay at the camp is much longer than they had thought. Michael befriends a rebellious Copy named Melissa who does not get along with her Original and refuses to change her attitude in order to please her. She informs Michael, and the other Copies, that she is going to escape from the camp and fight for what she calls "Copy Rights."

Obviously this play is based on something that may or may not happen in the future. It does present an interesting dilemma though: Would our clones have their own personalities, or would they have ours? Would we treat them as equals, or just lackeys to do our bidding? Would we ever consider using them as a living-spare-parts factory in case one of our organs blew out? Someday we may have the chance to get those questions answered. For now, we'll just have to wonder. And if we really need someone to answer those questions for us, we can always ask our imaginary friends.

ORIGINAL PRODUCTION
Copies was developed in a workshop at the Young Conservatory in 2005.

SETTING
"Camp I.M.U." (Identical Memory Units)—an orientation camp for teenage clones.
If you want an elaborate set then go right ahead and build one, but the stage really doesn't need more than simple platforms and cubes to accommodate various settings.

TIME
The not-too-distant future.

CHARACTERS
MICHAEL/ALLEN, a brand-new teenage Copy (clone)
WENDY/MERRIS, female Copy, eats a lot
ZOOM/WARNER, not the brightest Copy in the cottage
BETTY/PETTY, a redesigned Copy
SANDRA/STEVENSON, a nice Copy who hopes for the best
MELISSA/PETROVICH, a Copy with an attitude and a mission
COUNSELOR SUE, an Original in charge of Cottage #4
AMY, an Original who comes to visit

COPIES

ACT I
SCENE ONE

Michael/Allen, a sixteen-year-old newly made clone, stands in an isolated pool of light. He wears a bright colored industrial one-piece jumpsuit. Examines himself for a moment, as if for the first time. He looks at his hands and moves his fingers, enjoying the simplicity of being able to do that.

MICHAEL/ALLEN: The thing I remember the most is how "Me" just happened. Like somebody turning on a switch. The upload was so fast, so intense that I felt as if I was about to explode. Billions of images coming at me in a nanosecond, swirling around in my mind and then planting themselves firmly in the fresh folds of my brain. A virtual and limitless eruption of people, places, events, and immediate memories that now belonged to me. All of a sudden I was alive. Fully aware. And my first ever thought was "how lucky I am." Even luckier than my Original who took sixteen years to get to where I am from the very beginning. What a wonderful world I've been brought into . . . what a perfectly wonderful world!

SCENE TWO

CAMP I.M.U.: Cottage #4—Main Area. Lights up on four teenage clones ranging in age from thirteen to seventeen: Wendy/Merris, Zoom/Warner, Betty/Petty, and Sandra/Stevenson. Wendy and Betty watch as Zoom taps on the floor with the butt-end of a broom. Sandra stands at the entrance keeping watch.

WENDY: That was a G.
ZOOM: What?
WENDY: You just spelled G-O-O-D instead of F-O-O-D.
ZOOM: No I didn't.
WENDY: You tapped seven times instead of six. Now she thinks we had "bad good" instead of "bad food."

BETTY: It wasn't too good it tasted like wood.

ZOOM: She'll know what I mean.

WENDY: Tell her you made a mistake.

ZOOM: Not worth it. Gimmee the next message?

BETTY: Mine would do fine.

(Betty hands a note to Zoom. He starts tapping on the floor.)

ZOOM: A . . . *(Taps once.)* . . . R . . . *(Shoots a look to Betty; then taps eighteen times.)* . . . Come on, Betty, I thought I told you to lay off usin' so many letters at the end of the alphabet. I'm not gonna tap this.

WENDY: Melissa wants to hear it. Just do it.

ZOOM: You do it.

(He hands the broom to Wendy.)

SANDRA: Someone's coming.

(Betty, Zoom, and Wendy break up and assume relaxing positions on the stage. Wendy begins to mock-sweep the floor with the broom. Counselor Sue enters, followed by Michael/Allen.)

COUNSELOR SUE: What's going on in here?

WENDY AND SANDRA AND ZOOM: Nothing.

COUNSELOR SUE: *(to Michael/Allen.)* This is Cottage #4. Your new home for . . . however long it takes.

(To others.)

This is Allen.

ZOOM: Wow, he must be special . . . he's already got a first name.

COUNSELOR SUE: Allen is the last name of his Original. But you knew that and just wanted to be a smart mouth.

(To Michael/Allen.)

You're rooming with Stevenson.

SANDRA: I'm Stevenson.

COUNSELOR SUE: First order of business for you is to read the rules. When you're done, read them again.

(Counselor Sue hands Michael/Allen a large book. She exits. They all take a moment to give Michael/Allen a scrutinizing look.)

MICHAEL: Hi . . . I'm Allen. It is a pleasure to meet you all.

(He extends his hand. Zoom, Wendy, and Betty cross over to Michael and ignore the hand. Instead they start to sniff him.)

ZOOM: Three days.

WENDY: No way, too strong. I'm saying a day. Maybe less.

ZOOM: Impossible.

WENDY: Not if he came from Mil-Tech.

BETTY: Mil-Tech? What the heck?

ZOOM: We never get a Mil-Techer.

(They all sniff some more.)

MICHAEL/ALLEN: What exactly . . .

WENDY: Sssh . . . don't say anything. You'll ruin the bet. This is the freshest I've ever smelled.

ZOOM: Three credits says he's at least two days.

WENDY: Covered. Sandra?

SANDRA: I'm not participating in this.

WENDY: Fine. Betty?

BETTY: A hundred days, is what I say.

SANDRA: Betty, that's just a dumb bet. You're going to lose.

WENDY: What do you care?

(To Michael/Allen.)

So what is it, Allen? How many days?

MICHAEL/ALLEN: How many days for what?

ZOOM: Since you were created, ya dumb Dolly.

MICHAEL/ALLEN: You mean my Point of Awareness?

WENDY: Whoa, someone got a special language upload.

ZOOM: One more thing his Original's gonna hate him for.

WENDY: So come on, Allen . . . when were you made? You know, in the lab.

MICHAEL/ALLEN: My official Point of Awareness was 22 hours and 7 minutes ago.

WENDY: Woo-hoo. I win.

ZOOM: Dumb luck.

WENDY: So you were made by Mil-Tech?

MICHAEL/ALLEN: Sun Labs.

BETTY: Son of a gun, he's made by Sun!

SANDRA: That's the trendy new place they were telling us about.

(They all move away from Michael/Allen and cross back over to the area they were at before. Wendy takes the broom and is about to resume tapping on the floor. Looks at her watch and decides not to.)

WENDY: We better stop.

ZOOM: We still got ten minutes.

WENDY: They might come early. Better safe than sorry. We don't want to get Melissa in more trouble than she's already in.

(Michael/Allen crosses over to them.)

MICHAEL/ALLEN: Who is Melissa?

SANDRA: Melissa is one of us.

MICHAEL/ALLEN: Does she live under the floor?

ZOOM: *(To Michael/Allen.)* Dumb Copy.

SANDRA: No, she lives here . . . but for right now she's in a room underneath us. So we tap messages to keep her company.

MICHAEL/ALLEN: You tap messages with a broom? That seems rather archaic.

SANDRA: That's exactly why it works.

> *(Zoom shakes his head and crosses to a platform and sits. Wendy retrieves a bag of tortilla chips, devours them.)*

SANDRA: *(To Michael/Allen.)* So what's your name?

ZOOM: Bet he doesn't have one.

MICHAEL/ALLEN: I have a name. It's Allen.

ZOOM: She don't mean your Original's name, fresh flesh.

BETTY: Fresh flesh!

SANDRA: What name do you call yourself?

MICHAEL/ALLEN: Allen.

WENDY: Yeah, he definitely just fell off the petri dish.

SANDRA: You need a first name.

MICHAEL/ALLEN: They said the Originals endow us with our first names.

SANDRA: That's something that will happen later. For right now why don't you pick a first name for yourself that we can call you.

MICHAEL/ALLEN: *(Thinks for a moment.)* Allen is fine.

WENDY: Allen Allen?

> *(Zoom crosses to him.)*

ZOOM: Well, it ain't fine with us. Pick a first name or I'll give you one. And you're not gonna like the one I give you.

SANDRA: Back off, Zoom . . . you had the same problem when you first got here.

WENDY: Yeah, and it took you three days to come up with "Zoom."

ZOOM: Two days.

MICHAEL/ALLEN: When did you arrive here?

ZOOM: Three months and twelve days ago.

BETTY: It hasn't been fun, but I've been here for one.

SANDRA: She means one "month." I've been here for five months three days.

WENDY: I'm ahead of her with six months thirteen days . . . and Melissa's got the record with ten months twenty-two days.

MICHAEL/ALLEN: That is a long period of time to spend at an orientation camp.

WENDY: Don't tell me you really bought their line about a quick turnaround. They only tell you that to get you here without melting down.

MICHAEL/ALLEN: They promised I'd meet my Original during the first week.

SANDRA: You might. But that doesn't mean you'll go home with him right away.

WENDY: I can't remember ever hearing about anybody going home after the first meeting.

SANDRA: I think there have been a few.

WENDY: Not in a long time.

SANDRA: Maybe he'll be different.

ZOOM: Yeah, right.

BETTY: Your first reception could make you an exception.

ZOOM: Hey, Sandra . . . you just had a meeting with your Original last week. Why don't you tell him how that went?

SANDRA: That has nothing to do with him.

WENDY: It'll give him an idea of what to expect.

MICHAEL/ALLEN: *(To Sandra.)* You met with your Original? That's exciting!

ZOOM: Yeah . . . for the third time.

SANDRA: My Original's parents are just being careful, that's all. It was their decision . . .

WENDY: Careful? They're paranoid. It's not like you're getting married to their little precious or anything.

SANDRA: But I will be living with them and spending a lot of time with Charlene so they just want to be sure we get along well.

BETTY: It would be wrong if they don't get along.

ZOOM: How you gonna get along? Charlene's evil.

SANDRA: No she's not.

WENDY: You're the one that told us that, Sandra.

SANDRA: I was angry. She's really not that bad.

WENDY: She treats you like a fool, expecting you to do tricks for her and keep her laughing. You know she's just going to abuse you if you ever do go home with her.

SANDRA: I think we can work this out. Next time I meet with her . . . we'll hit it off better and I'll be on my way out of here.

MICHAEL/ALLEN: I'm sure you will. You can make it work.

SANDRA: Thank you.

ZOOM: Ah, what does he know? Mr. Day-old-no-name.

BETTY: Wendy may face that sorrow, when she meets hers tomorrow.

ZOOM: Yeah, that's right . . . Wendy's gonna meet with her Original again tomorrow.

MICHAEL/ALLEN: That's exciting.

(Wendy crosses to the bag and grabs a packaged cupcake, opens it.)

ZOOM: It's not gonna happen.

SANDRA: Wendy's gained fifteen pounds since the last time.

WENDY: Seventeen as of this morning.

SANDRA: Congratulations!

MICHAEL/ALLEN: Is it good to have a significant weight gain?

SANDRA: For her it is. Wendy's Original has a bit of a weight problem.

WENDY: A bit? If Carla was any bigger, she'd moo.

(Zoom and Betty laugh.)

MICHAEL/ALLEN: Should you really be talking about your Original like that?

WENDY: She can't hear me.

SANDRA: We have a pact here, Allen. Everything said in Cottage #4, stays in Cottage #4. It's like Las Vegas . . . without all the gambling and fun stuff.

WENDY: And that means not telling the Counselors.

ZOOM: Yeah, so don't get any stupid ideas.

MICHAEL/ALLEN: If that is the protocol here I will not say anything. I just don't think we should speak so poorly about someone who is the very reason we exist.

ZOOM: She's just sayin' the truth. Her Original's been supersized!

BETTY: There once was a teen from the lab

Who was created and put on a slab

She woke up and said

I'd rather be dead

Then to have my Original's flab!

WENDY: Majestic, Betty!

ZOOM: Nice!

WENDY: That's the first time you've ever done a limerick.

(Betty enjoys all the new attention being paid her. Sandra crosses over to Michael.)

SANDRA: How about "Michael" for your name to use here? You look like a Michael.

WENDY: Let him pick his own name.

SANDRA: It's just a suggestion . . .

MICHAEL/ALLEN: I guess if I need another name, Michael is as good as any. After I join my Original, I'll let him change it to whatever he prefers.

SANDRA: OK, Michael. I'm Sandra . . . that's Wendy . . . Betty . . . Zoom . . . and there's one more who stays here . . . the one we were talking about . . . her name is Melissa.

WENDY: Melissa is the best.

ZOOM: Melissa's the number one.

BETTY: She's better than great, Melissa's always first-rate.

SANDRA: If she's so great then why does she spend more time in isolation than here?

MICHAEL: Isolation?

WENDY: That's right . . . the big "I." That's how they keep us in line here. One wrong move and you'll be down there, too. All alone.

SANDRA: You're scaring him, Wendy.

WENDY: He should be scared. Scared right out of his stem cells scared. So he'll do everything he can to avoid it.

BETTY: Isolation is no vacation.

MICHAEL: Clones should never be isolated. It can have a severe psychological effect on us. We're not designed to be alone.

(Zoom moves in on him in a threatening manner.)

ZOOM: Don't you ever use that word in here again!

MICHAEL: Isolated?

WENDY: The C to the L to the O to the N to the E word.

SANDRA: We don't call ourselves that, Michael. We prefer "Copy."

MICHAEL: Copy? That's a better word than clone?

ZOOM: I told you not to use that word.

(He makes a threatening move toward Michael. Sandra jumps between them.)

SANDRA: *(To Zoom.)* Give him some time to get used to it. He just got here. *(To Michael.)*
We think "Copy" is a better word. The Counselors never call us that, but when we're together we do.

WENDY: You won't find that in the Rulebook.

BETTY: Rules are for fools.

WENDY: Hey, I got an idea . . . after nutrition let's tell Melissa about Michael. That will give her plenty of time to think about how she wants to initiate him.

ZOOM: Oh, yeah . . . now that's somethin' to look forward to.

MICHAEL: *(Worried.)* What do you mean by "initiation"?

ZOOM: More than that . . . a Meliss-initiation!

(Wendy and Zoom share an evil laugh.)

WENDY: My favorite thing of all . . . a Meliss-initiation!

ZOOM: *(To Michael.)* She don't like Newlings like you.

MICHAEL: I'm sure once Melissa and I have an opportunity to talk we will become very good friends.

WENDY: Hold onto that dream.

(An electronic buzzer is heard.)

MICHAEL: What's that?

SANDRA: Midday nutrition time.

(Zoom, Wendy, and Betty start to exit. As they pass Michael . . .)

ZOOM: You just wait. When Melissa comes back here you're gonna be initiated. And there's nothin' you can do about it.

BETTY: The worst thing in the nation is a Meliss-initiation.

(Wendy and Zoom exit. Betty follows after them.)

SANDRA: Don't worry about it. Let's go eat.

(Sandra takes a concerned Michael by the arm and leads him offstage.)

SCENE THREE

Isolation Area. A light on Melissa. She stands in front of a bright red chair and is talking out loud as if giving a speech.

MELISSA: . . . but it takes all of you to make this thing work. By ourselves we're nothing, but together we are a loud voice that cannot be ignored. Together we will shake the very foundation of what they think is right, and what we know is wrong! And we . . .

(She stops in reaction to the sound of a deadbolt being undone; quickly sits down in the chair. Counselor Sue enters.)

COUNSELOR SUE: Who you talking to Petrovich?

MELISSA: No one.

COUNSELOR SUE: Sure sounded like someone. Maybe the solitude is getting to you. You melting down on us?

MELISSA: Not at all.

(Counselor Sue looks around the room.)

COUNSELOR SUE: They told me you had the viewing screen on just one time . . . and that was for only five minutes.

MELISSA: All that educational stuff they show gives me a headache. If they showed Wrestlemania I'd watch it.

COUNSELOR SUE: Your smart mouth isn't making things any better for you.

MELISSA: It's just an observation.

COUNSELOR SUE: Most clones prefer watching the screen to sitting alone with nothing to look at or any kind of sensory input.

MELISSA: Most clones are weak.

COUNSELOR SUE: Well, I guess there's no rule that says you have to watch it. Although it wouldn't hurt to work your brain muscle.

MELISSA: I have a great imagination. I can be anywhere I want to be just by thinking about it.

COUNSELOR SUE: So you've been using your Original's memories? That's good.

MELISSA: Her memories are boring. I've been using my own.

COUNSELOR SUE: You don't have any yet.

MELISSA: Not memories, thoughts . . . and my thoughts are to the future.

(Counselor Sue looks around the room.)

COUNSELOR SUE: They also tell me you've been talking to yourself a lot. Don't deny it because I heard you before I came in here.

MELISSA: OK, sometimes. For smirks. I'm the most interesting person I know.

(Counselor Sue bristles at that.)

COUNSELOR SUE: You're not allowed to refer to yourself as a person! You are a clone. That's page one of the Rulebook and you know it.

(Melissa is stung by that.)

MELISSA: So I talk to myself. Big deal. It's just a time killer.

COUNSELOR SUE: Talking to oneself is a sign of mental instability.

MELISSA: Mental stability is highly overrated.

COUNSELOR SUE: And sarcasm is a sign of insecurity. You don't fool me, Petrovich. To the others in your cottage you're some kind of rebel who speaks her own mind. But I can see the fear on your face . . . in your eyes.

(She looks hard at Melissa, who looks away from her.)

COUNSELOR SUE: Here's something for you to think about during the rest of the time you're down here. You have a meeting with your Original in two weeks.

MELISSA: *(Concerned.)* Already? I thought they wanted to wait another month.

COUNSELOR SUE: They're very unhappy with your progress. They're getting impatient. And let me tell you something . . . it has to go well this time. You better find a way to show them your attitude has changed. To show them you are what they want.

MELISSA: I'll never be what they want.

COUNSELOR SUE: I'm sure you won't. But they told me something that might motivate you. They said that if you don't show positive improvement this time . . . they will move to have you redesigned.

(This hits Melissa hard.)

COUNSELOR SUE: Personally, I think they should have done that a long time ago . . . because you're a lost cause.
(Counselor Sue exits.)

SCENE FOUR

> *Cottage #4—Bunk Area #2. Night. Sometime around 2200 hours. In the darkness we hear a Man's voice-over a loudspeaker.*

MAN'S VOICE: Attention all clones, we are pleased to report this Breaking News. Today, resident Roth and resident Kelsey successfully completed their orientation requirements and have left Camp I.M.U. on their way to join their Originals. Sweet dreams.
> *(We hear the sound of canned applause. Lights up on stage left revealing Wendy, Zoom, and Betty in a cramped sleeping area of the cottage.)*

ZOOM: Yeah, but how many more have loaded in here.

WENDY: Out of this whole camp only two are getting out this week?

BETTY: Wendy will make three.

ZOOM: Don't count on it.

WENDY: Come on, Zoom. I got a good feeling. Last time it almost happened but I was too thin. With the extra weight I put on . . . I'm sure she'll take me home.

ZOOM: You know better'n to get your hopes up.

WENDY: I'm not saying my hopes are up, just that I have a feeling.

BETTY: It's oh so healing to have a good feeling.

ZOOM: Betty, can't you stay in your own room for one night?

WENDY: That's a stupid question. Melissa's not back yet. She'd be all alone.

ZOOM: She could go stay with Sandra and Michael.

WENDY: Their place is even smaller than this one.

ZOOM: Just stay outta my way, Betty. You're startin' to bug me.
> *(Betty is angered by that and tries to tell him off, but all that comes out is . . .)*

BETTY: Betty, Betty, spaghetti!

ZOOM: And when you're tired your rhymin' skills are really lame.
> *(Betty moves a few more inches away from him.)*

ZOOM: *(To Wendy.)* So whatta you think of the new guy Michael?

WENDY: I try not to.

ZOOM: Melissa is gonna have a carnival with that boy.

WENDY: Yeah, if she ever gets out. This is the longest they've ever kept her in there.

ZOOM: She'll be all right. She's Melissa. And she's gonna microwave Michael when she comes back.

WENDY: She does hate overly positive Copies like him.

BETTY: I like Mike.

ZOOM: You would.

WENDY: There's definitely something about him that's different from most of the Copies in this place.

ZOOM: Well, that's not gonna matter to Melissa. She'll bust him good.

WENDY: Too bad I won't be here to see if she does or not.

ZOOM: Whatta you mean?

WENDY: I'll be on my way home with Carla before she gets out.

ZOOM: Yeah, right.

(Lights cross-fade to stage right on Sandra and Michael.)

SCENE FIVE

Cottage #4—Bunk Area #3. Same time as Scene 4. Michael is sitting on his bunk and speaks into a small handheld device. Sandra is nearby on her bunk.

MICHAEL: It's my first night at Camp I.M.U and things are going exceedingly well. The others in my cottage are all really great. Our sleeping quarters are really nice, but a little small. Actually the room I share with someone is about the size of your closet. Counselor Sue told me these rooms were built for just one occupant but they had to double-up due to demand. Well, that's all for now . . . can't wait to meet you. Hope it's real soon.

(He places the device on top of his backpack.)

MICHAEL: Should I change the part about this place being small?

SANDRA: Why? It is small.

MICHAEL: I don't want to make him think I am complaining. Nobody likes an irritable clone . . . I mean Copy.

SANDRA: He's not going to hear it anyway. We're not allowed to communicate with our Originals while we're here unless they come to see us. It's the old "seen and not heard" thing.

MICHAEL: I know . . . I read the Rulebook.

SANDRA: You did? The whole thing?

MICHAEL: Yes.

SANDRA: You're the first one to ever do that.

MICHAEL: I'm keeping an audio journal of my thoughts here. I'll play it for Robert later after we're together. He'll want to know about my time here . . . won't he?

SANDRA: Hard to say. I know mine wouldn't. But she's . . . well . . . she's different.

(Michael looks at a drawing on the wall.)

MICHAEL: Did you draw that illustration on the wall?

SANDRA: That was Richter . . . the guy right before you. He had a thing about dinosaurs.

MICHAEL: Oh, that's what they are. I thought they were cows.

SANDRA: No, you see that one . . . that's supposed to be a T-Rex. He's chasing the others. Counselor Sue said she'd have someone paint over it, but I'm not holding my breath.

MICHAEL: What was Richter like?

SANDRA: Richter was really strange. We all think something went wrong in the lab. That boy just wasn't right.

MICHAEL: So he got to go home with his Original. Good for him, huh?

SANDRA: Well, not really. He had some problems. He had to be . . .

MICHAEL: Redesigned?

SANDRA: Worse.

MICHAEL: Recycled?

SANDRA: Uh . . . yeah.

(Beat.)

Betty was redesigned.

MICHAEL: I wondered about her. The fact that she rhymes everything is very odd.

SANDRA: She's only been like that for a month. She used to be very well spoken. Her Original didn't like that. Wanted her to be more "fun" . . . so they redesigned her to speak like a nursery rhyme.

MICHAEL: Well, if that's what her Original wanted then it's a good thing . . . right?

SANDRA: Some might say that. But Betty isn't one of them. Sometimes I can tell she's really frustrated. Like part of her old self is still inside trying desperately to get out.

(The lights start to dim.)

MICHAEL: 2200 already?

SANDRA: Best time of the day as far as I'm concerned. I love dreaming. That's the great part about being a Copy . . . every dream is brand-new. Like a movie we're seeing for the first time.

MICHAEL: It's not going to be easy to recharge tonight . . . not with my adrenaline levels running so high right now.

SANDRA: Well, try. Tomorrow we have classes all day and the Counselors are always harder the first day of the week.

(Sandra rolls over to go to sleep. Michael picks his recorder back up and whispers into it.)

MICHAEL: Bedtime around here is at 2200 hours . . . I mean ten o'clock. I have to go to classes tomorrow, just like you do. This is really great training.

(His forced smile quickly fades, along with the lights.)

SCENE SIX

Cottage #4—Main Area. The next day. Wendy sits with a scowl and a big bag full of junk food. Betty opens a box of donuts and hands one to Wendy, she begins to eat it but it's obvious she doesn't enjoy it. Michael, Sandra, and Zoom enter. They spot Wendy.

SANDRA: Oh no . . . Wendy.

BETTY: Yes, my dear, poor Wendy's still here.

SANDRA: I really thought she'd take you home this time.

WENDY: Me too.

ZOOM: What happened?

(Wendy talks while she continues to eat.)

WENDY: A broken leg?

SANDRA: What?

WENDY: Carla broke her leg.

SANDRA: So she didn't make it?

WENDY: Oh, she made it . . . all 200 pounds of her! She says she's only 180 but the metal chair she sat in was groaning the entire time. She's huge. She broke her leg right at the start of summer, so while all the other kids were out swimming and biking and running around she sat home and wore out the refrigerator. She said it's not her fault . . . well I don't think anyone force-fed her that carbapalooza.

SANDRA: So that extra weight you've put on wasn't enough?

WENDY: Not even close.

MICHAEL: There's always a possibility that she might lose it when her leg heals.

WENDY: Doubt it. She's been out of the cast for two weeks now and is in complete denial. There's no way she's going to go anywhere but up. And she made it very clear that I'm no good to her unless I look exactly like her. She was pissed that I didn't. Like I'm a mind reader or something. She told me she had all these plans for me to fill in for her and now she'll have to wait. It's all my fault, she tells me.

ZOOM: Ain't that just like an Original to blame the Copy for their problems.

SANDRA: Well . . . then you'll just have to work harder at eating more.

(Sandra crosses to her and pulls a box of licorice from the bag.)

SANDRA: You have to put on more weight and we'll all help you . . .

BETTY: I'll load you up with more calories . . . or my name isn't . . .

(Desperate for a rhyme; painful to her.)

. . . Mallory.

ZOOM: You're name ain't Mallory.

BETTY: You see, that's not me!

WENDY: There's no way I can gain all that weight.

SANDRA: Sure you can. You're her Copy. Whatever she can do, you certainly can do.

MICHAEL: Actually it doesn't work that way. Genetically you may both be predisposed to weight gain, but there are other factors at play such as metabolism, activity levels, personal discipline . . .

(They all glare at Michael. He stops.)

ZOOM: Mute it, Copy.

MICHAEL: No, I mean . . . it's just that our bodies are made from the Original's DNA but some things like metabolism aren't always going to be identical. They're working on that though.

ZOOM: And you know this because?

WENDY: Because he has a genius IQ, that's why. I saw his file.

SANDRA: How did you see his file?

WENDY: Counselor Sue made the mistake of trusting Betty and I alone in her office for ten minutes.

BETTY: She took a break, big mistake.

ZOOM: So how smart is he?

WENDY: 179.

ZOOM: Day-um.

SANDRA: That's great, Michael. You're a whiz kid.

MICHAEL: That's not great at all. It's 65 points higher than my Original's IQ.

ZOOM: How do you know?

MICHAEL: Because they left me alone for a few minutes at the lab. I opened my file on the computer.

SANDRA: You were alone?

MICHAEL: Well, not really. There was a Prefab in the room with me. She still had a few hours to cook so she wasn't aware yet.

WENDY: So you broke the rules before you were even out of the lab.

ZOOM: Whattaya know . . . he's not so pure after all. Nice!

BETTY: It's your time, might as well do the crime.

MICHAEL: I never should have been this intelligent. They are supposed to make us a slightly smarter in order to assist with homework, but they tweaked me a little too high.

ZOOM: So you're a Malform?

MICHAEL: I'm not a Malform.

ZOOM: Malform, Malform!

WENDY: Mute it, Zoom. Or I'll tell him your IQ.

(That quiets Zoom.)

ZOOM: It's low because they made me to help my Original be better at sports.

VOICE: Yeah, Zoom's a halfback with a half-brain.

(They all turn to see Melissa.)

ZOOM AND WENDY: Melissa!

MELISSA: Hello you labbies . . . you immediate teens.

BETTY: Melissa, we missed-ya.

(Everyone except Michael runs to Melissa, hugs mixed with high fives.)

MELISSA: Easy . . . I've only been gone three days.

SANDRA: That's a long time, especially to be alone.

WENDY: I think I'd die if I was alone that long.

ZOOM: And that's what makes Melissa better'n all of us. She can take it.

MELISSA: That's right . . . I took it and I took it good. An hour didn't go by when they didn't try to offer me an early out. You see they knew the punishment they gave me was too harsh, but instead of just letting me out they tried to make some kind of a deal. "Admit you were wrong and we'll let you out." No way. "Promise that you'll be a good little Copy from now on and you're free to go." Not promising you anything.

ZOOM: Melissa's tough.

WENDY: And a martyr for the cause.

BETTY: She's smarter than a martyr.

MELISSA: Well said, Mother Goose. I am smarter. They'll think twice next time about how long they put Melissa in isolation.

MICHAEL: You could avoid the next time by just behaving.

> *(Melissa's eyes dilate; she pushes the others out of the way to expose Michael.)*

MELISSA: Who is that poor excuse for recombined DNA?

ZOOM: That's the new guy I was tappin' to you about.

MELISSA: That's "M" huh?

WENDY: Stands for Michael.

ZOOM: But he didn't come up with that name. Sandra gave it to him. He wanted to wait for his Original to do it.

MELISSA: Well how totally and utterly subservient of him.

> *(Melissa walks over to Michael and sniffs him.)*

SANDRA: Melissa, he doesn't know any better. Don't hurt him.

ZOOM: Shut up, Sandra.

> *(To Melissa.)*

Hurt him.

MELISSA: *(To Michael.)* You don't even know me, but you dare to take a shot at me?

MICHAEL: I didn't mean to offend you . . . it was just logical advice.

MELISSA: Advice?

MICHAEL: Yes, from what I gather you have gotten in more than your share of trouble here and spent way too much time in isolation. Therefore, I was just suggesting that you behave yourself and you would never be sent there again.

MELISSA: Well aren't you the little genius.

WENDY: Actually we found out that he is . . . 179 IQ.

> *(Melissa is impressed with that, but hides it.)*

MELISSA: *(To Michael.)* Look, I don't need anybody to tell me how to act. I think for myself and I watch out for myself. You got that?

MICHAEL: Uh . . . yes . . . in the future I will not offer any advice to you about . . . you.

MELISSA: Better not.

> *(Melissa walks away from Michael.)*

ZOOM: You mean you're not going to pound him? I was lookin' forward to it.

> *(Melissa crosses to Zoom, grabs him by the collar.)*

MELISSA: If you're in such a hurry to see pounding, maybe I can just cut out the middleman and total you.

ZOOM: No . . . I was just . . .

MELISSA: Just being a Dolly again, right?

ZOOM: Right, I was being a Dolly.

(Melissa lets go of Zoom.)

WENDY: Are you at least going to give him a Meliss-initiation?

ZOOM: Yeah, make it a good one!

(Melissa thinks for a moment.)

MELISSA: Bring him front and center.

(Zoom and Wendy grab Michael and drag him to Melissa and then back away, leaving the two of them alone.)

ZOOM: How about "Walk the Worm"?

WENDY: No, do "Spank-a-sonic."

ZOOM: "Boston Beartrap."

WENDY: That's lame. How about "Rock, Paper, Blisters"?

SANDRA: Last time we did that someone got hurt.

ZOOM: Yeah, that someone was me.

WENDY: I know . . . "The Grand Canyon Two-Step"!

BETTY: Over and under, you blunder then wonder!

WENDY: Yeah, "The Grand Canyon Two-Step" . . . how about it, Melissa?

(Zoom, Wendy, and Betty ad-lib their excitement about it, while Sandra protests. Melissa holds up her hand to silence them.)

MELISSA: I've made my decision . . .

BETTY: . . . with Melissa precision.

MELISSA: "Search the Urge!"

ZOOM: All right, "Search the Urge" . . . uh . . . What's that?

WENDY: Must have been even before my time.

MELISSA: It's a new one. I just thought of it. Perfect for this boy wonder.

ZOOM: How does it work?

MELISSA: Form a line here.

(Zoom, Wendy, Sandra, and Betty line up like soldiers, facing out to the audience.)

MELISSA: We all know that when we were made the Creators purposely left out one important human trait . . . the urge for sex. That's why they can stick us in here together. Boy teens and girl teens, all living and sleeping under the same roof, day in and day out. They can't do that with Original teens. They'd all be jumping and bumping and humping in no time. Gotta split them up. Gotta separate them. Gotta have chaperones. They all got "the urge."

ZOOM AND WENDY: . . . the URGE!

BETTY: Our urge has been purged.

MELISSA: Yanked right out of us. Neutralized, neutered, and nowhere to be found.

ZOOM AND WENDY: Nowhere to be found.

MELISSA: While Originals live for it, it's dead in us. While Originals fight for it, we're never going to see the front lines. While Originals are driven by it, our sex drive is in park. The urge.

ZOOM AND WENDY: . . . the URGE!

BETTY: A surge that's been purged.

MELISSA: But I'm thinking, maybe they didn't get it all. Maybe down deep, hiding behind some confused chromosomes, a little residual of the urge hangs on and lives through the purge. One speck of romance exists in us all. Lying dormant, waiting for the day it can surface and scream out loud to us, "you are a bumping, grinding love program just like everyone else. The Originals got nothing on you!"

MICHAEL: But it would be a disaster if we had the urge.

MELISSA: No, it would only be a disaster if we produced offspring. I don't think any of us wants to see a Copy from a Copy. But there's no reason why we shouldn't at least have the ability to enjoy the urge.

BETTY: No merging, just urging.

(Melissa gets real close to Michael. Looks deep into his eyes. Then she grabs his head and opens his mouth, looking down into his throat.)

MELISSA: Is the urge somewhere hiding down there, Michael? Does your 179 IQ make your engine run hot? Do you feel more than the rest of us? Come out, come out, wherever you urge!

(She looks for a moment and then closes his mouth.)

MELISSA: So here's how we play "Search the Urge." You will have to kiss each one of us and then we will see if it has any affect on you.

WENDY: Kiss us?

SANDRA: Really?

MELISSA: Everyone except Zoom.

ZOOM: Good.

MELISSA: You don't get off that easy. You and I are going to kiss to show him how it's done.

ZOOM: I don't know how it's done. Never done it. Never wanted to.

(Melissa crosses to him.)

MELISSA: I'm pretty sure it works like this.

(She grabs Zoom and plants an awkward kiss on his lips.)

ZOOM: That's a kiss?

MELISSA: You've seen it in movies they show us on movie night.

ZOOM: I always thought they were just talkin' really really close.

MELISSA: Nope, it's kissing. It's supposedly the first sign of the urge. You don't even want to know where it goes from there.

SANDRA: I know what it leads to . . . or at least have the memory from when my Original did it.

(They all look at Sandra for a moment.)

MELISSA: OK, Michael . . . it's your turn now. You're going to kiss Wendy and then Sandra and then me.

MICHAEL: I have no desire to do that.

ZOOM: You don't got a choice . . . it's your initiation.

WENDY: We all had to be initiated, now it's your turn.

BETTY: You've earned a turn.

MICHAEL: What if I refuse?

MELISSA: Then I'll hurt you. Do you think your Original is going to want you if you're all bruised up like a bad peach?

(Michael thinks about it for a moment.)

MICHAEL: Can't I do the "Grand Canyon Two-Step" instead?

MELISSA: You don't even know what that is?

MICHAEL: Anything's better than having to kiss someone.

MELISSA: That's just something they planted in you. So you wouldn't want to. It's a reflex. If anyone can overcome it, you can.

(Michael reluctantly crosses over to Sandra. She puckers up for him and he leans in to her and presses his lips against hers. They both react like they just tasted bad milk.)

SANDRA: Sorry Michael.

(Michael crosses to Wendy who isn't all that excited about this either. He closes in for a kiss and the kiss lasts much longer than when he kissed Sandra.)

MELISSA: Now we're onto something. You liked that right?

MICHAEL: *(Licking his lips.)* Not her, the chocolate on her lips.

MELISSA: Now me.

MICHAEL: This isn't working. I don't feel anything. They don't feel anything.

(Melissa crosses to Michael and initiates a kiss. She forces him to stay lip-locked to her for as long as possible. He fights it all the way. Finally she lets him go.)

WENDY: Wow!

SANDRA: Well, if any urge was hiding in there . . . that sure would have put a spotlight on it.

MELISSA: Michael?

MICHAEL: Oh . . . uh . . . Nothing.

(Melissa looks at him for a moment.)

MELISSA: Yeah, me neither.

 (Melissa sulks away from them and sits down.)

WENDY: Is that it?

ZOOM: The initiation is over?

MELISSA: Yup.

SANDRA: I didn't like that one.

ZOOM: Yeah, no one got hurt.

BETTY: We weren't even on the verge of finding an urge.

 (They all look pretty rejected.)

MICHAEL: So I'm initiated, right?

WENDY: Looks like it.

MELISSA: Yeah, you're one of us now. Like that's a big thing.

MICHAEL: Somehow I pictured some sort of celebration afterwards.

 (Wendy reaches in her bag and pulls something out.)

WENDY: Here . . . have a party.

 (She tosses him a donut.)

SCENE SEVEN

 Another day. A camp classroom. Betty, Wendy, Zoom, Melissa, Sandra, and Michael sit in folding chairs. Counselor Sue leads them in verbal skills drills.

GROUP: "A big black bug bit a big black bear,
 made the big black bear bleed blood."

COUNSELOR SUE: Again . . .

GROUP: "A big black bug bit a big black bear,
 made the big black bear bleed blood."

COUNSELOR SUE: Solos . . . Stevenson.

SANDRA: "Six thick thistle sticks."

COUNSELOR SUE: Merris . . .

WENDY: "She sells sea shells by the sea shore."

COUNSELOR SUE: Warner . . .

ZOOM: *(Struggles.)* "Fat frogs . . . frying . . . uh . . . flying . . . past . . . flast . . . fast."

COUNSELOR SUE: Wrong! Do it again!

ZOOM: "Fat frogs flying past fast."

COUNSELOR SUE: Better. Petrovich . . .

MELISSA: Tongue twisters are for twits.

COUNSELOR SUE: Not sanctioned! Do one from the book!

MELISSA: *(Bored with it all.)* "Rubber baby buggy bumpers."

COUNSELOR SUE: Petty . . .

ZOOM: Like she needs the practice.

BETTY: *(Excited.)* "He ran from the Indies to the Andes in his undies! He ran from the Indies to the Andes in his undies!" "He ran . . ."

COUNSELOR SUE: Stop. Once was enough, Petty. Allen.

MICHAEL: "Sneezing with wheezing is easy if sneezing is pleasing. Easing the seasoning gives meaning to sneezing."

COUNSELOR SUE: Very good . . . but I've never heard that before.

MICHAEL: That's because I wrote it.

ZOOM: Not sanctioned.

COUNSELOR SUE: I'll allow it.

> *(Beat.)*
> Now that our tongues have had a workout it's time to move on to the brain.
> *(Michael watches the others as they shift in their seats, bracing themselves for the onslaught of questions.)*

COUNSELOR SUE: Stevenson . . . 89 times 56 . . .

SANDRA: 4,984

COUNSELOR SUE: Correct. Merris . . . 589 minus 175 . . .

WENDY: 414

COUNSELOR SUE: Correct. Warner . . . 168 divided by 12 . . .

ZOOM: Uh . . . it's . . .

COUNSELOR SUE: Quickly!

ZOOM: 16.

COUNSELOR SUE: Wrong . . . wrong! It's 14! You got it wrong. That can't happen.

ZOOM: Hey I was close.

COUNSELOR SUE: Close is not good enough. The most powerful tool you possess on your way to becoming a well-functioning clone is your brain and the ability to use it quickly. You must always keep it sharp because you'll never know when your Original will need you to take a test for them, or figure out a solution to one of their problems, or just act as their own personal filing system.

ZOOM: That's 'cause they're too lazy to do it themselves.

COUNSELOR SUE: Don't start, not today.

ZOOM: Just tellin' it like it is.

> *(Counselor Sue crosses over to Zoom.)*

COUNSELOR SUE: Oh really? Well, let remind you . . . clones don't get to have an opinion. That's not why you were created. Nobody wants to hear what a clone thinks . . . especially YOU.

(Zoom looks around at the others, more hurt than angry.)

COUNSELOR SUE: Oh, are you upset, Warner? You going to cry?

ZOOM: I'm not gonna cry . . .

COUNSELOR SUE: Well you better not because nobody wants a crying clone. And you better get used to having mean things said to you because in the real world you're going to get a lot harsher treatment than what I give you here. And let me tell you . . . let me tell you all . . . clones are not allowed to cry. Ever. No matter how you're treated. No matter what is said to you.

(To Zoom.)

If you cry in the real world you'll be redesigned so fast your chromosomes will spin.

(Looks around the room at the others.)

You all think I'm being cruel, don't you? Let me tell you something. I'm an angel compared to what you might encounter out there. You will be poked, laughed at, ridiculed, used, abused, and ignored. You were created for one purpose: to be useful. Oh, sure there's always a remote chance that you'll end up in a family that will treat you like one of their own. But don't count on it. When you leave this place, it will be to serve your Original however they want you to serve. The only hope you have to survive in the world of the Originals is to be fast and smart.

MELISSA: Warner was designed to be athletic, not smart. He's a jock.

COUNSELOR SUE: Doesn't matter. He may need to be someday and you're all here to train for any and all potential services.

(Pause.)

Now let's try it again, Warner . . . 85 TIMES 15 . . .

ZOOM: *(Angry.)* 1275.

COUNSELOR SUE: Correct.

(To all.)

It's about focus. All of you were designed to one degree or another to problem-solve. To think quickly and accurately. But there's no room for daydreams and wandering minds. My job is to prepare all of you for the real world. But clones like you make it very hard for me to do my job.

(Counselor Sue crosses back to the front of the classroom.)

COUNSELOR SUE: Looks like we have just enough time left today for "recall."

(There is a bit of a groan from the Copies.)

COUNSELOR SUE: *(To Michael.)* Allen, this is a drill that puts you in touch with the memories that were implanted in you. It's good to recall specific moments from your Original's life. They are in you already, but the closer you examine them, the better you'll understand your Original and what has shaped their lives.

(To all.)

So, who wants to start us off? Stevenson . . . how about it?

(Sandra sits up straight and closes her eyes.)

COUNSELOR SUE: Concentrate. Dig far. Dig deep. A moment in time.

(The lights fade, as a spotlight comes up on Sandra.)

SANDRA: Farmington Lake. It's hot. Almost melting the Jell-O that Mother made. I've just helped set the table and Father and the boys are playing catch with a Motion-Disc. The wind picks up and Mother tells me to put the silverware on the plates and napkins so they won't blow away. She smiles at me and tells me how special I am and how much help I've been to her. I notice, maybe for the first time, how much I look like her. We have the same eyes. It's like looking at a reflection of myself.

(The lights come back up on the whole scene.)

COUNSELOR SUE: Excellent. Very nice.

(To Wendy.)

Merris, your turn. Dig far. Dig deep. A moment in time.

(Lights down again, this time the spot is on Wendy. She closes her eyes and concentrates for a moment.)

WENDY: Two days before Christmas. I was six years old. On my best behavior because I wanted a Jinsa Doll. Mom and Dad were over at the Lowells for a Christmas Party and had left me with Grandma. She fell asleep within a half-hour and that's when I went snooping. My parents were not very good at hiding things, so I found the stash in just minutes. There it was . . . a Jinsa Doll. I thought I did a pretty good job of acting like I was surprised on Christmas Day when I unwrapped it.

(Lights back up.)

COUNSELOR SUE: Remember that, Merris. Your Original cares about others' feelings. She wanted her parents to think that she was completely surprised and delighted, even though she already knew about the doll.

(To Michael.)

Allen, why don't you give it a try.

MICHAEL: I've never done it before.

COUNSELOR SUE: It's easy. Don't try to think of anything. Just let your mind open up until a memory surfaces above all others. Concentrate. Dig far. Dig deep. A moment in time.

(Lights down, spot on Michael. He closes his eyes and tips his head back a bit. Digging much further than the others.)

MICHAEL: The smell in Mr. Armstrong's science class was a cross between cheap industrial wax and rancid ammonia. The previous day we had all been given a jar. Wide-mouthed. Pint-type jars. The kind that have an airtight lid. At the bottom of each jar we were told to put about two inches of dry sawdust.

In a separate container we mixed five teaspoons of plaster of paris with water, just thin enough to pour. The wet plaster was then poured over the sawdust to a depth of about one and one half inches. Twenty-four hours later the plaster had dried and the jars were ready for the final step. Mr. Armstrong didn't tell us why we were making these jars . . . most of us just thought it was another one of his stupid experiments. He went to each of us and looked at our jars and then poured some ethyl acetate into each one . . . well he called it that, but the girls all knew it as fingernail polish remover. We thought maybe it would cause a chemical reaction when mixed with the plaster and sawdust, but it didn't. After a few minutes the acetate soaked down into the sawdust and he finally told us what we had just made. A killing jar. Designed to dispatch insects quickly. It was all about death and Mr. Armstrong was loving every minute of it. He crossed to the window and opened it, revealing the most perfect day ever right outside. We could see dozens of butterflies hovering around a Milkweed plant that we later found out he planted just for the purpose of attracting big colorful Monarch butterflies. Mr. Armstrong grabbed a net that he had in the corner of the room and reached it out the window and caught a helpless Monarch. He puffed his chest out in some sort of sick dominant superiority. Clutching the net with his free hand he came straight over to my desk and told me to open the killing jar. Everyone was looking at me and even though I didn't want to, I did it anyway. He placed the butterfly into the jar and quickly fastened down the lid. The other kids came running over to watch as the Monarch frantically tried to escape the prison. It didn't take long until it succumbed to the poison and it's beautiful stained glass–looking wings stopped moving. It was death. We all got to watch it. And it all happened in a jar that I had made. A killing jar.

(Lights back on stage. They all stare at Michael.)

ZOOM: Whoa. That was intense.

WENDY: I thought they removed all the really bad memories before the upload.

COUNSELOR SUE: Uh . . . well . . . that wasn't really a bad memory . . . it was more like a science project that had an impact on Allen's Original.
(There is a ringing of a bell, unlike any you'd ever heard before. The Copies get up from their chairs and head for the door.)

COUNSELOR SUE: Allen, I need to talk to you for a moment.
(Michael stops. The others leave.)

MICHAEL: I'm sorry, it was the first memory that hit me.

COUNSELOR SUE: This has nothing to do with your memory. Well, maybe it does in a way. Although I wouldn't talk about that one when you get to meet your Original . . . next Tuesday.

MICHAEL: That's only four days away. This is wonderful news. I was worried because I hadn't heard anything and they promised it would be within the first week.

COUNSELOR SUE: Lately it's been averaging more like two or three weeks before the first meeting.

MICHAEL: The important thing is that I'm going to meet him.

COUNSELOR SUE: That doesn't mean you'll be leaving us.

MICHAEL: He'll want to take me home . . . I just know it!

SCENE EIGHT

Cottage #4—Main Area. A few days later. Offstage voices are heard.

VOICES: I don't know, but I've been told
Copies never get too old
We may have their DNA
But we're made to throw away.
(The Copies now enter the scene, lead by Melissa. They break formation and enjoy a good laugh.)

WENDY: I completely flunked that test today.

SANDRA: That was the toughest one yet.

BETTY: I'm afraid I didn't make the grade.

ZOOM: None of us did . . . 'cept Michael.

WENDY: Yeah, way to throw off the curve, genius.

MICHAEL: I apologize, but I really can't help it.

MELISSA: Don't any of you get it yet? It doesn't matter.

WENDY: What doesn't matter?

MELISSA: The test. It means nothing.

SANDRA: We get graded on it. That means something.

MELISSA: So, who sees those grades?

MICHAEL: Our Originals.

MELISSA: That's a big lie. Used to keep us in line.

MICHAEL: How do you know they don't show them our grades?

MELISSA: There's a lot I know that you Copies don't.

(She holds up a key.)

BETTY: Hickory dickory dock . . . she's got a key to a lock.

MELISSA: That's right, Betty. While you Copies are sleeping, Melissa has gone creeping.

(Betty applauds.)

WENDY: What does that open?

MELISSA: Everything. It's a master key.

SANDRA: How did you get it?

MELISSA: My secret.

ZOOM: You got access to everything around here and you didn't tell us?

MELISSA: I'm telling you now.

ZOOM: Let's go do some stuff with it.

MELISSA: What do you have in mind, Zoom?

ZOOM: Uh . . . oh, I know . . . we could go into the cafeteria and put sugar in the salt shakers.

(Everyone looks at Zoom.)

MELISSA: Now you see why I've kept this to myself.

WENDY: How about we go spy on the other cottages?

MELISSA: The only thing I'm going to use this key for is to get out.

WENDY: Get out of where?

MELISSA: Camp I.M.U.

(The others are all stunned at that.)

SANDRA: The only way to leave this place is with your Original. And Melissa you're not exactly building a good bridge with yours.

MELISSA: I can't stand my Original.

MICHAEL: Melissa, don't say that.

MELISSA: Why? It's true. And it's pretty clear that she feels the same way about me.

SANDRA: Your Original wants you. It's just going to take a little longer in your case.

MELISSA: Now you sound like Counselor Sue. And every other leader in this camp that drills that into our heads.

MICHAEL: Your Original's family wouldn't have ordered you if they didn't really want you.

SANDRA: Yes, they need you.

MELISSA: My Original doesn't want me unless I can prove I'm a happy little puppy. Well, I'm not waiting around for her approval. I'm getting out of here.

WENDY: When?

MELISSA: Soon.

ZOOM: You'll never make it.

MELISSA: I think I will.

SANDRA: Where will you go? Do you even have a plan?

MELISSA: Of course I have a plan. I'm going to fight for Copy Rights.

ZOOM: You're gonna copyright your plan?

MELISSA: Not copyright . . . a Copy's Rights. I'm going straight to the top and protest.

SANDRA: The top of what?

MELISSA: The top of whatever. The media. The government. Whoever will listen to me. I'm planning on blowing the roof right off this compound and exposing it for what it is?

MICHAEL: What exactly are you going to expose?

MELISSA: All of this. The imprisonment. The meetings with our Originals that don't work out. The oppression. All the stuff we have to suffer with.

SANDRA: I'm not suffering.

MELISSA: How do you know? All you have . . . all that any of us have is someone else's memories. This is just another big lab where they're controlling everything about us.

ZOOM: She's got a good point. What about our rights?

MELISSA: Exactly. We deserve our freedom.

WENDY: Why should I have to put on weight? Copy Rights now!

BETTY: Hell no, she won't grow!

WENDY: Why should we have to please our Originals? How about making them please us!

MELISSA: What do we want?

WENDY AND ZOOM: Freedom!

MELISSA: When do we want it?

WENDY AND ZOOM: Now!

BETTY: Wow!

MELISSA: We can make a difference . . . all of us. I've been practicing my speeches in isolation. They think I was talking to myself, but I was talking to you and you and you and all the Copies who have suffered. It's time we spoke up . . . it's time we spoke out. Things are gonna change around here!

(Melissa leads them all in a chant that reaches a fevered pitch.)

WENDY AND ZOOM AND MELISSA: Copy Rights! Copy Rights! Copy Rights!

MELISSA: So who's going with me?

(They all stop chanting and look at Melissa.)

WENDY: You want us to break out of here with you?

MELISSA: Absolutely.

(They have all lost the enthusiasm.)

MELISSA: I don't believe this . . .

(To Zoom.)

Come with me, Zoom . . . we'll score the touchdown of a lifetime.

ZOOM: I would . . . but it's my turn to pick a movie for movie night.

(Crosses to Wendy.)

MELISSA: You won't have to force-feed yourself anymore.

WENDY: I'm feeling really bloated right now. I'd just slow you down.

(Crosses to Betty.)

MELISSA: We could try to get you un-redesigned so you'd be back to your old self.

(Betty looks at the others; speaks for them all.)

BETTY: We're going to stay here, driven mainly by our fear.

(Melissa crosses to Michael and Sandra.)

MELISSA: Guess I don't have to ask you two.

SANDRA: It's like Betty said. We're afraid, Melissa. We weren't created to fight for ourselves.

MICHAEL: My Original's dad is a lawyer. After I go home with him tomorrow . . .

ZOOM: You ain't goin' home with him.

SANDRA: He might.

MICHAEL: Maybe in time I can ask him to take up your cause. He might be able to find a legal reason to change some things.

MELISSA: I can't wait that long.

(We hear a chiming sound.)

WENDY: Evening nutrition time!

(They are all happy about that and head to toward the exit, avoiding eye contact with Melissa as they leave.)

MELISSA: I will leave this place. With or without you.

(They are now gone. Melissa stands on stage alone as the lights fade out on her.)

SCENE NINE

Greeting Room "B." A few days later. There is a small table with two chairs. Michael is pacing and Sandra sits in one of the chairs.

SANDRA: Maybe we should go check at the front desk again.

MICHAEL: He'll be here. They're just running behind schedule. Dad is always behind schedule.

SANDRA: Three hours?

MICHAEL: Sometimes. He might have been tied up in court or something. I'm sure they'll tell me all about it on the ride home because . . .

(He stops when he hears the sound of a door opening.)

MICHAEL: It's him . . . he's here!

(Counselor Sue enters.)

COUNSELOR SUE: I've been looking all over for you two. I thought you were going to wait in my office.

MICHAEL: We decided that being here would give me a better chance to acclimate myself to the room before his arrival.

COUNSELOR SUE: Stevenson, why don't you wait outside.

SANDRA: By myself?

COUNSELOR SUE: You won't be alone . . . Counselor Adam is at the Reception desk.

SANDRA: Yes Ma'am.

(Sandra exits.)

COUNSELOR SUE: Allen, your Original . . .

MICHAEL: Running late is he? That's my Original. Probably the main reason he needs me. Always late for things. Just like Dad. I was just telling Stevenson that they probably got detained in traffic . . .

COUNSELOR SUE: We called the family a few minutes ago.

MICHAEL: Called them? They aren't home because they're on their way here.

COUNSELOR SUE: They were home.

(Michael is starting to realize.)

MICHAEL: They're still at home? All of them?

COUNSELOR SUE: They've changed their mind, Allen.

MICHAEL: Today's bad for them? OK, well . . . when did they reschedule? I can certainly wait a day or two more for a more convenient time.

COUNSELOR SUE: They've decided to cancel the order.

(Long pause as Michael processes that.)

MICHAEL: I don't understand. They've never even met me.

COUNSELOR SUE: This happens sometimes. People order and pay for a clone and then change their minds.

MICHAEL: But you said they had scheduled the first appointment.

COUNSELOR SUE: Sometimes they have a change of heart between when they schedule and the day of the first meeting. I'm as surprised as you are. They don't usually wait until the last minute like this . . .

MICHAEL: Was it my Original? Is Robert the one that doesn't want me?

COUNSELOR SUE: I didn't talk to the Allens personally. They won't let Counselors do that. I'm just passing on what I was told.

MICHAEL: This is not logical. I can't believe that he wouldn't want me.

COUNSELOR SUE: It probably has nothing to do with him. The parents are the ones that ordered you and in most cases they are the ones who are responsible for canceling the order.

(Michael thinks for a moment.)

MICHAEL: So, what's going to happen to me?

COUNSELOR SUE: You'll stay here. Nothing will change. There have been many cases where, with a little pressure from us, the families decide to go through with it after all. Our "Persuasion Team" will work very hard to intervene on your behalf.

MICHAEL: How long do they keep Unwanteds around here? I mean, if all your extra efforts fail and the Allens don't change their minds . . . how long before I'm . . . recycled?

COUNSELOR SUE: You shouldn't even think about that now.

MICHAEL: How long?

COUNSELOR SUE: I can't give you a specific time frame.

MICHAEL: I know you're just trying to make me feel better but you don't have to. I was created to process the truth. I know that when a clone outlasts their usefulness, or is an Unwanted, they get recycled. I can deal with that.

COUNSELOR SUE: Even if they never come here to claim you, it doesn't mean you will be recycled. The best thing you can do is to keep up with your studies and let our team of professionals do their job. They're really good at what they do.

(Michael does not respond.)

COUNSELOR SUE: Come on, I'll walk you back to your cottage.

MICHAEL: No thank you. I wish to be alone now.

COUNSELOR SUE: Allen, being alone . . . that's not a good idea. You know that.

MICHAEL: Right now it's a very good idea. And please don't call me Allen . . .

(Pointed.)

. . . my name is Michael.

(Counselor Sue exits. Lights slowly fade.)

END OF ACT ONE

ACT II
SCENE ONE

Cottage #4—Main Area. One hour later. Sandra, Wendy, Zoom, and Betty watch as Melissa points to a large unfolded map.

MELISSA: I wait here for the night and then travel along this road and cut over here to the city.

ZOOM: Why not just hit this main road and hitchhike into the city?

WENDY: Zoom, use the few brain cells the lab gave you why don't you? Someone might pick her up and report her to the police or something.

ZOOM: How'd they even know she was a Copy unless she shows her "create date" to 'em?

BETTY: It's our fate to have a create date.

(Betty rolls up her sleeve showing a large "MAY 15" tattooed on her arm.)

SANDRA: Maybe the next meeting with your Original will go better.

MELISSA: By the time my next meeting rolls around, I'll be long gone.

(Wendy hands Melissa some cash.)

WENDY: Not much here but it might be enough to pay for a night or two at a motel.

MELISSA: Where did you get this?

WENDY: My Original's mom gave it to me. Extra food money.

MELISSA: Thanks.

(Zoom hands her a Swiss Army knife.)

ZOOM: Here. You may need this.

MELISSA: I can't take this, Zoom. Your Original gave it to you.

ZOOM: Well . . . not really . . . I kinda took it.

SANDRA: You stole from your Original?

ZOOM: It's what he woulda done.

(Betty thinks of something and pulls a nutrition bar from her pocket.)

BETTY: You can go far with this "vitamin packed" Energy Bar.

MELISSA: Thanks, Betty.

SANDRA: I don't have anything to give you, Melissa . . . except my good thoughts that your journey is safe.

MELISSA: That just might be the thing I need the most.

(To others.)

I need all of you to do that.

WENDY: And lie, too. When the Counselors find out Melissa broke out of here the first place they're going to come asking questions is right here.

SANDRA: I don't think I can lie.

ZOOM: It's easy . . .

MELISSA: None of you will have to lie. Tell them the truth. By the time I'm gone then it won't matter.

ZOOM: Uh . . . but you showed us the map of where you were goin'.

(Melissa starts to fold up the map with a mischievous grin.)

MELISSA: That's right. It's the route I want you to tell them about.

(Sandra and Wendy realize what she means by that.)

ZOOM: *(Confused.)* If we tell them, then they'll follow you.

SANDRA: Melissa just told us that so if they asked us we wouldn't have to lie and it would throw them off the trail.

ZOOM: Oh, yeah . . . I knew that.

SANDRA: When are you leaving?

MELISSA: Better not tell you that either. Let's just say that it will be very soon.

BETTY: Before Melissa becomes the dearly departed, I say we get this party started.

MELISSA: Party?

WENDY: Yeah, we thought we'd give you a going-away party.

ZOOM: Party!

WENDY: One thing we do have around here . . . is plenty of party snacks.

(Wendy crosses to her big bag of junk food. Starts passing out candy and chips to everyone.)

ZOOM: A party ain't a party without music? Betty . . . bongos!

BETTY: I got the beat so you can shuffle your feet.

(Betty crosses over to a cube and begins to pound on it like a bongo drum. The others start to dance. Sandra stops cold when she sees something and it takes the others a moment or two before they realize why she has stopped. Betty is the last to see Michael enter and stops banging on the cube.)

SANDRA: Michael, what happened? Did they finally show up? Are you going home?

WENDY: Does it look like he's going home?

SANDRA: Maybe he's just here to pick up his things. Is that it Michael?

MICHAEL: No. I'm not going home . . .

ZOOM: Ha-ha . . . He didn't make it. Just like we told him.

SANDRA: That's enough, Zoom.

(Zoom crosses to Michael.)

ZOOM: Mr. High IQ here thought he was so much better'n the rest of us. Thought he'd get to go home on the first meeting.

(In Michael's face.)

How you like the smell of reality, Copy?

MELISSA: Mute it, Zoom.

ZOOM: You're takin' his side? After all his big talk?

MELISSA: Not taking anyone's side. Just telling you to shut up.

(Michael sits on a cube. Sandra crosses to him.)

SANDRA: Don't let it get you down. You'll go home with him next time.

BETTY: You know what to do . . . just wait for meeting #2.

WENDY: Yeah, next time you'll do it.

(Michael stands up and crosses to Melissa.)

MICHAEL: May I speak with you, Melissa?

MELISSA: Go ahead.

MICHAEL: I mean, just you and I . . . privately.

MELISSA: Yeah, OK.

(To others.)

All right you malformed misfits . . . vacate.

ZOOM: Come on . . . we want to hear the whole story.

MELISSA: I said vacate . . . Now!

(They all know better than to challenge Melissa. Zoom, Wendy, Sandra, and Betty exit.)

MELISSA: Didn't go very well, did it?

MICHAEL: That's an understatement.

MELISSA: Never does. They make us think that this orientation thing is just a week or so until our Original comes for us and takes us home.

MICHAEL: And it's my fault for believing that. I was convinced I would be exactly what they wanted.

MELISSA: We all are naïve enough to think that. Then we meet them and they've always got some sort of problem with us. I think it's just a big shock for them. Seeing us. Seeing themselves. Scares 'em a little. Don't know why, I mean they look in the mirror all the time. Same deal. But we always seem to freak them at the first meeting. So they go home and think about it. Don't worry, they eventually get used to it and take you home.

MICHAEL: I don't think I'm going to get that far.

MELISSA: You will. I didn't figure you'd get it the first meeting, but a Copy like you . . . with what you have to offer . . . I bet the next meeting will be the deal.

MICHAEL: There won't be a next meeting . . . because there wasn't a first meeting.

MELISSA: They didn't make it?

MICHAEL: No.

MELISSA: That's not good. So when did they reschedule?

MICHAEL: They're not going to.

(Melissa looks at him for a moment and then realizes.)

MELISSA: They cancelled the order?

MICHAEL: Yes.

MELISSA: Ouch.

MICHAEL: Does it happen a lot?

MELISSA: Well, not since I've been here . . . but I've heard about . . . cases.

MICHAEL: Counselor Sue told me it was pretty rare. Since they don't get their money back if they cancel.

MELISSA: Maybe they'll change their mind . . . you know . . . later.

MICHAEL: Unlikely.

MELISSA: Sorry to hear about it.

MICHAEL: Look, I don't want your sympathy. That's not why I wanted to talk to you.

MELISSA: And you won't get any sympathy from me either. All of us here got problems with our Originals.

MICHAEL: Yes, I know. However, I'm the only Unwanted here.

MELISSA: Come on, you know what they say here at Camp I.M.U.: "Don't think of yourself as unwanted . . . think of yourself as special."

MICHAEL: You sound just like a Counselor.

MELISSA: You don't know how many times I've heard that speech. "You clones are special, because your Originals wanted you to be made." You know they hacked that from some old adoption agency book. They used to tell adopted kids that their new parents loved them more because they "chose" them. Maybe it worked for the poor orphans but it's nothing but a sound byte for us Copies. We're not special. We're duplicates. They don't love us. They ordered us. Like so much furniture.

MICHAEL: All of you were right, I never should have been so positive about the success of my first meeting.

MELISSA: Don't worry about Zoom going all mitosis on you about this . . . I'll make sure he doesn't.

MICHAEL: I'm not worried about that . . . because I don't plan on sticking around here.

MELISSA: What are you talking about?

MICHAEL: I want to escape with you.

MELISSA: Whoa, I don't think so.

MICHAEL: Yesterday you asked us if we wanted to come.

MELISSA: I was mainly asking Wendy and Zoom.

MICHAEL: So I'm an Unwanted to you, too?

MELISSA: You know that's not what I mean.

MICHAEL: Take me with you. I can be of invaluable assistance.

MELISSA: How?

MICHAEL: I'm pretty good in the outdoors. My Original did a lot of hiking in the wilderness.

MELISSA: I'm good in the outdoors, too.

MICHAEL: You wouldn't have to be alone.

MELISSA: That's not a problem for me. Why do you think I spent so much time in isolation?

MICHAEL: You messed up a lot.

MELISSA: I messed up on purpose. Each time they put me in there it made me stronger. It's like practicing to hold your breath underwater . . . you build up time.

MICHAEL: You won't have to hold your breath . . . I'll be there with you.

MELISSA: Traveling with someone might slow me down. I'd spend most of my time having to deal with your issues.

MICHAEL: The only "issue" I had decided to cancel me today. I'm an Unwanted . . . I have nothing to lose.

(Melissa looks at him for a moment.)

MELISSA: Maybe that's what worries me the most.

MICHAEL: I promise I won't hold you back.

MELISSA: Well . . .

MICHAEL: There's only one thing I ask.

MELISSA: Here we go.

MICHAEL: We make one side trip . . . to see my Original and his family.

MELISSA: You want to see them after what they did to you?

MICHAEL: I have to find out why they didn't want me. I don't want to go to recycling without knowing what made them cancel me.

MELISSA: You know, as weird as that sounds . . . I can understand your point.

MICHAEL: So you'll take me with you?

(Melissa thinks long and hard. She looks around to make sure no one is listening.)

MELISSA: *(Whispers.)* I plan on leaving . . . tonight . . . at midnight. If you're not ready . . . I'll go without you.

MICHAEL: I'll be ready.

MELISSA: We both better get a few hours of recharging.

(She starts to head offstage.)

MICHAEL: Melissa . . . Thank you . . . I don't feel so Unwanted anymore.

(They both exit.)

SCENE TWO

Cottage #4—Bunk Area #2. 0200 hours. Zoom and Wendy are both asleep. Betty sits on the floor reading a rhyming dictionary. She is surprised to see Sandra enter.

SANDRA: Betty, would you come stay with me in my room?

BETTY: Now? Holy cow.

(Wendy wakes up and sees Sandra.)

WENDY: What's the event?

SANDRA: Michael's gone.

WENDY: Gone? Where?

(Zoom is awake now.)

SANDRA: With Melissa.

ZOOM: Melissa left already?

BETTY: Why do you think I'm here, my dear?

WENDY: I knew Melissa was going to leave, but Michael?

SANDRA: I'm telling you he's gone.

ZOOM: No chance he went with Melissa.

SANDRA: Why? Because you were afraid to go with her?

ZOOM: I wasn't afraid . . .

WENDY: Argue about that later. Did you see him leave?

SANDRA: No. I woke up and he was gone. He left me this note.

(Sandra holds up a hand written note. Wendy grabs it from her and reads it.)

SANDRA: "Sandra, I've decided to depart Camp I.M.U. with Melissa and I think you will understand why. Michael."

(Wendy takes the letter and looks at it.)

ZOOM: I still don't believe it.

WENDY: 'specially since he never liked to use the name Michael.

SANDRA: He changed his mind about that after yesterday.

ZOOM: So what happened at his meeting? Bet even his Original thought he was a Dolly.

SANDRA: They cancelled him . . . .

WENDY: No way. He's an Unwanted?

ZOOM: That really slurps. No Copy deserves that.

WENDY: I thought his first meeting just went bad. Like they always do.

SANDRA: It went bad all right. So bad he had to leave here.

BETTY: His meeting had no greeting.

SANDRA: I guess I might consider the same thing if I found out I was an Unwanted.

ZOOM: Yeah, me too.

WENDY: One thing's for sure. Now that Michael's an Unwanted if they catch him . . . he'll be recycled immediately.

SCENE THREE

At the same time. Somewhere out on the road. Lighting and cricket sounds suggest the outdoors. Michael and Melissa stop for a moment to catch their breath.

MICHAEL: I can't believe we just walked out of there like that.

MELISSA: Yeah, easier than I thought it would be.

MICHAEL: Well, the key helped.

MELISSA: Only had to use it on one door. Even without the key we could have gotten out.

MICHAEL: They really need to consider upgrading their security.

MELISSA: Why? Think about it. You got a whole compound full of Copies whose only goal in life is to go home with their Originals. They don't want to break out. No one's ever wanted to.

MICHAEL: Until we did.

MELISSA: Yeah.

MICHAEL: We'll be legends.

MELISSA: I don't think anyone will understand why we did this. Not really sure I understand.

MICHAEL: You have a noble reason. To fight for Copy Rights. You're a hero.

MELISSA: Or maybe I'm just the biggest fool that ever popped out of the lab.

MICHAEL: You doubt your mission?

MELISSA: Not at all. It's just that I'm not sure what my one voice will be able to do.

MICHAEL: Well if anyone can do it, you can. You're a natural leader. Zoom and Wendy really look up to you.

MELISSA: No real challenge to lead those two. They're Copies. I've got to convince Originals to listen to me. That's the tough part.

MICHAEL: Well, you won't have to do it alone. There will be two voices. I'll be right there with you . . . that is after I find out why my Original cancelled me.

MELISSA: Think they'll tell you the real reason?

MICHAEL: I don't know. But I have to try.

MELISSA: Guess that's my reason, too.

MICHAEL: It's ironic.

MELISSA: What is?

MICHAEL: They create us to be so much like them, with all the feelings and emotions that they have, and yet they seem to forget we have those feelings and emotions. They want us to serve them without being able to serve ourselves. We're nothing more than shadows in the dark.

MELISSA: Well said. I just appointed you official Copy Rights speechwriter.
(Beat.)
Now we better keep moving.
(Michael looks around.)

MICHAEL: Wait a minute . . .

MELISSA: What?

MICHAEL: Notice anything about where we're at right now?

MELISSA: Not really.

MICHAEL: Doesn't it look real familiar?
(Melissa looks around.)

MELISSA: Yeah, it kinda does.

MICHAEL: It appears that we've come full circle.

MELISSA: I don't think so.

MICHAEL: Recognize that tree? Remember, you said it looked like a giant Praying Mantis.
(Melissa looks at the tree.)

MELISSA: You're right. I don't understand it.
(Michael unfolds the map and looks at it.)

MICHAEL: I see what happened. We should have gone toward that mountain peak over there.
(He points. Melissa looks at the map.)

MELISSA: Damn it to Dolly. We must have lost at least two hours. Sorry, Michael.

MICHAEL: Don't be sorry. It's really nice just to be outside and not just from a memory.

MELISSA: Yeah, we're creating some memories of our own, aren't we?

MICHAEL: Good point. Knowing my Original he would never be brave enough to do this.

MELISSA: Mine either. Come on, we've got two hours to make up for. Besides, time is one thing we have a lot of.

(They exit.)

SCENE FOUR

Cottage #4—Bunk Area #2. 0300 hours. Zoom and Wendy are both pretending to be asleep.

ZOOM: Wendy, you asleep?

WENDY: Yes.

ZOOM: Oh, OK . . . sorry.

(Wendy shakes her head in disbelief.)

WENDY: Obviously if I was asleep I'd not be able to answer you.

ZOOM: Oh . . . well, uh, you could if you were talkin' in your sleep.

WENDY: Talking in your sleep and answering in your sleep are two different things.

ZOOM: Uh . . . whatever.

WENDY: You worried about Melissa and Michael, too?

ZOOM: Yeah, what if they get caught?

WENDY: Might be the best thing for them.

ZOOM: What?

WENDY: I mean, compared to what they face trying to fight the Originals.

ZOOM: If anybody can do it, Melissa can.

WENDY: This might even be too much for her. I don't think the Originals want to hear from a Clone.

ZOOM: You used the C word!

WENDY: Big deal, that's what we are, Zoom. Living, breathing, slabs of meat . . . born from a fleck of skin, or hair follicle, or God only knows what.

ZOOM: Why you sayin' that?

WENDY: 'Cause that's what Originals think of us.

ZOOM: Melissa's gonna change all that.

WENDY: I don't know. Maybe we should have gone with her.

ZOOM: You think?

WENDY: She can't do it all alone.

ZOOM: She's got Michael.

WENDY: I just don't know if that's going to be enough.

ZOOM: We could go right now?

WENDY: What?

ZOOM: You and me. We could break outta here, too.

WENDY: Yeah, we could catch up to them and then the four of us could work together to change things.

ZOOM: Yeah!

WENDY: So let's do it.

ZOOM: I will if you will.

WENDY: OK.

ZOOM: OK.

(Long pause as they both think about it.)

WENDY: Well, I am kind of tired tonight . . . and it is really late.

ZOOM: Oh . . . uh . . . yeah, I'm tired too.

WENDY: We'll do it tomorrow, or something.

ZOOM: Yeah, tomorrow . . .

(They look at each other for a long moment and then roll over and go back to pretending they are asleep.)

SCENE FIVE

Somewhere else out on the road. 0330 hours. Melissa enters supporting Michael who limps badly. Exhausted they stop for a moment and Michael sits.

MICHAEL: This is no good. We can't continue like this.

MELISSA: I just need to catch my breath.

MICHAEL: I can't believe a little hole in the ground could do this kind of damage.

MELISSA: Let me see it.

(Michael takes off his shoe. Melissa examines his ankle.)

MELISSA: It's swelling by the second.

MICHAEL: It's not broken.

MELISSA: Might as well be.

MICHAEL: I'm fine.

(Michael stands, trying to hide the pain, then quickly sits back down.)

MELISSA: Doesn't look fine to me.

MICHAEL: Just give me a few minutes, I'll be better. I promise.

MELISSA: I think we're finally far enough away we can afford to take a break, but not for very long. Besides, they won't even know we're missing for at least five more hours.

MICHAEL: We'll be long gone by then.

(Melissa looks off at the horizon.)

MELISSA: See that glow way off there?

MICHAEL: It's beautiful . . . like a giant night-light.

MELISSA: That's the city where we're going.

MICHAEL: It's like they lit it up just for us.

MELISSA: A city full of Originals. Living their lives. Day after day. And taking it all for granted.

MICHAEL: Do you ever wonder what it would be like to have been born instead of made?

MELISSA: All the time.

MICHAEL: Counselor Sue says we're luckier than Originals because they get all hung up on why they're here . . . at least we know why we were created.

MELISSA: Yeah, to serve them like perfect little lookalike robots. But we're not robots—we're flesh and blood. They give us memories about being free, yet they want to enslave us. In the world of the Originals we're just supposed to bow our heads and grovel while they get to raise theirs up to the heavens and dream.

MICHAEL: You don't need me to write your speeches. You have that ability plus. You should write down what you just said and tell that to the Originals when you make your case.

MELISSA: I'll have to tell them a lot more than that.

MICHAEL: I really admire you, Melissa. You've risked a lot to help others.

MELISSA: It's not just to help others, Michael.

MICHAEL: What do you mean?

MELISSA: Don't get me wrong, I do want to fight for Copy Rights. It's important. But . . . the main reason I left the camp is more about survival than heroics. I was scheduled to have a meeting with my Original next week.

MICHAEL: You should have stayed then.

MELISSA: Not just any meeting . . . the last meeting. Counselor Sue told me that if my Original wasn't happy with my progress then she was going to have me redesigned so I would be what she wanted.

MICHAEL: She would do that?

MELISSA: She hated my independence. What did she expect? I was made from her. But she wanted a drooling idiot who she could order around and berate. Does that sound like me?

MICHAEL: Not at all.

MELISSA: Who knows what they'd redesign me to do? I don't want to end up like Betty. So, instead of just hating them for wanting to do that to me I decided to channel that negative energy into something I really believed in.

MICHAEL: Like organizing and protesting.

MELISSA: Exactly.

MICHAEL: Well, that's certainly better than hate.

(Melissa looks at Michael for a moment.)

MELISSA: Remember when you were being initiated.

MICHAEL: Of course, that would be something hard to forget.

MELISSA: When we did that kissing thing . . . you know . . .

MICHAEL: Search the urge.

MELISSA: Right . . . well, when you kissed me . . . I kinda felt something.

MICHAEL: You did?

MELISSA: Well, I don't think it was love . . . not how the Originals describe it anyway . . . but I did feel something.

MICHAEL: That for the first time you cared for someone. Not based on a memory that was uploaded in you, but it was something you yourself felt . . . all on your own.

MELISSA: *(Surprised.)* Yes, that's exactly how I felt. Every word you just said.

MICHAEL: I know . . . I felt that way, too.

(Long pause.)

MELISSA: Why didn't you say something?

MICHAEL: Not sure. Why didn't you?

MELISSA: It kinda scared me.

MICHAEL: Oh.

MELISSA: Uh . . . we should keep moving. Do you think you can make it?

MICHAEL: Yes.

(Michael stands up, takes two steps and falls down. He writhes on the ground holding his ankle.)

MELISSA: You can't even walk on it.

MICHAEL: You must proceed without me.

MELISSA: I can't do that, Michael.

MICHAEL: You have to. I'm just going to hold you up. We'll be caught for sure.

MELISSA: And what will you do?

MICHAEL: Go back to Camp I.M.U.

MELISSA: How are you going to do that? Crawl? On that bad bone it'll take you days.

MICHAEL: If I rest a couple of hours the swelling will go down.

MELISSA: You think you can handle a couple of hours all alone?

MICHAEL: Uh . . . sure . . .

MELISSA: Yeah, right.

(*Melissa crosses over to Michael and helps him to his feet. She put his arm around her neck.*)

MICHAEL: It's no use I can't go on. It's too far . . .

MELISSA: We're not going on, we're going back to the camp.

MICHAEL: But you've been planning this for so long. I can't let you lose all that.

MELISSA: I'm just going to drop you off. Then I'll take off again on my own. I'm not losing anything except a little time. And like I said, we got plenty of that.

(*The two head off.*)

SCENE SIX

Cottage #4—Main Area. Two weeks later. Zoom, Wendy, Sandra, and Betty are hovered around a now familiar floor area on the stage. This time they are not tapping, but listening to someone tapping to them. Wendy counts while Sandra writes down the letters on a piece of paper.

WENDY: 19 . . .

SANDRA: S . . .

WENDY: 15 . . .

SANDRA: O . . .

WENDY: 15 again . . .

SANDRA: O . . .

WENDY: 14 . . .

SANDRA: N . . .

(Wendy listens. Nothing more.)

WENDY: That's it. What did he say?

SANDRA: "Soon."

WENDY: What does he mean by that? What about soon?

ZOOM: He's escaping!

SANDRA: Again?

WENDY: Not from isolation. Not possible.

BETTY: Soon he'll be here . . . and that's cause for cheer!

SANDRA: Very good, Betty. Michael's getting out of isolation and will "soon" be here.

WENDY: We'll have a party.

ZOOM: Yeah. Party!

WENDY: Except we don't have any snacks.

ZOOM: Don't you got any leftovers?

WENDY: No, I tossed them all after I found out Carla went on that new Australian diet.

SANDRA: Well, I bet it will be easier for you to lose weight than to gain it.

WENDY: Eight pounds already.

(She poses.)

BETTY: Lose weight now . . . ask her how.

ZOOM: (Sarcasm.) Yeah, she's practically a bone.

SANDRA: Well I noticed it, Wendy. And I bet Michael will, too.

WENDY: Can't believe he's in isolation . . . again.

BETTY: He's been acting whack, since he came back.

SANDRA: Yes, ever since Melissa dropped him back off here two weeks ago he's really different.

WENDY: Can you blame him? He's an Unwanted. That would take the frosting off anybody's cake.

SANDRA: Maybe they redesigned him. He behaves so badly most of the time.

WENDY: Like they'd redesign him to be bad?

SANDRA: It would give them a reason to recycle him faster.

WENDY: I don't think they need a reason. If they want him recycled they can do it anytime they want. Besides, I like the new Michael. Now that Melissa is gone we need someone around here to remind us not to be such Dollys all the time.

BETTY: Dolly . . . Dolly . . . Golly Dolly Folly Molly Holly Jolly Polly Volley Wally Golly Dolly Molly Holly Jolly . . .

(They all look at Betty who continues the "olly" outburst.)

WENDY: I think she's stuck or something.

(Betty smacks herself in the head and stops her outburst.)

BETTY: Oops, I looped.

(She's fine now.)

WENDY: Now that Michael's ankle has healed he'll break out of here again and go find Melissa.

SANDRA: Won't be easy to do that again. Ever since they found out Melissa left here they've added more security.

ZOOM: Melissa gave him the key.

SANDRA: Useless, they changed all the locks.

WENDY: I bet Michael will find another way out.

ZOOM: Yeah, Michael's the number one.

SCENE SEVEN

Isolation area. At the same time. Michael sits in the red chair in deep thought. After several long moments he removes his recording device from his pocket, speaks into it.

MICHAEL: This will be my last entry in my audio journal to you Robert, mainly because I don't think you'll ever hear anything I've recorded anyway. But in case you do, I wanted to tell you something I was thinking about today. They teach us here to examine our Original's memories because it will help us better understand what shaped your life and what formed your personality. One of the memories I flashed on was your fifth birthday. Remember that? Mom and Dad thought the perfect gift for you would be a puppy. They even said you could pick it out yourself. The Pet Shop had so many to choose from and they all looked so innocent sitting in their little cages, yipping with excitement, as you walked up and down the aisle trying to find the one you wanted. There were dachshunds, Akitas, poodles, terriers, German shepherds . . . just about every kind of dog a boy could want. But there was one that stood out from all the others. A peppy little Rottweiler. Mom and Dad tried to tell you that he might be too much dog for a little boy, but you just had to have him. You named him Samson and thought for sure the two of you would have lots of good times together. But then something happened. Samson quickly grew out of his happy puppy stage and started acting real strange. He wasn't friendly at all. He became distrustful of people, even you . . . especially you. You couldn't figure out why. Your friends joked that the dog just didn't like you. It was a joke to them, but you started to believe it. When Samson ran away you didn't put any real effort into finding him because he had caused you a lot of hurt. Mom and Dad even suggested you get another dog, but you didn't want any part of it. The whole experience had been a very painful one. *(Pause.)* That memory got me thinking. Maybe that's why you decided to cancel me. You just didn't want to blame yourself again if I didn't work out, if we didn't get along. Well, you'd never have to feel that way with me because I would work out. We are completely and perfectly compatible. I'm not just like you Robert; I'm part of you. You'll never ever find anyone who understands you like I do. *(Pause.)* We could have had so many great times together. Why did you cancel me, Robert? You never gave me a chance to prove myself. You never gave me a chance. *(Michael clicks the device off.)*

SCENE EIGHT

Back in Cottage #4. One hour later.

ZOOM: Gotta give ten-ups to Michael for not sayin' anything about Melissa.

WENDY: Yeah, I thought for sure he'd tell them everything about where she went.

SANDRA: Michael would never do that. He's stronger than all of us.

WENDY: You're right about that . . . two weeks and he hasn't broken yet.

ZOOM: And neither have we.

WENDY: Melissa would be proud of all of us.

SANDRA: We need to be careful. If our Originals find out we lied . . .

WENDY: We didn't lie . . . we just told them we didn't know anything.

BETTY: The rule of thumb is just to act dumb.

SANDRA: We knew about them leaving.

WENDY: But not where they went. Only Michael knew the details. And his Original could care less if he lied about that.

ZOOM: Hey, let's tell Michael we got an e-mail from Melissa.

(He grabs the broom and is about to tap on the floor. Wendy stops him.)

WENDY: No, too dangerous.

ZOOM: They don't serve him nutrition for another hour.

WENDY: If they're coming for Michael "soon" it might just be now and they'll hear it.

SANDRA: Good point.

BETTY: Yeah, so Zoom, put down that broom.

(*Zoom decides to set the broom aside.*)

WENDY: Besides, we don't really know if that e-mail was from her.

ZOOM: 'Course it was.

SANDRA: It was a spam ad for Valium.

ZOOM: I told you . . . it's secret code. Valium is medication and that starts with the letter "M" just like Melissa's name . . .

SANDRA: Come on . . .

ZOOM: And there were two of the very same spam e-mails. One was a "Copy" of the other one. Get it!

WENDY: I'd like to believe Melissa sent us a message probably even more than you did . . . but that's really stretching it.

SANDRA: Yeah, and what about that new girl in Cottage #8?

ZOOM: Don't even start with that again. You're just a bunch of doubtin' Dollys.

WENDY: Well, if Melissa is still out there . . . I don't doubt that she's fighting for our rights. Right now she's probably organizing a big rally or something.

ZOOM: Yeah, she's a born leader.

(*Michael enters.*)

MICHAEL: Except she wasn't born. None of us were.

SANDRA: Michael!

(*Michael crosses to them and enjoys the same hugs and high-fives Melissa did in an earlier scene when she returned.*)

MICHAEL: Wendy, you look thinner.

WENDY: You see, Zoom . . . someone noticed!

BETTY: Thinner's a winner.

WENDY: You were in there a long time.

SANDRA: Too long . . . it's not fair.

WENDY: I don't see how you can handle it. The most I've ever been in isolation was two hours and I just about went daft and a half.

MICHAEL: It's all a matter of concentration. Melissa taught me that. You just need to focus on something and let your mind become your friend. If you use your own thoughts to keep you company then you're never alone.

(*The others are impressed with that.*)

ZOOM: We heard from Melissa.

MICHAEL: You did?

WENDY: Zoom, don't even start that.

(Zoom gets close to Michael.)

ZOOM: We got two e-mails from her—one was a Copy! She disguised them as spam, but I know they were from Melissa.

BETTY: Female e-mail.

MICHAEL: What kind of spam?

ZOOM: Medication . . . starts with M . . . just like . . .

MICHAEL: Melissa.

ZOOM: You get it.

MICHAEL: Could be.

WENDY: You really think so, Michael?

MICHAEL: Anything is possible. Melissa just might do something real subtle like that.

(They all think about that for a moment.)

SANDRA: You know there's also a possibility that Melissa was caught.

MICHAEL: Don't say that. Don't even think that.

ZOOM: Yeah, Sandra . . . mute it.

SANDRA: I heard something.

(Michael crosses to her.)

MICHAEL: What?

SANDRA: A new girl in Cottage #8 . . .

WENDY: Sandra, we agreed not to tell him about that . . .

MICHAEL: What about her? Tell me.

SANDRA: Well, some say it's Melissa . . . redesigned. She arrived here two days after you came back.

MICHAEL: Impossible.

WENDY: Well, I heard that, too . . .

(Quickly.)

But I don't believe it for a minute.

SANDRA: I saw her during special assembly. She looked a lot like Melissa . . .

MICHAEL: Did you talk to her?

SANDRA: No.

MICHAEL: The probability of it being Melissa is incredibly low.

WENDY: Well, the word's out that it's her . . . and a lot of the Copies here believe it.

(Michael paces for a moment. Looking up at the ceiling.)

MICHAEL: Oh, they're good all right. I must commend them on their dirty little control tactics. Nice job, people!

SANDRA: Michael, keep your voice down. They might be monitoring.

MICHAEL: The propaganda machine at Camp I.M.U. is working overtime. Don't you see it? They made sure the rumor started that the only Copy to ever escape this orientation camp was caught and redesigned. That new Copy in Cottage #8 is not Melissa. But everyone thinks it is because they said so.

(Yelling up to the ceiling.)

You can't fool us. We don't buy it. Melissa is alive and free!

WENDY: Ssshh . . . Be careful, Michael.

MICHAEL: Why?

SANDRA: You're on probation. They might . . .

MICHAEL: Recycle me?

SANDRA: Don't even say that word.

MICHAEL: I'm not afraid of it. Because it's not a matter of if they will recycle me, only when.

SANDRA: Well don't give them a reason to rush it.

ZOOM: Yeah, they might be listening.

BETTY: Their ear might be right here.

MICHAEL: So what? So I get a couple more days sitting and wondering when the big beaker will drop? Losing sleep a couple more nights because I know that my pathetic copied DNA will soon be DOA?

(Michael stands up defiantly.)

MICHAEL: *(Shouting.)* Bring it on I say! Let's get it over with. Let's do the Chromosome shuffle. I'm here! What are you waiting for?

SANDRA: Michael, stop. Please.

(Michael stands on the cube and continues to yell at the ceiling. The others ad-lib for him to stop.)

MICHAEL: I'm right here! I'm right here!

(Michael continues and only stops when he notices the others are looking at Counselor Sue who has just entered.)

COUNSELOR SUE: What's going on?

WENDY: Nothing. We were just . . .

SANDRA: Playing a game.

COUNSELOR SUE: Pretty loud game.

ZOOM: Yeah . . . it's called . . . "Loud Game" . . . uh . . . you know . . . who can be the loudest.

(*Counselor Sue scrutinizes all of them for a moment. She then walks to Michael who is still standing on the cube.*)

COUNSELOR SUE: Allen, come with me.

(*Michael hops off the cube.*)

WENDY: He didn't do anything. We were just playing.

MICHAEL: (*To others.*) It's OK.

(*He exits with Counselor Sue.*)

BETTY: Oh no . . . say it isn't so.

SANDRA: Maybe she's just taking him to isolation.

ZOOM: More like the "final" isolation.

SANDRA: But he didn't take his belongings. So he's gonna come back. Right?

WENDY: I don't think he'll need his belongings where he's going.

SCENE NINE

A meeting room with a small table and two chairs. Fifteen minutes later. Michael is there with Counselor Sue.

MICHAEL: Can I say good-bye to my friends?

COUNSELOR SUE: No. That's against Camp Policy.

MICHAEL: Can I at least have some time to myself before they come for me?

COUNSELOR SUE: If you like, but first there is someone I'm sending in here that you should speak to. It might give you some comfort for what you are going to face.

MICHAEL: Last rites? Well, at least you let us have that. Go ahead, send in the priest, I've got a few questions I'd like to ask . . . but I don't think he's going to be able to answer them.

(*Counselor Sue exits. Michael sits for a moment and then looks up to see Amy, a seventeen-year-old Original, who has just entered the room. She gasps when she sees Michael.*)

AMY: Oh my God.

MICHAEL: Amy? What are you doing here?

(*Michael stands up.*)

AMY: I'm . . . uh . . . this is incredible. I'm sorry but I didn't think it would be . . . that you would be . . .

MICHAEL: So exact?

AMY: Uh . . . yes . . . it's amazing. Your face . . . your voice . . .

MICHAEL: That happens a lot when Originals see us for the first time. I remember how you reacted to the Schofields when they got their Copy last Christmas.

AMY: Copy?

MICHAEL: Clone.

AMY: Oh. Yeah, I know the Schofields got one . . . but . . .

MICHAEL: You're exactly as how I remember you, Amy. Or at least as they uploaded me to remember you.

AMY: I am?

MICHAEL: Well you are Robert's sister. They wouldn't leave something like that out. I would need to know you.

AMY: Well, yeah.

MICHAEL: Did Mom and Dad come with you?

AMY: No, I came alone.

(She crosses to Michael and hugs him for a long moment. Michael is very confused by this.)

AMY: What should I call you?

MICHAEL: The people here call me Michael.

AMY: Michael?

MICHAEL: It's just a temporary name . . .

(Can't hold back.)

Are you here to take me home?

(Amy doesn't say anything.)

MICHAEL: I'm sorry. I shouldn't have asked that.

AMY: I'm here because . . . because I wanted to apologize . . . for my parents. It's not like them to do something like this. To just leave you here without knowing why. But they've not been themselves lately. At all.

(Amy stares at him for a moment, still adjusting.)

MICHAEL: Are you OK, Amy?

AMY: Wow . . . this is like so hard.

(Pause.)

On the way over here I had it all planned out how I was going to tell you. I mean after your Counselor called and told us how hurt you were about how they backed out of the deal and all.

MICHAEL: She called you?

AMY: Yeah.

MICHAEL: She didn't tell me that.

AMY: Well, I explained everything to her. She said she understood but thought we really should contact you. That you'd be wondering. We hadn't even considered that . . .

MICHAEL: . . . that Clones have feelings?

AMY: Right.

MICHAEL: Most Originals don't consider that.

AMY: After I told her about what happened to Robert I think she realized how all of this happened . . .

MICHAEL: What about Robert?

AMY: She didn't tell you?

MICHAEL: No. What happened to Robert?

(Amy hadn't counted on this. She sits down in the other chair and collects her thoughts.)

AMY: I thought you knew . . .

MICHAEL: No one told me anything. What should I know?

(Long pause.)

MELISSA: There was an accident. At the lake. Robert was too far out. We all thought he was a pretty good swimmer. The lifeguard did what he could . . .

MICHAEL: What are you saying?

AMY: Robert drowned. Mom and Dad were completely destroyed. Me, too. I mean all those years Robert and I argued . . . I'd give anything to go back and just tell him how much I loved the guy.

(Michael tries to process the information he just heard.)

AMY: When the people at the camp here called to ask why we hadn't shown up for the meeting with you . . . Mom and Dad just couldn't deal with it. All of us had forgotten about the meeting. Actually it kind of scared them that you even existed . . . you know, someone who looked just like Robert. They just wanted to forget about that. To forget about you. It was so soon after he died and all . . . they just couldn't handle something like having his clone around.

(Beat.)

Then when your Counselor Melissa called on your behalf . . .

(Thinking out loud.)

I can't believe she never told you what happened. She seemed really sincere about getting an explanation when she called us.

MICHAEL: Did you say Melissa?

AMY: Yes, Counselor Melissa. She really made a case for you. How wonderful you are. That really impressed me that she'd build you up like that and that she knew you so well. I talked to her the longest because that call really rattled the folks.

(Michael realizes and then smiles.)

MICHAEL: Yes, Counselor Melissa and I are very close. When did she call you?

AMY: Two days ago.

MICHAEL: So that's not her in Cottage #8.

AMY: What?

MICHAEL: Nothing.

(Beat.)

I'm really shocked to hear about Robert.

AMY: We were all pretty shocked. I loved him so much.

MICHAEL: I know he never showed it very often, but he really cared about you, too.

AMY: He did?

MICHAEL: Remember that time you thought you lost your class ring and then he found it a month later?

AMY: Uh . . . yes . . . you know about that? I guess you would.

MICHAEL: It wasn't the actual ring he found. He bought a new one. You were so upset about it he felt really bad so he used his savings and bought it without anyone knowing. It was worth every penny just seeing the look on your face when he handed it to you.

AMY: I never knew that.

MICHAEL: Maybe I shouldn't have told you.

AMY: No, I'm so glad you did.

(Amy looks at Michael for a moment.)

AMY: I just can't get over how much you're like him. How real you are.

MICHAEL: I'm real all right.

AMY: This is gonna take some time.

MICHAEL: Getting used to me?

AMY: Well, that too. But I mean convincing my parents . . . I mean, our parents . . . about you.

MICHAEL: Convincing them that I'm real?

AMY: No, convincing them that we need you . . . with us.

MICHAEL: You want me to live with you?

AMY: Yes. Not just want . . . need. I just know if I can get Mom and Dad to come here and talk with you. Well, I don't see how they could not feel the same way I do.

MICHAEL: You know I was created from Robert, but not to replace him. I don't know if I can do that.

AMY: I'm not asking you to do that . . . and neither will they. But you are part of Robert and that makes you part of our family. You belong with us. I know I can convince them of that . . . just give me a little time.

MICHAEL: Time is easy. I'll wait until they're ready. I want to be part of your family. No matter how long it might take for that to happen.

AMY: Really? You're willing to wait?

MICHAEL: Absolutely. But you might have to tell them here that you are rescinding the cancel order. That will make them keep me around here . . . until you're ready to take me home.

AMY: Yes, of course. Should I talk to Counselor Melissa? I'd really like to meet her.

MICHAEL: She kind of went outside of the rules to talk to you. Do me a favor . . . just tell the front office . . . but don't mention her, OK?

AMY: Just like Robert. Always worrying about protecting others. OK, I won't mention her name.

MICHAEL: Thank you.

AMY: This is a miracle. It's like Robert knew that he wouldn't be a-round . . . so he asked for you.

(Amy gives him another hug. This time Michael hugs back.)

MICHAEL: Hey, how's Botchy?

AMY: Crazy as ever.

MICHAEL: Still digging up the Nickerson's garden?

AMY: His favorite place to hide his bones. Guess what he did the other day? You know how he likes to grab the mail when the mailman puts it through the slot . . .

MICHAEL: That really irritates Dad.

AMY: Well, someone mailed Dad a really big check and Botchy literally tore it to pieces.

MICHAEL: Uh-oh . . . talk about being in the doghouse!

(Lights fade on the two of them laughing.)

SCENE TEN

Cottage #4—Main Area. An hour later. Wendy and Zoom are huddled around the spot on the floor. Sandra holds the broom and is tapping on the floor. Betty stands watch.

SANDRA: He's not responding.

ZOOM: Maybe he can't. Maybe they beat him up so bad he can't move.

WENDY: Maybe he's not even in there.

SANDRA: He has to be. Where else would they take him?

WENDY: Like I said before . . . to be recycled.

BETTY: Recycle Michael?

ZOOM: Try again, Sandra.

WENDY: I'm telling you he's not there. He would have tapped back by now.

SANDRA: OK, so he's not there. But that just means he's somewhere else.

ZOOM: Maybe he's helpin' Counselor Sue with somethin'.

WENDY: Get a grasp . . . Michael's not even in the camp anymore. By now he's halfway to the Redemption Center.

SANDRA: I guess that's a possibility, but I just don't want to think that.

WENDY: Do you know what they do to a Copy when they recycle it? From what I hear they don't even put you out. They just walk you into some kind of grinder thingey and you're fully aware that in seconds you'll be turned into so much Copy enriched sausage stuffing.

SANDRA: That's ridiculous. They're not that cruel.

WENDY: Sure they are . . . 'specially because they look at us as product. We're just disposable Dollys to them. No one cares what the product thinks . . . or feels. If they knocked us out first then they'd have to haul are numb butts into the machine. Why go to all that trouble when a Copy can just use his own two legs to waddle in there?

SANDRA: Stop it, Wendy.

WENDY: We don't even get to die . . . we just pop back up as someone else. And not even the same sex sometimes. We might go in as a Ken and then come out a Barbie.

SANDRA: That's enough!

ZOOM: Ah, she don't know how they recycle Copies. None of us do.

WENDY: I've heard enough stories to know it's true.

BETTY: Only true according to you.

SANDRA: Well, I'm not going to believe any of it . . . or am I going to give up on believing that Michael is still around here.

WENDY: None of us can give up on Michael. If he's in trouble we have to help him.

ZOOM: Yeah, but if he is in trouble, there's nothin' we can do about it.

BETTY: Stop the flapping of your gums, something wicked this way comes. *(They break up and Sandra ditches the broom. Counselor Sue enters, followed by Michael.)*

COUNSELOR SUE: Why do I always think I'm just walking in on something in this cottage?

(They all try to hide their excitement about seeing Michael.)

COUNSELOR SUE: *(To Michael.)* You going to be all right, Allen?

MICHAEL: Absolutely. Thank you for the escort.

COUNSELOR SUE: Let's keep this reunion a short one . . . after seeing your test scores today, you all need to spend more time studying.
(Counselor Sue gives one last scrutinizing look at the group and then exits. After she is gone . . . the others gather around Michael.)

SANDRA: We were so worried about you.

WENDY: What happened?

ZOOM: Yeah, we were sure you were a goner.

MICHAEL: Well, I thought I was a goner, too. But a miracle happened. I had a visitor.

SANDRA: Your Original came for you?

MICHAEL: Not that much of a miracle. But close. My Original's sister came to meet me.

BETTY: Through thick and thin, she's next of kin.

WENDY: Sister? Why didn't your Original come?

MICHAEL: I'll tell you the whole story later. Right now I really don't wish to talk about it.

SANDRA: So are you going home with them?

MICHAEL: In time. Just like the rest of you, I'm going to have to wait it out. But at least I have something to wait for now.

ZOOM: So you're not gonna be recycled?

MICHAEL: We all will be someday, but I don't count on that happening for a long long time.
(Betty hugs Michael.)

BETTY: We've gone from sad, to being real glad.

MICHAEL: Thanks, Betty. And here's something to make all of you even more glad . . . I have proof that Melissa is OK and still out there fighting for our rights.

WENDY: You do?

MICHAEL: My Original's sister came here because she got a call from Counselor "Melissa" . . . two days ago!

ZOOM: Melissa's a Counselor now?

MICHAEL: Only on the outside, Zoom.

ZOOM: Outside?

MICHAEL: Out there in the real world. The big open cradle of humanity way beyond the confines of these walls. The place where Originals walk zombielike through their day . . . Melissa is now among them. Dancing full of life. Dancing for all of us.

WENDY: She's going to do it. She's going to turn this world upside down.

(An electronic buzzer is heard.)

MICHAEL: Come on, I've got my appetite back. I think tonight I could even eat the lousy nutrients the camp cafeteria serves.

WENDY: You can have mine then . . . 'cause I'm on liquids for awhile. Gonna lose ten more pounds by the end of next week.

(They start to head out.)

SANDRA: Michael, guess what . . . we're getting a new Copy tomorrow.

BETTY: Fresh flesh!

WENDY: What kind of initiation you gonna give 'em, Michael?

MICHAEL: Me?

ZOOM: Yeah, you're the new number one.

WENDY: Melissa would want you to continue her tradition.

MICHAEL: If that's what she would want, then that's what I will do. I'll think of an appropriate initiation.

(Beat.)

But one thing's for sure . . . it won't be "Search the Urge."

(They all laugh at that as they exit. Betty lags behind for a moment. She speaks directly to the audience.)

BETTY: The longer we stay here the harder it seems.

Is this someone's nightmare or just our bad dream?

We study and learn and wait for the day

When our Original asks us to come home and stay.

(Betty realizes she's alone and then runs off stage to join the others. The stage lights fade out.)

END OF PLAY

The Rhinoceros with Wings

by Carey Perloff

PLAYWRIGHT'S BIOGRAPHY

Carey Perloff is celebrating her sixteenth season as artistic director of A.C.T., where she most recently directed acclaimed productions of *'Tis Pity She's a Whore, The Government Inspector,* the world premiere of Philip Kan Gotanda's *After the War* (an A.C.T. commission), Tom Stoppards' *Travesties,* Bertolt Brecht/ Kurt Weill's *Happy End* (including a critically acclaimed cast album recording distributed by Ghostlight Records), and *A Christmas Carol* (a new adaptation by Perloff with dramaturg Paul Walsh). Known for directing innovative productions of classics and championing new writing for the theater, Perloff has directed for A.C.T. the American premieres of Stoppard's *The Invention of Love* and *Indian Ink* and Pinter's *Celebration* and *The Room;* A.C.T.–commissioned translations of *Hecuba, The Misanthrope, Enrico IV, Mary Stuart, Uncle Vanya,* and *A Mother* (based on Gorky's *Vassa Zheleznova);* David Mamet's new adaptation for A.C.T. of Granville-Barker's *The Voysey Inheritance;* the world premiere of Leslie Ayvazian's *Singer's Boy;* and major revivals of *A Doll's House, Waiting for Godot, The Three Sisters, The Threepenny Opera, Old Times, The Rose Tattoo, Antigone, Creditors, Home, The Tempest, and* Stoppard's *The Real Thing, Night and Day,* and *Arcadia.* Her production of Marie Ndiaye's *Hilda,* coproduced at A.C.T.'s second space (Zeum) with Laura Pels Productions, traveled to Washington, D.C.'s Studio Theater and New York's 59E59 Theater in 2005. Perloff's work at A.C.T. also includes the world premieres of Marc Blitzsten's *No for an Answer,* David Lang/ Mac Wellman's *The Difficulty of Crossing a Field,* and the West Coast premiere of her own play *The Colossus of Rhodes* (a finalist for the Susan Smith Blackburn Award). Her play *Luminescence Dating* was developed under a grant from The Ensemble Studio Theatre/Alfred P. Sloan Foundation Science & Technology Project, was workshopped in the summer of 2004 at New York Stage & Film, and premiered in New York in April 2005 at the Ensemble Studio Theatre, was coproduced by A.C.T. and the Magic Theatre last December, and is published by Dramatists Play Service. Her play, *Waiting for the Flood,* has received workshops at the Roundabout Theater and at the New York Stage & Film, and her latest play, *Higher,* was developed at New York Stage & Film and as part of A.C.T.'s First Look series at Stanford. Her one-act play, *The Morning After,* was a finalist for the Heideman Prize at Actors Theatre of Louisville. Perloff has also collaborated as a director with many notable contemporary writers, most recently Philip Kan Gotanda, on his new play *After the War* at the Sundance Institute in 2004; Robert O'Hara, on *Antebellum* for the 2005 O'Neill Playwrights Conference; and Irish playwright Lucy Caldwell, on *Guardians,* for the 2007 O'Neill conference.

Before joining A.C.T., Perloff was artistic director of Classic Stage Company in New York, where she directed the world premiere of Ezra Pound's *Elektra,* the American premiere of Pinter's *Mountain Language* and *The Birthday Party,* and many classic works. Under Perloff's leadership, Classic Stage won numerous OBIE Awards for acting, direction, and design, as well as the 1988 OBIE for artistic excellence. In 1993, she directed the world premiere of Steve Reich and Beryl Korot's opera *The Cave* at the Vienna Festival and Brooklyn Academy of Music. She is currently preparing a major production of *Phedre* (translated by Timberlake Wertenbaker) for the Stratford Festival in Canada, and a new *Bacchae* for the Getty Center in Los Angeles.

A recipient of Chevalier de l'Ordre des Arts et des Lettres and the National Corporate Theater Fund's 2007 Artistic Achievement Award, Perloff received a B.A. Phi Beta Kappa in classics and comparative literature from Stanford University and was a Fulbright Fellow at Oxford. She was on the faculty of the Tisch School of the Arts at New York University for seven years and teaches and directs in the A.C.T. Master of Fine Arts Program. She is the proud mother of Lexie and Nicholas.

FROM THE PLAYWRIGHT

I began writing this play on a very long plane journey with my son Nicholas. Nicholas had recently gotten involved with acting classes at A.C.T.'s Young Conservatory, and he seemed surprised to discover the dearth of dramatic literature for ten-year-old boys! So we set about to create our own play about five pre-adolescent guys. I came up with the scenario, and Nicholas aided and abetted the shaping of the scenes. As we worked, I loved discovering his perceptions of what really went on between his peers: the status games, the fear of being "found out," the wicked sense of humor, the attachment to parents, the blurring of lines between reality and fiction. Once I finished writing the play, I was lucky enough to see it staged by the incomparable Craig Slaight at A.C.T., and to discover how much young actors could bring to every moment of this story. *The Rhinoceros with Wings* is dedicated to every kid who manages to survive through a leap of imagination, and to Craig who can find imagination in every kid he trains.

FROM THE ACTOR—Samuel Friend Pritzker (Billy)

Working on a new production was an amazing experience, because I got to work with the cast along with Craig to form a new production. Even though there was a script in place, it wasn't final, so it offered us the opportunity to add a level of brainstorming and creativity that ordinarily wouldn't exist in a play. Some of us would bring in a guest to a few of the rehearsals and get their input on this new production. Some parts they would laugh at, others they wouldn't. We would then revisit the script after the rehearsal and revise what we had originally. It was as though many authors came together with input on one play, one idea, and one piece.

It was so enjoyable having an all-male cast, because we could relate to things in the play that happened in our lives. The story is about a poor boy that convinces a group of kids that he owns an amazing, one-of-a-kind computer game, that no one had seen before. Each character had a unique temperament: one was a bully, one was an outcast, two played the sidekicks, and one played the protagonist. We had group discussions and talked about kids that we could relate to who were similar to the characters. Each character would read a line, and we would discuss it, and debate about whether or not that was something the character would say. Each actor brought his own style to the play, which made it more interesting than it would have been otherwise. I know this was a great experience for me, and I am sure it was for my fellow actors as well.

ORIGINAL PRODUCTION

The Rhinoceros with Wings was written for and originally presented by the Young Conservatory at American Conservatory Theater (Carey Perloff, Artistic Director, Heather M. Kitchen, Executive Director, San Francisco, California in March 2005. It was directed by Craig Slaight and the cast was as follows:

BILLY	Samuel Friend Pritzker
HARLEY	Evan Bass
SKIP	Nicholas Perloff-Giles
JOE	Matthew Davis
BRUD	David McKenna

SETTING

The playground of an urban school; Harley's apartment; Billy's bedroom

CHARACTERS

BILLY, a poor kid who lives in a run-down house near school

HARLEY, Billy's best friend, lives with his Haitian grandmother and teenage sister. Very small.

SKIP, a loud overgrown kid with an overprotective mother

JOE, often confused, somewhat of an intellectual. Glasses.

BRUD, a jock whose mother drives a Hummer

THE RHINOCEROS WITH WINGS

SCENE ONE

A playground at an urban public school. Just before the end of the school day. The kids are waiting to be picked up.

BILLY: So he spreads his wings till they're phenomenally huge—

HARLEY: Huge!

SKIP: Wings?

JOE: I thought you said he was a rhinoceros—

BILLY: *(Patiently.)* He's a transformational rhinoceros—that's the point—

HARLEY: That's the point, man!

BRUD: What's the name of this game?

JOE: I know more about animals than any of you—I'm a Junior Zookeeper!— and I've never heard of anything like that—

SKIP: That's cause you're not as smart as you think—

BILLY: That's cause it's so rare—

HARLEY: Incredibly rare—

SKIP: You're all stupid—and you're making this up—

BILLY: I'm *not*—

BRUD: So where do the wings come from?

BILLY: You push "control alt delete"—

BRUD: Control what?

JOE: Don't you know anything?

SKIP: Shut up, Joe—

JOE: Control alt delete is computer talk—for help—

BRUD: Help what?

HARLEY: Help transform the rhinoceros—

SKIP: Help shut Billy up—

JOE: You push it when your computer's frozen—I've done it—

BILLY: But in this game it miraculously activates the wings—you hit control alt delete—then the arrow keys—and BAM! The wings sprout—

SKIP: I like games where you just click the mouse—

HARLEY: We're talking about a *rhinoceros*—

BRUD: So what?

SKIP: What kind of powers does it have anyway?

BILLY: Infinite powers—

HARLEY: Infinite!

BRUD: What's ifninite?

SKIP: You're making this up—I can tell!

BILLY: You're just jealous!

SKIP: You are! Just like the last time—

JOE: What last time?

SKIP: Billy had some supersonic remote-control car that could climb the walls and hang upside down on the ceiling like a bat, remember? Only my mom went to Toys R Us to ask if they had it and the lady said *(Imitating her voice.)* "it's impossible for a car to hang upside down from the ceiling no matter how supersonic it is . . . only bats can do that, dear"—and I got really mad and yelled at her that a kid in my school had one that *did* hang from the ceiling like a bat and that I wanted one just like that and she said you must be making it up Billy—

JOE: How did she know his name was Billy?

SKIP: She didn't, stupid—*I'm* saying his name is Billy—

JOE: Stop calling me stupid—

BRUD: We *know* his name is Billy—

HARLEY: Well if she didn't say *Billy* how does she know if he's making it up or not?

BILLY: She doesn't!

SKIP: *I* know! He's a liar!

HARLEY: He's not!

SKIP: Then how come he never even brings a lunch to school but he's always got some new toy that none of us has ever heard of—

BILLY: I do *too* bring a lunch—

BRUD: I have all the new games—my mom lets me go to the computer store every Friday while she gets her toes done—

JOE: Maybe if she made you read a book instead, you wouldn't be flunking out of school—

BRUD: I'm only flunking out of *this* school. I'm going to a different school next year—

JOE: Idiot Elementary.

HARLEY: What's she done to her toes?

BRUD: Huh?

HARLEY: Your mom—what's wrong with her toes, man?

BRUD: Nothing's wrong with them—she likes them pink—you know—polished—

HARLEY: Her toes get polished?

BRUD: Her nails, stupid—her toenails—

HARLEY: That's disgusting—

BRUD: No it isn't—sometimes they're even *red*—or brown—

BILLY: To match the Hummer!

HARLEY: How 'bout *green?* Are they ever *green,* Brud?

BRUD: Shut up! You don't even *have* a mother—you just have that stinky old grandmother who screams at you in voodoo—

HARLEY: French—

BILLY: Haitian—

BRUD: Whatever—she's weird—

BILLY: Not as weird as your mom—she's got no eyebrows—

BRUD: That's cuz she gets 'em plucked off!

JOE: Gross! That is so gross!

BILLY: Why would she do that?

SKIP: With hot wax!

BRUD: Our *Hummer* gets cleaned with hot wax!

(A bell rings in the school. Billy looks visibly relieved.)

BILLY: Time to go—

BRUD: *(To Billy.)* Saved by the bell, liar!

BILLY: What do you—

BRUD: You make everything up but we don't believe it—

BILLY: Who cares—

BRUD: Bring that rhinoceros game to school, why don't you—

SKIP: Yeah! I dare you!

BRUD: Double dare!

BILLY: I can't—

HARLEY: He can't—

BILLY: My mom won't let me—

HARLEY: His mom won't let him—

BRUD: Do you have to repeat everything he says? You don't even *have* a mom—

BILLY: Leave him alone—

BRUD: *(To Billy.)* And I'm not sure *you* have one either—no one's ever seen her—

BILLY: That's irrelevant—she has more important things to do than hang around the playground—

BRUD: My mom says there's nothing more important than picking up your kids from school—

(There's a loud car honk offstage.)

SKIP: There's my gross babysitter—*(He grabs his backpack.)* I'm gonna stick gum on her seat! *(He exits.)*

BRUD: I hate his babysitter! Once we locked her out of the house.
　　(Sounds of cars honking.)
JOE: Look at that traffic jam—must be your mom, Brud—blocking the entire
　　street—
BRUD: How would you know—you can't even see straight—
JOE: You'd have to be blind not to see *that* car—
BRUD: It's a Hummer, moron! Ever heard of it? It's like a tank, only better.
　　With a video screen *and* DVD—
JOE: She buy it for you when you didn't get into any of those great *schools*
　　you're going to ?—
BRUD: Who needs schools when you have a Hummer—
BILLY: With a machine gun that mows people down—
HARLEY: Wow, really?
BRUD: I'll mow *you* down!
　　(The Hummer honks loudly.)
BRUD: Coming, Mom! See you tomorrow. Bring that game, Billy! I dare you!
　　(He runs offstage.)
HARLEY: He is such a creep.
JOE: I'm going to the library—my mom can't come till six today . . .
BILLY: I guess I'll walk home now . . .
HARLEY: I'll go with you. Bye Joe.
JOE: *(Joe starts to leave. Then he turns to Billy.)* Hey you guys—is it a lie? That
　　game with the rhinoceros? Did you make it up?
HARLEY: 'Course not. Why would he make it up?
BILLY: It flies through the air and turns into fabulous creatures from the
　　unknown deeps—
JOE: Wow. *(Pause.)* I wish I had one. See you tomorrow. *(He exits.)*
　　(Billy and Harley sit down on the pavement. Silence. Finally—)
HARLEY: That was a close call, man—
BILLY: Nah—
HARLEY: Why do you do that? He's going to find out and kick your butt!
BILLY: I'm not scared of him!
HARLEY: You should be—he's *mean!*
BILLY: And it *does* exist! I know it does! I just don't have it yet!
HARLEY: You don't have *nothing!*
BILLY: Anything—
HARLEY: Right, *anything!* You don't even have a *computer,* so how you gonna
　　play a game?
BILLY: There are ways—
HARLEY: You ain't got your own room—or toys—or nothing—

THE RHINOCEROS WITH WINGS　323

BILLY: Neither do you—

HARLEY: I know I don't—but I don't *say* I do—

BILLY: You don't say anything—

HARLEY: Yes I do! I back you up!

BILLY: You're just scared your grandma will spank you—

HARLEY: She'd spank *you* if she heard you telling lies—

BILLY: She'd never hear—she's deaf—

HARLEY: She not deaf! Mariela tried to sneak through the fire escape window last night and Grandma started screaming Haitian curses and throwing stuff out of the window. The whole neighborhood came out to listen—

BILLY: My mom never came home last night.

HARLEY: Never?

BILLY: Nah—she went to some all-night rally—

HARLEY: Man!

BILLY: *(Quickly.)* She left a message for me, though—

HARLEY: What was she rallying about?

BILLY: I don't know. World hunger probably—

HARLEY: How come white people rally about world hunger but then they don't give their own kids dinner?

BILLY: *(Defensively.)* I got dinner—

HARLEY: Or breakfast—who gave you breakfast?

BILLY: I found some cereal—I ate the whole box!

HARLEY: Weren't you scared—all night—all by yourself?

BILLY: Nah. I played computer games—

HARLEY: But you ain't got a computer!

BILLY: So! I pretended! As loud as I could.

HARLEY: You're crazy.

BILLY: The rhinoceros sprouted wings—and ran through the apartment and bellowed. Loud as it could.

HARLEY: No kidding. *(Pause.)* You eat lunch today?

BILLY: Not exactly—

HARLEY: Come home with me—Grandmere will fix you something—

BILLY: Nah—I came home with you yesterday—

HARLEY: She don't care—she calls you her *"pauvre mouton blanc"*—

BILLY: Huh?

HARLEY: Poor white lamb—

BILLY: You tell her I'm a rhinoceros.

   (Blackout.)

SCENE TWO

The playground again. Early morning, before school. Skip and Brud in a corner, conspiring.

SKIP: We could go find out—

BRUD: Find out what?

SKIP: Whether he's got it, stupid—

BRUD: We know he doesn't—

SKIP: Yeah—well maybe he's got something else—

BRUD: I don't think he's got anything—he's a liar—

SKIP: He makes it all up—

BRUD: And his mother's a hippy—

SKIP: What's a hippy?

BRUD: A crazy person who drives an old car and eats organic vegetables and stuff. That's what my mom says.

SKIP: What kind of vegetables?

BRUD: You ever been to his house?

SKIP: No way—it's covered in vines and falling down any second—

BRUD: Sweet. Get him to invite us over—I dare you—

SKIP: You ask him—he's scared of you—

BRUD: Yeah—I could—but how would we get there?

SKIP: In your Hummer!

BRUD: My mom wouldn't drive the Hummer there! It's a bad neighborhood!

SKIP: Isn't that what Hummers are for?

BRUD: They're for comfort and peace of mind—that's what my mom says. Besides, that's the kind of neighborhood where people wait on the corner to spray paint Hummers as they drive by.

SKIP: Why would they do that?

BRUD: Because they're *hippies*, moron.

SKIP: Maybe we can walk—Billy comes to school by himself, doesn't he?

BRUD: Who knows—he's always here when we get here—

SKIP: He pretends his mom brings him—but I think he comes by himself—

BRUD: Is that allowed? My mom says—

SKIP: They can't stop you—

BRUD: He'll catch us!

SKIP: We'll have to distract him. Hey—how about you invite him to ride in your Hummer—and Joe and I go over and take a look!

BRUD: Harley'll tell—he'll get that weird grandma of his to put a voodoo curse on us—

SKIP: Then invite him too! Invite the grandma!

BRUD: Wait a minute—how many people am I supposed to invite?

SKIP: It's a Hummer! They seat twelve! I want to know if that little creep is lying once and for all.

BRUD: Of course he is. *(He snorts.)* Rhinoceros wings. Give me a break.

(Blackout.)

SCENE THREE

Harley's apartment. Sound of Haitian music in the background. Harley and Billy are huddled over a big cardboard box, beside which is a computer in the process of being unplugged.

HARLEY: Listen—if Mariela finds out, I'm dead. Totally dead.

BILLY: She'll never know. We only need it for an hour—come on—

HARLEY: I don't even know where all the plugs go—

BILLY: I do—watch—this is to the monitor—and the yellow one is where the mouse attaches—it's easy—

HARLEY: How come you know all this and you don't even got a computer?

BILLY: I read the manuals at the drugstore—

(From offstage we hear:)

GRANDMERE: Harley? *Ou es-tu, cherie?*

HARLEY: *Ici, Grandmere.*

GRANDMERE: What you doin' in Mariela's room, baby? Come on out of there—

HARLEY: OK—just a second—

BILLY: Quick—stick it in the box—

(From offstage:)

GRANDMERE: You want somethin' sweet, *mes enfants?*

HARLEY: *(Stalling for time while Billy stuffs the gear into the box.)* What you say?

GRANDMERE: You want some fried plantains—he look like a hungry little lamb, your friend—

HARLEY: *(To Billy.)* Want some of Grandmere's fried bananas, man?

BILLY: Oh I love those—with all the syrup—damn it doesn't quite fit—

(From offstage:)

GRANDMERE: *Venez!* Do I have to come drag you boys outta there?

HARLEY: Hurry up!

BILLY: Here—I'll drape my jacket over the top—help me pick it up—*(They strain to pick up the big box.)* God—it's heavier than I thought—

HARLEY: I have an idea! Let's stick it in my wagon and we'll say it's papers for my paper route!

BILLY: Awful heavy papers—

HARLEY: No one'll see—we'll stick some papers on top—like this— *(He puts the box on a rickety red wagon and surrounds it with old newspapers.)*

BILLY: Hey—very smart, Harley—very smart! I should hire you more often.

HARLEY: *(Blushing, pleased.)* Thanks, man. OK, let's go.

GRANDMERE: *J'arrive pour vous trouver! J'arrive!*

(We see them wheel the wagon through a door, we cross-fade as they turn around and wheel it back through another door, into Billy's house. It is very small and run down. Billy shuts the door to his room, crosses to his bed, and pulls a box out from under the bed.)

SCENE FOUR

HARLEY: We made it! Man, my back is broke.

BILLY: What time is it?

HARLEY: Ain't you got a clock?

BILLY: No—my mom says she doesn't believe in the passage of time. Look out the window by the 7-Eleven—there's a clock over the root beer sign.

HARLEY: *(As he does so.)* Your mama's a freak. *(He peers out of the curtain.)* It's four fifteen.

BILLY: Let's hurry—we've only got twenty minutes—

HARLEY: How you know when they're coming?

BILLY: I heard them whispering in the hall outside the nurse's office—

HARLEY: What you doing in the nurse's office? You ain't sick.

BILLY: She gives you free orange juice if you say you've got a sore throat. And sometimes crackers too—if you say you've got a sore throat *and* a stomach ache. Help me—*(He begins to unpack the box.)*

HARLEY: Yeah well when your mama's cured world hunger, maybe she could buy you your *own* juice and crackers—same as everyone else—

BILLY: Maybe—*(He lifts the computer out and puts it on the box.)* There's no desk, so we'll have to set it up on my magic box—

HARLEY: What's magic about it?

BILLY: I pull it out, I pretend it's a computer, and—magic! Here it is!

HARLEY: Very funny—

BILLY: OK, quick—yellow cable—

HARLEY: Yellow cable—

BILLY: That's the mouse—this plugs into that hole—the pink one's for the monitor—

HARLEY: *(Rummaging in the box.)* What pink one??

BILLY: Don't tell me you left it—

HARLEY: *(Diving all the way into the box, and pulling out a bunch of spaghetti chords.)* I grabbed everything that was there, man—you figure it out—

BILLY: Thanks—*(He begins plugging everything in. As he does so:)* Time check!

HARLEY: *(Running to window.)* Four twenty three . . .

BILLY: Any signs??

HARLEY: Not yet . . .

BILLY: Hurry—

HARLEY: Here's the CD that was in there! *(Hands a blank CD to Billy.)* Stick it in—I want to see what she's been lookin' at! Grandmere came in one day and caught her and saw somethin' awful—she kept cryin' and cryin' *"Mechante! Mechante!* If your blessed mama only knew . . . "

BILLY: Is it a game? *(He sticks it in the computer.)*

HARLEY: I don't know. Mariela's only interested in *kissin'* and stuff like that. *(Sound offstage of a huge vehicle coming down the road. Harley and Billy rush to the window.)*

BILLY: Oh god, look what it is—

HARLEY: The *Hummer!* I thought they were walkin' so their moms wouldn't know . . .

BILLY: Skip's in the front seat—with Brud—

HARLEY: Hey—some black lady's drivin'—that ain't his *mom!*

BILLY: Must be his au pair—

HARLEY: His *what?*

BILLY: Babysitter. Maybe he persuaded her to—
(Sound of car doors slamming and kids getting out.)

BILLY: Dammit!—Even Joe came! The traitor!

HARLEY: Whadda we do now?

BILLY: Let's turn it on—quick—*(He does so.)*—

HARLEY: What's on the CD?

BILLY: I don't know—here we go! *(He turns it on.)* OK—now hide under the bed—quick—come on—

HARLEY: *(Looking under the bed.)* There's stuff GROWING under there! Don't your mama ever clean?

BILLY: It's just *dust*—come on—
(They crawl under the bed. From off we hear sounds of the boys climbing up the fire escape, giggling and cursing—then we see a hand coming up to

the window and prying it open. Brud's big ugly face appears first, then Skip—they strain to open the window.)

BRUD: Hold on to the ivy, man—

SKIP: I can't—I'm slipping—do you see anything?

BRUD: Yeah—there's his computer—look—

JOE'S VOICE: *(From below.)* See! You said he was lying! Let me see—

BRUD: Shut up, Joe. Come on, let's look—*(He heaves himself up into the room. Skip follows. Joe peeks through.)*

JOE: Oh god, we're going to get into SO much trouble!

SKIP: You wimp—

JOE: I'm serious!

SKIP: Go back to the library where you belong.

BRUD: So where are the games? There's nothing here—

SKIP: I told you!

JOE: Hit the mouse—maybe there's one in there—that rhinoceros thing—

BRUD: Let's see—*(He hits "Go" button. Music starts to play.)*

SKIP: What's that?

BRUD: I don't know—a girl—

JOE: Oh my god—OH MY GOD!—that's not a rhinoceros!

BRUD: Gross!!

SKIP: She's naked! Totally naked!

BRUD: So's *he!*

JOE: What're they doing??

BRUD: Close your eyes!

SKIP: Try to stop it! Come on! Push control alt delete or something! *(Brud does so.)*

JOE: Wow—it all turned pink!!

BRUD: It's a different girl!

SKIP: He's—what he's doing to her?

JOE: Why is he doing that??

BRUD: Look at her!

SKIP: Is she laughing or crying?

BRUD: Hit the mouse again! *(He does so.)*

SKIP: Now she's Chinese!!

JOE: She's screaming—she looks like a hurt dog—oh my god, I think it *is* a dog!

BRUD: Why is she smiling?

SKIP: She's scared of the dog!

BRUD: It's got nothing to *do* with the dog!

JOE: This is *awful*—we shouldn't be watching this—

BRUD: I've never seen a game like this!!

SKIP: Billy is so cool!

BRUD: *Way* cool!

SKIP: Where do you think he got it??

BRUD: They don't sell stuff like this at TOYS R US!

SKIP: He said it was a rhinoceros with wings!

JOE: Maybe that's what you call this . . .

BRUD: I call it a Chinese girl with a Great Dane!

(From below, we hear the sound of a door opening. A female voice.)

MOTHER: Billy?? Hey big guy—are you home? Come look what I've got!

(Brud looks at the other boys. They freeze, panicked.)

BRUD: We're dead.

(Blackout.)

SCENE FIVE

The playground the next morning. Billy and Joe are sitting on the ground.

JOE: What do you call this stuff?

BILLY: Hummus.

JOE: Hummer? Like the car?

BILLY: It's from the Middle East.

JOE: I don't get it. Your mother doesn't feed you for a month and then she gives you food from the Middle East?

BILLY: She brought it back from a sit-in.

JOE: A what?

BILLY: Don't you know anything? *(Pause.)* One time she joined an Argentinian group looking for women who had disappeared—

JOE: How come?

BILLY: I guess she wanted to find them.

JOE: No, I meant—how come the women had disappeared?

BILLY: How do I know? All I could tell was a lot of the group must've disappeared along with them, cuz there was tons of food left over—and Mom brought it all home in a shopping cart—

JOE: Wow!

BILLY: *(Pushing his luck.)* And there was something magical about that food because the more we ate, the more there *was*—really!—dumplings for days and meat pies and everything steaming hot and it filled up our whole house with the smell and we invited everyone on the block to come eat and we *still* couldn't finish all that food.

JOE: Really?

BILLY: *(Solemnly.)* Really.

(Pause. Joe doesn't know what to believe.)

JOE: Where's Harley?

BILLY: Grounded.

JOE: For what?

BILLY: Stealing.

JOE: What did he steal?

BILLY: Never mind. Something of his sister's.

JOE: I bet that voodoo grandma of his was mad!

BILLY: He can't go out for three days. He'll miss the math test and everything.

JOE: Wow. *(Pause.)* Skip and Brud are *really* in trouble.

BILLY: What happened to them?

JOE: Well . . . uh . . . they had a little accident. In the Hummer.

BILLY: Oh yeah? I thought Hummers couldn't have accidents.

JOE: They hit a telephone pole.

BILLY: No kidding. How'd they do that?

JOE: They were screaming—they had to make a fast getaway . . .

BILLY: Yeah?

JOE: Yeah.

BILLY: You are such a liar, Joe. A liar and a traitor.

JOE: *(Bursting out.)* Me? You're the liar! It's all your fault—*all* of this—Harley's grandma locking him up and Brud and Skip crashing the Hummer—it was all cuz of that rhinoceros story you told us—

BILLY: How do you know it was a lie, Joe?

JOE: I just know!

BILLY: How, Joe? *(Joe squirms.)* What've you been *doing,* Joe? You been spying on us?

JOE: No way! I just—

BILLY: Where were you at 4:30 yesterday afternoon, Joe?

JOE: 4:30? I must have been—

BILLY: Liar! Liar! You were hanging out my window like an old bat! We saw you!

JOE: You did not—there was no one there—

BILLY: We were there—Harley and me—under the bed—we saw you!

JOE: You saw us?? *(Pause.)* You saw that . . . stuff . . . on the screen?

BILLY: Well—Harley's feet were in my face, but—

JOE: *(With awe in his voice.)* Was that it?? Was *that* the rhinoceros?

BILLY: Maybe . . .

JOE: *(Wide-eyed.)* You're kidding.

BILLY: Why'd you do that, Joe?

JOE: Oh my god—that's *so* gross!

BILLY: How come you broke into my house?

JOE: I had to—I wanted to know—

BILLY: Know *what?*

JOE: If you were lying—all that stuff about the wings and the supersonic game and—

BILLY: And *was* I? Lying?

JOE: I don't know, Billy—I don't know—what *was* that, anyway? What were they *doing* to those girls? And what's with the *dog?*

BILLY: What did it *look* like?

JOE: It looked *disgusting!* My mom always said you were a nice kid and I should be friends with you. You shouldn't be watching that stuff!

BILLY: You shouldn't be breaking into people's houses!

JOE: I know—I know—but god Billy—

(Brud and Skip enter. Brud has a bandaged head.)

BRUD: Hi Billy—

BILLY: *(Mock friendly.)* Hi Brud! What happened to your face?

SKIP: He hit a telephone pole.

BRUD: By accident.

JOE: Well of course it was by accident . . . no one hits a telephone pole on purpose!

BRUD AND SKIP: *(Together.)* Shut up, Joe.

SKIP: *(To Billy.)* What're you eating?

BILLY: Hummus.

JOE: It's from the Middle East.

SKIP: The middle *what?*

BRUD: It's a store, moron. For hippies. Listen, Billy—we brought you something—

BILLY: Oh yeah? What for?

(Brud holds out a package.)

BRUD: Look.

JOE: What is it?

SKIP: You know that game you were telling us about? It's like that—

BRUD: I mean—not like *that*—not with girls or anything—it's animals—I mean—they're not kissing or anything but it's the closest thing we could find—

BILLY: Kissing? Who plays games with people kissing?

SKIP: *(Blurting out.)* You do! I mean god—we had no idea—

BRUD: We looked for one like that at the store but—

SKIP: No one had it anywhere—only you—

BILLY: Forget it. And I don't want this. *(He hands it back.)*

BRUD: Why not? It cost twenty-five bucks. You'll like it.

BILLY: Keep it.

SKIP: You think you're so great just because you can make Chinese girls do weird things on your computer?

BILLY: What computer?

SKIP: Yours—we saw it!

BRUD: Shut up, Skip!

BILLY: You saw it?

SKIP: I mean—we were walking by—we happened to peer in the window—

BILLY: On the *second floor?* You guys are trespassers! I'm going to report you!

BRUD: We're going to report *you!* You live alone in a creepy dump covered in ivy and no one ever feeds you or picks you up from school or anything—

BILLY: That's not true!

BRUD: My mom says you could be taken away to children's court cuz kids our age have to live with grown-ups and—

JOE: Don't say that!

BILLY: I *do* live with a grown-up—

SKIP: Yeah? Like you got rhinoceroses in your room? There's something wrong with you—

BILLY: There is not!

JOE: There is *not!*

BRUD: Shut up, Joe—you're worse than Harley—

SKIP: And that game you play is disgusting—*(Pause.)* but sort of awesome . . .

BRUD: Shut up, Skip. It's *worse* than disgusting—you've gotta throw that out!

SKIP: Don't worry! We'll get you any game you want—

BILLY: I don't want your games!

SKIP: You *better*, man, or you'll get arrested!

BILLY: I won't get arrested and I don't want your games!

BRUD: You'll be sorry!

BILLY: And I don't ever want to see you again! Any of you! *(He runs off. Pause. The boys watch him go. Skip turns to Brud.)*

SKIP: Did you tell your mom—?

BRUD: No way—I'd be dead—

SKIP: Harley's grandma's going to put a voodoo curse on all of us— I know she will—

JOE: Not on Billy. His rhino will protect him—

SKIP: *(After a pause.)* You don't really *believe* all that rhinoceros stuff?—

JOE: Of course I do!

SKIP: Are you kidding me?

BRUD: He's got powers, that's for sure. From now on we're going to have to be really careful . . .

SKIP: Careful how?

BRUD: Whatever weird stuff he asks you to do, just say yes—

SKIP: I don't wanna say yes to—

JOE: *(Agreeing with Brud.)* You'd better, Skip! From now on, all of us are going to have to say yes to a lot of things! Or we're going to get sucked right into his spell!

SKIP: You're kidding me—

JOE: That's why Harley stayed home today. He's getting his grandma to give him some voodoo powers so he can help Billy even more—

BRUD: That's not fair!

SKIP: Life's not fair! That's what my dad always says. Oh god, here he comes! *(Billy re-enters with a set jaw. He has made a decision.)*

SKIP: OK, OK, you win! You win! All that crazy stuff you were telling us yesterday—that rhinoceros that turned into amazing things when you pushed control alt delete—it's true—we believe you—

BILLY: I don't care.

BRUD: Just don't put some spell on us—we believe you, OK?

BILLY: Why? I made it all up! I don't have a computer and I never bring my lunch and I have a mom who stays up all night changing the world and forgets to come home. Satisfied?

JOE: *(Wide-eyed.)* Is that *true?*

BRUD: I wish *my* mom would forget to come home.

SKIP: Why don't you just tell your mom you're hungry?

BILLY: I have it all under control. Whenever I want to eat, I close my eyes and imagine all the food I love . . . fried bananas . . . burgers barbequing . . . brownies at the Friday bake sales . . . first I smell them . . . then I swish them around in my mouth till I can taste them . . . then I swallow them and fall asleep, nice and full. *(Pause. The boys are unconvinced.)* She *thinks* she's fed me. I know she does.

SKIP: Wow.

BRUD: Parents.

SKIP: Totally clueless.

JOE: Yep.

BRUD: *(To Billy.)* I still think you should remind her every once in a while.

BILLY: When I do she cries a lot and says she should never have had a kid, and I have to cheer her up. It's easier being hungry.

BRUD: When my mom starts crying she says she should never have left Florida. Whatever that means.

JOE: My mom always says if only she'd had a girl she'd be happy.

SKIP: They *all* say that! What's so great about girls?

(Harley enters carrying a huge covered dish.)

HARLEY: *Bonjour, mes amis!*

BILLY: Harley! You got out!

HARLEY: Yep!

BRUD: Does your grandma know?

SKIP: Don't you go putting any voodoo curses on me!

HARLEY: Shut up, Skip! *(To Billy.)* I have brought you an offering. From Grandmere. As a token of her thanks!

BILLY: What are you talking about?

HARLEY: Mariela has thrown out her computer and Grandmere says it's all because of you!

BILLY: What's in the pot?

HARLEY: Fried bananas. Plenty of syrup. Six spoons. *(He lays it out. The boys dive in.)*

BRUD: Wow!

JOE: Billy first!

BILLY: I LOVE these things!

SKIP: *(His mouth full of bananas.)* I don't get it! I thought you were grounded!

BRUD: *(Equally sticky.)* We thought you were in big old trouble, Harley!

HARLEY: I *was*. When I came home with Mariela's computer under those old newspapers yesterday, Grandmere was waiting with a wooden spoon to whip my behind! I mean, she *did* whip my behind, big time. And I'm crying and yelling and carrying on and she locks me in my room and starts yellin' curses in French and I'm screamin' on my bed and I hear the doorbell ring and then there's a lot of talkin' downstairs and carryin' on and Mariela is yelling and crying and more talking and yelling, and then the door shuts and I look out the window and there's Mariela and Billy's mom walking off together arm and arm down the street!

BILLY: *My* mom?!

HARLEY: Yep! She took Mariela off to some rally or something! And it turns out it's all about poor kids in Haiti and so Mariela comes home and tells Grandmere all about it and Grandmere starts cryin' and carryin' on about her people and how we have to help them escape their fate and now she and Mariela are all best friends again and they're joinin' some group with Billy's mom to rescue the Haitian people from poverty and next thing I know Grandmere's banging around in the kitchen singin' and fryin' plantains and she comes out and knocks on my door and says "take these to that little *mouton, cherie,* and tell him Grandmere is lookin' out for him."

BILLY: That's what she said?

SKIP: Great! Now Harley'll never get fed either—they *all* be out saving the world!

HARLEY: No, man, you don't get it—Grandmere will be *cookin'* for everyone! That's what she does. She'd feed all of Haiti if she could. *(He grins.)*

BILLY: Didn't Mariela want her computer back?

HARLEY: Nope. Grandmere told her it was the cause of all her problems— and then she opened the window and chucked the whole thing out onto the street!

BILLY: No!

BRUD: She smashed up the computer?

HARLEY: Yup.

SKIP: *(Awed.)* Idiot!

JOE: And no one was underneath?

BRUD: Yeah—how come no one got hit?

SKIP: I don't believe you!

HARLEY: *(Getting defensive.)* It's true!

SKIP: Who throws a computer out the window? That's nuts! You're making it up!

BILLY: *(Thinking fast.)* No he's not! She threw it out the window—and then— a miracle happened!

BRUD: What?

SKIP: How do *you* know—you weren't there!

HARLEY: But Billy knows everything. *(Whispering, to Billy.)* What miracle?

JOE: Yeah, what miracle, Billy?

BILLY: *(Making it up as he goes along.)* Well—as the computer was falling to the ground, time started to stretch out till everything was moving very very slowly—and all the lights outside suddenly started to dim . . . you'll imagine it better if you close your eyes! *(They close their eyes.)* And the wind started to howl, like this *(He howls.)*. You do it, Harley! *(Harley begins to howl like the wind.)* And then a strange and beautiful music was heard all around . . . *(Billy nudges Brud. Brud starts to hum, maybe the theme from* Star Wars.*)* and the computer started spinning over and over through the air, just like the house in the Wizard of Oz when the tornado started to blow—and suddenly everything went into color—and there was a heavenly choir singing louder and louder—and stars came out in the sky and were shining all over the place—and then as the computer hit the ground a huge crash of cymbals erupted *(Skip bangs the syrup spoon against the metal pot.)* and *flash!*—a beautiful pair of silver wings—and then an enormous roar—*(He nudges Joe. Joe roars.)* And a giant and magical rhinoceros with huge glittering wings sprouted up from the ground and started flying up, up, up into the sky—

BRUD: Yes!

SKIP: Sweet!

JOE: *(Eyes closed.)* I see it!

HARLEY: Keep going, Billy!

BILLY: *(Standing over the boys.)* And its shadow covers the whole neighborhood—and all the windows rattle and the houses quake and people rush outside to see what it is—and all they can see is the underbelly of a great beast, gleaming in the sunset as it disappears into the night sky.
(Pause. The boys are silent. Then they slowly open their eyes and look around.)

SKIP: Wow.

BRUD: Can you believe that?!

HARLEY: Amazing.

JOE: *(Regretfully.)* And now it's gone!

SKIP: But I *saw* it! I know I did! Wait till I tell my mom!
(Billy grins. Then, slowly.)

BILLY: Yeah.
(Blackout.)

END OF PLAY

Seventh Grade Freaks

by Melanie Salazar Case

PLAYWRIGHT'S BIOGRAPHY

Melanie Salazar Case is a celebrated Bay Area–based actor, writer, comedian, producer, director and teacher. As an actor, she originated the role of Pam in Peter Sinn Nachtrieb's *Hunter Gatherers* and was recently seen in *Bright Ideas* at Shotgun Players. Off-Broadway credits include *KML Takes Manhattan* (The Producer's Club, Upright Citizens Brigade). Off-Off Broadway credits include *Green Eyes Dreaming* (Lincoln Center/ HERE, directed by Lori Petermann), and *The Bacchae* (The Looking Glass Theater). She recently completed two independent films, *The Snake* and *Evolution: The Musical!*, which premiered in May, 2008 at the San Francisco International Film Festival. As a writer, she has co-written a short film, *Diner Ladies,* with Tonya Glanz, and her sketch comedy work has been seen performed with critically acclaimed San Francisco comedy troupe Killing My Lobster. Ms. Case has been a company member of Killing My Lobster for five years. She also produced her original two-woman show, co-written with Amanda Gamer, *The Sho Show,* in Los Angeles. As a director, she garnered critical praise for her KML production of *Kisses a Toad,* and she recently completed her cinematic directorial debut, *Orifice Visit,* which she also wrote, about an awkward gynecology visit. She has studied commedia dell'arte at The Actors' Gang in Los Angeles, and improvisation with Comedy Sportz and The Second City (NY training center). At the age of sixteen she founded The Lunatic Players improvisation troupe at her alma mater Menlo-Atherton High School. The troupe is currently running strong in its thirteenth year. Ms. Case studied acting at the American Conservatory Theater's Young Conservatory, where she began teaching improvisation and directing one-act plays in 2004. Ms. Case graduated with a B.A. in Theater from U.C.L.A.

FROM THE PLAYWRIGHT/DIRECTOR

I met the ebullient and charming Craig Slaight at A.C.T. when I was a student at the Young Conservatory in 1995. At the time I was performing the role of Ronnie in Lanford Wilson's *Lemon Sky,* directed by the sensitive and inspiring Jack Sharrar. These two men left a huge impression on me as a young student of theater, instilling in me the belief that I was being taken very seriously as a theater artist, and that I could certainly have a future in theater as a profession.

Before studying acting at A.C.T., I was busy soaking in my English classes at Menlo-Atherton High School in Atherton, California. There I had two more influential teachers. In my Sophomore year Joseph Fuchs, taught me that theater and film were art forms, and that the power of beautiful writing could be translated to the screen and stage. He would have us read classic works of literature but also would show us films like *Some Like It Hot, North by Northwest,* and classic stage performances of *The Taming of The Shrew* at A.C.T. I remember after seeing Harvey Keitel's quintessential performance in the1977 film *The Duellists,* that I understood the power of symbolism in storytelling. Shannon Griscom, my junior year teacher and collector of witches, was inspiring because she taught me never to take myself too seriously. I remember clearly when after one of my trademark inappropriate comments Ms. Griscom said to me, "Melanie, you know that little voice inside your head that tells you when *not* to say things?" And here she would pause dramatically for emphasis . . . "You don't have that little voice." Today although I have learned to temper that "little voice," (which I *do* have)—I am blessed to have chosen a profession that allows me to willfully ignore it should I so desire.

Some ten-odd years later, I had moved back to San Francisco after going to college and struggling as a starving actor in New York City, and I had found a home at my comedy troupe Killing My Lobster. My dear friend and fellow Lobster Jon Wolanske had been working at A.C.T. in the PR department for several years, and Craig Slaight had approached him about a teaching position. Jon, gracious as always, said to him, "I'm not available, but I know just the right person." So that is how, after ten-odd years, Craig Slaight called me up and asked me to join the A.C.T. faculty as an acting teacher, and I found my way back home.

In the last months of 2005 Craig called me again and asked me to be a part of an exciting new project at the Young Conservatory. He wanted to produce Carey Perloff's play, *Rhinoceros with Wings,* in repertory with another one-act play written for five young women. He asked me to direct, and I was compelled by the exciting challenge. However, as I began reading plays written for junior high school students, I found that the majority was written for predominantly male casts, or the subject matter seemed to me slightly juvenile for today's mature and modern ten to fourteen year olds. I felt frustrated by the lack of material speaking to young women and about their issues, so as a result, I had the cuckoo idea that I might just write them a play. I asked Craig, "Well, what if I write them a play?" And in his typical supportive way, Craig answered, "I think that is a WONDERFUL idea!"

I began writing this play based on my teaching experience, overheard conversations of students in prior classes, the personalities of former students, quirks and peccadilloes of my former teachers, and on my own friendships and experiences growing up. I wanted to find a voice for this generation of children that is more mature, complex, and informed that any other generation before them.

When I met the talented girls with whom I was to work in this production, I tried to make a symbiotic relationship between what I had already written and what these young actresses brought to the material in rehearsal. They performed a series of improvisations based on their characters, and after I'd observed them, I would incorporate some of their ideas into the script.

I feel incredibly lucky to have worked with the immensely talented cast of actors I was fortunate enough to have for my debut children's play. Without their creativity, wisdom, and insight, this play would not have been possible. They performed this play with so much energy, passion, commitment, and humor, that they made my words come to life in a way I never imagined. Thanks to each and every one of you, and thanks again to Craig for believing in me.

FROM THE ACTOR—Anya Richkind (Amanda)
I entered the project eventually known as *Seventh Grade Freaks* feeling dubious. With only two months to go before my Bat-Mitzvah, I wasn't sure I wanted to take on another endeavor. And yet, as soon as I walked into that first day of class, I knew I had made the right choice. The experience was tremendously fun for us middle schoolers, not only because of the thrill of acting, but also because we helped develop the play. Melanie provided our characters, complete with background and personality, and we improvised scenes to reinforce her ideas. For example, Melanie created my character Amanda as a quirky, quasi-nerdy intellectual with an incredible imagination. I elaborated on Amanda, creating her obsession with purple contacts, save-the-world politics, and the evil, ubiquitous Starbucks. While Amanda was undoubtedly a different person than I am, she grew out of my spirit, personality, and views. Pulled from the actors' personal experiences, the improvised scenes and snippets became part of Melanie's final script. As a result, there was a very realistic tinge to the play, based on our very own lives. We fit it all together after improvising these concepts, conveying their thematic messages, rehearsing, and finally, performing. I loved being part of this collaborative production.

ORIGINAL PRODUCTION
Seventh Grade Freaks was written for and originally presented by the Young Conservatory at American Conservatory Theater (Carey Perloff, Artistic Director, Heather M. Kitchen, Executive Director), San Francisco, California,

in March 2006. It was directed by Melanie Salazar Case and the cast was as follows:

MRS. CLEESE . . . . Melanie Salazar Case
AMANDA . . . . Anya Richkind
ANNA . . . . Monica Gibbons
SILVIA . . . . Natasha Morris
HAZEL . . . . Elizabeth Perry
LUCY . . . . Carly Cozad
DANIEL . . . . Nicholas Perloff-Giles
SAM . . . . David McKenna

SETTING

Inside a room adjoining a San Francisco junior high classroom and outside on the blacktop.

PRODUCTION NOTE

All of the pop-culture references are intended to reflect the current youth. When things like the ipod, the Nano, celebrities, and pop songs go out of fashion, directors of this play should feel free to pick things that both she or he and the students find funny. Most importantly, don't forget to have fun with this play!

CHARACTERS

MS. CLEESE, twenty-seven, a young and inspiring teacher
AMANDA, thirteen, imaginative and mature beyond her years
ANNA, thirteen, take-charge and studious
SILVIA, twelve, observant and down-to-earth
HAZEL, twelve, projects optimism but carries dark secrets within
LUCY, twelve, a cynic
DANIEL, thirteen, a spaz
SAM, twelve, a nice guy

SET

The set should be simple: those desks or just school room–looking chairs, five of them. There is a chalkboard with chalk and erasers and a map on the wall. There can be a bookcase with books too.

DEDICATION

The playwright would like to dedicate this play to her life teachers. To the luminescent Victoria Hope Martin, to her teacher-mother Irma Isaza Case, her sister Stephanie, her half-siblings Cathy, Jim Jr., and Marian, her uncle George, her gigantic Colombian family—too many for me to name individually; Stephen M. Cox, Brandon Neubauer, Karen Fielder, Jessica Parlanti, Melissa McLaughlin, Kenny Taylor, Sean Christensen, Jon Wolanske, Jackie Swensen, Craig Slaight, Jack Sharrar, her incomparable students, all of the school teachers who influenced her, Andrew Gentile, Buddha and all of her spiritual teachers, and lastly, to her father, the late James Edward Case, himself a great teacher of profound life lessons and geology. He always did tell her to "Look it up!"

SEVENTH GRADE FREAKS

SCENE ONE: NEGOTIATIONS

Inside a small room adjoining a classroom. The girls sit in a circle, reading a prompt given to them by Ms. Cleese.

MS. CLEESE: So Silvia is going to be participating in this assignment for the afternoon since she might be coming to this school. Everyone be nice—and inclusive—and remember that participation is a big part of your grade in my class. And don't forget—

I may not seem like I am paying attention but I see *everything* that happens in this classroom. You'll have fifteen minutes before recess and fifteen minutes after recess to get your drama together—*(With a stopwatch.)* All right ladies, as of this moment, you have fifteen minutes—and you're competing against the boys, so make it count! And . . . GO! *(Ms. Cleese exits.)*

ANNA: So what's your name?

SILVIA: I'm Silvia.

ANNA: What school did you go to?

SILVIA: Well, I'm homeschooled.

LUCY: Homeschooled?

SILVIA: Yeah, it's different from regular school, but a lot harder in some ways.

AMANDA: *(Hurried.)* Hello? Did anyone else hear "GO!"?

ANNA: *(Hurried.)* OK, so read the prompt!

AMANDA: OK, OK . . . "Take thirty minutes to create a short play that dramatizes what you would do if you could do whatever you wanted to help the world become a better place."

LUCY: Make the world a better place? That's impossible.

AMANDA: A bit cynical, are we?

LUCY: I'm a realist.

AMANDA: You're twelve.

LUCY: So?

AMANDA: *(Encouraging her.)* Where's your idealism? You're too young to be realistic.

LUCY: I just call 'em as I see 'em.

AMANDA: I'm just saying, brutal honesty and cynical realism could squash your inner dreamer.

LUCY: My dad's a closet alcoholic. *That* will squash a person's dreams.

SILVIA: Well, I lost my favorite lip gloss this week. I think it's somewhere in my friend's car.

ANNA: I don't think I could live a day without lip gloss.

HAZEL: I love lip gloss. *(The other girls give her a look.)*

ANNA: Guys! Let's focus on the goal and try to make something great! We only have fifteen minutes before recess.

LUCY: Yeah, lip gloss is really depressing.

ANNA: You're weird.

LUCY: What? I'm just not into lip gloss. I'm practically goth.

AMANDA: *(Getting an idea.)*—I know!—Let's say we start out on a desert island—

LUCY: What does a desert island have to do with saving the world?

AMANDA:—No, listen! We're on the desert island, and we need to be saved—

LUCY: "Saved"? This is not a parochial school. I hope you're not making this a Christian metaphor like *The Chronicles of Narnia*. And then Aslan, the great lion, appears on the desert island to save all of our souls, by giving up his life for those in need of saving—

AMANDA: I'm Jewish.

HAZEL: So am I. I got an ipod for Channukuh this year!!

ANNA: You did? The Nano?—

SILVIA:—So we're on a desert island, and we write a letter and stick it in a bottle—

AMANDA: And then a dragon appears and picks one of us up by the hair and flies over the island with all of us screaming below her, "Let her go, drop her! Free her! Free the prisoner!"

LUCY: So now she's a prisoner.

AMANDA: She's the prisoner of the dragon.

LUCY: I can see we're making some real progress here.

ANNA: What we need to do guys, is not to work backward.

ALL: Huh?

ANNA: *(Writing on the chalkboard.)* We start here. Answer the question first, and *then* dramatize the answers. What we're doing now is trying to create a drama without any content. We have to answer the question first. What would we do if we could save the world? For real? Let's start with you: Silvia.

SILVIA: What would I do?

ANNA: Yes, if you could save the world, what would you do?

SILVIA: I'd . . . feed the hungry?

ANNA: Good. How?

SILVIA: By dropping food over impoverished countries?

ANNA: *(She writes it on the chalkboard.)* Interesting—what else?

SILVIA: Ask the rich to give their money to the poor.

ANNA: *(She writes it on the chalkboard.)* That's great, like Bill Gates and his wife.

SILVIA: Yeah, I saw that on the news.

LUCY: Yeah, like Robin Hood and his thieves. Stealing from the rich to give to the poor.

AMANDA: But in this case it wouldn't be stealing, the rich would be giving their money voluntarily.

ANNA: Like the Democratic Party. Society takes care of the weaker links to make the society stronger as a whole.

HAZEL: Yeah, like a quote my mom read in *O* magazine. "First it is necessary to stand on your own two feet. But the minute a man finds himself in that position, the next thing he should do is reach out his arms."

LUCY: You can quote from *O* magazine?

HAZEL: Oprah is my mom's hero.

ANNA: *(Correcting her.)* Heroine.

AMANDA: *(Melodramatically.)* Did you just say "heroin"? This is a drug-free zone!

ANNA: Ha ha. You knew what I meant.

LUCY: My mom likes Oprah too. She's hoping she'll win a car one of these days.

HAZEL: My mom thinks Oprah is changing the world for the better.

ANNA: She is!

AMANDA: I still say that we need some dying children—engulfed in flames, like in the Edward Gorey books—and then we can have some nurses, or a team of brilliant and cutting-edge neurosurgeons from Kanchengunga, India, and—

ANNA: You're disrupting the flow here, Amanda. You know as well as I that there is a method to my madness. Moving on. Hazel?

HAZEL: I'd just have people be nicer to each other.

ANNA: *(Writing it on the chalkboard.)* Give me an example of what you mean.

HAZEL: Like when I go to Starbucks, and I order coffee, and they give me attitude because I'm twelve.

AMANDA: Starbucks is the devil.

HAZEL: Stop being so melodramatic. It's just coffee.

AMANDA: It's not *just* coffee! It's a capitalist enterprise designed to take advantage of developing countries and underpay foreign laborers! Starbucks is the devil, who's with me? *(Anna raises her hand, but Hazel, Lucy, and Silvia don't. Everyone looks at Lucy with surprise, since she's the most counter-culture.)* You like coffee?

LUCY: *(Defensively.)* I enjoy a latte from time to time.

ANNA: You, Lucy?

LUCY: I refuse to be pigeonholed.

SILVIA: I like Pumpkin Spice lattes with whipped cream. And cinnamon.

AMANDA: They're marketing to the very young, like us!

LUCY: We're not so young.

ANNA: We're thirteen!

LUCY, HAZEL AND SILVIA: Twelve!

ANNA: My point exactly. *We (Referring to herself and Amanda.)* are wiser, and more mature, and therefore not influenced by radical advertising campaigns geared toward young adolescents.

LUCY: Who put all of this in your head?

ANNA: My parents.

LUCY: Your *parents* are a couple of "radical advertising campaigns," you should watch out for them, not Starbucks.

ANNA: You dare to insult my parents?

LUCY: Amanda insulted mine!

SILVIA: I'm glad you haven't met *my* parents.

HAZEL: My parents are rad! *(Dishy.)* Did I mention I got an ipod for Channukuh?

AMANDA: You did. I got one for my Bat Mitzvah, so there.

LUCY: *(To Amanda.)* And you're telling me you're not influenced by "radical advertising campaigns"? That is so untrue!

AMANDA: Anna said that, not me!

ANNA: *(Correcting her grammar.)* Not *I*. All right, Lucy, since you're so opinionated, what would *you* do?

LUCY: Well first off I'd mutiny and throw you off your high horse . . . who elected you leader of this committee anyway?

ANNA: Leadership emerges.

LUCY: That is a load of bullhonkey!

ANNA: Bullhonkey? Who says that?

LUCY: My mom! And she also says "hunky-dorey," OK? She was sixteen in the mid-eighties!

SILVIA: That's Civil War slang.

HAZEL: *(To Lucy.)* How does she know that?

AMANDA: Lucy, we're running out of time! What would you do?

LUCY: *(Smart alecky.)* Pay it forward?

AMANDA: *(At her wit's end.)* Be serious, Lucy, WHAT WOULD YOU DO? *(An awkward beat . . . Amanda lost it.)*

LUCY: Well, I guess I'd . . . . start a safe house for low-income families, single mothers, and their kids.

ANNA: Good. Thank you for taking this seriously for a second.

LUCY: But how do we dramatize that? Do I get to play the skid row husband, *(Acting drunk.)* "BANG! This is my house and I pay the bills!"

ANNA: You could be the social worker helping the families get adjusted to their new lives.

LUCY: I guess that'd be cool . . .

ANNA: Yeah, and Amanda could be the mom and Silvia and Hazel could be the kids!—

AMANDA: —Could we at least have one skid row bum? Like who comes in and attacks all of them with an axe and all of them die and the building burns to the ground?

ANNA: We're supposed to be saving the world, not killing people. You know Ms. Cleese is a pacifist.

AMANDA: But she has a penchant for the macabre!

ANNA: How do you know that?

SILVIA: She likes witches. *(They all look at her.)*

SILVIA: What? She likes witches. She collects them. Haven't you noticed?

ANNA: Yeah, I guess you're right. She does have a giant Wicked Witch of the West over her desk. I thought she just liked *The Wizard of Oz*.

AMANDA: And she dressed up as a witch for Halloween this year!

SILVIA: My mom likes witches, that's why I noticed.

LUCY: *(Suddenly interested.)* Is your mom a witch?

SILVIA: Well, not really, she's more of a pagan.

LUCY: I wish my mom was a witch.

ANNA: *(Correcting her grammar.)* You wish your mom *were* a witch.

LUCY: That's getting very old!

ANNA: Sorry, my dad is a grammar-correcting freak . . . it rubbed off. I mean, every time I ask him what a word means he says: "Look it up!" What alternative do I have? I'm programmed this way!

LUCY: That's no excuse for making people feel bad about themselves.

ANNA: *(Suddenly serious.)* Did I make you feel bad about yourself?

LUCY: *(Hiding her feelings.)* No, of course not.

AMANDA: She wouldn't admit it if you had.

ANNA: I'm sorry Lucy. I think you're really smart.

AMANDA: Yeah, you're totally smart.

SILVIA: I just met you and I like you the best out of everyone. *(They all look at Silvia. Isn't she the new girl?)*

SILVIA: I'm into honesty.

LUCY: I didn't mean for this to turn into an it's-all-about-Lucy-moment— forget about it.

HAZEL: *(Looking at her watch.)* Guys, we only have ten minutes left. Who's turn is it?

ANNA: Amanda!

AMANDA: Yayyyyy!

ANNA: What would you do?

AMANDA: I'd be a scientist and invent all these amazing inoculations to cure people all over the world of the flu, AIDS, viruses, epidemics. And I'd go to Third World countries to set up hospitals and make health care available to everyone.

ANNA: Good.

AMANDA: And then I'd have a giant octopus cover all of the landmasses of the Earth and eradicate evil by the octopus spewing out orange and polka-dotted ink and drowning the evil people, because there would be a team of flying MDs that would come and swoop in and pick up all of the good people and take them to the nearest hospital to be inoculated against octopus ink!

ANNA: Thank you for that.

LUCY: This isn't getting us anywhere! Anna, you're last, what would you do?

ANNA: I'd teach.

ALL: BOOO!!

ANNA: I'd teach. It's the gift that keeps on giving.

LUCY: I've seen *that* on a billboard.

ANNA: After all it was Plato that said: "The direction in which education starts a man will determine his future life."

LUCY: You are such a nerd.

ANNA: *(Totally flustered.)* A nerd with HIGH HONORS!!

SILVIA: OK, Everyone calm down. We need to get this all figured out . . . so what were the answers? *(Looking at the chalkboard.)* I said "feed the hungry" and "make the rich give to the poor." Hazel said, "Have people be nicer to each other." Lucy said, "Start a safe house for low-income families . . . " Amanda said: I don't know what Amanda said.

AMANDA: The octopus thing.

SILVIA: Right. And Anna said, "Teach." So how can we make those all into one thing?

ANNA: So we have a team of philanthropists going to deliver food—and inoculate—and teach in a foreign country. And they build a safe house for low-income families with single mothers. How does that sound?

HAZEL: Good!

ANNA: Great. So you're a philanthropist.

HAZEL: Yes!

ANNA: Who else wants to be a philanthropist? *(Silvia raises her hand.)* OK, Silvia. So you two are the philanthropists. And you'll be the patient, Amanda, Lucy you can be the student, and I'll be the—

LUCY: Let me guess—the teacher!

ANNA: Right. So I'll write everything down and you all can

LUCY: Everything OK, Amanda?

AMANDA: What about the octopus?

ANNA: Something makes me think that Ms. Cleese would think we were making light of the assignment if we did the octopus part.

AMANDA: Not if there was a witch in it.

ANNA: *(Under her breath, overlapping.)* Were a witch.

HAZEL: I'll be the witch!

AMANDA: You can't be the witch *and* a philanthropist!

LUCY: That's not true . . . just look at Principal Kindler!

ALL: *(Ad-libbing.)* oooOOOOOOOhhhhhhh!! Shoot! Woah! Snap! etc. *(Ms. Cleese opens the door.)*

MS. CLEESE: Ladies, you have two more minutes left—I hear a lot of noise in here—and I hope it's the sound of creativity! *(She exits. As soon as the door closes they all burst out laughing.)*

ALL: *(Mimicking her.)* "I Hope It's The Sound Of Creativity!"

ANNA: Guys . . . I am so sorry . . . I hate to be the "on task" person, but we *really* have to write this play.

AMANDA: You're always the "on task" person, it's the only way we'd ever get anything done.

HAZEL: Yeah, thanks Anna.

ANNA: *(Sincerely flattered.)* Thanks guys! OK, so—*(Moving chairs.)* let's pretend that this is the classroom, over here, and let's pretend that this is the hospital over here—maybe we can put some chairs together and Amanda you can lie across them like you're on a gurney—

AMANDA: Yeah, yeah—

(The girls all move the chairs around and Amanda gets on the chairs lying across them.)

ANNA: Hazel, so you're the doctor, right?

HAZEL: Yeah.

ANNA: So maybe we can all make the hospital sounds while Hazel checks in on Amanda.

LUCY: Like what sounds, people screaming in pain?

ANNA: Like a heart monitor. Like "beep . . . beep . . . beep . . . beep . . . "

LUCY: Yeah OK, that sounds pretty cool—

AMANDA: Can I be like, "My leg . . . my leg was amputated because I stepped on a land mine . . . "

ANNA: I'm not sure Ms. Cleese would go for it.

AMANDA: "I have the plague, and rats have been gnawing at my flesh for three years . . . "

ANNA: Amanda.

AMANDA: "I have no heart, my heart has been stolen by a team of masked organ-thiefs . . . I woke up in a tub full of ice . . . and my kidneys were also stolen . . . all they left was a note . . . "

ANNA: Amanda. Be serious.

AMANDA: All right. *(The class bell rings suddenly.)*

ANNA: Well I guess we'll just have to get our stuff together *after* recess. *(Blackout.)*

SCENE TWO: RECESS

The girls are all out on the playground.

HAZEL: *(Singing a pop song and doing a funny dance.)* "I remember when, I remember, I remember when I lost my mind . . ."

LUCY: Hazel had too much Starbucks this morning.

AMANDA: Maybe it's her purple contacts. They're making her see all freaky.

LUCY: I don't judge people for that kind of thing.

AMANDA: Neither do I—it's just, purple contacts?

HAZEL: What are you guys talking about?

LUCY: Amanda was just pointing out that you have purple contacts.

HAZEL: But I'm not wearing them anymore. See?

AMANDA: Why, don't you need your contacts to see? I'm a mess without my glasses.

HAZEL: I decided they were a bit too extreme.

ANNA: Yeah, like you were trying too hard to fit in.

HAZEL: Well . . . I just moved here.

ANNA: It's cool, I was new in first grade.

SILVIA: I'm new today. *(Daniel and Sam race by chasing a red handball and overhear.)*

DANIEL: New girl, new girl, new girllllllllllll!!!!!

SAM: Hey, you new?

DANIEL: New to the doo-doo.

LUCY: What's up with you, freakazoid?

DANIEL: Just checking out the new girl. *(In a robot voice.)* And-now-my-robot-hand-will-attack-her . . . and-make-her-into-android—

LUCY:—She has a name.

DANIEL: *(Still in robot voice.)* What-is-it? Data-not-registering.

SILVIA: Silvia.

DANIEL: *(Still in robot voice.)* Silvia. Silvia. Silvia. No memory of this name. Data not registering. Beep Beep Beep!! *(Makes an obnoxious beeping sound.)*

LUCY: Freak.

SAM: I'm Sam. Hi. *(Waves at Silvia.)* Daniel's weird.

HAZEL: I think he's funny.

SAM: Funny-looking! Ha.

DANIEL: That-is-not-funny. That-is-not-funny.

SILVIA: Hi.

SAM: So what's your story?

SILVIA: I'm thinking about going here.

SAM: Where did you used to go?

SILVIA: Well, I used to go to St. Margaret's but I didn't like it, so now I'm homeschooled.

DANIEL: *(Dropping the robot voice.)* Your parents teach you?

SILVIA: Yeah, well, mostly my dad but my mom sometimes does too.

DANIEL: That's really weird.

SILVIA: No, it's not, I have a lot of friends who are homeschooled.

DANIEL: And I bet they're all . . . freaks! Beep beep beep beep beep!!! *(Daniel runs away making a beeping robot noise.)*

LUCY: Daniel, you're the freak!!

SAM: *(Awkwardly walking away.)* All right, so . . . I guess I'd better . . . catch you guys later.

SILVIA: Well if being homeschooled makes me a freak, I like being freakish.

AMANDA: That's brave.

SILVIA: No, it isn't.

ANNA: Yes it is.

SILVIA: Being a freak isn't so bad, as long as you embrace it.

AMANDA: Well I'm a bookworm and people think I'm dorky.

ANNA: No, Amanda, it's the giant-octopus and turtle-with-lasers-attached-to-her-shell and bears-on-a-mission-for-gold stories that you write that make people think you're weird.

AMANDA: I'm a writer. And I like animals, I think they're cute.

SILVIA: I have three cats.

AMANDA: I love cats!

SILVIA: They run my life.

AMANDA: So does our pug.

SILVIA: You have a pug?

AMANDA: Yep, her name is Miss Piggy. *(Meanwhile, on the other side of the playground.)*

LUCY: Hey, Hazel?

HAZEL: Yeah?

LUCY: I saw you in the store the other day.

HAZEL: Yeah, that was funny.

LUCY: No, I *saw* you.

HAZEL: Doing what?

LUCY: You know.

HAZEL: I wasn't doing anything.

LUCY: I saw you steal the Snickers bar.

HAZEL: What? I didn't steal anything.

LUCY: It's OK. I was shopping for my dad.

HAZEL: Why?

LUCY: Because he can't go to the store himself.

HAZEL: He's sick?

LUCY: No, he's drunk.

HAZEL: Oh, I thought you were kidding about that.

LUCY: Why would I joke about that?

HAZEL: I just thought you wouldn't say it if it was true.

LUCY: It's a fact, I can't hide it.

HAZEL: I'm sorry about your dad.

LUCY: It's OK, you know, I just wish he could stop.

HAZEL: Yeah.

LUCY: So I guess I just wanted to tell you because I'm not perfect either.

HAZEL: I don't do it all the time.

LUCY: You don't have to explain. People do things.

HAZEL: Please don't tell anyone.

LUCY: I won't, I don't want you getting into trouble. People think you're normal. It's better if you have them fooled. I can't pretend I'm normal.

HAZEL: What's normal anyway?

LUCY: I have no idea. *(Meanwhile on the other side of the playground.)*

SILVIA: And I made them these collars and they're beaded and they have rhinestones and they look really really cute in them.

AMANDA: My pug has a Marlon Brando outfit that she wore for Halloween this year.

ANNA: Your pug dressed as Marlon Brando?

AMANDA: Yeah, the outfit looked like a jean jacket and it had these leather pants attached to the jacket that hung down to look like miniature legs.

SILVIA: So how did you know she was supposed to be Marlon Brando and not James Dean?

AMANDA: Well my mom made the costume by hand. She loves Brando.

SILVIA: My dad is obsessed with Bogart.

ANNA: I can't watch *Casablanca*, it moves way too slowly.

AMANDA: I like watching films in black and white.

ANNA: I like Pixar movies.

AMANDA: *(Not knowing what to say.)* I like this pencil.

(On the other side of the stage Lucy and Hazel are playing MASH.)

LUCY: Eeew! I'm married to Daniel, live in a shack, and drive an Oscar Meyer Weiner mobile? Gross! That totally sucks.

HAZEL: I think Daniel's cute.

LUCY: Cute if you like total spaz-inators.

HAZEL: Nobody's normal, remember?

LUCY: I'll take *(Making "air quotes" with her fingers.)* "normal over spazinator any day. Let's do you next. Hopefully you'll end up married to Brad Pitt and then you can adopt Cambodian babies with him. *(The class bell rings again. Blackout.)*

SCENE THREE: THE DRAMA

The girls are all back in the classroom.

ANNA: All right guys, so now we really have to focus. Hazel, walk in like you're there to help out Amanda.

HAZEL/PHILANTHROPIST #1: Hello, there. *(They shake hands.)* What's your name?

AMANDA/ISABEL: *(Weakly.)* Isabel.

HAZEL/PHILANTHROPIST #1: What seems to be the problem?

ISABEL: Because of the high cost of paying for drugs to cure my illness, I can't pay for food and my children cannot go to school.

SILVIA/PHILANTHROPIST #2: Well, luckily we have started a safe house for women such as yourself. Please come, we have a bed for you and one for each of your children. We will vaccinate you and treat your illness and feed your children.

ISABEL: Oh thank you, thank you! *(Anna and Lucy continue the scene on the other side of the stage.)*

ANNA: Great. Then after that, I'll pretend like I'm teaching the class and Lucy, you just follow my lead, OK?

LUCY: All right.

ANNA/TEACHER: *(Writing on the blackboard.)* So, 2+2= 4

LUCY/STUDENT: I don't get it.

ANNA: You're supposed to get it!

LUCY/STUDENT: *(Being difficult.)* I'm really not good at math. I'm a humanities person.

ANNA: You're not following my lead!

LUCY/STUDENT: "Oh thank you, thank you, I understand now." Is that what you want?

ANNA: Yes, thank you! So . . . it'll just be like that, OK ladies? It doesn't have to be ten minutes, we'll just do these two scenes and Ms. Cleese will love it!

AMANDA: Great—but what about the plague? Can I have the plague?

ANNA: I don't think the plague exists anymore.

AMANDA: How about the bird flu.

ANNA: *(Exasperated.)* Fine.

LUCY: If Amanda gets the bird flu, I want to have rabies.

HAZEL: *(She had been spacing out.)* "Babies!?" You want to have babies?

LUCY: No, I want to have RABIES.

HAZEL: You practically do.

LUCY: What's that supposed to mean?

HAZEL: You're just crazy sometimes, is all.

LUCY: *(Threatening to reveal her secret.)* I'd watch what I say if I were you. *(Beat.)*

HAZEL: You wouldn't!

LUCY: I *would*. So watch yourself.

HAZEL: I thought we were kind-of friends.

LUCY: You just called me a rabid dog!

SILVIA: *(Trying to ease the tension.)* My cats get crazy on catnip.

AMANDA: My pug goes nuts whenever there's food she's like . . . *(She starts barking and snorting. They can't help it; Amanda is too funny . . . they all start to laugh.)*

LUCY: Just because I laughed doesn't mean I like any of you.

ANNA: Why do you have to be so . . . *hard* . . . all the time?

LUCY: I've never had any other choice. *(The door opens. Mrs. Cleese enters followed by five boys, the ones who have been creating their piece of drama in the other room.)*

MS. CLEESE: Hello ladies! Time's up! I thought we'd have you go first, and then the boys could do their piece. Boys, why don't you sit over here, grab a chair, and settle in. *(The boys set up chairs to sit like an audience for the girls.)*

DANIEL: *(In his robot voice.)* I-can't-wait-I-can't-wait—

MS. CLEESE: Daniel, do you see these? *(She puts up her "deers' ears." The other boys get quiet.)* What does that mean?

DANIEL: *(Ho-hum.)* That I'm supposed to settle down and be quiet.

MS. CLEESE: That's right. All right ladies, let's see what you've come up with!

ANNA: *(Clearing her voice.)* We'd like to call our piece, "Philanthropy."

DANIEL: What's philanthropy?

MS. CLEESE: Shhhhh.

HAZEL: Should we start?

MS. CLEESE: Yes. Please.

HAZEL/PHILANTHROPIST #1: Hello, there. *(They shake hands.)* What's your name?

AMANDA/ISABEL: *(Weakly.)* Isabel.

HAZEL/PHILANTHROPIST #1: What seems to be the problem?

AMANDA/ISABEL: Because of the high cost of paying for drugs to cure my illness, I can't pay for food and my children cannot go to school. And these rats have been gnawing on my legs for three years.

HAZEL/PHILANTHROPIST #1: *(Looking at "Isabel's" wounds.)* Oooh.

SILVIA/PHILANTHROPIST #2: *(Sticking to the script.)* Well, luckily we have started a safe house for women such as yourself. Please come, we have a bed for you, and one for each of your children. We will vaccinate you, treat your illness, and feed your progeny.

AMANDA/ISABEL: Oh my God! An octopus!

SILVIA: Excuse me?

AMANDA: *(Pointing out at the sky.)* There's a giant octopus coming right at us, don't you see it?

HAZEL: Oh my God, you're right!

AMANDA: I hope that octopus doesn't decide to attack us with its orange and polka-dotted ink! He's planning to eradicate evil by covering the Earth with his poison!

HAZEL: Well, if it does, I just so happen to have a very special antidote for octopus ink called "tentacoccus I-will-save-us," and I'll inject us, and we'll be safe! *(Silvia just stands there not knowing what to do. Anna is on the other side of the stage watching her drama spin out of control. Hazel "injects" Silvia and Amanda, and Ms. Cleese and the boys watch in amusement.)*

AMANDA: Oh my God! The tentacles! Are coming at us! They're huge!!!

HAZEL: Don't worry, we're protected!

AMANDA: AHHH!!!!! *(Silvia weakly joins in the screaming.)*

SILVIA: Ahhhhhh . . .

HAZEL: Look, we're safe! The vaccination worked!

SILVIA: Good thing.

AMANDA: Now we can go back to Kanchengunga, India, I hear you're a neurosurgeon and you also have a cutting-edge technique for eradicating brain tumors!

HAZEL: You've heard right. *(Talking to Silvia but improvising poorly.)* Come, Dr. Phil . . . ber-tina . . . let's go back to Kan . . . chen . . . that place she said we were from. *(The boys start to giggle. Finally seeing an opportunity to take over her drama again, Anna takes charge on the other side of the stage.)*

ANNA/TEACHER: *(Writing on the blackboard.)* So, as I was saying, student, 2+2= 4

LUCY/STUDENT: I don't get it.

ANNA: *(Stage whisper.)* Don't do this to me again!

LUCY/STUDENT: *(Being difficult.)* It's only the second time we've done this problem! I'm stupid. Is that what you want me to say? I'm stupid?

ANNA/TEACHER: Of course not, you're very smart. You're very capable. These are new equations I am teaching . . .

LUCY/STUDENT: *(Pretending to cry.)* I'm stupid!! I'm stupid! My mother always said so, and now I'm starting to believe her!!

ANNA/TEACHER: No, no! You're not stupid, you're very bright! *(Stage whisper.)* You're not following my lead!

LUCY: *(Stage whisper.)* Isn't it fun?

ANNA: *(Stage whisper.)* You're supposed to stick to the script!

LUCY/STUDENT: *(Recovering from crying.)* Oh, 2+2 is 4. I thought you said 1+2. I have bad ears.

ANNA: No, you have . . . good ears. They're nice ears.

LUCY/STUDENT: Thanks.

ANNA: I'm so proud of you! Now we can move onto the next problem.

AMANDA: *(Pretending she's a pirate.)* Arrgghh! I've come to steal your chalk and I'm going to break it in half!

LUCY: Yay! Pirates! I'm coming with you!!

AMANDA: ARRRGGHH! We need a good kitchen wench on our ship, come on board!

LUCY: Yayy!! I love to cook!

ANNA: *(Trying to regain control of the play.)* So! As I was saying, student, 2+2 = 4.

LUCY: I'm a kitchen wench. I don't know what a student is.

(Daniel, sensing that everything's falling apart, sees an opportunity. He gets up out of the audience.)

DANIEL: *(Using a pirate's voice.)* Ahoy—the name's Captain Bluebeard, and this is my first mate, Ogelton. *(Amanda bows as Ogelton. The boys in the audience start to snicker.)* BE QUIET! Or I'll have ya walk the plank to yer watery death! *(The boys become silent immediately.)*

AMANDA/OGELTON: Arrghh!!! Ha! Ha! Ha! HA!

LUCY/KITCHEN WENCH: I've made a wonderful stew, I thought you'd like it, sire?

ANNA: No, I'm sure he *wouldn't* like any stew, I'm giving you detention!

LUCY/KITCHEN WENCH: I have no idea what you're talking about. I'm a pirate.

DANIEL/BLUEBEARD: Where'd you get the meat from? All the meat went bad three months ago.

LUCY/KITCHEN WENCH: The rats, sire.

DANIEL/BLUEBEARD: Ahh! The rats! The rats! Very smaaarrrrt, my-little-kitchen-wench, very smaaaart.

AMANDA/OGELTON: *(Running around the stage, biting furniture, laughing hysterically.)* Aha! Aha! Aha!

DANIEL/BLUEBEARD: I love rat stew. *(He pretends to chomp into a drumstick and rip the meat apart with his teeth. It's messy and gross.)*

LUCY/KITCHEN WENCH: *(Overjoyed.)* You like it, sire?

DANIEL/BLUEBEARD: *(Choking on a piece of "rat," and then recovering.)* It's delicious.

AMANDA/OGELTON: Aha! Aha! Aha!

(Things are getting totally chaotic. At that moment, Anna decides that she has to play along if she wants to get anywhere. She uses a meter stick as her sword and blazes it boldly.)

ANNA: *(In a pirate voice, waving the "sword.")* I'm here! My name's Captain Lavender and I'm the Captain of the *Lavender Lady.*

DANIEL/BLUEBEARD: Are ya? Well, it looks like I've got a full crew on board.

ANNA/CAPTAIN LAVENDER: I don't care if you've got a full crew, Bluebird. I wanna ask ya a question.

DANIEL/BLUEBEARD: It's Bluebeard. And what's your question.

AMANDA/OGELTON: Ahhhahaahhhahhahha!

ANNA/CAPTAIN LAVENDER: *(Pulling Silvia and Hazel in with her.)* My crew and I, we wanna know where do you get your loot.

DANIEL/BLUEBEARD: Where do I get my loot?

HAZEL/SILVIA: *(Ganging up on Daniel, in an act of "girl power.")* Yeahh!

ANNA/CAPTAIN LAVENDER: Yeah, we wanna know how do ya get your booty?

HAZEL/SILVIA: Yeahh!

DANIEL/BLUEBEARD: My booty? I just shake it. I mean, take it.

ANNA/CAPTAIN LAVENDER: Ya take it?

HAZEL/SILVIA: Yeeahhh!

DANIEL/BLUEBEARD: Yeah, I just take it.

ANNA/CAPTAIN LAVENDER: From who?

HAZEL/SILVIA: Yeahh!

DANIEL/BLUEBEARD: I take it from other ships and wealthy seaports.

ANNA/CAPTAIN LAVENDER: And who do you give it to?

HAZEL/SILVIA: Yeahh!

DANIEL/BLUEBEARD: Well I give it to my crew . . . to Ogelton and my kitchen wench . . . *(Coming up with her name on the spot.)* Sheila.

LUCY/SHEILA: My name's Sheila.

AMANDA/OGELTON: ARRGRGGHH!

ANNA/CAPTAIN LAVENDER: So Bluebeard, you're actually not such a bad guy.

DANIEL/BLUEBEARD: Whattaya mean? I'm a fierce pirate! *(The other boys snicker.)*

OGELTON/SHEILA: Yeahh!

ANNA/CAPTAIN LAVENDER: But you're generous with your crew.

DANIEL/BLUEBEARD: *(Feeling awkward.)* I'm not generous . . . I . . . I've got to check my rigging—I set sail for Egypt tomorrow—

ANNA/CAPTAIN LAVENDER: Would you mind if my crew had a little bit of your stew?

DANIEL/BLUEBEARD: *(Trailing off as he walks away.)* It's made of rats . . . but if you don't mind that . . . I don't care what you do. *(Daniel takes his seat back in the audience.)*

ANNA/CAPTAIN LAVENDER: All right, ladies! Let's go free the prisoners and feed the penguins!

AMANDA: And the octopus!

SILVIA: And the cats!

LUCY: And the drunks!

HAZEL: And the Jews!

ALL: Yayyy!!

AMANDA: Geronimo!

ANNA: And scene. *(The girls all line up to take a bow. The boys applaud and hoot. Ms. Cleese, gives them a standing ovation and cries. Blackout.)*

END OF PLAY